A Walk Against The Stream takes a look at the experiences of a young national service officer in the Rhodesian Army. This is a true story – encompassing all 18 months the author spent at Victoria Falls, Rhodesia – facing enemy territory just across the Zambezi River in Zambia.

Initially allocated to 4th Platoon, 4 Independent Company Rhodesia Regiment (RR) as a subaltern – and later on as a 1st Lieutenant in Support Company 2RR – the story starts with the author's training and subsequent deployment to the operational area. The events that unfold contain interesting military encounters, with battles against the Zambian Army and local terrorists clearly depicted. The style of writing flows easily and graphically – drawing the reader into a half-forgotten world.

But there is also another aspect to the story: the human side of it. It is an examination of the author's love of a country falling apart and the relationship that he forms with a local woman in the village; their love, hope and dreams snatched away by unfolding events. This is a riveting personal tale – interspersed with interesting facts and dozens of photographs. All the names and places are real – including the battle scenes with ZIPRA and the Zambian Army.

Tony Ballinger (born 13 April 1955) was raised in a modest, but happy home in Salisbury, Rhodesia. He attended Admiral Tait Junior School – followed by Churchill High School, where he enjoyed athletics, rugby and swimming. Preferring travel to tertiary education, he set off on a three-year working holiday around the world – undertaking varied roles such as a clerk, carpenter's assistant, lifeguard and assistant train driver (the latter being in Sydney, Australia).

Within two weeks of returning to Rhodesia, the author received call-up papers to do his compulsory 18 months' national service. While at Llewellin Barracks in Bulawayo, an offer was put out for any candidate with an 'O' level education and above to apply for a trainee officer selection course – to be run at the School of Infantry in Gwelo. The author underwent a very stiff five-day pre-selection course – and out of 300 eligible men, only 13 were selected to go to the School of Infantry. One of the successful 13, he found awaiting him a very stiff and demanding course – at the end of which only three men were commissioned; the author being one of them.

Initially transferred to command 4th Platoon 4 Independent Company RR, he went on to serve in 1 Independent Company RR, Support Company 2RR – and then finally, he became a weapons and tactics instructor in PATU (the Police Anti-Terrorist Unit) based at Morris Depot, Salisbury.

Tony has an avid interest in studying current geopolitical events – linking them to prophecies in the Bible – and is currently writing a book on the subject matter. He is married with two children and currently lives in Salisbury in the UK – something he finds ironic as he was born in Salisbury, Rhodesia.

A WALK AGAINST THE STREAM

A Rhodesian National Service Officer's Story of the Bush War

Tony Ballinger

Helion & Company

Helion & Company Limited
26 Willow Road
Solihull
West Midlands
B91 1UE
England
Tel. 0121 705 3393
Fax 0121 711 4075
Email: info@helion.co.uk
Website: www.helion.co.uk
Twitter: @helionbooks
Visit our blog http://blog.helion.co.uk/

Published by Helion & Company 2015
Designed and typeset by Bookcraft Ltd, Stroud, Gloucestershire
Cover designed by Euan Carter, Leicester (www.euancarter.com)
Printed by Lightning Source, Milton Keynes, Buckinghamshire

Text © Tony Ballinger 2015
Photographs © as individually credited
Cover: A soldier patrolling against the backdrop of Victoria Falls © Craig Bone.

ISBN 978 1 910294 43 7

British Library Cataloguing-in-Publication Data.
A catalogue record for this book is available from the British Library.

For details of other military history titles published by Helion & Company
Limited contact the above address, or visit our website: http://www.helion.co.uk.

We always welcome receiving book proposals from prospective authors.

I dedicate this book to my wife, Coral. Thanks honey for putting up with my mood-swings and long absences while writing this story.

To Roy Orchard, Dave Kruger and Tom Shipley. You paid the ultimate sacrifice and we will never forget you.

Contents

List of Photographs

Introduction & Acknowledgements

This is a true story – based on my personal experiences in the Rhodesian Army. All of the character names, places and events are real – although one or two scenes are narrated in the third-person to allow continuity.

I do not claim to have achieved anything spectacular during my experiences in the Rhodesian bush war, but I continue to have a deep love for that country and felt I should put my story forward to complement the tapestry of other fine works on this subject.

Whether you see one corpse or a hundred, you are forever changed – and the innocent youth that you once were is gone for good.

So this is a story of lost youth, lost love and the loss of a country loved more deeply than the other two.

I would like to thank Craig Bone very much indeed for painting the picture on the cover; I cannot express my thanks enough Craig, that an artist of your calibre would do this for me. Thank you.

Prologue

I eyed the seething mass with barely-disguised hatred and my mind began to float and wobble as if I was imprisoned in a horrible nightmare – and as Prince Charles's speech dragged on, so my eyes latched onto the Union Jack and I realised 90 years of white rule had begun with the raising of that flag – and was now ending with the lowering of it. Fifteen years of rule under the green and white flag of Rhodesia was forgotten already – and as I stared at the flag with floodlit, phosphorescent grass blocking out most of my teary vision, so images of people formed in my mind.

They were images of dead people – people like Dave Kruger, Roy Orchard and Tom Shipley – spirits of people who were now only memories or names on a gravestone. And as they formed before me like a developing photograph, so the tears ran freely down my cheeks to mingle with the dust that held their bones – and I knew the country I loved was no more.

I didn't really hear the roar of the people or the rush of the jets, or the explosions of the cannons as the hour of midnight heralded in Zimbabwe. I could only feel a breeze and see a bright horizon of swaying fields of corn – their heads proud in the bright sunshine. I couldn't hear the noise, for the sound of half-forgotten voices and laughter echoed and rolled down the halls of my mind; and as I stood there, seeing but not seeing the perpetrators of Rhodesia's downfall, so I knew that it was time to go; that we would have to seek another land as beautiful as her – if that was indeed possible.[1]

---

1   This scene depicts the night I stood in Rufaro Stadium watching the Union Jack come down on the night of 18 April 1980. I was extremely angry and emotional that night – angered by the fact that it wasn't the Rhodesian flag being lowered. It was like our nation never existed; emotional because the memory of my dead friends were still fresh in my mind.

Chapter One

A night can be a long time – a long time when you've got nothing to do but think. I must have been half-asleep though, because the jolting coach suddenly pulled me back to consciousness – or was it the dread of tomorrow that woke me? That pit of fear in my guts?

The coach lurched again – some bloody amateur driver no doubt. The steam engine hooted several coaches ahead. Orange platform lights flashed by – momentarily lighting my cabin. I put my hands behind my head and stared up at a ceiling I could barely see. What a dark, horrible hole. Some stupid bastard had wired up all the windows with steel mesh. No air and someone's feet stank horribly in the bunk below.

I stroked my face where my beard should have been. It felt all naked and squashed-in. I'd cut myself laughing at me in the mirror… was that really me?

The steady rhythm of wheels on steel and the cradle-like motion of the train tried to soothe me into sleep, but it didn't work. My brain was alive and the night dragged on endlessly. Thoughts popped in and out of my head. Was it only a few weeks ago? The horse ranch in the Cape… wild and free spaces with purple mountains in the distance. Green grass and fresh air. Days of hot sunshine, wine and carefree laughter; riding until my arse was sore.

"You stupid bastard!" I spat at the ceiling.

I tried turning on my side – hoping to shut out my thoughts, but it was no good. Time for a piss and some fresh air. The military policeman was still there in the corridor – red peak cap above bloodshot eyes.

"Where youse goin'?" he shouted.

"For a piss."

"For a piss, who?"

"Piss, who?"

"For a piss, sergeant!" he stabbed at his sleeve.

"For a …"

"Stand to tenshun!" he bellowed.

How the hell do you stand to attention in a lurching train?

"Youse in the army now, so start actin' like it! If I says jump, you jump you little prick; you got me?!"

"Sir!" accompanied by a feeble attempt to stand to attention.

"I'm not a fucking sir, you little prick! I work for a living!"

More stabbing at the sergeant stripes.

"Sergeant!"

"Louder, boy!"

"Sergeant!" I screamed.

"Better," he said smugly. "Now have yer piss and fuck off back to bed."

"Sergeant!"

"And hurry up, you wanker. I don't want you whining in the morning that you're all tired and worn out, you little mommy's boy!"

"Sergeant!"

I disappeared into the poorly-lit, urine-smelling cubicle. Some bastard had pissed over the floor and it was squidging up between my toes. I balanced myself as best as I could and pissed into the stainless-steel trap. In front of me, staring back from a fly-blasted mirror, was the image of a young man – a man too young to die.

It was a cold grey morning as the troop train pulled into Heaney Siding. I scanned the windswept sky and guessed it would rain soon. Hundreds of heads bent this way and that as men eyed their surroundings. Some still had beards and long hair; others wore beads and denims. They were just kids like me – cannon fodder. There was the same desultory air about all of us and few talked. We were strangers.

The wheels clack-clacked slower, until finally we stopped. A small brown suitcase containing all my worldly possessions was already in my hand. The MP from the night before jumped down from the train – his immaculate boots making a crunching noise on the ballast as he landed. He ran his eyes over the men staring wide-eyed at him through the windows.

"What the hell are you mommy's boys waiting for?!" he bellowed.

The hissing train emptied its human cargo like maggots being squeezed from a wound and we tumbled out into the cold, damp air – shivering as much from fear as from the cold.

There were tall men, short men, fat and thin men, but we all had something in common… We were all white. Four-hundred of us moved slowly like a herd of cattle over to the protection of the station house – and there we stood for two hours without a word being said to us. It was clearly a case of hurry up and wait.

"Stupid fucking army," someone said.

The drizzle and the cold wind became more intense – and by the time a convoy of 15 trucks arrived, we were all wet, miserable and shivering. Several MPs hopped from the lead truck and began giving orders. Four-hundred cold, miserable and wet men threw their luggage aboard and hauled themselves into the rickety old vehicles – the wiser ones sitting immediately behind the cab to gain shelter from the icy wind. Squashed in like sardines, the convoy bounced down the dirt road to Llewellin Barracks seven kilometres away.

Nothing ever looks appealing about a military base. This camp was no exception. It was old, run-down and looked very unwelcoming. Senior recruits jeered and insulted us as our convoy trundled into camp.

"Woo! Smell the fresh puss!" they taunted. "You give me a hard-on!" followed by male masturbation gestures.

"Green like my spleen," another shouted.

The guys in the trucks gave them twos ups and threw empty coke bottles at them.

"Fockin' fresh puss!"

The trucks pulled up in a huge square just behind some old hangars. It started to drizzle again and I was wet, hungry and miserable. Several raincoat-clad officers stood in a small group – eyeing us with disapproval. A sergeant barked at us to de-bus. Hundreds of feet made contact with the concrete floor and after the shuffling and coughing ended, the sergeant addressed us.

"Listen in!" he shouted – his voice echoing around the hangar behind him.

"The first thing we're gonna do is break youse up into three companies starting from my left to the right."

By then, our numbers had grown to about 600 because men from Matabeleland had arrived by car instead of by train.

"You lot there in front of the vehicles will be 'A' Company," a Pommie sergeant pointed with his finger.

He marched forward and made a clear division between men – striking one poor sod a cruel smack for being too slow. Then, moving along the lines, he hived off 'B' and 'C' Companies. I found myself in 'B' Company.

"Now that's sorted out, all you mommy's boys will dump your personal kit in that hangar, then form up in front of me again!"

Several men made a move to comply with the instruction.

"Stay where you are!" screamed the sergeant, "I've not given you the order to proceed!"

Six-hundred faces turned and eyed him in stony silence. Enjoying his 15 minutes of fame, he paced slowly along the front rank of men – eyeing them from below his beret.

"Get away!"

Twelve-hundred shoes made a loud echoing racket as we doubled into the hangar to dump our personal kit wherever we could find a place. What chaos; what sheer bloody stupidity. The attempt to form up again sent the sergeant into a towering rage – his beer-red nose matching the rest of his face.

"Wankers, bloody wankers the lot of you. Shit, you must be the worst load of crap to come our way. Form up! Form up!"

After a long time… Silence again.

"It's time for your medicals. You see that hangar there?" he said, pointing to his right. Six-hundred faces stared in blank resignation.

"'A' Company will go first, mount the spectators' stand and proceed singly to be processed, understood?"

No answer.

"Understood?" he bellowed.

"Yes, sir!" 600 times.

"Oh shit!" I mumbled to myself, "he's not a…"

"I'm not a fucking sir!" he spat out with contempt. "I work for living. I work for a living!" he repeated – glancing nervously at a group of officers who were staring grimly at him.

"'A' Company, 'A' Company 'shun!"

It was a pathetic attempt by untrained men to stand to attention. The footfalls sounded like wet cowshit flopping on tarmac. Some saw the humour of it and cackled among ourselves.

"Silence, you wankers! Think you're any better?" he yelled at us.

Facing 'A' Company again, he commanded them to right turn.

This conjured up more chuckles and sniggers.

"'A' Companeeeeee! By the riyaat, quick march!"

Two-hundred men began marching to the hangar. Some started on the wrong foot, others tripped over feet in front of them; some arms swinging forward, others swinging back – beads and long hair flapping. It was like watching a centipede on drugs. I almost cracked up, it was so funny.

Then came our turn – and it was just as hilarious. What a cock-up. We entered a huge, brightly-lit hangar – 'A' Company snaking ahead of us through a maze of tables and cubicles. I went with 'B' Company onto the spectator stand. I was shivering with cold. We inched forward, one man at a time, until I reached a bored-looking group of men with piles of folders.

"Name?" asked a spotty youth in uniform.

"Ballinger."

"Initials?"

"AJ."

"AJ what?"

"I only have two initials."

"AJ what?" asked the youth – stabbing at his corporal's chevrons.

I groaned inwardly. What a stupid little prick.

"AJ, corporal."

He scribbled a lot of details before I moved on – by then clutching a brown folder.

"Strip," ordered an orderly.

I looked self-consciously at the rest who had already stripped off – relieved to see they had kept their underpants on. There were brown men, well-muscled men, skinny, hairy – all different shapes of shivering humanity. Above the murmur of 400 men whispering to each other, I could hear the sergeant bawling at 'C' Company outside. Next was a man in a white coat who took my pulse before and after a few step-ups, then weighed me.

"Tubby unfit civvy, hey? We'll soon sort that out."

Next, the dentist's cubicle.

"Good teeth," the kindly man said, "should last you a long time. Next!"

Then a cubicle to get my eyes tested. A man dropped some liquid in them which made my vision blurry. He wrote something in my folder.

"Next!"

I staggered off – my eyes watering and feeling half-blind.

"Next!"

I vaguely made out a table in front of me. A male orderly glanced at my file, then came around to my side of the table.

"Drop your pants."

"What?"

"I said drop your pants."

"Cough," he said softly and cupped my balls in his hand. I felt sick and wanted to vomit.

"'A' category," he said, signing my folder.

"Next!"

It was only afterwards that I learned that a couple of nurses had been giggling in the background as they watched men removing their underpants. I guess it was when they saw Mark Faccio's cock that they stopped giggling and became silent – very silent.

❧—❧

Later on, the three companies were marched by individual sergeants to a massive, dingy storeroom that smelled like a mixture of soap and denim.

Having just dressed, I was pissed off when told to strip again. This was made more difficult because my left arm was screaming from my 'three-in-one' jab.

There we were – 600 half-blind and half-crippled men on our first day in the army. The gooks were going to have a field day with wankers like us.

"Attennn … shun!"

We looked at an immaculately turned-out guy with a pace stick wearing a 'Mickey Mouse' watch on his right wrist – a symbol of authority we would later come to dread.

"Pack your civvies in your suitcases and form up in a line; 'A' Company first."

After doing so, we slowly edged forward – brown folders in hand. There was a long trestle table with about a dozen white clerks and perhaps two dozen black labourers standing behind them. To our left towered rack after rack of everything imaginable. Boots, canteens, sleeping bags, camouflage shirts, trousers, T-shirts, mosquito nets and so on. My first stop was for long denim trousers known as 'combat trouser, long'.

"Size?"

No 'please' or 'thank you' from the arrogant tin god…

"36 waist corp."

"That's corporal to you!"

"Corporal!"

Two pairs of size 36 trousers were thrown at me. I glanced around and saw that everyone was having something thrown at them – like a carnival where you threw things to get a prize.

Next: 'combat shirt type sleeve, long'.

Why was the language backwards in this crazy place?

"Size?"

"Seventeen neck, corporal," I said smugly – at last getting the hang of this rank-addressing system.

"Sergeant!" hissed the narrow-eyed three striper. "Three stripes, see!"

"Sergeant!" I agreed.

Two 'combat shirts type sleeve, long,' were tossed in front of me.

And so it went down the line. Boots, socks, brushes, tins of polish, T-shirts, sleeping bags, mosquito nets, helmets, belts, webbing, 'stick' boots. I stuffed it into a duffel bag which was only big enough to take half the load thrown at me.

Outside, it was drizzling. 'A' Company was ordered by their sergeant to get dressed into uniform. We followed suit. We sat on the cold concrete and battled to put on socks, boots, belts and shirts – all 600 of us, grunting, cussing and swearing at the unfamiliar kit.

"Form up!" someone bellowed.

I craned my neck and looked along the front row of men inwardly smiling at this pathetic attempt to be soldiers. We hadn't yet had haircuts, so we looked like a picture of Dutch Army troops I'd once seen. They were allowed to keep their long hair – even if it meant putting it up in nets!

"What a joke," Pete Wells whispered.

"Mmm," I concurred.

More sergeants and corporals arrived – and two hours later, we'd been divided into 30-man platoons.

A rat-faced corporal adopted a position in front of us.

"Youse pricks is first platoon, 'B' company. Pick up your shit and follow me. At the dubble!" he yelled.

There was a mad scramble to pick up everything and run like the clappers after the corporal, while attempting to stay in some kind of drill formation. I glanced left and saw a small, dark-skinned fellow with a uniform far too big for him. His helmet was bobbing on his head, his shirt sleeves went over his hands and his trousers were baggy. To cap it all, he had a big smile – despite having two front teeth missing. I cracked up laughing.

"This is youse barracks!" the corporal said as we stood – lungs heaving in front of an old, red-brick building.

Why does *everything* in a military camp have to be red-bricked?

"Get in there and store your civvy shit in the lockers. Put the rest on your beds."

There was a mad rush to get inside. Why the rush? Who knows. I headed for the furthest corner. I vaguely remembered someone saying that guys close to the door got it rough on inspections.

I'll always remember the smell of that barrack room. It was not a horrible smell – a smell of beeswax floor polish and soap mingled with fly spray, so common in government buildings of the day.

I dumped my civvy clothes in the locker and my military kit on the bed just as I had been told. I then sat down and waited to see what would happen next. I didn't have to wait long.

"Form up outside in ranks of three. At the double!"

There was mad rush for the door – boots skidding and sliding on the immaculate floor. We formed up facing the corporal. He went up and down the line telling men to tuck their shirts in, tie their laces correctly, clip their belts correctly. But we still had beads and long hair.

"All beads and personal jewellery off!"

Off it came – quickly stuffed into our pockets.

"Platoon. Everything – and I mean everything – is done at the double here. You will run at the double, you will eat at the double, you will shit and piss at the double. *Verstaan julle?*"

"Corporal!" bawled the platoon in acknowledgement.

All around us I could hear men shouting 'corporal' or 'sergeant'. Men running everywhere.

"Platooon, riyaaat face!"

A pathetic attempt to turn right was followed by insults and threats of instant death from the corporal.

"By the riyat... Quieeek march!"

It was the usual cock-up, but a slight improvement nonetheless. We followed the corporal at a stiff pace. Then the command: "Dubble!"

I hated running at the best of times, although in my brief 20-year lifespan I had achieved a degree of success in the UK running with Andy Ligemar on the beach at Prestatyn in Wales. He ran for his county and if my memory serves me right, he eventually represented the United Kingdom. Not that I could keep up with him. I think in his good-humoured way he just idled alongside me as we covered the vast expanse of beach at low tide.

A memory that will always remain with me is of Andy streaking ahead on one run, way ahead, jetting up and over a sand dune and then out of sight. This was followed shortly afterwards by a screaming, enraged apparition covered from head to foot by what looked like mud. It was only when I got closer and down-wind from him that I realised it was crap. Black, smelly crap of the foulest kind. Andy ran back towards me – eyes open in terror and disgust, his mouth a pink hole against a black background. I doubled up with laughter and rolled halfway down the sand dune. I caught a glimpse of him diving into the ocean some distance away to wash himself. It turned out he'd run straight through an open gate into a sewer pond. The wind had blown a sandy crust over the foul-smelling goo and it looked just like the beach.

I remember those runs too, to reach the caravan where I made love to a raven-haired beauty who used to go apoplectic with delight seeing me running up all tanned and muscular to her front door.

"You!" screamed the corporal – rousing me from distant memories.

"Corporal?"

"Concentrate on what you're doing or I'll ram a stick up your arse and ride you like a bloody witch on a broomstick."

"Corporal!"

We approached another red-brick building. I figured you had to be a moron to be in the army as a regular and that it would take a moron's moron to be the architect of such shitty buildings.

Great, I said to myself. It was time to get shaved bald.

We filed in despondently and took turns to sit in the equivalent of an electric chair. It was a barber's chair manned by a young soldier. Some guys had tears in their eyes as their dark, blonde and red locks cascaded to the floor. The buzzing clippers swept remorselessly back and forth like a miniature lawn mower.

It felt even colder with our bald heads exposed to the elements as we formed up outside, then doubled back to our barrack block. It was almost sunset on our first day in the army.

"Get your mess tins and get over to the canteen. On the double!"

The day's light entertainment had made me forget just how hungry I was. I hadn't eaten since the night before and the thought of food made my stomach gurgle.

The canteen swarmed with bald men – their scalps white from a lack of exposure to the sun. We formed up in a long, snaking queue as we headed for a line of Bain-Maries packed with steaming hot food. It wasn't great, but there was plenty of it and we licked our lips as it was splashed and slapped onto our stainless-steel trays, with pudding sliding into gravy and vice versa. But we didn't care. We were young and starving and our stomachs thought our throats had been cut.

Scalding tea that tasted remarkably like copper sulphate washed it down.

"You reckon they've got chemicals in here to keep our dicks down?" my neighbour asked – looking suspiciously into his metal cup.

"Nah," said another, "it's only the taste of the cup."

"Balls," commented another. "My brother says they lace your drink with that blue shit that keeps your pecker down. They don't want horny soldiers raping everyone in town."

"Fat chance we'll see town for months," I said.

Everyone looked gloomily at me. No pussy for months. That's impossible!

We queued to wash our dishes, but by the time I reached the trough it was a greasy slimy liquid decorated with bits of floating vegetables. I realised why my brother had said volunteer for nothing, but always be at the front of the food queue.

After dumping our utensils at the barracks, we were ordered to form up and follow the corporal 'at the double' to the lecture hall. It was a long run and we were soon puffing and burping as half-digested food slopped around in our stomachs. However, we soon got into that type of rhythmic step that soldiers down the eons have used. Hwump hwump went our boots in unison. I suddenly felt proud and strong.

The lecture hall was curved like the seats of a cinema, with a large brightly-lit stage. Chatter mingled with the sounds of men settling into their seats, but soon there was silence – barring the odd cough and the clearing of throats.

"Battalion, battalion… Shun!"

There was the sound of men rising to their feet – standing stiffly to attention.

A tall, uniformed, dignified-looking man in his early-fifties strode onto the stage. He stood in front of the lectern, cleared his throat and spoke into the microphone.

"I am Lieutenant Colonel Roley, your overall course commander for the remainder of your stay with us." He eyed the audience before proceeding.

"Be seated."

Six-hundred men obeyed – shuffling into a comfortable position.

"I don't need to tell you men why we are here. To put it simply, we are at war. Society has chosen that in times of war, men must fight for their country and for their way of life. You are not fighting for the benefit of individuals, but for the survival of our Rhodesian way of life. We're facing a ruthless and determined enemy whose resources, compared to ours, are virtually unlimited."

He paused and took a sip of water before continuing.

"I believe we have right on our side, which is to hold back the wave of tyranny and lawlessness that is sweeping post-independent Africa. We can boast of having one of the best police forces in the world and a constitution that guarantees safety and security for its citizens. Law and order is paramount in our society and none of the countries that have become independent to the north have maintained law and order. It is your task to hunt down the enemy who will destroy us. You already know about the murders that have taken place to date. Tribesmen massacred, farmers killed, property destroyed.

'You are fighting for your country's survival and the communists are backing the enemy. Communism is not the kind of 'freedom' that any of us want. We lie north of the Republic of South Africa, which sits abreast of the strategic Cape Sea route – a route that carries most of the West's oil from the Middle East. We are pawns in a very big game, and if the communists kick us out of here, they will be one step closer to grabbing the Cape of Good Hope. The enemy's propaganda machine demands that we be unseated from power because we are white supremacists – racists, if you will. That is their excuse for arming and training our enemy, who sadly, are our own countrymen.

'As for our own kith and kin applying sanctions on us… what can I say? Is it the reward we deserve for rushing to Britain's defence in their hour of need in both World Wars? Is this the reward we get for our soldiers laying down their lives in more numbers per thousand of population than any other Commonwealth country that fought? I guess not.

'It does speak of the proud traditions of our army – our pride as a young nation. We have won battle honours in North Africa, Sicily, Italy, the beaches of Normandy and in Burma. Our pilots helped to turn the Nazi tide in the air – both as fighter pilots and as bomber crews.

'Learn well what your instructors will teach you in the coming months. War is a serious and nasty business, and some of you sitting here today will not be alive at the end of your national service. So learn your trade well."

The talk ended abruptly and we stood to attention as the colonel left the stage. He had had a sobering effect on us and we sat down again in silence. Some of us were going to die.

We watched various films after that – one about the dangers of catching VD and how to avoid it. This perked us up because anything to do with sex was okay with young men. Insults were hurled such as: "you got a blobby nobby, Phil" with Phil responding: "yeah, got it from your mom" and so on. Another film dealt with the organisation of the army and the roles of various units.

The last movie shocked me. It showed pictures of dead tribesmen and dead civilians; dead gooks; but thankfully, no dead soldiers. This was the ugly, true side of war. This wasn't acting where tomato sauce is poured on an actor. Here we saw brains plopped out of heads, intestines wrapped around torsos, animals maimed, cows with eyes missing and a foetus dangling on the end of umbilical cords. Savagery – there was no other word to describe it.

Whether we were racists or elitists or not is another story, but at least we weren't savages with no sense of law and order or a moral code. I just couldn't understand why the West wanted us to hand our fine little country over to Mugabe and his followers. The colonel had put that straight at least. We were just pawns – totally expendable in a massive world-wide power struggle. How gullible we were at that time.

I felt even more determined than ever to do my bit to keep this mindless tyranny at bay. I went to bed exhausted. As I crept into my rough cotton sheets, my mood sunk really low. I once again stared up at a ceiling I could barely see, thinking of Jess and the purple Hottentots Holland Mountains in the Cape – her blonde hair blowing in the wind as her mount charged ahead; laughter and smiles and sun all around. My heart ached so bad that night and tears stung my eyes as I drifted slowly into sleep.

Chapter Two

Some people are 'springers' and some are 'crawlers'; some people greet the day with a wide smile and a spring of expectation. I hate such people because I most definitely fall into the second category. To me, waking is a luxurious privilege. You can stretch and yawn and turn over one more time – pulling the warm blanket over your ear. It's time to delay the coming day, not to embrace it.

For a 'crawler' to be screamed awake at 0430 is possibly the most awful thing after a visit to the dentist. Blinding white lights snapped on followed by: "Up, up uuppppp!" Beds tipped over, sleep-drugged men with erections scrambling dazed, confused and direction-less. This is the precise reason for dawn attacks. They are effective because sleep-drugged men make useless defenders.

"PT kit on at the double!"

Thirty men scrambled for shorts, t-shirts, socks and tackees – the local name for trainers.

"It's still fucking dark," whined my neighbour. "Only bats and idiots are awake."

Then out into the stinging cold air. It's barely April and bloody cold already. The semi-desert scrub reflected back at us around the camp's well-lit perimeter.

"Form up... Form upp!"

We did a few stretching exercises and then we were off. I found it hard-going to begin with and felt a stitch approach then fade away. We were back in that swaying rhythm of 30 men running in step – and I must admit, I enjoyed the sound. Eventually, after a long run, we reached a rugby field. Off to the east, the first faint pink-orange glow of the sun was breaking through hazy clouds above the horizon.

We did a whole range of exercises: sit-ups, push-ups, star-jumps, more sit-ups and then piggy-back races between the goalposts. Our hot steamy breaths puffed into the cold air like steam engines. After an hour of this, we formed up dripping with sweat for our run back to the barracks, where we arrived back at 0600.

"Youse have 30 minutes to shit, shower and shave and be formed up here again in combat kit, undastood?"

"Corporal!"

We made a mad dash for the barrack block, stripped off, grabbed a towel, a bar of soap, a razor and headed for the showers. It was a toss-up having a hot shower and then shaving in cold water, or shaving in hot water and having a cold shower. There just wasn't enough hot water to go around. I decided on the former and felt the bliss exhilaration of hot water cascading over me. What a lovely feeling after a run; you just felt so good. Everywhere, white arses wiggled and jiggled. Mirrors steamed up – hands wiping it off to shave before the steam fogged it again.

I was done and was about to double out the shower block when I caught a glimpse of the biggest cock I had ever seen. A couple of other guys were staring without making it too obvious. The guy was facing towards us – head back under the shower, his fingers running over his bald head and eyes shut. His dick, full and thick, almost touched his knees. I stood there – transfixed like a rat before a viper – and with embarrassment bordering on jealousy, I ran from the room.

And so the 'Italian Stallion' came into our lives. It was Mark J. Faccio and he became a legend in our company – winning all 'cock on the table' competitions until our national service ended 18 months later. And he always had a gorgeous girl or two on his arm whenever our rare liberties came around. What could they have seen in the man? Yeah, right!

Another mad scramble for breakfast. This time I got it right: hot food and clean water in the trough. Dreading another run, I was pleasantly surprised to hear that we had to report to the lecture hall, although we still moved at the double. It was only our second day in the army, yet we somehow felt more professional already and less like 'fresh puss'.

Colonel Roley strode on the stage, followed by the usual 'attention', then 'be seated'.

"Listen in," he said.

"Llewellin Barracks is where the majority of you will train, but we have reached the stage where we commence our NCO and officer selection programme."

He paused for dramatic effect.

"Those of you without an 'O' level standard of education, stand up and leave the hall."

About half left. I felt a thrill of excitement. Me, an NCO or even an officer? The thought hadn't even entered my head.

"The rest of you will begin a three-day selection course identical to the commando selection course used by the British Army in the Second World War. The course is not designed to see how much brawn you have, but to see if you can think," he tapped his head.

"You'll be asked to talk on a piece of string without pause for three minutes to see if you have fluent thought processes. You'll be given a multitude of tasks and exercises to perform, like getting a prisoner over an electrified fence with three poles and a rope and so on. Those lucky enough to pass this selection will go to the School of Infantry in Gwelo to train as platoon commanders."

I was stunned, amazed. Just think... I could possibly shit on a corporal for once. Wouldn't that be fantastic? I left the hall a new man and ran with a sense of purpose back to the barrack room. There were only about 30 percent of us left. The rest were probably on another run at the double somewhere.

Within an hour, we had white numbers pinned to our chests and backs and we were doubled to a part of the camp I had not seen before. It looked like a massive open-air jungle gym with ropes, 44 gallon drums and nets all over the place. The other 200 or so men were already there.

I can't remember much of the next three days, except to say it was mentally and physically demanding. It wasn't so much to see if you could finish your tasks in the allotted time, but to see if you could think towards the goal of getting your task finished and to lead, inspire and encourage men in the process.

I got to talk for four minutes on a piece of toilet paper without any prior warning. Just try that some time; it's not easy – and it was done while we were hungry and fatigued both mentally and physically. I also had to get a 44 gallon drum out of an enclosure with six poles and two pieces of rope. We all knew how much that bloody drum could weigh, and in all honesty I only managed to raise the drum up to the top of the fence before it crashed to the floor. I felt an idiot. But what I didn't realise was that I was being marked on how I led the men in the exercise.

Day two saw the numbers drop to about 100 and I was still in the running. Late nights, reduced food levels and more tests. I had to show the course instructors how I would escape from a prisoner of war camp and why? They constantly asked why? How would I set up an ambush. Everything was: Why? Why? Why?

At the end of day three, only 13 of us remained.

Strangely – and out of character with the army – we were allowed a single beer in the canteen that night. It felt like the last meal before an execution.

The train clack-clacked to a halt at Gwelo Station. It was a chilly day, but at least the sky was clear and the place seemed clean and bright, with palm trees tilting in a gentle wind.

I had never been to Gwelo before. It was a small town situated centrally in the country. Its main purpose was to serve farmers and host the massive Bata shoe factory – its only claim to fame. A three-tonne Bedford was waiting for us. An immaculately-uniformed sergeant stood by the cab – boots gleaming and his beret tilted at that 'how-the-hell-does-it-stay on?' angle.

We formed up in two rows – standing to attention and looking straight ahead… our upper vision obscured by our combat caps, or 'cunt caps', as they were affectionately known.

"My name is Bartlett, Sergeant Bartlett, and I am your course sergeant."

He eyed us with steely-green eyes.

"It's my job to turn you lower-than-shark-shit specimens into leaders. How the fuck I'll ever do that I don't know, 'cos you're the worst-looking part of pathetic humanity I have ever seen."

We later learned that was the standard greeting at the School of Infantry when we heard other 'fresh puss' being welcomed in the same way.

Bartlett flicked his head in the direction of the truck and we clambered aboard. The old petrol engine kicked into life. I was nervous and excited at the same time. We drove south-west for a few kilometres on a nice tarred dual carriageway. We passed a large hill to our left – a hill I would come to despise – but that was for later. Turning left, we headed past a guard post with the sign 'The School of Infantry' on it. Eventually, we stopped at the back of a neat complex of barracks. Thankfully, they were not red.

Bartlett got down from the cab and in simple sign language motioned to us to follow him. We walked past a double-storey barrack block to our left. We later learned that was where the regular trainee officers stayed. We turned right and right again down a small passage. Bartlett stood to one side and indicated with a nod that we had reached our barrack room.

The same smell! Soap and beeswax polish mixed with fly spray.

"You have five minutes to dump your stuff and form up outside in full combat kit," Bartlett snapped.

We entered the room and I took the third bed on the left. A long row of concrete lockers with steel doors divided the room down the middle. The barrack block was only half-full. We still had no idea how to piece our webbing together, and trying to do that and put it on at the same time proved impossible. Well, that was the idea wasn't it?

"You're late!" Bartlett screamed. "If I say five minutes, I mean five minutes!"

"Sergeant!"

"You see that big tree on top of the hill?"

We turned to look. My stomach slumped. Shit, that was a long way off.

"Go! Get away!" Bartlett screamed in our ears. "The last one back repeats it!"

A mad scramble of slipping and sliding boots on gravel and we were off up a well-worn path to the top of the hill – water bottles and food pouches slapping on our hips.

Run, slip, run. Heart thumping, gasping for air, run more, run, run, run. Who the hell was behind me? I glanced back – two others. Thank God for that. Up to the tree, touch it, then down again – slipping, sliding, racing. Bleeding hands grasping at thorn bushes. Dust in the air and lungs fit to burst. Forming up in front of the sergeant.

A skinny, dark-haired guy called Sandberg was last. No sympathy for him, poor bugger!

"Again!" shrieked Bartlett.

We heaved air into our lungs and watched the poor bugger race off again – relieved we were not him. But as it turned out, we were no luckier by any means…

"Follow me," Bartlett said, crooking his index finger – an evil glint in his eye.

We followed him to the back of a shed. Shit, we had only just got to Gwelo and this was full in our face already! I felt completely disorientated. In front of us was a 44 gallon drum and two long gum poles, with bits of rope tied between the two poles to form a harness.

"Meet 'Felix'," Bartlett smirked, "he loves riding to the top of the hill… just loves it."

I groaned inwardly.

"Put him in the harness and carry him up the hill."

We pushed the poles apart and rolled the heavy drum onto the ropes.

"Hey, you shark shit! You scratch the paint on 'Felix' and you'll do the hill again and again until you drop, do you hear me?"

"Sergeant!"

We gingerly rolled 'him' into the harness, but the poles were only long enough for two men either side. A 44 gallon drum weighed about the equivalent of a 50 kilogramme sack of cement for each of the four men. That's not too bad on level ground.

We began at a slow pace towards the hill – the drum swinging in its harness.

"Those of you not carrying the drum, mark time at the double alongside it."

I ran on the spot as the drum progressed to the base of the hill. That's where we suddenly realised the full horror of what we had to do: carrying a drum to the summit without putting it down, at a 45° angle. The four men doing the carrying were already sweating and shaking after only a dozen or so steps. A few minutes later, they were begging to be relieved. Three men walked at the back of 'Felix' – holding onto 'him' so 'he' didn't slide out the back of the harness like a dead foetus.

It was my turn. I tried to scramble to the front of the gum pole, but I was too tall. It was better to have short men at the front. I eased in as best as I could behind a guy I came to know as Phil Laing and ripped two fingernails while trying to grasp the log before the damn contraption crashed to the ground. The pain made me angry – fuelling my muscles. I suddenly didn't give a damn and was raring to go.

But that enthusiasm and energy didn't last long. The weight that we were carrying might have been okay on a flat surface – and I am not a scientist – but somehow the 40° angle made it a whole lot heavier. It became a dead weight. A team effort was the only solution. It was a team effort or nothing.

My feet slipped and skidded over the pebbles that littered the pathway. Sweat stung my eyes and my breathing became laboured; my muscles screamed in agony. Someone developed the idea of walking behind the two men at the back and pushing upwards on their rumps. It helped by taking a few kilos off our shoulders. Twenty metres later, we changed teams again. Sandberg was back with us after his second time up the hill and he replaced one of the front guys. He was dripping with sweat and gasping for breath.

About seven changes later, we neared the top of the hill. We were shaking with fatigue; hands bleeding, knuckles shaved of skin. Knowing we were that close to the summit gave us hope and we surged forward to the top and gently eased the barrel onto the ground.

Bartlett appeared from nowhere.

"Who said you could put 'Felix' down?" he shrieked.

We stared at him in shocked disbelief.

"Who said you could put him down?!" he shrieked again.

We continued to stare dumbly at him.

"Right," he said, moving over to the drum. "Tip it up so that the plug is at the top!"

Four men scrambled to comply with the order. Bartlett reached into his pocket and removed a tool for unscrewing the metal cap.

"Empty it," he said.

The plug was removed and the drum laid on its side. The water splosh-sploshed, glug-glugged out onto the dusty ground – forming a little riverlet trickling down the hill. We licked our lips – suddenly realising how thirsty we were. I vaguely figured that he was doing it so we could carry the drum down empty... probably it was too dangerous going down with such a heavy load? Bartlett soon dispelled that idea.

"You will each make one full trip at a time to the tap down by the shed where you found 'Felix' and fill up both your water bottles, then bring them back to poor old thirsty 'Felix' and fill him up. Understood?"

I was dumbstruck. The drum would require roughly 200 water bottles to fill it. We each had two bottles, which meant 100 journeys to and from the tap. Divided by 13 men, it meant eight return trips each.

We just stared at Bartlett like condemned men.

"Get away you pieces of shark shit!"

He pointed down the hill – a smirk on his face. How I would come to hate, but eventually admire, that bastard.

We skidded down the dusty hill – creating a small sandstorm as we went.

"I really can't believe this," said Dave Kruger, my mate from high school. "We will never make it."

"Gotta try," said Pete Wells – a big man with a strong-looking face. "It's just a test; they can't kill us." The comment gave us hope.

We were about to fill up our bottles when we realised they were full already.

"Drink your fill and then top them up again," Ant Marsh said. I took a couple of swigs and replaced the water from the tap.

A few minutes later, we were done and turned to run back up the hill. Bartlett was at the base of the hill again! How the hell did he do that?

"I said you must fill up your bottles from the tap!"

"Sergeant?"

"The tap, the tap! Are you stupid? The tap!"

"They're already full," stammered Sandberg.

"You disobeyed an order – a lawful order," screamed Bartlett. "You must listen to orders carefully. It could save your tiny, pathetic lives you pieces of shark shit!"

"Sergeant!" we bellowed.

"Fill them up from the tap!" he hissed – bending slightly forward.

I became really angry at the thought of emptying my bottles, then refilling them. I couldn't see the sense in it. What an idiot Bartlett is – what a bloody lunatic. How the heck could this water be any different from the water already in the bottles? Stupid shit! Stupid, stupid shit.

It took five months of this stupidity to realise every order had to be obeyed to the letter.

Pete Wells led the way up the hill. He was a powerful man with massive shoulders and one of his steps was one-and-a-half of mine. He seemed to inspire us and we got going as quickly as we could. After about the third time to the top, it dawned on us that it wasn't a race and no time limit had been set. We settled into a kind of rhythm – just slumping one foot in front of the other – making sure we drank from the tap at the bottom of the hill just in case we suddenly found we had disobeyed some other bloody order.

Pausing at the top of the hill on my fifth climb, I let my eyes wander over the camp below. Immediately below us was the only double-storey building in the camp – and beyond that a further three or four barrack blocks at right angles to the double-storey. Further to the right, below leafy trees, was what looked like an administrative building – and beyond that some more buildings, a hangar, parade square and rugby fields. I came to hate all of it in the months ahead. Beyond the camp, in the distance, was the double-lane highway that brought us here – bordered by houses and a motel. The houses looked lovely in the bright sunshine, with hedges of bougainvillea and red and green roofs.

Towering behind all this stood the massive Bata shoe factory, where virtually every medium-priced shoe worn by every man, woman and child in the country was made. Beyond that, the African veld stretching to the horizon – still vaguely green from the rains that had ended six weeks before, but turning to that familiar golden yellowy-brown that is so typical of the winter bush in Africa. My mind came back to the present with a jolt when I realised I still had another three journeys to that bloody tap.

It was late in the afternoon as the sun was setting, when the final bottle of water spluttered into 'Felix'. Someone from a previous intake had painted a face on the drum and its eyes mocked us.

We were absolutely shattered. Our trousers were muddy; our shirts dusty; faces caked with sweat; mouths hanging open as dry as the dust beneath our feet – little white cakes of dried spittle at the corner of our mouths. Torn skin, torn denims and caked blood.

"Take 'Felix' down the hill," Bartlett said from nowhere.

We obeyed without question or a groan – and as usual, Pete was there to inspire us. We picked the poles up and started slowly down the hill. I was surprised that it was actually easier, as the weight of the drum helped us forward. Apart from a couple of near-misses where we almost dropped 'Felix', we arrived safely at 'his' shed.

My legs were trembling from exhaustion and I had a raging headache.

"You have 40 minutes to shower and change into PT kit," Bartlett said.

PT kit? We couldn't possibly do PT in this condition, but we obeyed nonetheless and after forming up into a squad, ran back to the barrack block (if you could call hobbling and limping a run). When I pulled off my combat boots, two huge blisters stared back up at me – one on the pad of each foot, others starting on both big toes and more on each heel. It was sheer agony walking to the shower block, which fortunately was only a few metres along a glass-smooth passageway.

The hot water was sheer ecstasy as it cascaded over me – literally draining the fatigue out of my body – and unlike Llewellin Barracks, there was an unlimited quantity of it. It was only when I got out of the shower that I noticed how bruised and red everyone's shoulders were. Mine were no exception. Putting on our PT tackies (trainers) was sheer agony. They were still new and stiff and made direct contact with our new blisters.

After forming us up, Bartlett led us at the double down to the canteen. It was a pleasant surprise as there were no more than about 30 men there. What really surprised us were the white porcelain plates we were handed and the civilised tablecloths on civilised-looking tables – and porcelain mugs instead of steel mess tins for the 'have as much as you like' tea. We could help ourselves to as much food as we wanted.

"Listen in," said Bartlett, "you are ordered to drink a bottle of milk at lunch and supper. Is that understood?"

"Sergeant!"

We each wolfed down two crumbed pork chops and a small mountain of mashed potato before tucking into various jellies and ice-creams. We regretted it later, because you cannot run on full stomachs – and we soon learned to eat well, but moderately.

After supper, we shuffled our way down to a small lecture hall where we saw the same movie we had seen at Llewellin, which we tried desperately not to fall asleep while watching. Unknown to us at the time, our course officer was sitting in a darkened room alongside us. I caught a glint of his glasses as he looked at us – a glint of light off glass that I would come to dread in the months ahead.

⁂

My head had hardly hit the pillow when the lights came on and Bartlett stood screaming in the doorway.

"Up, up upp!"

Dazed and sleep-drugged men staggered from their beds – some too slow for Bartlett's liking. He stalked down the right-hand side of the barrack block tipping men onto the floor – kicking their pillows and belongings everywhere. Dave Coleman, a territorial, had the corner of a bed land on his back – gouging out a chunk of flesh close to his spine. I was in a pair of underpants and a civilian T-shirt.

"Ballinger!"

"Sergeant!"

"Who gave you permission to wear civvy clothes in this place?" I could smell beer on his breath.

"Nobody, sergeant."

"Thanks to Ballinger, you can all go for a little run."

Cusses and threatening glances were flung in my direction.

We floundered around trying to find our tackies, socks, shorts and T-shirts. I almost screamed while putting the tackies on; the blisters were so big and tender.

Out into the cold air we 'ran'. I glanced at the barrack-room clock and saw it was 0130.

We turned left at the top of the passage, then left again towards the double-storey building. I was full of rage and pain as I hobbled along. I simply loathed and detested being woken up so rudely. I was designed to be a civvy – a couch potato par excellence. This was shit, man! Continuing left, we ran slightly downhill on tar and then right onto a dirt track. It was sheer hell – absolute agony. The dirt track got steeper and doubled back on itself as we shuffled and staggered uphill – the moon casting grey, dancing shadows through the trees.

After what seemed an eternity, a tower emerged through the brush ahead of us. It was obviously a communications tower because it bristled with aerials and dishes. A large red light stuck on top of the tower cast an eerie glow around us. It was our turnaround point.

We about-faced and charged down the hill again – the chilly night air making our T-shirts cling wet and soggy to our backs. It was 0230 when we returned to the barrack block.

"Inspection at 0530" mocked Bartlett before disappearing through the doorway.

We crashed wet and soggy back onto our beds and I cursed the day the army had sent me my call-up papers. But worse was to come – much, much worse…

At 0530 precisely, Bartlett again entered the room. We were still fast asleep. This sent Bartlett into a towering rage.

I don't remember being tossed out of bed. The first thing I became aware of was the mattress and bedclothes landing on top of me. From all around came the sounds of thuds, screams and cries.

"Up, up, get up you pieces of shit!" screamed Bartlett. "I told you bastards to be ready for inspection by 0530 hours! What the fuck are you still doing in your wank pits?!"

We made a pathetic attempt to form up.

"Clear this mess up, dress in PT kit and get to that tower now."

We obeyed like machines. Beds were righted; mattresses and sheets hurriedly chucked on top; damp T-shirts pulled over shivering torsos; painful feet shoved back into tackies.

Back to the tower on top of the hill again, still pitch-black – a faint orange glow to the east. Up, up, up and down, down, down again.

"I will be back at 0700 for another inspection. You'd better be ready, in full combat kit!"

It was an impossibility to get combat kit on and ready the place for an inspection in half an hour. It was simply not possible. We resigned ourselves to more punishment for failing the order, but it never came. Bartlett returned at 0700 and we doubled off to be served a fantastic, hot breakfast.

"Have a shit, shower and shave and be formed up outside the barrack at precisely 0830. Combat kit, webbing, the whole bang shoot. Got it?"

"Sergeant!"

We made bloody sure we were lined up at 0830, but we still had no idea how to wear our webbing properly ('nobody had told us'). Precisely on time, a man immaculately turned-out in Rhodesia Africa Rifles uniform crunched ballast beneath gleaming 'stick' boots as he approached us. It was the man behind the glinting glasses from the night before. Night before? Man, that seemed ages ago.

We dared not look directly at him, but stared straight ahead at some invisible target.

"Squad… squad, atten… shun!" bellowed Bartlett standing to our side.

Painful feet thumped the ballast in unison – well, almost.

"That was pathetic," hissed the man with glasses. He walked to our front and turned to face us. He wore a hat with one side pinned up – a green, cropped feather sprouting out of the fold.

"You are indeed lower than shark shit to me," the voice behind the glasses said. "I've been watching you since Llewellin and you are a pathetic bunch. How the hell we're going to win the war with wankers like you is beyond me."

I took a very quick look at his face, which looked almost pained.

"I am Captain Theo Williams and I'm your course officer. It's my job to make shark shit think, but how the hell I'll do that with you lot I'll never know."

What a greeting! What a warm embrace. Can you imagine shoppers being greeted at Harrods like that: "Good morning Mr and Mrs Shark Shit. Do your shopping, then get the hell outta here."

The man who we came to know as 'The Smiling Shit' stared at us in silence – almost sniffing the air.

"I promise you that for the first six weeks here, you will barely sleep; you will run everywhere; and Sergeant Bartlett and I will do our damndest to break you." He paused before continuing: "We will be simulating battle fatigue, and even while you are fatigued, you will be expected to think and act and lead because that will be your job for real one day. Do you understand?"

"Sir!"

"I expect you to obey every single command I give you to the letter. Understood?"

"Sir!"

'Because my friend 'Felix' – who, by the way, I introduced to the School of Infantry – will be waiting for you. Understood?"

"Sir!"

He walked slowly up and down the line – looking at each of us while we stared above his hat.

"Shark shit," he said softly – threateningly.

"Saren't Bartlett!"

"Sir!"

"Get this flotsam out of my sight!"

"Sir!"

We charged off down the hill at the double under the cool shade of trees, down past the admin block, past the RSM's office block – skirting the parade ground until we came to the Quartermaster's office near the hangar.

We entered one at a time. I was handed a brown card and my dog tags, which showed my blood group, name and service serial number – V93749 – and blood group ('O') stamped below my serial number. I signed for this on the brown card and put the dog tags around my neck before we were doubled off to the armoury.

I have always had a great love of weapons, and I was overjoyed when I was old enough to buy my first Bruno rifle. I'd bought it with my second paycheque while working for Internal Affairs at Plumtree on the border with Botswana. It was my first job after leaving school. It had been a memorable time working in Plumtree – getting pissed far too often for a young school leaver (so much so that the kindly assistant district commissioner, Jan Buitendag, told me I couldn't drink without his permission because I was still under-age). He embarrassed me no end because he announced this in front of my friends on the veranda of the only hotel in Plumtree. At that age, you are acting grown-up and want to impress people, don't you?

I hated him for that and set out to take the virginity off one, or both, of his two beau-tiful daughters, who were his pride and joy. Afrikaners are very strict with their women-folk, and for a daughter to lose her virginity outside of marriage was unthinkable – so that became my determined task and I spent many memorable moments trying to chat them up and take away their virginity (mine also for that matter), but I never succeeded.

I loved the smell in the armoury; oiled gun metal, grease and a faint odour of cordite and explosives. The racks were packed with rifles of all kinds – communist as well as NATO. We were issued with *Fabrique Nationale* (FN) 7.62 mm (long) NATO rifles and four magazines. Each held 20 rounds.

One side of the armoury had a line of 7.62 mm NATO general-purpose machine-guns – known to us as MAGs – with rows of gleaming ammo belts ready to go draped from an overhead insulated cable. We learned later that the belts were kept fully charged on standby in case the camp or Gwelo was attacked. One didn't have time to charge ammo belts in combat.

We received our rifles, magazines and cleaning kit. We signed for them before forming up in the bright sunlight outside. Bartlett showed us how to put the magazines in pouches and how to hold the rifle in the 'port' position, when we ran from one point to another. Basically, our left hand held the stock of the rifle and our right hand wrapped around the narrow part of the butt – carrying it at a 45° angle across our chest. This was better. Weapons in our hands at last! But still no ammo. What the hell do we kill gooks with?

Bartlett led us up the road at a fast pace, which I found uncomfortable because you need your arms to balance the swing of your legs (otherwise you sort of flop along with your water bottles and pouches flapping against your bum).

Up past our barrack block to the right, into scrub and brush on a dirt track. Thwump, thwump, thwump went our boots – our breathing laboured… sweat stinging our eyes. We ran for perhaps 20 minutes until we reached a small clearing at the head of a rifle range, where we were told to halt. Wet 'cow shit on tarmac' sounds followed because we didn't know how to come to a halt from a run. This pissed off Bartlett so much he made us run to the butts of the rifle range and back again.

We were ordered to sit on logs that had been built into little plastered granite supports – forming rudimentary chairs. They formed a circle and Bartlett stood in the middle.

"This is a rifle," he said, pointing to the weapon in his hands. He then chanted a little song that we had to repeat 10 times. "This is my rifle," pointing at the rifle. "This is my gun," pointing at his dick. "This is for fighting," pointing at the rifle. "This is for fun," pointing at his dick.

"If I ever hear any one of you call a rifle a gun, you will fill 'Felix' up on your own at the top of the hill. Do you hear me?"

"Sergeant!"

"Say it again!"

"This is my rifle, this is my gun; this is for fighting, this is for fun!"

"Again!"

For fuck's sake!

"This is my rifle, this is my gun; this is for fighting, this is for fun!"

"Again!"

And so on and so forth.

We spent the rest of the day learning how to put our webbing together properly and to strip and assemble our rifles. Make the weapon safe by removing the magazine – cocking once and pulling the trigger. We had to run to the butts and back because we didn't point the barrel at the sky when making safe, but 'nobody had told us' we whined. Then, pressing the release catch, we broke the weapon in half and slid the dust cover off the inner working parts – removing them – followed by various other bits and pieces behind the gas regulator and springs etc.

We did this perhaps 20 times – opening up scabs that had formed from slaking 'Felix's' thirst the day before. Each time we had to do it a bit faster, and then with our camo head-scarves tied over our eyes. The weapons were new and unfamiliar to us, so we ended up sprinting to the butts over and over again as punishment.

My watch clicked past 1800 as we staggered into camp. Despite being buggered, I was dying of hunger, but to our shared horror we got no food that night. Several guys dug deep into civvy bags to pull out private stores of food, but they were gone.

"Bloody bastards," shrieked Dave Kruger, "they've stolen my food!"

For a small guy, he could certainly pack it away.

Neil White just managed to shout: "Barrack room, barrack room, 'shun!" before Bartlett entered the room. We scrambled to attention at the foot of our beds.

"At ease," he commanded. "I'm here to teach you mommy's boys how to do bed packs for inspections. Gather around Wells's bed."

We gathered around Pete's bed and watched a ritualistic display unfold in front of us. We were shown how to position the mosquito net astride the pillows, make both pillows absolutely dead square with bits of fruit boxing under the cover; and position belts, brushes, towels and dozens of other items of paraphernalia in precise, measured spaces from the edge of the bed. The sheets had to be folded down in a special way, with the blanket tucked under the turned section of the sheet – all to exact measurements taken off a diagram.

An hour later, Bartlett pinned the diagram to the notice board, then bent down and pulled a candle and a spoon from a box – as well as a large tin of beeswax polish and two brushes.

"Ballinger, bring your 'stick' boots here."

I returned in due haste with a pair of brand-new drill boots that had been issued to us at Llewellin Barracks and handed them to him. He lit the candle and heated up the spoon until it was red-hot, before running the spoon quickly over the little plastic lumps on the surface of the boot. The heat of the spoon made the dimples go flat – the first step in an agonisingly slow process of 'boning' the boot into a shining, gleaming thing that you could shave yourself looking at.

Bartlett stood up and took one step back – and tipped up Pete's immaculate bed.

"All of you will have boned boots, bed packs and squeaky-clean floors for inspection at 0530. Is that understood?"

"Sergeant!" we bellowed.

"And you will sleep in your bed. Understood?"

"Sergeant!"

He eyed us grimly and strode from the room.

"How the hell are we going to do this?" bleated Sandberg.

"Shove it," said Piet van den Berg. "Stop whining."

"Listen in," said Pete Wells, "let's polish the floor and get some shuteye."

"You're nuts. Let's do the bed packs first."

"I tell you, if we disobey Bartlett and sleep on the floor to save our bed packs, we will be in deep, deep shit."

"We'll risk it," said Coleman.

"Suit yourselves, but let's at least get the floor polished first and then we can run a cloth over it in the morning to get rid of the scuff marks."

We nodded and started the long process of applying the polish – waiting 20 minutes for it to dry slightly and then putting an immense amount of elbow grease into getting the floor to shine. It took two hours to complete to any degree of success, but it looked good in artificial light anyway.

After that, the guys did their own thing. Big mistake. This is the army; there is no individualism at this stage of training, although it would be encouraged later. For now, we were being taught to think uniformly.

I decided to follow Pete's lead and jumped into bed – planning to be awake at 0400 to make my bed pack and dress in combat kit. Little did I know that a bed pack took at least an hour to prepare – let alone getting dressed in combat kit.

I lay on my back and stared at the ceiling as the quiet sounds of men putting their bed packs together filled the still night air.

My thoughts turned to four weeks previously when I'd received my call-up notice and the shock and horror that erupted from Jess when she read it.

"A year!" she spat, "a whole bloody year without you."

"I'm sorry babe, there's nothing I can do about it."

"Shit, Tony! Why the hell did we come to Rhodesia if you knew this would happen?!"

"It didn't occur to me. Perhaps I thought it wouldn't happen for a long time yet."

"A whole year – in a strange city without you…" Tears formed in the corners of her eyes.

"You've got the job at the university."

"Big deal! Big bloody deal! Shit, Tony!"

I took hold of her shoulders and her head fell onto my chest as she sobbed. She was a Yank from Connecticut and we had been together almost a year. I'd met her in an Australian pub and we made love on our second date – prefaced by a bit of dope in my mouth and a lot of my dick in hers.

Clattering, crashing noises wrenched me to the surface of consciousness like a bolt from a crossbow. I propped myself up on one elbow and watched, detached in a dreamlike state, as Bartlett tipped up one bed after another that had been made into bed packs – shouting and screaming at the occupants to get off the concrete locker tops and get into their bloody beds!

He didn't touch the guys that were under their sheets and I smugly thanked my lucky stars that I had listened to Pete. I looked at my watch – 0330 already.

I was cold, tired and hungry when my alarm clock went off at 0430. It was a struggle to get out of bed. The early stages of exhaustion were creeping in, and it was into this exhausted mindset that the instructors came charging like bulls in a china shop.

We staggered into our combat kit – less our webbing – and began the slow process of making the bed packs. We didn't have bits of fruit box packaging to square our pillows off, but we did the best we could. There was only one instructional diagram available and we shuffled to and from this like zombies to get the measurements of curled belts from the edge of the bed, brushes from the edge of the bed, hand towels from the edge of the bed and so on. None of us had remembered to bone our boots, which were standing in our lockers in the correct fashion. A big mistake.

By 0515 I knew we were not going to make it, and I resigned myself to the coming punishment. At precisely 0530 in walked Captain Theo Williams to the usual accompaniment of: "Barrack room, barrack room, 'shun!"

We crashed to attention as best we could, but nobody had told us how to come to attention yet. That would come later in exhausting drill sessions.

Williams took two steps into the room, and from the corner of my eye I saw his gleaming 'stick' boots slip out from him – his arms flailing wildly to correct his balance. My eyes shot forward and made contact with Pete Wells. Our tightly-clenched mouths began to tremble as we battled to stop a flood of laughter. Williams corrected his balance with the aid of quick reflexes from Bartlett and gingerly marched into the room. Bartlett was dressed in drill kit, wearing a diagonal red sash over his green and white RLI stable belt – his green beret with the silver bugle badge set at a rakish angle on his head.

Williams didn't say anything until he reached Sandberg's bed two down from mine.

"Pets!" he said with mock horror. "What's your name, shark shit?"

"Sandberg, sir!"

"Why are you keeping pets in your net? Dead pets at that," he said, craning to have a closer look.

"Pets, sir?"

"Look at the pets, Sandberg."

Sandberg swivelled around and saw two dead moths in his mosquito net.

"Moths," he said feebly.

"Pets!" spat Williams – licking his lips like a lizard. "We don't allow pets on government property, Sandberg."

"Sir!" shouted Sandberg – standing rigidly to attention.

"Sergeant," Williams turned to face Bartlett. "You know what to do. Burial at 1000 – standard grave sizes."

"Sir!" Bartlett smirked.

Williams lost interest after that – obviously satisfied that he had found what he wanted. What we didn't know until many months later was that 'pets' were a standard 'plant' in mosquito nets by the instructors – and ours had been duly installed while we were on the rifle range.

We had no breakfast. Instead, we had to double to the Quartermaster's office to collect picks and shovels. What bloody insanity was this?

At the barrack block, we had to put our dead pets into a matchbox (symbolising a coffin) and then double with it to the upper part of the rifle range – picks and shovels clanking along as we ran. By then, our rifles went everywhere with us and never left our sides.

"Your rifle must be closer to you than anyone in your whole life – including your mommies, you mommy's boys," Bartlett had mocked.

We reached an area that had obviously been dug before and we set about digging separate holes two metres long, two metres deep and a bit wider than our shoulders. The ground was hard and stony and it took us ages to get it squared away. Our hands were rubbed raw by the time we had finished.

At 1000 precisely, 'The Smiling Shit' appeared in a Land Rover, but remained seated.

"Carry on, Bartlett."

"Sir!"

Rotating to face us, Bartlett told us we were to bury Sandberg's pet, but it was to be done while we faced away from the graves. Matchbox in hand, Bartlett quietly dropped the box into one hole and a few pebbles into other holes to confuse us. We were then instructed to shovel the soil back into the holes.

"Return to the barracks and change into drill kit," Bartlett sneered.

We doubled off only to discover Williams had been in the barrack block and had tipped our kit all over the floor.

"For fuck's sake!" screeched Sandberg.

"What's the point of griping?" I snapped. "Your bloody pets did it for us."

"How the hell was I supposed…"

"Put a cork in it," shouted Pete Wells, "just get dressed, man."

We scrabbled around putting on shorts and shirts that should have been stiffly starched, boots that should have been boned and gleaming, berets that we didn't know how to wear and stable belts that we didn't know how the army buckled them.

Bartlett appeared, took one look at us and bellowed at us to double in our brand-new, unbroken drill boots back to the graveyard with picks, shovels and rifles clattering together. It was sheer agony. We were dirty, tired, thirsty, hungry and our blisters shrieked at us for mercy.

At the graveyard, Bartlett asked us which grave contained the 'coffin'. We had no idea, and nor could we. We had been facing the other way.

"Dig up the pets," Bartlett said.

We obeyed with heavy hearts. We were really knackered and my feet and hands ached like blazes. The 'pet' was discovered two hours later in Piet van den Berg's trench and we then had to bury it again – thankfully for the final time.

We staggered into camp towards sunset – and after spending an hour being taught how to wear our drill kit correctly, we were instructed to prepare for another inspection at 0530 the next morning.

"You had bloody better get it right this time," Bartlett snarled.

Most of us showered to let the hot water ease away our aches and pains, but my feet still hurt like hell and I could only hobble back to the barrack block. On entering, I noticed a couple of guys talking to an African man through the back window.

"What's up?" I said, shuffling up to them.

"Phillimon here reckons he will bone our 'stick' boots for 10 bucks each. He'll take them now and have them back by midnight."

"What if it's a trick?" I said.

"So what? What can they do to us they haven't done already?"

We agreed – and after writing our initials on the inside of the boots, we handed them to Phillimon. Ten bucks was a fortune to us (we only got $45 a month as recruits), but we figured it was worth it.

Time passed agonisingly slowly and midnight came and went. Still no boots. By then, we had polished the floors and shut all the windows to make sure that no 'pets' flew into our mosquito nets. We were still unaware they had been 'plants' all along. We had painstakingly ironed our shirts, shorts and squared away our berets with badges.

By 0230 we were beginning to panic about our boots, but just as Pete was about to go and 'find the fucker to knock his head off', he appeared at the window with another man carrying a big box.

The boots were absolutely immaculate and shone like a halo over a saint's head. We just couldn't believe it. Our pathetic attempts with spoons and candles had been hopeless.

"How the hell did you get them so good?" Ant White asked.

Phillimon gave a big toothless grin.

"Use iron *baas*, iron very good. Put in fire to make vely hot and then *fagga* polish *baas*."

"Chuffed!" we chorused.

Time for an hour's kip and then make our bed packs again. We slipped off into a deep sleep instantly.

It took ages for the alarm clock to rouse me – and when I awoke, I found I was almost crippled by stiffness, fatigue, aches and pains. It was sheer agony putting the bed packs together and dressing – especially putting on my boots (that seemed to have shrunk a bit after Phillimon's 'ironing' technique).

We were as ready as we would ever be when the wall clock read 0530.

I glanced around at the other guys – boots gleaming on a sparkling floor under shimmering white lights, shirts starched, shorts starched, berets sitting at that 'how-the-hell-does-it-stay-on-their-heads' angle. I felt strangely proud and strong with these men – experiencing a sense of comradeship that would last many years into the distant future.

Bartlett and Williams entered a few minutes late. This time, Williams entered the room very carefully indeed – the steel studs of his 'stick' boots tap-tapping on the floor like a predator's toenail as he progressed.

When he reached Coleman, he paused and looked closely at his uniform.

"Threads," he said, before moving on to Sandberg and then to me.

"Threads," he repeated – tugging at three or four loose threads on my uniform.

"Sergeant," he said, without turning to look at Bartlett, "these men are virtually undressed, wearing rags. A soldier wouldn't dress like this – threads hanging everywhere."

"Sir!"

"Punishment. PT, Bartlett."

"Sir!"

And off we went – not in PT kit, but in our shiny 'stick' boots to sprint along the tar road and do star jumps until our bodies shrieked for mercy – followed by endless piggy-back races on the rugby field.

It went on like this for six weeks – six weeks of sheer hell. We carried 'Felix' to the top of that hill 25 times before 'Phase One' was over. We never had a full night's sleep and had to double everywhere, but all the time we got fitter, harder and stronger.

Even when in a state of almost total mental exhaustion, we still had to go to the lecture hall and learn about patrol formations, convoys, ambushes, radio voice procedures, weapons training, 'Felix', shooting at the rifle range, assault courses, principles of camouflage, survival, silhouetting, unarmed combat, more 'Felix' and battle marches.

I hated those battle marches. We had to fill our rucksacks up with wet sand, fill our pouches up with painted rocks and drag a car tyre behind us for 15 kilometres. On one such march, I had to carry a machine-gun in addition to this load – and at the end of it, an assault course was waiting for us.

Phil Laing was feeling so weak on one assault course that he fell from the top of a 10 metre assault net and landed squarely on his back. He was badly winded and could hardly breathe. It was the first time I saw worry and compassion in the eyes of 'The Smiling Shit'.

Phil ended up in the infirmary at Thornhill Air Force base for a week – suffering from concussion and temporary memory loss.

On another occasion, we were bundled into trucks in the dead of night and driven 30 kilometres to Selukwe – a small mining town east of Gwelo. Charlie Pope was a skiver of note, but had the brains to phone for a taxi to collect him while the rest of us slugged it all the way back to camp – arriving bone sore in time for an impromptu inspection. Charlie, of course, had been sleeping on the back seat of a regular's car since 0100.

I remember trying to stay awake in the lecture hall. Captain Williams had put a bucket of cold water next to his desk and if he saw anyone nodding off, we were called forward and had to dip our heads under for a full 15 seconds. The shock of it worked wonders.

Severe punishment followed another episode when we were sent on a 20 kilometre-long run; four men to a large gum pole that we had to hump (in addition to full battle kit). After about six kilometres, we thumbed down a passing farmer in a 10-tonne truck, who gladly offered us a lift to the front of the camp – our plan being to de-bus about two kays from the front gate so that we wouldn't be spotted by guards or any other army personnel. But we hadn't banked on 'The Smiling Shit' deciding to check our progress in his personal Land Rover.

We were about a kay from our de-bus position when he saw us. I will never forget the look of disbelief on his face as we sped in opposite directions along the dual carriageway – nor the dread I felt when I saw his glasses reflect back at me through his cab window.

I can't remember the punishment for that episode, but it no doubt involved copious quantities of 'Felix' and more big, stinging blisters.

Many days were spent on the parade ground with Bartlett, who went through the arduous task of trying to teach us how to march – something I definitely had no skill at. I have always found difficulty in co-ordinating my hands and feet, as various girlfriends over the years have learned when trying to teach me to dance.

What a joke. I just couldn't get it right. I couldn't 'about face' – going through all those measured steps to turn 180°. I couldn't 'present arms', 'riyaaat turn' or even start off on the correct foot while swinging the correct arm.

It sent Bartlett, who was a superb drill instructor, into fits of rage and frustration as he watched my pathetic attempts to follow his orders. About the only thing I got right was coming to a halt, which I did well. I hated those days on the parade square as I was the only guy who didn't have a tea break during the long, long sessions conducted in the heat of the day. No, I had to march up and down looking at myself in a huge mirror positioned on one corner of the parade square – much to the delight and amusement of my comrades.

I reached a point where I began to doubt whether I would stay the course. I felt depressed thinking about Jess alone in Salisbury, but I wasn't the only one facing stress it seemed. I began noticing that Sandberg and Crowe were beginning to withdraw into themselves – becoming silent and indifferent to the usual banter that went on in the barrack room in the evenings. The long days of physical and mental stress and lack of sleep were beginning to take their toll on both guys. It didn't go unnoticed by Bartlett. He zeroed in on them like a shark sniffing blood and rode them even harder.

"What's up?" Pete asked Sandberg one night.

"I just can't take this fucking place any longer."

"It's just a test Brian. Remember what the 'Shit' said to us when we first arrived here. This is simulating battle fatigue, so just press on, man."

"I can't Pete. I've had it."

"Come on Brian, give it a go man. Things will ease up soon. You don't want to be rtu'd back to Llewellin, do you?"

"I don't give a shit anymore!"

And that was that. Crowe was sent packing when he failed to vault over an obstacle on the assault course after a five-mile run in full combat kit. A few days later, Sandberg vanished. It seemed like he had never been there. Two guys gone in the first six weeks. We were down to eight. Eight out of the 600 in our intake! (Brian died many years later in 2014 – a wonderful man full of the love of life. He became an exemplary medic during the bush war, saving many lives.)

The end of the first phase of training came to an end as quickly as it had started. Bartlett strode up to us on a Thursday afternoon while we were weeding the lawn outside the officers' canteen – or mess, as we called it. He had a smirk on his face.

"Listen in."

We stood rapidly to attention.

"It's the end of your first phase. You will be allowed to have a beer in the recruits' mess tonight and if you pass inspection in the morning, you will be allowed a 48-hour pass."

We could scarcely believe our ears – 48 hours of freedom.

"But cock the inspection up, and you will stay right here and weed the entire camp. Got that?"

"Sergeant!"

The one beer in the dimly-lit recruits' mess went down like liquid gold and made the lot of us instantly pissed. Alcohol does that to you when you are superbly fit.

"We can't cock up this inspection," Dino Quinn said, squinting at me.

"No chance," Pete chipped in. "It'll be the smartest barrack room in the galaxy. It had better be, because any guy who prevents me from getting my end away is mincemeat."

We just couldn't believe how pleasant this surprise break was and how much it meant to us. In the six weeks we'd been here, there had been no time off. It was grind, grind, grind up to 20 hours a day in some cases – and our Sundays were spent weeding lawns or getting our kit sorted out away for the next inspection.

We slept until 0330 and then slaved away until the inspection at 0600 – making sure the barrack room was completely spotless and that every net was minutely inspected for 'pets'. Windows and floors were shined to perfection, drill boots like mirrors, every thread on every item of clothing burnt off with a match, bed packs checked and re-checked against all measurements and then tested with a long ball of string to see if every bed was lined up with the next – including all the contents on them. Each guy checked his neighbour and then the guy opposite him. We couldn't have got it better if we tried.

At 0600 sharp, Williams marched in with Bartlett close behind him. Our boots made a uniform smacking sound as we came to attention – eyes fixed firmly ahead. My heart was in my throat as I watched them proceed from one man to the next – pausing here and there to look at something. Around he came until he was standing in front of me – looking at my bed and then at me… his glasses reflecting the overhead lights. Only one man to go… Dino Quinn. Will we make it, or won't we? Williams turned abruptly and stood on a steel trunk to wipe a white cloth over the concrete surface of the row of lockers. It was spotless. A perfunctory look at Dino ended the inspection. We got our passes.

Charlie Pope, Phil Laing, Dino Quinn and I squeezed into Charlie's green homemade VW Beetle, which looked like a cross between a dune buggy and a Pookie – a locally-designed mine detection vehicle. He affectionately called the monstrosity 'Pickles'. We were beside ourselves with joy as our passes were checked at the guardroom. Then we were off along the road in bright winter sunshine – dressed in crumpled civvies with not a care in the world.

My stomach gave a squirt of adrenalin when I realised yet again that I would be seeing Jess in three hours. We stopped off in Gwelo – feeling as tall and proud as kings – casting disapproving glances over all the 'soft' civvies around us.

"Civvies are such losers," Charlie said arrogantly.

"You're still a bloody civvy yourself," Phil snapped back.

"Piss off! I'm in the army now."

We bought beers, cokes and chips, had a piss in an alley and zoomed off down the road. What a tremendous feeling of freedom – roaring along munching chips and swigging beer. Freedom at last.

I fell asleep somewhere around Que Que, only to be wakened two hours later by a very red-eyed and pissed Charlie Pope – our driver.

A bolt of adrenalin shot through my system when I realised I had reached the University of Rhodesia's staff quarters, where Jess lived.

"Shit, man," I said to the others. "I feel like a bull off to the slaughterhouse."

The guys shouted typical sexual innuendo before disappearing in an oily cloud of exhaust fumes.

It looked a nice place to live. The double-storey building was surrounded by neat gardens and green, trimmed grass with large Jacaranda trees sheltering parked cars. I headed for the entrance and then up one flight of stairs to flat number eight. My heart was pounding when I stretched out my hand to knock on the door. Rather 'Felix' up the hill than this.

Jess opened the door on the third knock and the moment I saw her face, I knew trouble was brewing.

"Jess," I said, kissing the cheek she offered. It was not exactly the welcome I wanted.

"Hi hon," she said and walked back into the room. I was crestfallen.

"What's up babe?"

She shrugged her shoulders and her lips began to tremble – big salty tears forming in her eyes.

"What's up my love?" I said tenderly – pulling her into my arms. Her whole body trembled slightly, with tears forming in her eyes. She pulled away from me and busied herself in the kitchenette – taking two cups from the cupboard.

"Six weeks," she said – her back to me – while pouring tea, "six bloody weeks and not a bloody word from you."

I surveyed the interior of the room as she spoke and felt depressed looking at the rickety furniture and a crumpled bed through the bedroom door.

How could I explain six weeks of hell to someone? Six weeks of no sleep, no passes, no spare time, no telephones and 'Felix'. It all seemed so pathetic now – standing in front of her.

I walked up behind her and put my hands on her shoulders.

"It's been hell Jess. I haven't had a spare minute to myself the whole time, phones were banned and I hardly ever got any sleep."

"It hasn't exactly been a bed of roses here," she said unsympathetically. "This is a strange country to me, with strange customs and strange people. You were the only thread of security I had when I got here."

She turned and handed me a cup of lemon tea. Good old Jess – always the naturalist. I hated lemon tea, but it was good to swill the beer and sleep from my mouth.

We sat next to each other on a couch.

"How's your job?" I said, trying to change the subject.

"Not bad, actually. I'm the personal assistant to one of the professors – mainly admin, but I also help with research stuff."

"You look lovely, Jess."

It didn't have the desired effect. She stood up and walked to the window – looking outside.

"How long do you have?"

"Until late Sunday afternoon."

"Great," she said looking into her cup, "and how long until the next time?"

And to think I had been dreaming of seeing her for weeks.

"I don't know," I snapped. "I didn't exactly plan this whole thing."

An awkward silence followed. I sipped my tea, then put my head back and closed my eyes – suddenly feeling very tired.

I didn't feel her sit next to me, but I could smell her – that smell of hers drove me insane. Her mouth closed over mine – lips slightly parted, tongues gently exploring each other's. An electric thrill ran past my groin into the nape of my neck. I carried her through to the bedroom and threw her on the bed – her yellowy-blonde hair spreading over the pillow.

Our lovemaking was urgent, passionate and deep – lasting until well into the night – by which time we lay sweating in each other's arms deeply content and unaware of the world around us.

It was 8:30 a.m. the next morning when Jess stirred me gently awake – coffee in hand. We made love again before showering together.

"You're gorgeous," Jess said as she soaped me down. "The army's done wonders for your physique…"

"What's your excuse then?" I breathed into her mouth.

Brunch followed, but as we started to prepare it, we realised we had no milk and eggs. I offered to go get them while Jess tidied the flat.

It was lovely walking to the shops. It was a clear sunny day – cool and fresh. I turned left out the back gate of the campus and then along a leafy lane towards the shops on The Chase – heading for Bon Marche. I eyed the houses as I walked along – typical suburbia. Two-car garages attached to large houses on an acre of land, swimming pools, tennis courts and trimmed hedges. Water sprinklers tush-tush-tushing away, the sound of kids slashing in water and the thwa-plonk of tennis balls striking racquets. Servants clad in white ferrying copious quantities of meat and drinks to barbecues, or 'braais' as we called them.

Did *they* know or care who I was, though? Did they know I had been through hell for weeks on end to learn the trade of killing – to protect them? Would they offer me a beer or even listen to my stories? I figured not and the thought of it made me feel slightly depressed. I don't know why, but time stands still in the army – and my six-week absence from civilian life seemed like six months. Everything looked just that little bit foreign and alien to me – almost like I didn't belong there anymore.

"Your brother's just been here," Jess said, taking the groceries from me.

"Why didn't he stay?"

"Had to get back to something. He left a surprise for you."

"What?"

Jess tossed a set of keys at me from the table. I recognised them immediately. His car keys.

"Ah, fantastic!" I said looking at them. "We can go for a drive in the country, babe."

"We'll need this then," she said, holding up a bottle of wine.

"More importantly, this," I said, rolling up a blanket with a naughty look on my face.

We packed a basket of wine, cheese, bread and a salad for the tree-hugging Jess. Everything had to be 'natural', she would say in her Yank accent.

"I just can't get over my *boet* letting me use his car," I said, admiring the neat interior of the 1275GT Mini.

"*Boet*? What does '*boet*' mean?" Jess asked. She pronounced it 'boot'.

"*Boet*? It's afrikaans slang for 'brother'. You've got a lot to learn *vrou*."

"Shit, man. What does 'fro' mean?" she giggled.

"'Woman' – that's what it means. 'Woman'… you beautiful specimen."

I put on my sunglasses, turned up the stereo to full volume, engaged reverse and zoomed backwards. The car retraced my steps back to The Chase and past the shops – a quick chicane – and in a few seconds we reached second street extension. I felt like a million dollars as we zoomed past the last set of traffic lights; Standard Bank sports club on the left and then into the wide open country.

Mazoe Valley was one of the lushest farming areas in the country and it hosted a massive orchard of orange trees – many hundreds of acres in size – fed by a large, shallow dam surrounded by blue hills and bush. It produced the locally-famous Mazoe orange crush – a superb cordial when mixed with ice and water. In fact, no other cordial has met its quality in any of my travels. Most Rhodesians would agree.

The dam didn't quite make it as a tourist destination, but nonetheless, it had a hotel just past the dam wall with a nice pool and band area. It was a place I had often visited during many happy weekends when I was younger.

The road leading to the dam passed through some of the most fertile farms in the country. They were neatly bordered by rows of pine trees that acted as windbreaks. Lands were neatly tilled and many were showing a full crop of mealies. The steep hills bordering the road were covered in large msasa trees. They have the unusual beauty of their leaves turning red (before they turn green) in summer. We would always know that it was a sign that we were going to have good rainy season if the msasa trees turned deep red early.

"I'm loving this!" Jess shouted above the roar of the car engine.

We stopped at the little kiosk by the dam wall and bought ice-cold cups of Mazoe orange – as well as a bag of oranges to take home with us. While we were parked, a convoy of army trucks pulled into the kiosk area – the guys 'coo-cooing' and whistling at Jess, much to her delight.

For a brief second, I was back at Gwelo with the guys – getting ready for a training exercise or off on some formidable route march.

"Penny for your thoughts," Jess said, still waving at the guys. "Jealous huh?"

"Far from it. I was just thinking of something else… seeing all those guys."

We finished our drinks and headed down the winding road past the dam wall, through towering 'yellow fever' thorn trees and up to the hotel on our left. I was shocked. It was my first dose of Uhuru – the new 'freedom' in Rhodesia – as the winds of change swept down from the north. I took in the rusted kids' swings, the empty swimming pool, the long grass fighting for dominance over a wild bougainvillea where the band members used to play the favourite hits of the day. The hotel roof was rusting and the odd corrugated iron roof sheet was beginning to peel off at the ridge. A white man came down the steps and got into a pick-up before driving off – obviously a 'few sheets close to the wind'. Laughter came from within the bar. We parked the car and decided to investigate.

I led Jess into the dimly-lit interior, which brought back memories of me standing at the same door whining at my dad to bring me a coke and a packet of Willards cheese and onion chips. My eyes adjusted to the gloom and I suddenly realised we were the only white customers there. A dozen or so black faces turned to look at us.

"Not my cup of tea," I said sourly – pulling Jess out the door.

Blacks hadn't been allowed in white establishments before, but now they were swamping them. On the drive out, while showing Jess the orange orchards, the little black kids didn't seem to smile and wave like they used to do when I was a kid.

"It's all changing, Jess – and I don't think I'm gonna like the end result."

"You can't stop these people enjoying what you enjoy Tony."

"True Jess, but what we build up, they take away. It's a clash of cultures more than race. I don't give a shit that their skin's black; it's a cultural thing."

Suddenly, the bush no longer looked friendly, but strangely ominous. I had been away from Rhodesia for several years – working my way around the world. It was the first time since my recent return that I was seeing change – albeit subtle change. Buildings were not freshly painted, pot holes were appearing in the roads and there were hardly any young white males in the streets. Military vehicles were everywhere, shortages of all sorts of things were creeping in and luxuries were disappearing.

We decided to stop at a picturesque spot on the way back to town near Mazoe boat club, but there again I found my favourite fishing spot overrun with locals, who would twist their upper bodies to look at us as we drove past. I carried on out the other end and after paying two dollars' entry fee to the boat club gate guard, settled in among some large msasa trees at the water's edge.

"This is nice," Jess said, making herself comfortable on the rug. I sat next to her, but my mind was far away.

"What's up, honey?"

"I dunno Jess. I'm a bit frightened by the changes I'm seeing. Nothing's the same anymore. This whole area used to be alive on the weekends; the hotel pool full of kids and young lovers necking under the trees, people queuing up for orange juice at the kiosk, canoes and boats on the dam – and look at it now… it's barren and full of ghosts."

"Well, hardly. It is getting on for winter, after all."

"It's change; that's what it is – not the weather – and it will never be the same again."

"You can't stop the majority from sharing what you have, Tony. It's not reasonable."

"That's okay for you to say. You have a country to escape to. Change for me and my culture is a death sentence."

An awkward silence fell between us.

"I'm sorry," I said after a long time. "You see, Jess, the kiddies' swings back there and the swimming pool? That's a microcosm of what every facility and tourist outlet in this country will come to. There will be no more young lovers necking under the trees anymore. We are, basically, in full retreat as a culture. Keeping what we have, including law and order, is like trying to walk against a stream – a very powerful stream."

Chapter Three

It was like entering Alcatraz when the guard lowered the boom behind us. My stomach was in a tight knot.

"Just bloody wonderful," Pete said, looking out the window.

We drove up the road that led to our barrack block – passing a group of regular recruits going in the opposite direction.

"What the fuck am I doing here?" lamented Charlie Pope in his slow drawl.

The road twisted to the left and right until we came to a small parking area reserved for recruits' cars. It was a cool day – bright and sunny like most winter days in Rhodesia. Shadows were lengthening as the sun started to set.

We hauled our suitcases and bags off 'Pickles'' roof rack.

We walked into our barrack block half-expecting Bartlett to run in and start screaming at us, but the place was empty apart from Piet van den Berg and Coleman.

"Guys," we greeted each other – stowing our civvy stuff away.

"What's the plan of action?" van den Berg asked.

"Inspection at 0600; combat kit with 'cunt caps'," Coleman answered.

"For fuck's sake," Pete said, "I should've left Salisbury at midnight tonight. I'm back too early!"

I decided to get a drink from the mess, but it was closed, so I followed my feet and ended up walking all the way to the top of 'the hill'. I sat on a rock watching smoke and steam from the Bata shoe factory curl up against the huge coppery sun as it slipped towards the horizon. I felt totally depressed. The last 24 hours had been unforgettable. We'd only left our bed to get something to eat or drink – making love for hours on end to Pink Floyd, Carlos Santana and America... lost in our own cocoon of joy and abandonment.

Jess had been devastated when 'Pickles' arrived to collect me. She stayed inside her flat because she didn't want the guys to see her red eyes and streaming nose from crying so much. I felt a real shit leaving her like that.

My mind returned to the present. Lights were coming on in the valley below and it was dark by the time I got back to the barrack block.

We were as ready as we could be for inspection at 0600, but oddly enough, Bartlett didn't look at us or our bed packs.

"Listen in," he said. "From today, there'll be no more bed packs and no more running at the double. Instead, you'll march as a squad and there will be inspections every Friday morning at 0700. Got that?"

"Sergeant!"

"But don't for one second think this place is turning into a holiday camp just because 'Felix' hasn't seen the top of the hill for a few days, if you get my drift?"

"Sergeant!"

"From now on, you will rise in the mornings at 0600 and be ready, beds made and room tidy to do PT in gym kit unless I tell you shark shit otherwise."

"Sergeant!"

"As for today, the lecture hall," he said, curling his finger to follow him.

We grabbed our lever arch files, pens and pencils and headed outside to form up into a squad – marching as best we could to the lecture hall situated to the one side of the admin block. 'The Smiling Shit' was already waiting inside for us.

"We start 'Phase Two' of our training today – the 'Classical Warfare' phase. As you know from your notes, there are generally three stages in the type of war we are fighting. 'Phase One' is the indoctrination and terrorising of the local population to subdue them. 'Phase Two' is the 'Insurgency', or 'Counter Insurgency' stage. This is the phase we are currently fighting. 'Phase Three' is total 'Classical War', when the country is at its weakest point of resistance.

'For the next few months, you will learn the art of classical warfare. This warfare involves the use of armoured or mobile infantry, tanks, artillery and air support. This was the kind of war your fathers fought in the Second World War. In your case Coleman, the First World War!"

It was a joke from 'The Smiling Shit'! We didn't know whether to laugh or not, which resulted in an embarrassing silence and a throat-clearing exercise from Williams.

Williams turned back to the board and chalked in big bold letters 'THE ATTACK'.

And so, 'Phase Two' began. It was up at six each morning, followed by an hour of intense, gut-twisting PT before shit, showering and shaving before a big hot breakfast. There was as much tea as you wanted without the blue 'keep your pecker down' chemicals in it. I felt great – fit, healthy and young.

Felix was still dished out occasionally, but whether we had adapted or not, those eyes on the drum weren't able to mock us like they had before. For some reason, the grind up the hill didn't seem to bother us anymore.

Nor did the five-kilometre run to the end of 'the hill' and back every time we made a cock-up, or said something stupid to 'The Smiling Shit'. Without realising it, we were being moulded into a team – a team that depended on each other for moral support and encouragement. We trusted each other.

The next two months was gruelling, but it was also very interesting. I felt good learning about stuff I had always been curious about anyway.

A couple years before when in high school, I had collected all the military clippings from the local newspaper I could find. There were pictures of men in uniform, men in training, men in convoys and RLI guys smiling from the pages of the news magazine. I had attended every single army march-past through the city of Salisbury and had watched with youthful wonder and glee all the aircraft roaring overhead as rank after rank of men marched below. I grew up loving the army and had planned ambushes and attacks with my toy soldiers up to the age of 16. My mates, all involved in the never-ending pursuit of girlfriends, used to mock me.

We learned how to patrol, attack, set ambushes, drive in convoys; how to react to an attack in convoy or on foot; digging shell-scrapes covered in camouflage at the end of each day. We learned about 'H' hour; how to form up for a company or platoon attack; how to build sand models for giving orders; how to employ the effective use of artillery and mortar support; how to 'talk in' aircraft to strike a target. It went on night and day ad nauseam.

The night ambushes were very realistic, with trip flares and live tracer bullets lighting up the night – claymores thudding and crashing around us as they exploded. We did co-ordinated attacks with the air force at Katanga and experienced the thrill of Hawker Hunter strike aircraft zoom over us as we attacked an 'enemy' position, using live ammunition.

Watching a Lynx push-pull aircraft drop a large bomb was a thrill – especially when a rear echelon admin girl (obviously some officer's 'ground sheet') got blown off her feet from the intensity of sound and shockwave from the bomb. Pete Wells, Ant Marsh and I laughed at her white petticoat flapping in the wind – arse up in the air.

"Gives me a hard-on," Pete whispered in my ear.

The paperwork and theory came in volumes – resulting in us having to stay up until the early hours of the morning studying for tests that came around every week as regular as clockwork.

After our PT and morning inspection on Fridays, which occasionally resulted in 'Felix' going for a joyride, we would have our breakfasts and cram in a few minutes of study time before our exam at 1100 on the dot. Fail two tests in a row and you were returned to unit or rtu'd back to Llewellin – a positively horrendous thought for all of us.

I have a good memory, so the tests were no problem, but three others fell foul of them. Suddenly, Dave Kruger, Piet van den Berg and Coleman were gone. We were down to six men. Five reserve or territorial sergeants on a refresher course brought our numbers back to 11.

I was particularly shocked that Piet van den Berg was rtu'd because he was a tough soldier and invariably came first in most physical activities, but he seemed to struggle with communications in all its forms – and an officer could not fall victim to that. I heard a rumour later in the war that he passed selection for the Selous Scouts – perhaps one of the toughest outfits in the Rhodesian Army.

During our free hours, which were rare and far between, we would cram into the recruits' pub – rubbing shoulders with regular recruits from all the main battalions in the army. We were allowed two beers each – and most importantly of all, we could make phone calls from the cubicle next to the gents' toilet.

My calls to Jess were initially full of bounce and excitement, but as the weeks went by I detected strain in her voice, which left my gut twisted and knotted after I hung up. I tried to reassure her all would be well – as much trying to convince myself – but I knew in my heart that we were splitting apart. Her letters became less frequent, and then dried up altogether.

'THE DEFENCE' Williams scrawled on the board.
We learned the art of defending against an enemy attack – digging interlocking and zig-zagging trenches that could not be seen from the ground or only partly from the air. We learned the art of setting up machine-guns on fixed lines, erecting barbed wire and positioning dummy anti-personnel mines in channels that would force an attacking enemy into our chosen killing field. The digging left large, stinging blisters on our hands.

The nights were bitterly cold. Gwelo and the Somabula Flats were notorious for their bitter winters, where the wind chill factor permitted by the treeless landscape cut right through our tunics – leaving us shivering until the first rays of sunlight warmed us up again. The funny thing was, we never got sick – so much so for those stupid adverts on TV where you had to wipe away every germ to keep your family safe. We ate meals on top of green fungus in our mess tins, and I can honestly say I was never healthier in my life.

'THE WITHDRAWAL'.
"Not something we plan to do in our army," quipped Williams, "but we must show you how to do it so you are not routed and end up in a stinking POW camp.

'The art of 'The Withdrawal' is that you must leave sufficient men in contact with an attacking enemy while withdrawing your major force to erect a new line of defence in the rear. The essence of this is the timing. The German general in charge of the defence of

Berlin in the Second World War was famous for his ability to detect an imminent Russian attack – moving his men to a secondary position before the main attack fell. In this way, he cost the Russians over a million casualties in their attack on Berlin."

A million men... a million men! What horrors went on there?

"Part of the strategy of defence is that you must patrol your environment. While intelligence is important in the attack, it's equally important in the defence. If you can't see an attack coming, you're dead."

The Chinese perfected the art of deception during their attacks in the Korean War when they poured in their tens of thousands over Allied bases. This caused some of the fiercest defensive battles in any war. The Korean War is now called 'The Forgotten War'; so few people know about it today.

After two months, the theoretical phase came to an end. It was time to put what we had learned into practice.

"Listen in," Bartlett said as we stood to attention in the barrack. "At 1000 tomorrow morning we'll depart by vehicle to Bulawayo, where you will be reunited with your wank partners from Llewellin. You will be ready with all your classical warfare kit, helmets, webbing, bayonets, packs, sleeping bags, rifles, the works. Got it?"

"Sergeant!"

"It is time to see if you shark shit can lead instead of follow like a bunch of mommy's boys."

"Sergeant!"

The three-hour drive to Bulawayo was a welcome break – and as cold as it was, we chattered away on the back of the truck like a bunch of kids on a school outing. Well, we were kids really, but we felt mean and threatening in our full classical war combat kit. Boots, denim trousers, shirt, combat jacket, webbing, rifles and helmets covered in strips of camouflage material. Our white epaulettes identifying us as officer cadets made us feel very cocky indeed, but the reality was that they were just strips of cloth. We enjoyed de-bussing at a garage to buy cokes and chips and look threateningly at the wide-eyed faces of the locals who dared to look at us.

It was mid-afternoon when we drove through the gates of Llewellin and I thanked God I hadn't been rtu'd here. What a dump the place looked.

We felt cocky enough to shout 'fresh puss' at a bunch of recruits as we bounced towards the rugby field, where we camped for the night.

The next morning at 1030 we left Llewellin for Essexvale at the head of a 20-vehicle convoy. It was an impressive site with over 130 men dressed in full classical warfare kit pouring through the streets of Bulawayo. People stopped to stare, but we had been instructed not to wave back. We had to look disciplined and military-like. The remainder of the 600 men from our intake had been ferreted away to regular units or specialist units like mortars, tanks, armoured cars and artillery. Some had been downgraded to 'B' category to serve as drivers.

Although I had been with these men for a few days before we went to the School of Infantry, it was good to see them again. Dave Kruger, Piet van den Berg and the rest waved self-consciously when they saw us – not knowing whether to salute or give us a twos up.

Essexvale, like most of Matabeleland, is a dry, inhospitable place with rolling hills interspersed with wide flat pieces of land and thorn bushes.

We were allocated about 20 men each. The territorial sergeants acted as our platoon sergeants for the exercise. It was acutely embarrassing having 20 men stomp to attention in front of me when I was introduced as their officer cadet. After all, in Bartlett's eyes, I was still lower than shark shit.

I suddenly realised I had to put into practice what I had learned, which was intimidating. While the men unpacked and the rear echelon men erected tents and kitchens away to the rear of our defensive position, the officer cadets were given a briefing about the current situation in our 'war game'.

We were facing a possible enemy attack in battalion strength, with light tanks and armoured cars in support. Our position straddled the only road through the area – about five kilometres from a small bridge in enemy territory. We were to select the best defensive ground and dig in for their attack. I was dropped into the deep end straight away – and after receiving call-signs and radio frequencies, I was told to select the best defensive position and 'dig in'.

Returning to my men, I took a clipboard and wrote down their names – amused that Dave Kruger, my school buddy of long standing, was among them. His presence made it seem like cowboys and Indians, really. Dave, sadly, was killed by a landmine about a year later.

I divided the men into squads of eight and allocated each squad a trainee corporal – men who had been on the LTU, or Leadership Training course, at Llewellin. Each squad received a radio and call-sign.

Taking my map, I quickly established the boundaries of my platoon area. Then leaving the men behind, I went forward with the sergeant to reconnoitre our defensive positions. Satisfied that my left and right flank linked up with the platoons on either side of me – and that we had sufficient elevated ground to build machine-gun nests – I briefed each corporal to start digging bunkers and trenches.

Walking behind me, every step of the way, was an instructor – men mainly from regular army units like the Rhodesia Light Infantry. This fine unit had a nickname, 'The Saints', and everywhere I went, I was accompanied by my own 'Saint' – making notes on a clipboard.

Being an officer cadet did not exempt me from digging trenches and bunkers – and I mucked in with the rest. We had to go far into the rear areas and cut logs to cover our bunkers – followed by a deep layer of sandbags and soil removed from the trenches. They were then carefully camouflaged. I instructed my men never to use the same route to each bunker twice, as this would form a path that could be clearly seen from the air. My 'Saint' ticked something on his clipboard.

The ground was stony and it was tough work getting to the correct depth, but by 2300 we had finished the bunkers. We would start the trenches the next day. It was hard work and all I'd eaten that day was two boiled eggs and a slice of bread. In the tradition of the British Army, whose traditions we followed closely as colonials loyal to the crown, the officers ate after their men had eaten their fill. Needless to say, the mountain of food brought up to us in stainless-steel tureens disappeared like lightning – leaving us poor officer cadets with virtually nothing (the scraps, if you will).

By the time I had done my rounds (checking on my men, ensuring that guards had been posted), it was 0100. I was totally knackered, thirsty and hungry. Slipping into my sleeping bag, I reflected on the past day's work. I felt I had done reasonably well and there was one thing for sure: I was a lot fitter than my men thanks to 'Felix' and 'The Smiling Shit'.

The attack came in at about 0400 – that time of night when you are drugged by sleep and totally disorientated.

"Stand to!" I shouted above the din of automatic fire and mortars.

Men poured from holes all over the place – scrambling to find helmets and equipment. I made a mental note that must not happen again. The guys must know where their bloody stuff is; that's where the fine line between life and death is drawn – in the detail.

"Shit," said Dave Kruger, standing next to me. "That's live ammo they're using."

I stood transfixed – watching the red tracer arc above our heads, probably at treetop height, and shivered as each mortar round landed about 200 metres to our left to give the impression of a real attack.

Quickly realising that I wasn't a follower anymore, but a leader, I sprung into action – grabbing hold of the radio handset, calling headquarters to tell them we were under attack. I imagined a 'Saint' ticking a box on a clipboard somewhere.

I called each squad leader in turn and told them to fix bayonets and prepare for an infantry attack. Faint glints of helmets and bayonets filtered out the dark bush as the men obeyed my orders.

Although it was only a mock attack, it was extremely realistic and frightening – and we stared into the gloom waiting for the inevitable 'enemy' assault. It came in the form of a company of demonstration troops specially trained for these exercises, and they appeared through the cordite-smelling dust like ghosts in the night – silhouetted against several flares that they tripped. It was actually quite frightening, and I could easily imagine count-less soldiers down through the ages seeing this for real.

"Fire!" I screamed at my men and into the handset at the same time.

A cacophony of sound and lights erupted all around me as over 130 men down the line opened up with blank cartridges – the flash hider of each barrel spewing out sparks and cordite. The enemy infantry came on, with pre-selected men falling to the ground in increasing numbers until the attack faltered and died; the 'survivors' turning and running for their lives.

It was remarkably real and exciting, with attacks continuing for four nights in a row – denying us the rest our brains screamed for. Coupled with poor quantities of food, it became a real test of my ability to lead and to remember that all the while, my 'Saint' was circling in the background.

On the third night, I was tasked to lead a recon patrol to a nearby bridge to see if it was strong enough to support the weight of tanks – information vital for headquarters to see if armour should be sent to reinforce our position. Other officer cadets were tasked with leading defensive patrols.

I must admit I was totally buggered and disorientated when the eight of us set off. I didn't have a clue where to go in the pitch-black night. For a reason I will never know or understand, my 'Saint' told me to follow him. Maybe he wanted to get the exercise over and done with so he could get some sleep himself?

He led me through thickets, over roads and fences, in and out of river lines and after about two hours, we approached a small concrete bridge that spanned a river. 'Enemy' guards were pacing back and forth – and in the distance, two instructors sat by a fire drinking beer no doubt.

Leaving my men, I crept forward with my sergeant and looked the place over through binoculars. They didn't help much, but they slightly amplified the starlit sky enough for me to see what was going on. I couldn't get any closer as the ground was flat on my side of the bridge. I made a mental note of what I had seen and slid back to join my men. I followed my 'Saint' blindly back to my bunker – only to be awakened by another attack an hour after I had fallen asleep.

I was completely shattered when I reported to the course commander to give him a debrief on the previous night's operations. This took over an hour in a hot tent.

Then, while my men dug more trenches, I had to complete admin returns – giving the platoon strength, ammo supplies, food and water requests and so forth to headquarters. Then I had to pick up a shovel and dig alongside my men. After this, it was down to the tureens to eat scraps gain.

On the fourth night of the mock attack, we were told not to fix bayonets – and I knew something was up. An attack came in at 0300, which 'succeeded' and the demonstration troops poured over our trenches – firing blanks at us. It was shocking and mind-numbing – and all the while, I had to run around giving orders to men as best I could. It was time for the 'withdrawal' phase – although if this had been real, we would all have been dead or in POW camps.

The withdrawal is really just a repeat of the defence, except we had to simulate 'leap-frogging' backwards to a new defensive position, where thankfully, we only had to dig 'shell-scrapes' – coffin-sized holes half a metre deep. All the while, the 'Saint' circled like a vulture – making notes.

After five days of starvation, I told the guys that if they couldn't be reasonable and leave me some food, they would bloody well dig trenches until they died. Not surprisingly, I ate pretty well that night.

The attack, to me, was the most interesting and exciting part of the war game – although in reality, I couldn't think of anything more dreadful than running across a flat piece of ground with men firing automatic weapons at you; weapons so powerful they were capable of decimating a company assault in seconds.

To prevent such a massacre, it was essential that the enemy position was 'softened up' or suppressed in such a way that they would either be dead in their trenches or sufficiently cowed not to fight back. We achieved this in platoon assaults by laying down extremely heavy fire on the enemy position with two or more machine-guns, while the remaining infantry manoeuvred themselves onto the flank or side of the enemy position (depending on the terrain that offered the most cover to manoeuvre). This was known as a 'flanking attack', which had the added advantage of making the enemy defend two fronts at the same time – thus weakening his response.

The attack was expected to be costly in terms of lives, because the attacker was exposed while the defender was sheltered – overlooking his chosen killing ground. For this reason, the attacking force should always be at least three times larger than the defending force. But how do you know how large the enemy force is? The answer, simply, is intelligence.

Intelligence was gathered by patrols capable of snatching prisoners for interrogation; or from specialist forces like the SAS, who could monitor movements deep in the enemy's rear; or intelligence gathered from aerial photographs.

In classical war, you knew where the enemy was and he knew where you were, so there wasn't the secrecy of the terrorist slipping into the night. Here, we faced trenches and tanks and artillery, which meant we could gather our own intelligence.

For the first three days of the attack phase, we practised platoon attacks; learning how to put down suppressing fire; then flanking the enemy position using live rounds. It was quite hairy to say the least, and I quickly learned that a loose helmet can be as dangerous as a karate chop to the neck, so I tightened the chin strap well every time I put it on.

After each enemy position was 'taken', we had to swing in the direction that the attack was going in case the enemy decided to counter-attack. You always had to end up facing the enemy. At night, we dug in again – ensuring that the machine-guns were well-camou-flaged and had a clear field of fire.

For the men, this was exhausting work – but for the officer cadets, it was bone-crushing. Not only did we have to do what the men did, but we had to plan, organise and give orders, which often meant making new sand models in the fading light to give and receive orders. We had to do all the admin that a classical war formation loved generating.

By the end of the ninth day, I had lost so much weight that my denims barely stayed up and the puppy fat I had carried most of my life was gone for good. We spent the tenth and final day of the exercise learning the big one, where all three platoons came together to launch a company attack. Because of the three-to-one ratio to assure the success of the attackers, we would be attacking an enemy force no bigger than a platoon in strength. The 'enemy', as usual, was a platoon of demonstration troops commanded by Ant Marsh, who had rather cleverly twisted his ankle so that all he could do was hobble around or stand up in a trench.

During daylight hours, we learned how to form up near the start line, or pre-assault area. The men would move forward and lie down in the actual formation the attacking force would choose.

Because daylight frontal attacks would be virtual suicide against modern weapons – as was seen in the First World War – it had become the entrenched practice for most attacks to go in at first light. This was when the enemy was sleepy and his reactions sluggish, or at last light when the human eye cannot easily detect accurate information – thus making an attacking force of 100 men suddenly look like 200 men.

This happens when a reduced level of light causes the cones in the retina, used during the day, to 'switch off' – thus allowing the rods in the cornea of the eye to take over for night vision. At this point, it is difficult to distinguish shapes, numbers and movement

– and is, therefore, one of the favourite times of the day for military commanders to attack. Indeed, an attack at last light had the same effect. New Zealanders became specialists in the night attack, as the Germans and Italians found to their cost in the Western Desert of North Africa during the Second World War.

At 1630 on the last night of the exercise, an attack at last light was decided upon and all 135 of us marched silently out of camp – led, to my surprise, by Phil Laing. We were blackened up and carried only our weapons, radios and webbing. To ensure we were totally silent, all metallic objects were removed and we had to jump up and down to see if we 'rattled'.

Our target was a set of trenches at the top of a gently-sloping rise overlooking a large treeless field that we would have to traverse. We walked until the wintry sun had disappeared below the horizon – at which point we squatted by the side of the road until it got too dark to see. A 'Saint' then took over from Phil Laing and led us to the bottom of the slope – setting us up in rows in our assault positions. In front of us was the dull green glow of several lights that demarcated the front of the assault position. The lights were specially made to emit hardly any reflection and only faced in one direction: towards us and not the enemy.

I lay down on the cold earth waiting for the command to attack – resting my head on my outstretched arms; my helmet too heavy to look up for long periods. We waited for what seemed an eternity for the command to 'go', and when it finally came, we stood up and began walking forward at a fast pace – looking left and right to keep our dressing.

Spreading out from left to right – two platoons in line abreast at the front, with the third platoon forming the second wave – we marched steadily up the hill with bayonets fixed. In a real battle, our supporting artillery, mortars and heavy machine-guns would be pounding the enemy – forcing him to keep his head down – thus enhancing our chances of success and survival. That night though, all I could hear was the rustle of the men's boots passing through the short stubbly grass. For some reason, this sounded sinister, like a long snake slithering up behind you.

We kept going – our breaths short and sharp as the incline of the hill worked against us.

I turned to look around and was impressed by the sight of 100 or so men – arms locked forward on their rifles, bayonets pointing forward, surging ahead. It was impressive indeed – especially since the poor light made us look like 200 or more men.

At 50 metres, the front ranks were ordered to take aim and fire – slowly and deliberately – as we walked at a stiff pace. This was necessary because, by then, the supporting artillery and heavy machine-gun fire would have ceased firing, so it was up to us to do our own suppression of the enemy forces.

At 30 metres, a great cry went up and we charged forward – screaming at the top of our voices, drunk with excitement – into the enemy trenches firing at anything that moved. Scared blackened faces looked up – trying vainly to raise weapons in confined spaces to fire back at us. We totally eliminated the 'enemy' position, then moved slightly beyond the trenches before returning to them.

When all the noise and excitement had abated, I reported to the company commander by radio that the position had been taken. I then did my rounds to assess casualties and expenditure of ammunition. I also ordered a two-man listening post to move about 100 metres down the opposite slope in the direction that the enemy had 'fled' so they could warn us in case of a counter-attack.

After a lengthy debrief under hissing gas lamps, we were marched back to the main base camp, where a surprisingly good meal and cokes awaited us.

"Shit," Ant Marsh said hobbling up to me – coke in hand, "if that'd been the real thing, I would've shat in my pants. I have never seen anything so scary as you guys charging up the hill towards me. I didn't know whether to run or fight – even though it was only an exercise."

On a Thursday afternoon, after a particularly demanding inspection which we nearly failed, we humped 'Felix' up the hill for the final time.

"You," said Charlie Pope – affectionately tapping the top of the drum, "will be full of holes when I leave this place."

We just knew, that being a long weekend, the instructors would want time off with their families, or beer, or both. It was debatable though if 'The Smiling Shit' and Bartlett felt any compassion towards us, but indeed they did and we got a 72-hour pass. We had to report back any time before our 0600 PT run on Monday morning.

"I'll take my kit with me and leave Salisbury at two in the morning," Pete Wells said.

"Don't expect me to give you a lift so late," Charlie replied. "It's cutting things too tight."

"Relax. Phil's getting his dad's BMW. I'll come with him."

It was close to 2100 that frosty winter's night when I tapped on Jess's door. I hadn't told her I was coming so I could surprise her. My heart was thumping in my chest. Music filtered down the hallway.

Jess opened the door as far as the safety chain would allow and her eyes grew big – jaw dropping slightly. She made no attempt to let me in.

"Tony?"

She stood there transfixed.

"Aren't you going to let me in?"

"Tony," she repeated dumbly – her face bright red.

"Who is it?" a male voice called.

Jess looked back and then at me. She could see the look of disbelief on my face. "Great," I said, having nothing else to say.

"Tony, I'm sorry. It got so lonely here."

"How long?"

"Four or five weeks. I don't remember."

She ran a hand past her ear – pinning loose hair behind it.

"Great," I repeated.

"I wanted to tell you, just didn't know how. Can't really believe it's happened."

There was movement behind her and a slim, long-haired man wearing only underpants came up and looked at me through the crack of the door.

"Who is he?" the man asked – resting his hand on her shoulder.

Jess looked at the floor.

I don't remember kicking the door in or physically throwing the man against the wall, but I do remember hitting him hard until blood and snot smeared his face.

"Tony, please go!" Jess said, pounding ineffectually on my shoulder. "I'm sorry, but please go. It's not his fault!"

I looked at her tear-stained face for the last time and walked off into the night. Two years of my life had gone in less than five minutes. What was that all about?

I was angry and charged with adrenalin so I didn't notice the six kilometre walk to the Monamatapa hotel in the centre of town.

It was only when I reached the gents' toilet that I saw caked drops of blood on my face and right hand. I washed it off and headed into the main bar, which was bursting full of yuppies – all happy and hot in the confined space – faces reflecting joy and laughter. I ordered a beer and sat in the far corner. It was long into the night when I staggered to a hotel room and fell fast asleep – face down on soft white pillows.

I don't remember much of Friday and Saturday night because it passed in a drunken stupor, but I vaguely remember hooking up with some young female travel agents from South Africa – invited to Rhodesia to sample the tourist spots and hotels first-hand.

I sat in a silence all the way back to Gwelo, while Charlie Pope and Phil Laing bragged about their conquests, real or imaginary.

Chapter Four

"Your last six weeks here will be spent studying counter-insurgency," 'The Smiling Shit' said, writing 'COIN' on the blackboard. "COIN is the abbreviation given to the counter-insurgency phase of war. You will remember that it is first the indoctrination of the local population and then the terrorisation of the local population.

'Rhodesia's been in the COIN phase of this war for four years – and as time progresses, you will see the size of the insurgent groups getting bigger and bigger as they convert to a classical war footing. For now, though, you will invariably bump small groups of terrs – possibly numbering as few as two or three or as high as 30 or so.

'God help you if you're in a stick of four or eight men and you bump into 30 gooks. That could be quite hairy."

Without realising it, Williams prophesied an event a year into the future when Theo Nel, one of our corporals and an exceedingly brave man, took on 12 (reinforced to 30) ZIPRA gooks in a contact, which earned him the Bronze Cross of Rhodesia for his exemplary leadership and bravery. Theo progressed to become a sergeant in the RLI and was the only man to pass his Selous Scout selection course near the end of the war.

❧—❧

Sweat stung my eyes as I stooped to inspect the footprint. I blinked it away irritably. The heat was as overpowering as the silence.

I gave the thumbs-up to the man next to me. He smiled – the white of his teeth contrasting with his blackened face. We were onto them again. The bastards had almost lost us in the rocky ground. I looked back at the stick I was leading, but could barely see them.

"Open ground in front of that gomo",[1] I whispered to the tracker next to me. "Could be a problem?"

"Ambush," he nodded.

A faint static-filled voice broke radio silence.

---

1   Gomo: Pronounced quickly on the tongue – 'Gommo'. Rhodesian slang for a hill.

I saw slight movement near a large rock on the hill. I could actually see one of the bastards. My heartbeat accelerated.

The tracker had seen him too.

"We'll work our way around the side of the *gomo* and take him by surprise."

My FN felt heavy in my slippery hands. My heart was thumping – adrenalin pouring into blood vessels.

I belly-crawled back to the eight-man stick I had with me – propping myself up on the trunk of a leafy mopani tree.

"One Three Alpha, this is One Three," I spoke into the radio handset.

"Go ahead," the metallic voice said.

"We've seen gooks on a *gomo* about 100 metres due north of me, copied?"

"Copied."

"Wait for me. I'll come back to form the assault group and work our way around to attack from the east, copied?"

"Copied."

I looked forward at the hill once more.

"Pass the word down the line," I said to the corporal, "gooks in the *gomo* directly ahead. Give us covering fire when we attack from your right front, from the east. Got it?"

"Yes, sir," he nodded and licked his lips.

"Get the machine-guns into the best possible positions; they're worth 20 men each. I'll depress my handset three times when we are ready to assault, but only open fire when you hear shots. Make sure your fire swings left as we advance."

He nodded and crawled away to give his orders, while I slithered back to the main body of about 20 men. I briefed the sergeant and two corporals and waited while they passed my instructions down the line. We rolled quietly out of our backpacks; webbing, radios and rifles only.

Blackened, sweaty faces gawped back at me as I slithered to the right of them to take the lead.

"Let's go," I said to the corporal.

We walked slowly into the thick bush – spaced far enough so that we didn't create a target, but close enough to see each other.

There were a number of rocky outcrops on the way to our start line, and for a brief moment I became lost and disorientated. There was a risk that the gook I had seen was a sentry, and the main body was somewhere in the matted growth and rocks ahead. A close quarters contact could occur at any time. Fortunately, the hill we were targeting was prominent, with a large boulder and tree close to the top. I caught a glimpse of it from time to time as I moved through the undergrowth.

We reached our assault position 20 minutes later. I spread the men out as much as possible – carefully avoiding twigs and sticks that might crack underfoot. My heart thumped and my ears buzzed.

I made eye contact with the corporal and nodded my head in the direction of the enemy. It was time to go. I depressed my handset three times – getting two bursts of static in response. We emerged from the undergrowth in a long, raggedy line that had to sort itself out as we moved towards the hill. I thanked God that it wasn't a completely bare area. I had chosen the line of attack well.

A long, tearing burst of automatic fire shredded the silence and there was chaos all around me. I saw two men drop to the ground from the corner of my eye. I didn't need to tell the men anything – they were already firing. The noise was ear-shattering and dust flew everywhere.

Above the roar of our own weapons, I became vaguely aware of our supporting machine-guns opening fire to our left.

It was my job to keep order and momentum in the attack, but everyone seemed to have disappeared. Where the hell was everyone?

"Keep going," I bawled at the top of my lungs. "Keep going!"

We were close to the hill now.

"One Three Bravo, begin swinging your fire slowly left," I yelled into the handset. I couldn't hear a reply. I just hoped Duff heard me and had swung the machine-guns slightly to his left. I had no wish to get cut to ribbons by my own covering fire.

We reached the bottom of the *gomo*. Rocks and trees towered above us. I had completely misjudged the size of this hill. Everything looked like an enemy. Everything was happening so fast. I'd read that in the Battle of Britain, those huge aerial dogfights suddenly dispersed until only one or two planes were slugging it out over a wide area.

That is what had happened to me. I simply couldn't control so many men in such rough terrain any longer. It was one-on-one and I had to leave it to the individuals to sort out.

I focused directly ahead and began climbing slowly. Only what happened directly in front of me mattered. Higher, a little higher, rifle pointing forward. Heart pounding. Something ahead to the side of a tree trunk moved. I double-tapped two rounds at the fleeting figure. Did I hit him?

In Hollywood movies, they come staggering around with tomato sauce over their chests – saying a few choice words before they 'died' at one's feet. But I could see jack shit! Was the bastard dead or wasn't he?

I inched my way forward – firing steadily into the undergrowth – but nothing was there. I'd missed him, but he could be anywhere. My chest tightened – expecting bullets to come crashing into me – but nothing happened. The noise was indescribable and despite the size of my assault force, I could only see the odd man here and there.

I knew by then that although only a few minutes had passed, that One Three Bravo's ammo must be getting low. I decided to change them into a stop-group. I crouched behind a rock and called 'Duffy' on the radio.

"One Three Bravo, One Three Bravo, move south west of the *gomo* and see if you can cull any runners."

I repeated the order – hoping that Duff had his ear pinned to the radio as we'd been taught. There was no way I could even hope to hear the answer, so I continued moving forward and up. Up! Up! Up!

I thought I could see the top of the hill, so I moved forward again – accelerating slightly to catch up my men.

A shadowy figure stepped out of a small cave to my left, and as I swung to face the threat, the gook fired a long burst at me.

"You're dead, you wanker!" Bartlett shouted above the noise – and then put a whistle in his mouth and blew like crazy.

The cacophony of noise died down to the odd 'thwack, thwack' of weapons – then silence.

"Form up in the open area," Bartlett shouted.

Men materialised from everywhere – some higher up the hill than me, others lower down. 'Dead men' stood up and dusted themselves down.

We gathered around Bartlett in the centre of the clearing – dripping sweat and swigging water. Williams appeared from nowhere and the 'sergeants', 'corporals' and 'officers' followed him to a tent about 100 metres away to be debriefed, while Bartlett did the same to the troops.

It was the fourth time we had done the exercise that day – and we had to do it at least three times more. No exercise was the same. Each had its own variable, like gooks ambushing the attacking force heading for the assault position and so on.

The debrief was intensive and thorough. I was corrected for trying to deploy such a large assault group in thick bush without knowing the enemy's strength. It would have been preferable if I had split my platoon into three – forming a stop-group to kill gooks fleeing the contact area – having a fire-support group of two machine-guns and three riflemen and a smaller, more manageable assault force to lead the attack.

"Other than that, Ballinger, not too bad," Williams said, concluding the debrief.

We had lunch under the trees, and afterwards we started the exercise all over again, with another course member being the 'officer' and me the 'sergeant'.

The whole time this was going on, we had 'The Smiling Shit' and a couple of 'Saints' hovering around us like avenging spirits. I was wondering when will it ever end?

We finished our training in late August 1976 – just as the weather was getting warmer and the trees were beginning to leaf. Nature was waiting for the November rains to sweep away the dust and grime generated in the dry winter months.

We were allowed a few beers in the mess that night, and for once I relaxed and enjoyed the companionship of my course mates. Whatever the future held for me, I had done my best. I sat in the mess with the other guys and looked at the plaques and paraphernalia from previous intakes – letting my eyes linger over the plaque we had donated the week before. It was a small tyre attached to a board by a piece of rope, with intake number '152' stencilled above it. The tyre commemorated our many battle marches dragging a car tyre behind us.

The motto printed beneath the tyre: 'Ask of me anything but tyres', was a parody of what 'The Smiling Shit' had screamed at us in the lecture hall: "Ask of me anything but time, gentlemen, anything but time!"

"I never thought the day would come," Pete Wells said, sipping his beer.

"Me neither," I replied. "It was really intense."

I sat for awhile remembering the last six weeks of our COIN training. Learning how to track enemy spoor, set ambushes, patrols (river-line patrols, fan patrols, every kind of patrol). Setting up a bivvy, camouflage, calling in air strikes onto gook targets. Emplaning and deplaning from Fireforce helicopters, first aid, mortars, rifle-range work, map-reading exercises, on and on and on for weeks at a time. Receiving orders, giving orders, walking miles through the bush, sleeping rough and cold. A real journey to Shamva, to track real gooks spotted in the area.

And now that it was over, where would we be posted? Hopefully, not to some shitty place with buffalo beans – a plant with fibres which were so itchy, that the victim could go almost insane if they touched his skin. Maybe the eastern Highlands, with mountains, valleys and frigid water stocked with trout? What about the south-east of the country, where stubby mopani trees and elephants abound?

Kariba in the north maybe, with its vast man-made dam covering thousands of square kilometres? Or Centenary and beyond… Fireforce country, Mukumbura land.

The Brits used to sing: *'It's a long way to Tipperary, it's a long way to go'*, while the Rhodesians sang: *'It's a long way to Mukumbura, it's a long way to go.'*

In a few hours we would know our fate, but for now we enjoyed each other's company, got totally pissed and went out to punch 'Felix' full of holes.

The next morning, five of us – only five men out of the 600 in the intake – stood at ease outside 'The Smiling Shit's' office. This was it: the culmination of many months of training. Even at this late stage, we could 'fail' the course by getting lower than a sergeant's rank, such as a corporal or even a lance corporal's rank.

My stomach was fluttering when Pete Wells was called in first. 'The Smiling Shit' was torturing me by starting from the lowest letter of the alphabet. Pete came to attention and was marched in by Sergeant Rumble, who had replaced Bartlett in the closing week of the course. Pete was gone for about 10 minutes. When he emerged, he was smiling and returned to his position in the squad.

"Marsh."

Same thing again, but this time he was gone for almost 20 minutes.

"What you get?" I hissed at Pete – two men down from me. It was a rhetorical question in my opinion. He would definitely be commissioned – perhaps even get the Sword of Honour.

"Lieut," he whispered back.

Good, I was glad for him.

I was just pondering the thought that if we were being called in alphabetically in reverse order, then Kevin Torode should have gone into the office before Marsh. Maybe the name-calling was just random?

Ant Marsh came out smiling – mouthing the word 'Lieut'.

"Ballinger!"

For a split-second, I forgot how to march. I started off on the wrong foot – really cocking it up. Coming to a halt in front of Williams was pathetic, but I hoped my salute looked smart enough.

"Ballinger," the 'Shit' said looking up at me. Light from the doorway reflected off his glasses so I couldn't see his eyes. "Ballinger," he repeated – looking down at a folder, then up again. "What can I say about you? I really battled to come to a decision about you."

"Sir," I responded neutrally.

"There are some good and bad traits about you. Let's start with the bad traits."

He flicked through a few pages of the folder.

"You are not good at long-distance runs. In fact, you came last in almost every one of them. I nearly failed you on that alone because an officer has to be fit and tough enough to lead his men in every situation."

"Sir."

"However, I will give you credit for having finished every run and battle march, so you got points for persistence. Not every run to or from the enemy is at full speed, but it does require grit – and you continually showed that quality. The thing that troubled me the most is that you lack self-confidence and the ability to stamp your authority on your men. You want to be friends with them – to be popular and liked. This is a disturbing trait in an officer because some of the decisions you may have to make will be to let your men die, or to commit men to a certain death if the need arises. This becomes hard if you become too pally-pally with them."

"Sir."

He paused – glancing down at the folder again, reading a few notes. I felt stiff and uncomfortable – sweaty in the rising heat in the office.

"Your strengths," he said looking up at me. "You're an academic. You came pretty near the top of every test. You're observant and have a natural ability to grasp facts quickly.

'You have a good tactical mind – perhaps the best on the course – and it was this trait, revealed in the classical war phase, that stood out the most. Your advance, withdrawals and associated planning was very good indeed."

I felt encouraged and knew it was unlikely I would get less than sergeant.

"Generally," 'The Smiling Shit' went on, "you did reasonably well. But you are some-what of a contradiction Ballinger; not sergeant material, nor the type of guy that shits on men to discipline them. Then you are not quite physically fit enough to shine as an officer. You walk well, but you lack long-distance stamina."

He paused and again studied the folder. Surely I couldn't be failed because I was totally breathless after a six kilometre run? No assault on an enemy position would be more than 100 metres – and I had the stamina to walk long distances. What's the problem? My confidence nosedived again.

"In the end though, I figured that as you climb up the ranks, your tactical mind will be more valuable than your lung-power, so I have decided to commission you. Well done Ballinger."

I couldn't believe it. I felt as if I had been poleaxed. Joy and relief flooded my being. 'The Smiling Shit' stood up and extended his hand to shake mine – a smile on his face, a smile that for once wasn't malicious and nasty.

"Well done."

"Sir!"

"Well done, sir." Sergeant Rumble said, saluting.

I stared at him shocked and confused. I was no longer lower than shark shit. I was being saluted by the course instructor.

"It's customary to return a salute," Williams said dryly.

I hastily saluted Rumble and then Williams.

He handed me a slip of paper to take to the quartermaster to get my shoulder pips. I then marched out the room with Sergeant Rumble.

"What you get?" Phil whispered.

"Lieut."

"Thought you'd failed," Marsh said, without humour.

"So did I. Believe me, so did I."

Of the 600 men called up during the first week of April, only three of us were commissioned – a 0.5 percent success rate. Phil Laing was promoted to sergeant and we remained very close friends. He was horribly murdered in December 2003 in post- independent Zimbabwe when, as an accountant for a tea estate, he was forced to drink five litres of acid while tied to a tree. His crime? He worked for a British-owned plantation – and at the time, a lot of hostile words were being directed by Mugabe towards the Prime Minister of Great Britain, Tony Blair.

Kevin Torode also got sergeant, but deserted in 1977 – a short time after being separated from his stick in the worst thunderstorm in the Zambezi Valley I have ever seen in my life. Charlie Pope and Dino Quinn were sadly rtu'd, but would later become a corporal and sergeant respectively.

That afternoon, we marched to the quartermaster's stores to draw our epaulettes. Wells, Marsh and I were handed two pairs of dark green material with a single embroidered pip on each of them.

I put them on my shoulder straps, and for once was allowed to walk back to my quarters. I was highly embarrassed when the RSM – a man before whom everyone quivered – stood at his door, saluting in my direction as I walked past.

Still unused to being an officer, I turned to see where the officer was whom I should salute, only to be chastised by the grim-faced RSM, who said:

"I am saluting you, sir!"

I prayed that a hole would open up in the ground and swallow me.

The next day was our passing out ceremony, and we went through a series of noisy drills and demonstrations for the sake of our proud and wide-eyed relatives – ending the evening in a lavish black-tie dinner that turned into a drunken brawl as we skidded around in our tuxedos playing Bezant and tug of war. Bezant was a quaint game that involved putting a metre-long stick between your forehead and the ground and then running around a fixed point before standing up. Once you were standing up, you were supposed to use the stick as a golf club to thwack an empty Bezant orange can into a goal – thus scoring a point.

The comical result was a lot of pissed penguin-looking officers staggering around uncontrollably – thrashing away at the air and leaves in an attempt to hit that damned Bezant tin into the goal. The level of danger and anticipation was heightened by us playing next to the swimming pool, where one or two unlucky idiots ended up.

I had the misfortune of wearing a rented tuxedo that was so big on me that it was pinned at the waist under my jacket. I don't remember it happening, but guys swore that my pants fell down during a dance with my lovely escort; my head nestled between her boobs – ecstatically happy and wearing a pair of mud-stained underpants.

Chapter Five

The weekend pass gave me a chance to return to Salisbury and spend the time with my brother and parents, but I wished I hadn't gone because I knew Jess was just the other side of the city. I talked to my family and watched TV without really seeing or hearing anything because my mind was on her and our two years together. It was all I could do to muster enough willpower to stay away from her.

At least I knew where I was going: 4 Platoon, 4 Independent Company at Wankie in Matabeleland. I had worked as a trainee district officer in Plumtree after leaving school, so I knew it was a hot and arid part of the country, with the massive Wankie National Park and the Victoria Falls forming a large part of the district.

Wankie's claim to fame was that its coal-fired power stations provided a major part of the country's electricity requirements. Their fuel source, top-grade coal, came from nearby mines that had a recorded reserve of 2,000 years' supply at current excavation rates. The coal fields covered thousands of square kilometres.

Pete Wells, Charlie Pope, Phil Laing and I were allocated to infantry units made up entirely of national servicemen, but led by regular officers. Ant Marsh was given the Sword of Honour, which surprised me really, and he was sent to the Rhodesia Artillery Regiment, where he had great fun bringing down fire on Russian-made T34 tanks when FRELIMO tried to expel Rhodesian forces during the *Operation Miracle* Cassino battle east of Umtali in 1976.

At 1800 on a Sunday early in September, the four of us drove to Wankie in Phil's green BMW to link up with the troops we were destined to lead for the next year. The journey to Bulawayo was familiar, but beyond that, it was new territory. I let my mind wander back to my childhood when I played rugby in Bulawayo and used to go fishing in the Maleme Dam with my brother and uncle Ronnie. It wasn't the huge fish we caught that stuck in my mind, so much as the beautiful girl whose name I have forgotten and whose big nipples pointed accusingly through her wet shirt after swimming in the cold water of the dam.

We passed through Bulawayo, which means 'house of slaughter' in the local Sindebele vernacular, at about midnight. We only stopped to refuel and grab a bite to eat at a takeaway.

"Who's been out this way before?" I asked from the back seat.

"Me," said Pete. The others shook their heads.

"Just our luck to be posted to a bloody desert," I said.

"You're nuts," Pete said. "We couldn't have got a better posting. There's bound to be female visitors in the Wankie National Park, and Victoria Falls is an international babe magnet."

Charlie perked up.

"You bet. Hotels, casinos, game parks and a Gary Player golf course. What more could a tourist want?"

We drove on in silence through the night. The car headlights cut a swath through the dark African bush, and here and there eyes reflected back from the darkness as a wild animal looked towards the strange metal monster that slid by.

Albert Ncube was born approximately the same year as me – 1955. I knew nothing about him at the beginning of my national service, but knew screeds about him by the end of it.

What made this tall, muscular Matabele man with narrow, yellow eyes turn into the killer that he became?

Perhaps it was because he had always been a petty thief and criminal – operating out of the huge, sprawling black townships around Bulawayo. Maybe it was because some white person had insulted and humiliated him in his youth? Maybe it was because he felt it was time to kick the Mukiwa's[1] ass out of Africa? Whatever the reason, the liberation struggle gave him the perfect opportunity to refine his ability to rape, pillage and murder to a fine art.

We arrived at our base camp at Wankie at 0700 on the Monday morning. It was already hot and humid as we emerged sore and stiff from the 900 kilometre drive.

Near the top of a fairly substantial hill – where we'd just parked – was the administration block, quartermaster's stores and armoury, while farther down by the gate we'd just entered was the vehicle repair depot. To the left of this were two long asbestos-cement barrack blocks – and behind the hill, there was another small barrack complex, which I discovered was the officers' quarters.

---

1   Mukiwa: Pronounced 'Mookeewa'. Black people nicknamed white people 'Mukiwa', which is a wild fruit with a white skin – hence the analogy.

The sound of ballast crunching under boots made us look around. It was our company commander, Major Charlie Pearce. We snapped to attention and saluted. He eyed our rumpled uniforms with distaste – running his tongue over his lips.

"You're our new lads?" he said.

"Sir!"

"Stand at ease, gentlemen."

We relaxed our stance and stood with our hands held loosely behind our backs.

Pearce looked at a clipboard in his left hand.

"Lieutenants Wells and Ballinger?"

"Sir."

"Wells, you get 6-Platoon; Ballinger, 4-Platoon; Laing, 5-Platoon. Ballinger, your second-in-command is Sergeant Torode. Wells, your 2 i/c is Sergeant Quinn."

"Sir."

'I looked around for where Kevin Torode was, but there was no sign of him.

"Some drivers have gone to the station to collect your men. They'll be back in an hour or so. I suggest you settle into your rooms in the meantime. Wells, you're in room eight and Ballinger, room seven." He pointed to the officers' quarters.

"Sergeant Laing and Corporal Pope, report to the CSM's office over there and he'll brief you about quarters."

"Sir."

"I'll call you when it's time to meet your men. Dismissed."

We came to attention, saluted, turned to the left and broke into normal step. Phil and Charlie took their bags and headed for the CSM's office.

Phil threw his car keys up to me. "Probably be safer parked near the officers' quarters," he said. Pete and I got into the car and drove about 200 metres to the neat little officers' complex that comprised a dining room, a mess and 10 single bedrooms.

"Ha! We get our own room." Pete paused in the doorway to his quarters.

The smiling black mess servant ferried my bags to my room. Once again, I breathed in the familiar beeswax, soap and fly spray smell. I looked through the window at a big hotel on a hill – beyond that, steep green hills fell away into the distance.

I unpacked and joined Pete in the dining room. I was still experiencing a thrill at being a newly-commissioned officer – and it appeared the perks were fantastic. Here we were being offered bacon, eggs and toast on porcelain plates and mugs of steaming tea. Less than a week before, we were 'lower than shark shit'. I could hardly believe the change in fortunes and how good it made me feel.

We were summoned to meet our men at 1000. After squaring our berets as best we could, we marched up the hill to meet them. I sweated from the heat as much as from the nerves in my belly.

When we crested the small rise by the admin block, we could see 94 men standing at ease in three squares. My heart thumped and skidded from excitement.

"Companeee… companee… atten… shun!" the CSM barked.

Ninety-four boots came crashed down on the tarmac.

The RLI CSM turned to salute Pete and I. It was the most amazing moment of my entire life.

"At ease, CSM," Pete said casually.

I couldn't believe he had said that so easily. I didn't have the guts to talk to a CSM like that yet!

Pearce came from his office and after the company had finished saluting him, he stood at ease and addressed us all.

"Welcome to 4 Indep Company," he said. "For those not familiar with this area, we are the only troops in an area the size of a small ocean – from Wankie National Park in the south, to the Matetsi River in the north and to the Botswana border in the west. We have thousands of square kilometres to protect using only 94 men."

He paused to let this startling fact sink in. Thousands of square kilometres with only 94 men. No wonder Rhodesia was like a sieve with many thousands of terrorists entering our borders from Zambia to the north and Mozambique to the east. It was only a thin line of national servicemen we had to defend the area.

"It's pointless patrolling away from the Zambezi River, which borders Zambia, because most of the bush around us is inhabited only by wild animals and a few farmers. The real target is the City of Bulawayo and the towns and farms en route to it. For this reason, your patrol areas will be mainly along the Zambezi River – both west and east of Victoria Falls. That's where the main gook crossings from Zambia have taken place to date."

I eyed the sea of faces while he spoke – recognising many of them. Pope smiled sarcastically at me when our eyes met – as if to say 'wanker!'

I smiled back at him.

"Lieutenant Ballinger," Pearce said.

"Sir!"

"Your platoon must be ready to leave at 0900 tomorrow morning to report to the police station at Victoria Falls, where you will meet the company 2 i/c, Captain Von Stranz. Here's the nominal roll of the men in your platoon."

He handed me a sheet of paper with 30 names neatly typed in black ink.

"You've been given three drivers and they will sign for the four-five[2] trucks that have been allocated to your platoon. You and Sergeant Torode will begin drawing stores as soon as you are dismissed from here. Report to the quartermaster's stores. He will know what to give you."

"Sir."

Pete's face looked really sour when he heard that he would remain with his platoon in the Wankie area – and he gave me that 'lucky bastard' look.

I spent the remainder of the day with my men – separating them into sections of eight, each led by a corporal. I looked from the name on the clipboard to their faces to try to memorise each individual.

The quartermaster was really switched-on and began the laborious task of issuing rifles, magazines, ammunition, radios, batteries, sleeping bags, stretchers, bayonets, helmets and the thousand-and-one other bits and pieces that infantrymen need to survive in the bush or during classical warfare.

I left Torode with the finer details, like signing for everything, and headed down to our vehicles with the drivers. Three five-tonne Mercedes-Benz vehicles stood in a row.

"Make sure they're all squared away, Corporal Furmston. All five tyres inflated, oil full, radiator full, fuel tank full, tool kit and jack in working order."

"Sir."

"Make sure you report anything missing or not in working order to me."

"Sir."

I walked back up the hill – relieved my first day was coming to an end. Pete and I headed straight for the bar when we reached the officers' mess.

"You lucky shit," he said, taking a long swig of beer. "Vic bloody Falls and all I get are ticks and gook huts."

"Someone has to keep the ladies happy, Pete."

"You lucky bastard! So near, and yet, so far."

We had a huge meal of T-bone steak, mash and veggies before confirming with Pearce that it was okay to go to the Baobab Hotel on top of the *gomo* we'd seen earlier in the day.

---

2   Four-five: A nickname given to one of our troop-carrying vehicles. The vehicle was a very good German Mercedes-Benz and was lined with various types of mine-proofing, like thick conveyor belting and sandbags under the benches and seats – with steel-reinforced conveyor belting bolted to the wheel arches. Water-filled tyres also absorbed blast shockwaves very efficiently. The vehicle could carry a 4.5 tonne load – hence the expression 'four-five'. A large, heavily-reinforced roll bar would protect its 10 seated and outward-facing troopers in the event of the vehicle rolling. A very good vehicle to hit a landmine in, even boosted mines didn't bother it much.

"Your first day here and you're acting like bloody tourists," he said with a smile on his face. "The system is that if you're not the duty officer, you can do what you like after hours, so long as we know where you are. Enjoy yourselves."

What a break. Off to grab some poor daddy's virgin daughter while the rank and file had to sort out their barrack block!

"RHIP," Pete said, quoting 'The 'Smiling Shit's' taunts about rank having its privileges.

We hopped into Phil's car and headed out the camp for the Baobab Hotel – named after the huge baobabs that grew in the surrounding countryside. African lore had it that one day the gods got angry and ripped up all the trees in this land and planted them upside-down, with the roots sticking up in the air. If you look at a baobab, you can see why this fable started; the branches do indeed look more like roots than normal branches. They carry a large bittersweet pod of fruit called tartar. We loved sucking away at that powdery fruit as kids before whining at our parents to buy us a coke to wash the sticky substance off the roofs of our mouths.

Multi-coloured lights surrounding the hotel winked at us through the leaves of the trees as we sped up the hill. We were full of excitement that we might meet some young ladies willing to share the euphoria of the day with us. But it was not to be. It was a Monday night and the pub was deserted apart from a few locals.

We bought beers and went outside and sat down near the steep edge of the hill – looking west towards Wankie and the power stations beyond it. The strangeness and unfamiliarity of the dark bush beyond the lights filled me with excitement, blended with dread. What lay out there and would I be able to cope? Would I do my job well?

I looked at the powerful, quiet man sitting next to me – a man who I looked up to and respected; who had encouraged and cajoled me through the toughest part of the selection course. Neither of us could even guess that in a few months' time, his leg would be shattered by automatic gunfire and his life changed forever.

The three-vehicle convoy carrying my platoon passed the camp's guardroom just after 0900. I had made sure that all communications were in order and had conducted a brief ambush drill rehearsal.

We turned left on the main road – maintaining a distance of about 80 metres between each vehicle. The idea was that if one or more vehicles hit an ambush, one would remain out of the killing ground and hopefully be capable of mounting a counter-attack or rescue of some kind.

The road curved to the left of the 4 Independent Company camp – now on the hill to our left – and continued through bends and curves until we came to the turn-off to Wankie town itself. The roadside at the junction had neatly-trimmed grass with a row of palm trees offering cool shade to a number of locals gathered around the fuel station buying bread, milk and cokes.

This was new territory to me now, and as signs of civilisation fell away behind us, I felt mildly apprehensive. The last complex we passed as we left Wankie was the base camp of 1 Independent Company – our sister company in Matabeleland. It looked run-down with the Rhodesian flag fluttering by the guard room. A bored-looking soldier was slouched over a parapet wall. The guys whistled and gave him the middle finger, but he didn't respond. I sat behind the driver facing outwards towards the bush on the right-hand side of the vehicle. To my left, a machine-gunner slouched over the cab with his belt-laden weapon pointing forward in case someone tried to blast us from the front with a RPG-7 rocket or rifle fire. To my right sat four men, three riflemen and a second machine-gunner at the back of the vehicle. Behind us, four more riflemen sat back-to-back, with us facing the far side.

We were heading north-west – and as we progressed, the short, stubby bush gave way to tall and graceful forests of hardwood. We drove out of the steaming valley and twisting hills surrounding Wankie, which trapped the heat in an oven-like furnace. Once outside town, the air was cool. An hour later, we stopped for a break among huge msasa trees; another hour and we reached the turn-off to Victoria Falls Airport – only 20 kilometres from the world-famous waterfalls.

"Look there," the machine-gunner to my left said.

I swivelled my head and looked through the windshield and saw 'smoke' spiralling up into the clear blue sky. It was a column of water vapour towering way above us.

"The smoke that thunders," I shouted at him above the whine of the engine.

"Vic Falls?"

I nodded and turned to face the front again – the wind flicking through my hair. After one more steep rise in the road, we entered the township of Victoria Falls – a very pleasant place by the look of it. A few tourists paused outside the reception area of Peters Motel to look at us trundle by. We freewheeled down the hill towards the commercial centre, and off to the left were rows of typical suburban houses with red, pink and orange bougainvilleas draped over fences or climbing into trees. On the right was a turn-off to the industrial sites and African township.

The towering spray from the waterfalls lay directly ahead, and I could just make out a glint of the waters of the mighty Zambezi River through the trees. That feeling of a holiday resort pervaded the whole area – making our presence feel somehow out of place. What were soldiers doing in a place like this?

But the tranquillity belied the reality of the situation, for only a few kilometres outside the town lay thousands of square kilometres of bush – hiding who knows how many enemy?

The police station appeared on the right and I shouted to the driver to turn into the driveway and park at the rear of the complex. There were plenty of army personnel around and tents and trucks were sprawled beneath huge leafy trees to the south of the camp. I called Corporal Orchard over to me.

"Tell the guys to de-bus and hang around while Sergeant Torode and I find out what the buzz is."

"Yes, sir."

Kevin and I entered a cool, fan-swept reception area and asked where Captain Von Stranz was.

"Right here," a voice said behind us.

We swivelled to face a ginger-haired man in his early-forties. We stood to attention and saluted.

"Relax," he said. "This isn't a training camp. We're a bit more casual around here. A simple salute will do."

"Sir."

"You're Lieutenant Ballinger?"

"Yes, sir," I nodded.

"I've been expecting you. Follow me."

We followed him down a brightly-lit passage – our boots squeaking on the highly polished floor. On the left was the main operations room, with a large map on one wall and a bank of radios and tables along another. Two signallers were smoking cigarettes and listening to the radios. We were ushered into a smallish office with a desk and three chairs.

"Take a seat," Von Stranz said, waving his hand at the chairs.

We took off our green berets and sat down. He took a cigarette from a case and tapped the filter twice before putting it in his mouth and lighting up.

"You're probably wondering who the other guys here are?" Without waiting for an answer, he continued: "They're Intake 146 – at the end of their time. They'll be heading back to civvy street. You're relieving them."

He took a drag on his cigarette – watching the blue smoke curl lazily up towards the ceiling before continuing.

"You'll be feeling pretty disorientated, so I'll bring you up to speed."

He stood up, took hold of a ruler and pointed at the map behind him.

"This is where we are," he said, waving at the map with the ruler. "There's Zambia to the north, Kazungula to the west – bordering Botswana – and to the east, absolutely fuck all."

He turned to look at us – a smile on his face.

"You couldn't have been given a cushier number than Vic Falls. I think there's only been one or two incidents here in the last two years."

I figured this guy enjoyed the lack of action. He looked the type who would prefer to sit out the day in the casino. He didn't strike me as very professional. He was far too casual.

"Get your guys squared away as best as possible and report back at 1400 for a full briefing – stick leaders included."

Kevin and I walked out to our vehicles. We did a quick tour of the camp and decided where to park and erect bivvies and so on.

"There's no defensive positions at all," Kevin said, looking around.

"Bloody holiday camp," I agreed.

Kevin signalled the trucks to come forward and spent some time positioning them the way I wanted it. I left the rest up to Kevin.

"Use about 40 sandbags and make a machine-gun nest over there. I want it manned from 2200 until sunrise. Set up a roster."

I decided to explore the camp some more and continued towards the south side, which eventually led me back to the main entrance of the building. Maybe I could glean some info from the guys in the ops room?

Halfway back to the main entrance, I came upon a freckled-faced subby reading a newspaper.

"You're the new guy?" he asked – looking over the paper.

"Yes."

"Welcome to Stalag 13."

I smiled and sat down on a canvas chair. He folded his newspaper and looked towards a nearby tent.

"Cook!" he bellowed.

A grubby, squat guy with a big belly ran over to us.

"Make the Lieut and I some ham sandwiches and a big pot of tea."

"Sir."

"Bloody holiday resort, this place."

"Just what Captain Von Stranz said."

"Von Stranz is a wanker – a real tourist. If the shit hit the fan, he'd fall to pieces."

I wasn't sure whether to feel happy or disappointed that we'd been given one of the softest assignments in the army. The north-east of the country and the area around Umtali was being hammered by gooks. Or was it just the calm before the storm? Only time would tell.

"I'm Graham Smythe, by the way."

"Tony," I said, shaking his hand.

"Where you from?"

"Salisbury."

"Bambazonke," he mocked in a Shona accent. It meant 'take everything'. The nickname had been given to our capital city because in sanctions-hit Rhodesia, it appeared Salisbury got everything it wanted, while other towns and cities struggled along with much less.

"I'm from Highlands, Prince Edward School."

"What a loser. I went to Churchill."

"You're the loser, my mate. Bunch of wankers at Churchill."

A school adversary sitting opposite me! The friendly rivalries between his school and mine were legendary – especially when we played rugby during Derby week. This culminated in the first teams playing international-quality rugby against each other, which drew huge crowds. We reminisced for a while before I changed the subject back to the army.

"Not been in action then?"

"Not a bloody sausage, boring as fuck here. Nothing but bloody ticks and snakes and wild animals out there – and that's just in the casinos!"

He threw his head back and laughed – as did I. The sandwiches and tea arrived.

"Stupid little prick still can't make tea after 18 months," he said, sipping his tea.

It did taste awful. How the hell can you ruin tea like that? Anyway, the sandwiches were good and I wolfed two down quickly.

"How often does he send you out on patrol?"

"Eight days out and four days in town guarding the bridge. Don't worry – it's a piece of cake. It'll be old hat after a week or so and then all the nice parade ground manners you've arrived with will dissolve into a 'couldn't give a fuck' attitude."

I felt annoyed that our training would culminate in this – a slow, rotting stagnation… perhaps the worst environment to try and keep men motivated and disciplined in. I was determined I wouldn't end up like this.

"You'll be just the same as the rest of us," Graham said, as if reading my mind. "You're no different, you know."

I felt irritated by him and decided to go and see how the guys were doing and to unpack my own stuff and set up a bivvy against the wall of the police station. I pondered whether each guy should dig a shell-scrape, but quickly decided against it, which was wrong. Maybe some of Graham's lacklustre attitude had rubbed off on me already?

At 1400 Sergeant Torode, three full corporals, three lance corporals and I entered the ops room. The guys on the radio looked bored and made no attempt to rise or salute me. Von Stranz handed us clipboards and indicated we should sit.

Behind him was a large map of our operational area. A few coloured pins were stuck into the map – primarily along a thick blue ribbon that represented the Zambezi River, going from west to east.

"There's not much I can brief you gents on really. We've had a few sightings of terrs to the west of the chalets belonging to national parks, which resulted in follow-ups, but no kills. Other than that, it's setting ambushes along the river front at likely crossing points and conducting cross-grain patrols in the mornings.

'The extreme west of our operational area is the border with Botswana – starting from the Caprivi Strip, where Botswana, Zambia and Rhodesia meet at Kazungula – down along the Botswana border to Pandamatenga, east to the Matetsi River and then north-east along the Matetsi River back to the Zambezi River. It's thousands of square kilometres gents.

'Most gook river crossings are to the west of us – and when you get to know the geography of the place a bit better, you will understand why. The river to the west of Vic Falls is wide, very wide in some places – up to 600 metres with slow-flowing water. But to the east, it's a narrow gorge with the same volume of water in it, so the flow is rather wild to say the least. It's just not practical for the enemy to cross east of Vic Falls for many miles downstream, so for this reason we ambush the western leg of the river more than anywhere else – starting again at the confluence of the Matetsi and Zambezi Rivers to the east.

'Ops west will be conducted from this police station and Ops east will be headquartered at a keep called Jambezi, about 40 kays away." Von Stranz pointed a pencil at the map – highlighting the base's location.

"The guys based at Jambezi will have a company of 'Black Boots' to work alongside, so it's important that whoever gets posted there co-ordinates patrols with the 'Black Boots' OC. In general, though, the army patrols north of the Vic Falls to Jambezi Road, while the police 'Black Boots' patrol the villages to the south, and also along the banks of the Matetsi. The area to the east of the Matetsi River belongs to 1 Indep and a couple of companies of Rhodesia African Rifles, so it's strictly forbidden to cross the Matetsi River without clearance from me. Is that understood?"

"Yes, sir," we said in unison.

"Because of our limited numbers, your platoon will be broken up into seven sticks of four men each, with the remaining men acting as vehicle escorts. Whenever all seven sticks are deployed, your drivers and vehicle escorts will help guard the bridge over into Zambia or act as a small reserve for the village."

Von Stranz paused – looking at each of us in turn.

"Right, I know this is a bit of a bombshell, but I want you to deploy tonight. With the men of Intake 146 in camp, there are no ambushes set up along the Zambezi – and that's not good."

I swallowed involuntarily. Deploying so soon after arriving in an operational area was madness to me. I barely knew my men.

"Tonight, sir? We've just arrived."

"Relax, Ballinger. It's not the Battle for Berlin here."

I stared blankly back at him.

He looked down at his clipboard and peeled off eight pages of coding that enabled us to transmit co-ordinates and other information by code over our radios rather than in the 'clear', which would allow eavesdroppers to intercept.

He picked up a roll of maps of the area and handed us one each.

It was gone 1530 by the time he'd finished giving us our call-signs, likely ambush sites and boundaries between each call-sign. The boundaries were usually small rivers or a knot of hills or some other physical feature that demarcated our patrol area. Without these boundaries, friendly forces could bump into each other – often with tragic consequences.

I left the ops room feeling really concerned that despite having just arrived here a few hours ago, we were now expected to start an eight-day patrol on the first night of our arrival. I didn't like this one bit because if I felt totally disorientated, I'm quite sure my men felt the same way. It was just too soon; everything was too rushed. What was the big hurry anyway if there had been no action around here for two years? I would have preferred to settle in for a day or so for orientation purposes and maybe do a few daylight patrols near our ambush sites.

The sun was dipping towards the west in a huge ball of orange fire, and yet we still had hundreds of finer details to sort out. Packs had to be emptied of clothes and then re-packed with sleeping bags, ration packs (or 'rat-packs' as we called them), spare ammunition, medic kits and bivvies. Webbing had to be packed with magazines of ammo, grenades and other bits and pieces. Faces blackened up, combat caps sorted out, radios checked, call-signs confirmed, seating and de-bus arrangements made on the vehicles.

"I'm really pissed off with Von Stranz," I said to Kevin. "If any of my guys get injured or killed because of this fucking rush, I'll have his guts!"

Kevin nodded and carried on packing his rucksack. I was also concerned about the leadership qualities and abilities of my corporals because we had only interacted with them on three or four occasions in training.

"I think I need to speak to Von Stranz. This is bullshit," I said, throwing some cans of food into my rucksack.

I walked around the side of the building where Graham and I had tea earlier in the day, then up the floodlit steps of the main entrance hall.

"Where's Captain Von Stranz?" I asked the guy on radio duty.

"He's gone, sir."

"Gone? What do you mean, gone? Where is he?"

"Probably at one of the hotels, sir."

"Probably? You mean you don't know where your own commanding officer is?"

The man looked embarrassed and fiddled with a magazine he'd been reading.

"Who's the duty officer?"

"Sergeant Jackson, sir."

"Dare I ask where he is?"

"Having a shower at the Elephant Hills Hotel, sir. The army has an arrangement for us to use their showers near the golf course."

"And if the shit hit the fan, how would you get hold of him?"

"He's got a radio with him, sir..."

"Where's the reaction stick then?"

"The cops are on duty tonight. We share a roster with them..."

I was about to ask to see them or speak to their OC, but realised that it would be futile.

"God help this place if it gets attacked," I said, walking out the building into the dying embers of daylight.

The small convoy turned left out the gate and retraced its steps from our arrival this morning. All the lights were on at Peters Motel, with coloured party lights anchored around the swimming pool – people moving to and fro.

I was still seething with anger at our OC. It was like he wanted to get rid of us because we were mucking up his social life.

We turned right – or west – about two kilometres past the motel, and even though we were still close to the village, it was like it had been transported away by an alien spaceship. The bush outside the headlamps of the vehicle was pitch-black under a star-studded sky. This was all new ground for me. It felt like I'd arrived in a strange city and was then tasked to tell a local taxi driver where to go.

"Stupid bastard," I said under my breath.

It wasn't long until a small pile of painted stones came into view on the right-hand side of the road. They were the correct distance from the main Vic Falls to Bulawayo Road we had left behind us – and a dirt track ran off to the right towards the edge of the escarpment that formed the Zambezi Valley.

"Turn right," I shouted to the driver – a few feet from me.

I turned to look back at the vehicles behind me to make sure they were following, which they were. Large clouds of dust formed halos around the headlights behind us. The driver knew he had to go two kilometres and then stop.

A few minutes later, the driver pulled over to the side of the road – killing the engine and headlights. The other vehicles followed suit.

"De-bus and form up along the side of the road," I said into my radio handset. The sounds of 30-odd men climbing down from the vehicles filled the air.

I was temporarily night-blind, so I waited for it to clear for a minute or two before walking back down the line – counting the men and briefly chatting to each stick leader.

"If we hit an ambush, turn and face them with as much firepower as possible," I said to each stick leader.

Satisfied that all was in order, we started north towards the Zambezi River – now lying about 10 kilometres away. The ground was extremely sandy and it made tough-going.

Even though I knew that this was a low-risk environment, it was still new to me – and the tension made me grip my rifle tightly as I stared into the black void ahead.

After a few minutes, we'd settled into a steady rhythm – and thankfully, the ground was sloping downwards towards the valley floor, which made it a lot easier-going.

We walked for about 40 minutes until the bush thinned out, and there below us was the Zambezi River. My night vision was as good as it was going to get – and as I stared ahead, the whole valley floor seemed to notch a degree or two brighter under the immense carpet of stars above. It was an awesome sight, with the river glittering like a great silver serpent – the lights of Livingstone village to the right forming the serpent's eyes.

I used the view as an excuse to take a break and do a head-count. It was not uncommon for men towards the rear of a column to get separated on night marches.

Satisfied that all was well and that the men had alternately sat on each side of the road to offer all-round defence in case of an attack, I took my pack off and sat on a small rock. The muscles in my legs twitched as they relaxed.

Although my eyes took in the lovely view ahead, my mind focused on the map I'd looked at in the briefing room earlier on. Von Stranz had told me that the track we were on came to a distinct T-junction, and then sort of petered out in very thick, tall elephant grass. I'd decided that the T-junction would be our base for the night. I was not prepared to go tromping around with 30 men in an area I hadn't seen in daylight.

Five minutes later, and we were on the move again. I remembered from my route marches that getting up again after a walk could be painful because your muscles had stiffened and blood wallowed in your aching feet.

The river slowly disappeared from sight as we neared the valley floor – and for some reason or other, it made the place look dark and sinister. We not only had to contend with the gut-twisting thought of being ambushed, but the place was alive with wild animals and I sort of imagined that I was about to bump into an elephant or hippo – or even worse, a male buffalo.

A bolt of terror ran up my spine when this grey wall appeared in front of me. I looked out the side of my eyes to see what it was because peripheral vision is actually better than full-on vision in the dark. The wall did not move; it sort of just stood there – swaying gently. My radio handset hissed quietly in my ear.

"What the fuck is that?" I whispered to the man behind me. He shook his head.

I walked slowly forward – rifle butt crooked into my shoulder, ready to double-tap the thing if it moved. It just stood there.

"It's elephant grass… shit, thought it was a herd of them!"

The man behind me let out his breath and swore softly. We'd reached the T-junction.

When my eyes adjusted to the gloom, I could see that it was not a good defensive position to base up for the night. I looked back the way we had come and noticed a fairly flat ledge to the one side of the path.

It was quite a mission turning 30 men around and then re-tracing our steps 50 metres or more before turning left off the pathway. It was a perfect place to camp the night; at least, it looked like that in the dark.

I put the men into a large circle with machine-guns facing likely points of attack – telling each alternate man to unpack while his buddy kept guard, and then vice versa.

It was just gone 2300 by the time the guard was set. I lay back on my sleeping bag to look up at the awesome array of stars twinkling above my head and listen to the grunts of distant hippo, the screech of crickets and the waaa-woop of hyena out on a hunt.

My God, Africa is so beautiful and mysterious and harsh and kind all at once. What an amazing continent full of a multitude of different life! I lay there enchanted by her beauty; her terror; and her promise – drifting slowly down into a deep sleep that knew nothing… nothing at all.

It was quite probable, according to intelligence gathered later in the week, that Albert Ncube lay in his bed in Zambia staring at the same stars I did that first night.

I wondered what must have gone through his mind at the time. What were his fears? Was it the crossing of the swollen, black waters that teemed with crocodiles? Or the thought of going into enemy territory with little or no support?

What would happen if he or his men got injured? Where would they take him? It was a long, long way back to his base camp in Zambia. He would probably die on the way.

Ncube must have had all these thoughts going through his mind as he prepared to cross the mighty Zambezi, but it was equally obvious that he had the drive to get it done. What was it that drove him to leave the comfort of his home, go to Russia, Tanzania and Zambia to train as a comrade in the liberation struggle? To join Joshua Nkomo's shock troops, ZIPRA?

Maybe it was the promise of a white man's house, a car, a decent job or education – all the things that the present political system in his homeland denied him?

Or maybe he could already hear in his mind a white madam – a white bitch – squeal as he drove his bayonet into the inners that he had just spoiled with his semen?

Whatever it was that pushed this man forward was there that first night I lay looking up at the stars.

***

The sky was a faint glow to the east when the guard shook me awake. My spirits slumped slightly when I realised where I was. I had been dreaming something about getting married… having kids. Something normal.

"Is everyone awake?" I said, looking up at the guard's silhouette.

"Just about, sir." He moved off to gently rustle people back to consciousness.

I slid my feet into my boots, rolled up the sleeping bag and shrugged on heavy chest webbing.

"Kevin," I whispered in his direction. He walked at a crouch over to me.

"Get your stick ready as quickly as possible and go back about a hundred metres up the road to see if anyone picked up our spoor last night. Corporal Orchard, go down to the T-junction with your guys and see if any gook spoor is there. We'll be under those big trees having our breakfast, okay?"

The two men nodded their heads and quietly slipped out of camp with their men to determine if we had been seen the night before.

I waited until the remainder of the men were ready and then led them down to a dense patch of fever trees about 300 metres away to have our breakfast. It had been drummed into us to never eat where we slept in case the enemy had seen us go to ground – in which case, our dining room would become our coffin.

The men cooked in pairs: one doing the cooking, the other watching the surrounding bush, rifle at the ready. I put some butter and jam on a 'dog' biscuit while I waited for the water to boil on the small gas cooker we each carried. The biscuits were rock-hard and tasteless. It seemed their only purpose was to act as a platform for the jam, meat and other goodies we piled onto them. Having said that, if you soaked them overnight and fried them in butter and jam, they made superb pancakes – all soft and swollen.

I sat with my back against one of the trees – observing the men around me; boys more like it... kids. No doubt this was a fantastic adventure to them. Maybe some dads never took their sons camping and this was their first chance to catch up. Gas cookers hissed and men chatted quietly as they worked.

"Four Four Alpha, Four Four Charlie," the metallic voice of Corporal Orchard said over the handset.

"Go ahead."

"No sign of gook tracks, over."

"Copied that. Find a safe place to brew up and I'll call you when it's time to pull out."

"Copied."

"Four Four Bravo, Four Four Alpha," I said.

"Bravo, go ahead."

"How you doing there?"

"No sign of spoor either – just lots of elephant crap."

"Good one," I said, smiling. "Have your breakfast and standby for further instructions."

"Copied."

"Four Four Alpha, out."

I pulled a plastic-covered map out of my rucksack – as well as a list of codes. It was time to report back to headquarters at Vic Falls.

"Zero Four, Four Four Alpha."

Only static filled the handset when I let go of the transmit button.

"Zero Four, this is Four Four Alpha, over."

"Four Four Alpha, this is Zero Four," a sleepy voice replied.

"This is Four Four Alpha. We have November Tango Romeo, copied?" (November Tango Romeo – Nothing to Report)

"Copied."

"Our position is Shackle: Lima, Mike, Foxtrot, Lima, Zulu, Zulu, Whisky, Foxtrot... Unshackle," I said, reading off the code for the day.

"Copied."

"Four Four Alpha out."

I threw down the handset and took a big swig of the sticky-sweet tea that had just come to the boil. It was a beautiful day, with a cool breeze sighing through the branches overhead.

By the time we'd finished our breakfast and regrouped, it was nine in the morning. I posted sentries and then called the stick leaders together. I showed them where we were and where their patrol areas started. I drew boundaries on their maps in thick red ink and only prayed that they knew how to map-read. I was still angry with Von Stranz. We hadn't been shaken down well enough as a unit to be chucked out in the bush like this.

"Make sure you stick to your areas, guys. I don't want friendly fire killing our own men."

"Sir," they nodded.

"Be sensible. Remember what you've been taught – no fucking around. Make sure at least one of your guys is told where you are on the map every single day – plus your radio frequency and call-sign in case you get zapped. Understood?"

"Sir," they said, smiling.

There we were – seven sticks of four men to patrol and ambush 30 kilometres of riverfront. That was only four-and-a-bit kilometres per stick. Not bad, but it meant the western and easternmost sticks had to walk 12 or so kilometres to get into position.

Kevin led four sticks west and I led three sticks east – east towards a distinct bend in the river, with an even more distinct humped-back island called Chundu on the western edge of the bend.

We watched Kevin's men move off behind him – their blackened faces and camouflage blending extremely quickly against the background. I felt slightly emotional and strangely proud as they humped their heavy equipment along the path and out of sight through the elephant grass. It was a bit like a school teacher waving goodbye to his kids for the last time.

I took the lead – checking that all 11 men were well-spaced-out behind me – and headed downstream towards the island in the river.

The bush looked dense and threatening the night before, but in the sunny light of day it was sparse, but tropical-looking. Huge towering trees were draped in vines that dangled down to the dry, dusty earth – interspersed with rows of palm trees shivering in the mild breeze. These palm trees are unique because they require the powerful digestive juices of an elephant's gut to break open the thick, leathery covering of the palm-ivory seed, which it eventually exits in piles of elephant dung that forms a ready-made compost heap for the palm shoot to develop in.

Sentry baboons barked a warning to their troop – resulting in frenzied shrieks from the females and babies as they scattered into the treetops for protection.

The swollen, boiling waters of the Zambezi River were about 300 metres to our left as we moved cautiously ahead. I was staggered by the beauty and tranquillity of the place. It's as if time stood still here.

About an hour later, I said goodbye to Corporal Orchard's stick. He was a very handsome young man with a wicked smile and an eye for the ladies. They loved him to bits too. The little chip in his front teeth didn't seem to detract from his good looks. He was the type of guy that you couldn't dislike. He was always happy and upbeat, but sadly he died a year later in the same landmine that killed Dave Kruger and Tom Shipley.

"Don't do anything stupid, Orchard!"

"Yessir," he smiled – the little gap showing in his teeth.

We peeled away and continued east until I reached the west end of Chundu Island about an hour later.

"Right, Corporal Nel," I said to Theo Nel – the man that would one day take on a platoon or more of ZIPRA gooks virtually single-handed to win the Bronze Cross of Rhodesia.

"This is my pozzie – the western end of the island. You must go about another 40 minutes east until you cross a fairly substantial tributary… This one here…" I stabbed my finger at a spot on the map.

"Sir."

"That's your western boundary. Your eastern boundary is Hippo Creek. Understood?"

"No problem, sir."

As soon as Theo was out of sight, we withdrew to a thick spread of shrubs near a massive ant nest and prepared to make our lunch. It was too hot to eat though, and all I had was a cup of tea.

We'd been given strict instructions not to be seen at the river's edge during daylight hours, so I decided to let the men have a nap before our first night ambush. I set the guard and then lay back against the sloping bottom of the ant nest – feeling the warmth of the sun-dried clay through my combat shirt.

I cannot sleep in the daytime, so it was a wonderful afternoon just lying there in the cool shade listening to hippos cavort and baboons bark in the distance. It was a rare opportunity to unwind and forget about this stupid war – even though I'd just entered it.

※—※

Although I'd been born and bred in Rhodesia, I'd been away on a worldwide working holiday for the previous three years. I had been to the UK, Australia, Singapore, Thailand, Russia and then back to Rhodesia via the UK and my aunt's horse ranch in the Cape of Good Hope, South Africa. The horse ranch with Jess and the beautiful purply-blue Hottentots Holland Mountains in the distance…

My heart ached at the thought of it – well, maybe just that little bit less these days.

But it was the other feeling that bothered me. I had been away from my homeland for three years now. I hadn't followed the daily struggle against Mugabe and Nkomo's gooks; I hadn't witnessed the creep of Uhuru or the decline in services; I had not heard people talk in low voices about their neighbour's death while on active service, nor witnessed the horror of a massacre in the night in some darkened bush somewhere. I'd been away in first world countries having a gas – living life to the full and shagging anything with a skirt on it. And now this – ants and ticks and prickly heat down my back… to do what? To try and save a way of life that was already dying? I remember the swimming pool at the Mazoe Hotel – full of weeds and bat shit instead of laughing little kids; their moms all pissed on pink gin and suntanned everywhere except under their panties and bra straps. What the hell am I doing here?

The sun was getting down towards the horizon in the west – a magical, huge orange ball of fire with slivers of gold-lined clouds framing it – when I decided it was time to move. I crept a little way up the anthill and did a quick sweep of the surrounding bush through my binoculars to make sure the coast was clear.

We moved east for about 200 metres and then sat in another clompie of bush to have our final meal of the day. I made bully beef, rice and onions and washed it down with segments of orange and an insipid-tasting cool drink that was made from powder and water from my bottle.

I radioed our estimated locstat, or position, for the coming night and then moved off to our selected ambush site – pausing for total darkness to do a recce with one of the guys to the water's edge.

It was close to 2000 when we slid silently into position. We spread out facing the river – easing very quietly out of our rucksacks and positioning grenades within easy reach in front of us, two magazines out of our webbing for quick loading, and two left in the webbing in case we had to run like hell from the ambush position. I made sure Kenny, the machine-gunner, had all his belts ready to go. If gooks were going to land here, I was planning to rip them to shreds while they were still in the water.

The river sighed through reeds only a few feet away – and I noted with satisfaction that we were elevated about six feet above the dark water.

A slither of moon appeared to our left through the trees, and its light reassured me that we were at the eastern edge of Chundu Island – looking across approximately 400 metres of river at a farm homestead in Zambia; its security lights zig-zagging a reflection off the water. The faint sound of a generator reached our ears.

I knew from Von Stranz's briefing that the house opposite us was one of the few white-owned properties still left in Zambia on the Zambezi River. I wondered why the hell the owners wanted to stay in a grossly-corrupted country that hated white people?

The ambush, to begin with, was an exciting affair. This was for real – no more 'Smiling Shit' or 'Saints' hovering around me. The bullets we carried killed people and the bullets they fired back at us killed people also.

Two hours later though, my attention began to flag – and apart from the sigh of the river, crickets shrieking and gloworms playing tricks on my eyes, there was nothing to be seen or heard. I decided to set the watch at midnight, which would require the four of us to do about an hour-and-a-half of guard duty each before we would withdraw from the position just before sunrise.

At midnight, I told the guys to get some sleep and sat up – holding my watch in my hand to make sure I didn't fall asleep. I also made sure I wasn't silhouetted by sitting up.

The combination of darkness and tiredness can play funny tricks on your mind – and several times I almost panicked as shapes and shadows seemed to float past my vision. Was that something moving over there? What's that in the river… a dinghy? We had no specialist night sights at this stage in the war, and it was our eyes versus the gooks' eyes – and I knew for a fact that they had bloody better eyesight than we did, but then again, our hearing is better and it is that sense I depended on the most… now and again cupping my hands behind my ears to amplify the sounds around me.

But nothing happened – and at 0130 I shook the man next to me and sat with him until he was fully awake, before pulling on my combat jacket and lying on top of my sleeping bag.

During the cool hours of the morning, we withdrew from the water's edge for about half a kilometre to patrol east – looking for any signs of a landing or human spoor. This was a national park – closed to the public and, therefore, any footprint would belong to someone up to no good. Whether a poacher or a gook, they were both legitimate targets.

We ambushed slightly further east the second night – turning west to cross-grain for spoor. I was starting to feel bored with this place already. Time drags in the bush. It was beginning to make sense why Intake 146 looked like such a dishevelled bunch of idiots after patrolling here for a year.

I was having my breakfast when a call came over the radio.

"Four Four Alpha, Zero Four."

"Go ahead," I said.

"Sunray wants you to blindfold at the following locstat tonight. Ready to copy?"

(Sunray – military jargon for 'officer commanding' – wants me to set up a blindfold or ambush for him.)

"Go ahead."

The radio operator back in Vic Falls sent me a series of coded letters, which I repeated for confirmation.

"That's affirmative," the voice in my handset said. "Zero four, out."

I picked up my codes for the day and read them off against the letters of the alphabet just given to me over the radio. The codes worked by converting one letter of the alphabet into another one – varying the combinations every 24 hours. In this way, if enemy code-breakers unravelled any given code on one day, it would be out of date the next day.

"I bet it's halfway to the bloody moon," Kenny said, munching a dog biscuit.

"Not at all." I said, looking up and smiling. "We're almost sitting on it."

I looked at the river. We were at the western end of Chundu Island. No big deal; we did the east of the island for two nights and I guess the OC wants us to go west now.

"Why here?" Kenny asked.

"No idea. Maybe gooks have tried to cross here in the past, or maybe the boss has a feather up his arse."

I took a swig of the condensed milk-sweetened tea and pondered about our ability to inter-cept anybody in this huge wilderness. It was like a lottery moving from one position to the next at night… which was the right combination? We could ambush east of the island and the bastards could cross on the west. It was a bloody lottery I thought. And the prize? A possible hole in the head.

We patrolled to our western boundary in the late afternoon and then paused for the evening meal and weapons prep about a kay from the proposed ambush site. It was 2100 by the time we had settled into position – choosing a spot near a massive tree that enabled us to lie in the shadow it created from the glare of the moon above. We were about 20 metres from the river and had a small hump of soil just in front of us for protection. It was a perfect ambush position. I put Kenny on the right flank, with the remaining two men between him and me. This was deliberate. I liked starting guard first so that I could have a straight run of sleep until sunrise. It was lousy being in the middle of the men because you may have just fallen asleep and then you are wakened for guard duty.

For the first two hours, nothing happened. Some nasty insect was crawling around in the leaves in front of me – and I was more worried about getting stung by a scorpion or a centipede than any bloody gooks. Hippos grunted and cavorted around in shallows to our left. They are nasty animals and are probably more dangerous than crocodiles.

At first I wasn't sure I'd heard it, but it came again. The man next to me raised his head. He'd heard it too…

"Make sure the other two guys are awake!" I hissed into his ear. He rolled over and shook the man next to him – repeating the instruction to wake Kenny.

The noise came again. The proximity of the insect rustling in the leaves and the sigh of the river made it difficult to pinpoint what it was.

"Sounds like someone moving a metal trunk," someone said.

"Yes," I said. I cupped my ears and listened again. The clanking, sliding noise of metal on metal was quite distinct now – and then it stopped.

"I can hear a vehicle…"

"Me too," I agreed.

I raised my binos to my eyes and studied the opposite bank. The horizon appeared to have a halo of light over it – a type of glow that bobbed once or twice and then went out. I could distinctly hear a vehicle moving away to the east – accelerating.

"Must be the farmer coming back from a piss-up."

"Maybe. It's Friday night after all."

I thought about the house on the opposite side of the river – now hidden by the island in front of us. I thought about the manicured lawns that ran down to the river's edge and the beautiful blonde girl I had seen sun-tanning when I'd crept forward to get water from the river late one afternoon. What a contradiction; her beauty and innocence surrounded by normality, and here we were creeping around with weapons and blackened up with camo cream!

Nothing happened after that – and by midnight I started the first guard. I became sort of mesmerised by the millions of green flashes from gloworms skidding in and out of the reeds nearby. My thoughts returned to the vehicle we'd heard earlier.

If it had been the farmer returning from a piss-up, why did the vehicle accelerate away from the homestead? Had someone dropped him off? Or maybe it was the blondie getting a lift home from a night out? But what were those metallic noises – like steel trunks being unloaded?

I gave up the Sherlock Holmes bit and at 0130 handed the watch to the man next to me.

The report of vehicle activity to Von Stranz resulted in us having to ambush the same point that night, and then the eastern end of the island – where we could see the farmer's homestead – for another two nights. On the second night, a five-tonne lorry had arrived at the farmhouse – driving behind it to the west and out of our line of sight – followed shortly by scraping metallic sounds once again.

Boredom had set in and I began to feel slightly less serious about all our ambush techniques, our places to eat and other forms of discipline. There was clearly no-one anywhere near this place, and I felt, not for the first time, that this was a complete waste of manpower. We should be doing something else.

I wondered about how the other guys were faring to the west and east of me, but I figured it was just as dull. Their sitreps, or situation reports, were the same as mine... November Tango Romeo... Nothing to Report.

※—※

"Smell that," Kenny said suddenly, "it's gonna rain."

"Bullshit," Abbott replied, "it's only September!"

"I tell you, it's gonna rain," Kenny repeated.

I looked towards the east and decided that Kenny may be right. What should have been a brightening sky was blackened by cloud. If it was going to rain, we had better move it up to check for spoor.

"Pack up," I ordered.

It was our eighth day of ambushing and cross-grain patrols with nothing but tick bites to show for it. I was dirty, smelly, itchy and I'd had enough. We had watched the house to the east of Chundu Island for two nights in a row now – and despite the odd unusual comings and goings at all hours, nothing had happened.

"We'll go west to the big tree, fill up our water bottles and head south to the RV," I said to the guys. We spread out with Max on the MAG immediately behind me, followed by Abbott and Kenny.

The wind picked up as we walked – and that familiar 'about to rain' smell hit my nostrils. I love that smell, and I drew it deeply into my lungs. It was almost as if nature was rejoicing at the pending relief from the dry months of winter, but it was a little odd that it was about to rain so early in the year. It was only September – our spring, so to speak.

We'd been walking about 20 minutes when a fat drop of water hit the visor on my 'cunt cap'. I looked up at the heavens and got another drop straight in my right eye.

'Shit!' I said, wiping away the sting. "Just our bloody luck to get drenched before the vehicles arrive!"

"Sod's law," Max mocked in his lazy drawl.

"Great!" I moaned aloud. I hate being wet and cold!

We headed west to the giant tree we'd ambushed from three nights previously – and when we reached it, I put Max in a rear-facing position while Abbott and Kenny filled up our water bottles. "Which one of you wankers left a baked bean can for every gook on earth to find?" I said, picking it up. Nobody replied.

"I tell you, the next guy that doesn't bury his shit will be on orders. Okay?"

I looked at Max. He was smiling thinly through a new beard – his spectacles reflecting light like 'The Smiling Shit's'. Bastard. I would get that disrespectful son-of-a-bitch if it was the last thing I did. I kicked open a shallow hole to bury the can, and as I did, so I noticed footprints near the base of the tree... they were definitely not ours, or were they?

I was just bending down to have a look at the unusual shoe patterns when a wall of water swept over us – turning everything into a muddy pool within seconds. Raindrops thrashed the ground like millions of tiny bullet strikes.

Whoever those footprints belonged to – if indeed, they weren't our own – were gone for good.

I almost wept with relief when the trucks arrived to collect us. At least, that's what I thought they'd come for. I wanted to weep again when the driver handed me a letter from Von Stranz telling us that we were being re-supplied and had to spend another eight days in the bush.

"Bastard!" I spat. I was sick and tired of this place.

"Nice one!" Bomford said from Theo's stick.

Max looked sick – his bottom lip was quivering. I didn't know it then, but he was an alcoholic and his system was screaming for a fix.

"Another eight days?"

We refilled our packs with supplies – totally lacking in humour – but there was one consolation... the driver had brought us some cokes and a newspaper.

"Let's go," I said after we'd finished sorting ourselves out.

Back to the same boring routine. Ambush... patrol... ambush.... patrol. Nothing happened for the first two nights, but on the third we heard shots to the west. It turned out an elephant cow with a calf in tow attacked one of my call-signs and they had to fire into the air to drive it off.

"I can just see Calitz legging it in his sleeping bag," Max said sarcastically. "Hundred-metre sack race, ha!"

Late on the afternoon of the fifth day, there was a huge, rolling explosion towards the village. The noise echoed down the valley for ages.

"What the hell was that?" Kenny said.

"Landmine for sure!"

I picked up my radio handset and listened to a panicked plea from someone in Intake 146 requesting starlight – army jargon for a medic.

"…boosted landmine, sunray Four One Alpha needs emergency casevac!" crackled over the radio net.

"Copied that," a flustered radio operator replied. Not a nice prospect for some bugger having to drive into bush – that will soon become dark and ominous – to collect casualties. I was amazed Von Stranz allowed it – or maybe he wasn't even around?

It turned out that Lieutenant Smythe had gone out on the very last ride of his national service to collect his men from their final patrol, only to hit a boosted landmine – that is, one mine on top of the other! The 12 kilogrammes of explosive in each Russian-made TMH46 landmine is powerful enough to blow a civilian car into tiny bits of scrap. Two of them made a military vehicle virtually do cartwheels.

Smythe, lax and undisciplined after 18 months of doing nothing, was sitting on the water tank behind the driver's cab when the right front wheel detonated the mines – catapulting him 30 feet into the air to land in a thorn tree, which he promptly rolled out of and broke nearly every bone in his body.

C'est la vie – that's the way it goes…

❋—❋

At last, the seventeenth day of our enforced imprisonment in this god-forsaken backwater dawned.

"I'll kill the OC if it's a re-supply," Bomford muttered.

"He can't do that?" Max pleaded – looking at me for confirmation.

"He can do what he friggin' likes…"

Three trucks trundled into view – and as soon as I saw the guys beaming smiles from the back of them, I knew it was time for some civvy action for a few days.

"Lap straps and stay alert," I instructed all NCOs over the radio.

We took a different route into town this time. Instead of going back up the escarpment, we followed the river east towards Vic Falls village. It was rough, broken country with palm trees spaced along the riverfront. It was all new and interesting to me.

After about 30 minutes, we passed some dark green national parks' chalets off to our left. There were still civilians in them – as if nothing was happening a few kilometres to the west. What the hell did they make of that massive explosion a few days before? If it was me, I would've legged it out of there already.

A gate under a thatched building demarcated the boundary of Vic Falls National Park, and as soon as we passed through it, we were back on tarred road. We sped past the crocodile ranch to the right – briefly catching a glimpse of colourful civvies looking at curios and other touristy junk.

"This is more like it!" Kenny shouted above the roar of the wind and engine.

The massive thatched roof of the A'Zambezi River lodge came into view around the next bend. The arrivals area was packed with black and white zebra-striped minibuses with even more tourists shuffling about. The guys whistled and waved at a couple of gorgeous babes.

"That's more like it!" Max shouted when he saw them; they were one of his other addictions!

"What the hell's that?" Kenny said, pointing ahead to my right.

To begin with, it looked like a grey humped-back whale, but as the scenery unfolded rapidly in front of us, it became apparent that it was the thatched roof of the massive Elephant Hills Casino Hotel. Golfers paused to look at us race by. Lush manicured lawns rolled up several grassy terraces to a large swimming pool just below the veranda of the hotel. Babes in bikinis… this is more like it indeed!

It was three o'clock in the afternoon when we pulled into the police camp. Phil Laing stood next to Von Stranz as I de-bussed.

"Get the guys sorted out," I said to Torode, and then walked up to the OC – saluting. Both returned the salute.

"You look like shit, sir." Phil said.

"And smell like it too," Von Stranz said, smiling. "Give Sergeant Laing and I a debrief and then you and the guys can have the night off. The casinos are for officers and NCOs only."

"Sounds great, sir," I said.

I followed them down the brightly-lit hall to the ops room, where I spent the best part of 40 minutes showing Phil where we'd ambushed, what we'd seen and where we found watering holes slightly inland. Von Stranz listened without saying anything – his right hand balled into a fist under his nose. I guess I stank like elephant shit or bad cheese; take your pick.

"Get that stink off you, Ballinger. Tomorrow you'll be in charge of setting up our new camp by the Elephant Hills Hotel while Sergeant Laing deploys."

"Sir."

Phil and I walked down the passage back to the front door.

"What's it like down Wankie way?" I asked.

"Shit place – thousands of square miles of nothing. You've landed your bum in the butter, you jammy bugger."

"It's the first time I've seen the jam my mate; two-and-a-half weeks out there..." I scratched my balls.

"What news of Pete Wells?"

"He's back in Wankie for the time being – then back to the sticks."

"Okay, Phil. You coming out with me tonight?"

"Wouldn't miss it for anything, sir."

I went around to the back of the building and told Kevin the good news for all of us – better news for the guys with rank than the others.

"All weapons are to be made safe, Kev – ammo counted. The guys can go to the golf course for a shower and start their time off at 1800." He nodded and set about squaring things away.

Surprisingly enough, Von Stranz allowed me to use the Land Rover that belonged to his HQ, so Phil and I took off for a shower. Perhaps the bugger wasn't so bad after all?

It's hard to describe how incredible a hot shower is after living in your own sweat and filth for two weeks. I let it run hard and hot over my suntanned body – running my fingers through my hair again and again. It was a pure delight to sit on a toilet seat and crap into something that stopped the plop-plops from landing on your boots – and, unlike out there in the bush, I had no horseflies sucking on my dick while I was trying to do the business!

I felt like a new man when we headed back to the camp to drop off my dirty clothes. They were slimy from sweat and dirt and still crawling with one or two of the countless thousands of ticks we had encountered.

"Where do we get them washed?" I said to Phil. We'd deployed the same day we got here, so this was still new to me.

"Beats me," he said, shrugging.

I walked around to the policeman's staff quarters and very quickly made arrangements for one of the wives to do our laundry for a few bucks.

"Let's go," I said to Phil.

We jumped into the Land Rover and retraced our steps back to the 'Hills Hotel', but not to shower this time.

The sun was a massive ball of orange flame to the west when we arrived. What a place! Built on a medium-sized hill, the hotel afforded its plump hosts a magnificent view of the Zambezi River in the middle distance – just beyond the perfectly groomed holes of the golf course. A few warthogs were in the 'praying position' gobbling up sweet grass. The surrounding bush was thick and lush. Six elephants loitered around by one of the man-made water traps to our left.

"I'm starving," Phil said, so we ordered steaks and beer to eat on the terrace overlooking the swimming pool. Something stirred in my groin when I looked at a couple of babes in bikinis.

"There's all types of hunger!"

The beer and food made me feel really good. I was young, fit and alive – in better shape than poor Smythe lying in hospital in Wankie after his dance with death the other day.

"Let's see what's in there," I said to Phil.

We walked through a plushly furnished lounge with subdued lighting and thick carpets, past the reception area and down a passage to the casino. Heads swivelled here and there as people turned to look at us in our crisply-pressed camouflage uniforms, polished boots and stable belts.

"This is more like it, Phil. Come to daddy, baby."

The room was lavishly furnished in various shades of red. Several roulette tables were spread in an arc – at the end of which stood several blackjack tables. Male and female croupiers worked smoothly and efficiently over the tables, while waiters plied the punters with alcohol. Various shades of humanity placed bets with multi-coloured chips – stacking them in incomprehensible piles on the table.

"No more bets," the croupier in front of me said. The little white ball slowed and fell into a slot on the wheel marked with a zero. She swept dozens of chips away and only paid out a few splits. I watched this for a few minutes before gingerly putting 10 dollars on the table.

"The minimum is 20 dollars," the cold, unsmiling face said to me. I felt myself go bright red. I pulled out another 10 and in a few seconds, I had a pile of blue chips in front of me. I stupidly put the same number of chips on the black and the red. The croupier looked at me as if I was a moron.

"It's pointless backing red and black, sir. You can never win anything."

I realised my mistake and backed red. The other punters were watching me with sort of pitying looks. I felt really embarrassed and cleared my throat to cover it.

"Eight black," the croupier said, sweeping my stake away. Any hopes of buying a house in the plush suburbs of Salisbury lay crushed. Five minutes later, it was all gone. I felt stupid and dejected. Okay, so 20 bucks is no big deal, but the 12 dollars for the meal made it 32 dollars I'd parted company with in an hour. My measly pay was only a 120 a month.

"Let's bugger off," I said to Phil. At least he was wise enough to watch me waste my money while he sipped his beer.

We headed back to town. The lights had come on by now and the place looked quaint and colourful.

"Let's give the Vic Falls Hotel a go," I said above the roar of the engine. Phil nodded. Instead of turning right at the Wimpy fast-food restaurant – which would have taken us back to the police camp – we turned left, bumped over the railway line and then right at The Casino Hotel.

The Vic Falls Hotel turned out to be a majestic 'turn of the century' place in a colonial style with high ceilings and lazy fans stirring the air – the type of place you'd expect to see old colonial gentlemen with handlebar moustaches tittering away with ladies drinking gin and tonic.

"What a place!" Phil said.

We walked through the reception area and a plush lounge before we reached the patio. An awesome sight greeted us. The high French doors opened outwards to reveal one of nature's rare beauties. Magnificent mahogany trees framed the Vic Falls Bridge reaching over into Zambia – and to the left of it golden-red spray from the Falls clawed its way heavenwards. Each tiny droplet of water reflected the dying rays of the sun to create the illusion of a wall of flame over the gorge.

Immediately in front of the patio was a concrete dancefloor – at the head of which was a good African band playing a very credible version of '*Rock Your Baby*' by George McCrae. It was too early to dance, so most people sat at tables eating food, drinking wine and enjoying the scenery.

The tree which they sat under was enormous – and it looked even more beautiful with green lights shining upwards into the leaves. A queue of people snaked its way forward to be served meat, salads and vegetables at the braai to one side.

"I could get used to this," Phil said, ordering two beers.

We hadn't seen women for a long time – and both of us fell silent when a group of four girls went up to dance with each other. The sight of their tanned bodies and seductive motions made my lower belly tingle.

"Shit, I'm horny, man!"

"Me too, I could handle all four of them right now," Phil agreed.

But we were in uniform – and I felt stupid and out of place. What woman wants to dance with some army sucker? Or maybe they would? One of them kept looking over at us.

I could scarcely believe it when Phil got up and walked over to them. It was just so uncharacteristic of that reserved, gentle man. I admired him though. Doing that was harder, in my opinion, than doing an assault course. They gesticulated for me to join them, but I waved 'no thanks' and indicated with sign language to Phil that I was going to try the Casino Hotel to get my 20 dollars back. It was payback time!

It was only a couple of hundred metres back to the Casino Hotel. I parked the vehicle near the entrance and sauntered into the reception area. An African male receptionist looked at me without smiling. I took an instant dislike to him. Probably a gook sympathiser.

I went left and climbed the carpeted stairs towards the casino – turning back on myself to enter the slot machine room. This place was seedier than the Falls Hotel – definitely more run-down with waiters in frayed maroon tunics. I paused to order a whisky on the rocks before turning to push the swing door open into the main casino.

She didn't see me and I didn't see her, so we collided head-on. A tray full of betting chips crashed to the floor.

"Shit!" the girl with fiery green eyes said. "Why the hell don't you look where you're going?!"

"It was an accident… sorry, let me help you…" I bent down to help plonk them back on the tray.

"Not like that!" she snapped. "They each have their own place!"

I was taken aback by her attitude. I was a guest and didn't deserve to be treated like this. Besides, I had just spent two weeks in the bush protecting her frigging arse! I felt the blood rise into my ears – burning them.

"I'll leave it to you, then," I said, looking down at her. I couldn't see her face behind the shock of auburn hair, but it was hard not to notice the exquisite bulge of her breasts. I left her there as she continued to repack the chips for the next 10 minutes. I strolled over to a roulette table where a dark-skinned Mexican-looking man sat in a high chair.

"I see you've met Marilyn then?" he said, smiling. "I'm Fred McGraw, casino manager."

"Tony," I said, shaking his hand.

"One of Von Stranz's boys, or up from Bulawayo?"

"One of his."

"He's not a bad bloke – just been on holiday here for too long. He needs to go fight the war for a while."

I smiled at him and accepted my drink from the waiter.

"Quiet tonight, Fred?"

"Yes, bloody Elephant Hills gets all the punters. We're the poor relatives."

I looked around me. About six people sat at the bar in the right corner. A mere dozen or so people placed small bets with bored-looking croupiers. The square, high-ceilinged room had only eight tables in it – of which three operated.

"Mainly locals come here – bunch of bloody cheapskates," he whispered, and smiled at his own joke. I immediately liked Fred. He made me feel at ease.

"You been here long?" I enquired.

"Six years. It's going downhill fast though, Tony. It's this bloody war. Foreign tourists don't come here much anymore. This place used to be heaving with Brits, Americans... French... mainly South Africans and locals now. Not much foreign currency for our war-starved nation, hey?"

I felt mildly depressed – another slice of Rhodesia's new Uhuru in the making. Why the hell does everything have to go seedy and rotten in Africa – a continent with so much wealth?

The whisky tasted good, but I was suddenly very tired, so I sat at the head of the roulette table near Fred. Marilyn arrived and eased the tray of chips onto the end of the table furthest away from the roulette wheel. Her cheeks were flushed red and a bit of hair was stuck in the corner of her mouth. She did one of those swishing movements that only a woman can do and the errant strand of hair disappeared behind her ear. She caught me looking at her. A vague smile teased the corner of her mouth. Her eyes were electrifying.

"Change?" she said, suddenly.

"Pardon?"

"It means do you want to place bets," Fred cut in.

"Uh – I guess so," I said stupidly, and took out 20 dollars. I was determined to get something back after the earlier disaster. A pile of pink chips was passed to me. Marilyn spun the ball – spinning the wheel in the opposite direction. She kept her eyes lowered at all times – focusing on the table and the speeding white ball. It gave me a brief chance to study her glossy full lips, the bulge of her breasts and her well-painted fingers. She was rounded at the hips, but I like that in a woman – no twiggy for me, thank you.

"No more bets..."

The ball plinked into 32 red. I had a split on it and got 17 chips back. My heartbeat accelerated. Suddenly, that house and sports car seemed a reality. I increased the bet on 32 – as well as several numbers adjacent to it on the wheel. The ball was flicked into motion again – spinning slower and slower as gravity took over.

"No more bets, thank you... 11 black." I hadn't covered it – and suddenly my reserve of pink chips looked miserable. I decided on a 50-50 bet and backed red. It was 17 black and my chips were whisked away again. Another 20 bloody dollars gone! This is where gambling addicts will not let go and would pull out more and more money until they left drunk and broke late in the night.

"I shouldn't be saying this Tony, but nobody beats Mally. She's a real asset. Notice nobody came to join us at the table?"

"Thanks for the advance warning, Fred."

I felt foolish, irritable and tired all in one go. Ticks and elephant shit were suddenly very appealing in their simplicity. It was hard to gauge the smile in Marilyn's eyes. Was it victory or revenge?

"I'll bid you all farewell."

"You take care," Fred said. "Come back any time!"

"Mmm," was all I could muster as I got up from the table.

I drove back to see how Phil was doing. The dancefloor was alive with people and the sounds of George McCrae boomed out into the starlit African night. I sat and watched people turning slowly on the dancefloor for about half an hour before giving Phil a thumbs-up and throwing him the Land Rover keys. A nice walk back to camp would clear my head.

I turned right out of the hotel reception area. The night air was cool and full of the fragrance of frangipani. Bollard lights discreetly lit the way ahead. I passed the colonial-style railway station on my left and then walked for a short while back to the main road that led up to the police station. I hadn't a clue where I would sleep that night – and the thought of climbing into a stinking sleeping bag made me feel sick.

I was still pondering this unpleasant thought when I noticed a black Morris Minor pulled over to the side of the road with its hood up. I was pleasantly surprised when I saw Marilyn fiddling around with some wires on the engine.

"What seems to be the problem?" I said. Her eyes flashed immediate recognition of me in the gloom.

"If I knew that, I wouldn't be here."

I felt a hot rush of blood soar into my neck. It took a lot of willpower restraining the urge to smash the bonnet down on her head.

"Okay, I'll rephrase the question. How did it conk out? Slowly or suddenly?"

"Suddenly."

"Got a torch?"

"No, sorry."

If it conked out suddenly, the chances are it's an electrical fault. I asked her to switch the headlights on. They were bright and full of power. The battery was okay.

"Leave them on. It helps me to see a bit. Got a mirror?"

"Yes," she said – producing a small one from her handbag.

"Reflect the headlamp onto the underside of the bonnet. It'll give me a bit of extra light to work with." She did as she was told. I could see her black evening gown rustling in the gentle breeze out of the corner of my eye. It brought the smell of her into my nostrils. I just love the scent of a woman… it drives me mad with wonder and excitement.

I could feel – more than see – the wires in the engine, but as I traced them back to the distributor cap, I noticed the lead to the solenoid was hanging loose. I pushed it back into position.

"Try it now," I said. The engine fired first go. I closed the bonnet and walked round to her window. Her face glowed in the reflection of the headlights, but she stared ahead.

"Thank you," she said quietly.

"You're welcome."

I didn't know what else to say, but I desperately wanted this mysterious, gorgeous woman to stay with me a bit longer.

"Where do you live?"

"Up there – in the suburbs," she said, flicking her hand in the general direction of the campsite nearby. I had hoped for more, but nothing was forthcoming. "I have to go… thank you."

"You're welcome," I said stupidly for the second time – taking a step back to let her pull away.

I stood there transfixed watching that little black car drive up the road – its headlights casting a halo of light into the dark streets ahead. I so wanted to run screaming after her, but what was the point? She didn't know me and I didn't know her – and it looked like it was going to stay that way.

Three days passed since I'd bumped into Marilyn – and in the interim, I'd been given the onerous task of setting up our new base camp just east of the Elephant Hills Hotel. National parks had seen our plight – being based at the police station – and had very kindly allowed us to move into disused staff quarters just beyond the municipal campsite.

"You've gotta be joking," I said to Kevin as we climbed out of the Land Rover to inspect the buildings. The whole area was overgrown with tall grass and weeds. There was bat shit and hornet's nests in every room. There was even evidence of a vagrant living there.

"No point looking any closer, Kev. We need the guys and grass slashers for a start."

We returned two hours later with brooms, grass slashers, shovels, axes, picks, cans of paint and paintbrushes that we'd requisitioned from the local hardware store.

"Half of you guys start this end, and the other half from the other end," I said. Kev divided the group into two and the slashing began.

By the end of the second day, we had cleared the grass away and swept the rooms out. Ten men were 'volunteered' to start painting the rooms, while the others found rocks to form borders around the entrances to each barrack block. I intended to plant flowers in them. Several men began painting the rocks white as soon as they were in position. Von Stranz sent a requisition to a local construction company for all electrical circuits to be ripped out and made new – as well as all plumbing in the crumbling ablution block. He also asked for four security lights to be strategically placed at each corner of the rectangular-shaped property.

On day four, my entire platoon was bent over double planting chunks of grass that the estate manager of the 'Hills Hotel' had very kindly donated to us. Days five and six were spent erecting six bunkers – as well as a guard post next to the already-existing gate boom. Mid-Friday afternoon, a section of engineers arrived and put barbed wire all the way around the camp about five metres in front of the sandbagged defensive positions.

From the air, the camp buildings looked like a large capital 'I' – with the bottom cross piece making up the officers' and NCOs quarters – while the vertical link made up an ops room, officers' and NCOs mess and two barrack rooms. The top cross piece was entirely troop barrack rooms. The kitchen was situated to the west of this, with the ablution block to the right-hand side of the entrance.

"Time for some relaxation, I reckon," I said to Kev. We'd started to get on well with Von Stranz – and, as I expected, he allowed all of us to go to the Casino Hotel for a swim. What's more, he let us go in civvies so that it wouldn't look like an invasion at the hotel.

I'd been given a room to myself at the new camp, so I went inside and changed into shorts, slops and a T-shirt. I was relieved that I'd brought my costume with me.

It was a beautiful, hot sunny day – and the walk to the hotel was very pleasant. My guys were ecstatic that they could have some time off, and they bounced along in a big group laughing and talking at the top of their voices. I stopped to buy an ice-cream on the way, while the main body of men took a shortcut through the municipal campsite.

The pool area was heaving with masses of humanity – and the arrival of the 30 of us added to the general chaos. Kids and adults splashed in the crystal-clear waters. Beautiful women lay back on deckchairs clad only in bikinis, while tanned men applied suntan lotion to their lithe bodies. I changed into my dark yellow costume and ordered a drink from the bar set under a rambling masasa tree, with an orange bougainvillea growing high up into its branches.

It was great being young, tanned and bursting with health – and the feeling of being free, being a civvy for just a few hours, was hard to describe. I sat at the edge of the pool – dangling my legs into its cool, caressing waters, just watching the joy of kids splashing around and young lovers holding onto each other in the shallows. I put my drink in a safe place and slid easily into the water – letting it cover my head with a cone of silence. I rose to the surface and floated on my back – looking up at fluffy white clouds in the azure sky.

I bumped into someone's head and rolled over to apologise. It was her – the girl with the green eyes.

"Marilyn, we meet again."

"We seem to have the habit of bumping into each other."

I smiled. Her eyes caught the afternoon sun – making them look like burning emeralds. Her coppery skin contrasted sharply with the white of her bikini.

"Can I apologise by buying you a drink, then?"

The corner of her mouth turned down slightly, but her eyes smiled.

"Up there… in 20 minutes," she said, pointing to the Summit Bar of the hotel.

"Agreed," I said, smiling.

I told Kev where I was going and quickly changed back into my clothes. The lift slid quietly to the fourth floor of the hotel. The view was spectacular up there. Off to the left (or west) was the glint of the river through the trees, which led to a tower of spray above the Falls. Windows either side of me vibrated quietly from the millions of gallons of water cascading into the deep chasm. Directly ahead – through the boughs of magnificent trees – stood the amazing bridge that spanned over into Zambia. To the east was the gorge, steep and rocky – at the head of which was the Victoria Falls Hotel, just visible through the trees. The entire countryside was awash with greens, golds and yellows from the late afternoon sun.

"A penny for your thoughts," she said from behind me. I turned to look at her without making it obvious that I was blown away by her looks. The red dress she wore hugged her trim waist, moulded under her breasts – a compliment to the tan of her skin.

"You don't get much for a penny these days… What can I get you to drink?"

"A ginger square, please."

"Never heard of it."

"Try it. You'll be pleasantly surprised."

She sat at a table overlooking the Falls, while I went to the bar to order drinks. I turned to face her – leaning back on the bar counter. The mild breeze was tousling her hair – exposing a smooth neck.

"Thanks," she said as I sat down opposite her.

"I'm not good at this," I said.

"What?"

"Chatting to a beautiful woman. I get nervous."

"What for? I'm a person just like anyone else. You'll see."

She drew the golden liquid into her mouth through two straws. I did the same and was pleasantly surprised by the fruity alcoholic flavour.

"That's nice."

"See? I told you."

"I defer to your wisdom. Where are you from?"

"South Africa originally… Jo'burg. And you?"

"Salisbury."

"I worked there for four years at Meikles Hotel as a receptionist."

"Why'd you leave?"

"Time to move on, I guess… well, actually, things kinda fell apart in my life there."

"How?"

She paused to gather her thoughts – taking another deep draught of her drink. She was gorgeous – and the effect of her and the sun and booze made me want her so bad.

"I was married, Tony. It is Tony isn't it?"

"Yes."

"Well, as I said, I was married, but things fell apart quickly."

"Don't tell me. He had an affair?"

"You might say that."

"I don't follow?"

"He was gay. I caught him with a guy."

"You're kidding? I've heard of it before, but you're the first person I've met that's actually had it happen to them." I expected her to go deep into thought or cry or something, but she giggled. It was a deep, warm and infectious sound. The bridge of her nose crinkled. I laughed with her.

"Stupid bastard," she said. Her teeth were white against her tan.

"Why Vic Falls then?"

"A friend of mine told me the casino was looking for croupiers. I went back to Jo'burg to sort a few things out and contacted Fred."

"He seems a nice guy."

"Couldn't wish for a better boss. It's not a bad job, really. The tips make the difference."

She put her glass down and looked into my eyes. It sent an electric thrill up my spine. I knew in that instant that we would become lovers. I could sit back now and enjoy the anticipation.

"And you?" she said.

"When I left Salisbury three years ago, I worked my way around the world. I was a carpenter's mate in Essex, a lifeguard in Wales and a trainee train driver in Oz."

She giggled again – easing back in her chair, resting her feet on the bottom rung of the table.

"You're a train driver, ha!"

"It was a great job," I said defensively, "great pay and good perks."

She laughed again. I think the alcohol had just caught up with her. Ginger squares, as I discovered later, had a secret punch in them. They tasted like a cool drink, but kicked like a donkey.

"And then?"

"Well, that was at the end of my two-and-a-half years abroad. I had a Yank girlfriend and I had this crazy idea I would show her the greatest country on earth."

Something like jealousy flitted across Marilyn's eyes.

"Then the army got in the way…"

"And where's she, the Yank?"

"In Salisbury."

"You still going with her?"

"No, same thing as you. Caught her with a guy."

"Except she's not gay…"

We both laughed at that. I felt mellow and at home with her. She made me feel relaxed and comfortable – like putting on familiar gloves or a pair of slippers.

'What's your job up here, in the army?'

"To kill people."

"Oooh, I better watch myself then. I might become a target… no, seriously, what do you do?"

"I'm a platoon commander in the infantry."

"What's that then, an officer?"

"Yes, a lieutenant."

"Mmm, an officer, hey? How old are you?"

"Twenty-one."

"Shit, I'll be had up for cradle snatching."

"How old are you then?"

"Twenty-six in November."

"You're joking? You look younger than I do!"

"Why, thank you. Seriously though, you're only 21?"

"Yes." I felt embarrassed and stupid. She would probably tell me to go look for my dummy now. It made me anxious. I didn't want this to stop.

"A five-year age gap's nothing," she said simply. "Ten or 20 years maybe…"

"Even if the woman is the older of the two?"

"Why not? Men always get younger women. What's wrong with the other way around?"

"Dunno. It seems different… the toy-boy thing."

"Rubbish, Tony. Love conquers all barriers."

I felt relieved and smiled. The setting sun formed a halo around her hair. Colourful lights flicked on around the pool – and over in Zambia, street lights lit up.

"You've got lovely eyes," she said suddenly.

"Thank you. I was thinking the same thing about you earlier… prettiest I've ever seen in fact."

She smiled at me. I wanted to pull her forward and crush her into my arms. I was aching for her, but I knew it was too soon. Kev appeared next to me and cleared his throat.

"Sorry sir. The OC wants you back asap."

I could've screamed, but said simply: "Why?"

"There's been a scene down the road. The boss wants us to follow up, or act as stop groups."

"For shit's sake, why now?!" I screamed in my head, but merely nodded and downed the syrupy remainder of my drink.

"Sorry Mal, I have to go."

She looked as disappointed as I did, but smiled nonetheless.

"I hope we can catch up where we left off… some other time?"

"Yes, I want that very much," she said. I leaned forward and kissed her on the cheek – smelling that divine woman's scent. She squeezed my arm. "Take care, Tony…"

"Shit, Kev! Why now?" I said as the lift doors closed. "What's happened?"

"The boss didn't say."

"What about the guys?"

"They're already on their way back to camp."

I ran virtually all the way back – arriving there at last light. I made a cursory check of the men before entering the ops room.

"You're back. Good," Von Stranz said. We sat opposite the large wall map that used to be in the police station.

"A farm's been hit here," he said, pointing at a small red spot on the map. The location was roughly a third of the way back to Wankie. "PATU[3] are on-site at the moment, but a stick under Corporal Bosch will do the follow-up."

"What about Lieut Wells in Wankie?"

"Who?"

"Wells, Pete Wells – the other subby in 4 Indep. He's based at Wankie."

"I dunno. Maybe Major Pearce has him deployed elsewhere… anyway, your task is to get your platoon ready for backup in case it's needed."

---

3   PATU: Police Anti-Terrorist Unit. Paramilitary police – often made up by farmers or civilians from the cities – on call-up. They had a formidable reputation for being quick, accurate shots.

"What happened to the farmer?"

"He heard a noise outside and went to open the door. Got it in the chest. His wife ran out the back and hid in the bush... she's bloody lucky to be alive."

"What's their surname?"

"Cannings," Von Stranz said, looking at a clipboard, "No...sorry, Cummings, I think."

I imagined the horror of an incident like that; out on an isolated farm with little or no immediate help; the sheer terror and suddenness of it all; the helplessness of that woman lying in the bush waiting to be discovered... tortured... raped... skewered on a bayonet.

"The farmer's wife said the gook that did it was tall and muscular, with evil yellow eyes. He seemed to enjoy firing into her husband – all the while shouting and screaming what he would do to her when he caught her."

I was pissed off that I'd been called away from Marilyn, but under the circumstances, who could complain? After all, we were here to kill people like this big evil bastard.

I went straight to work with Kevin Torode – making sure that everything was sorted out in the platoon for a possible deployment at daybreak. Stores, ammo, radio batteries, maps, radio frequencies, call-signs, boundaries of friendly forces and so on and so forth. It was about 2230 when I decided that all was in order.

Would it be wise to pop back to the casino and see Marilyn? I looked at my watch, then at the remnants of my guys heading for bed, and decided against it. If we were needed, it would be an early rise – and I needed my beauty sleep.

We were all awake and ready to go at 0530, but Von Stranz didn't arrive until 0615. He ordered coffee and sat yawning in front of the ops map – feet up on another chair.

"It's wait and see now," he said, glancing up at me. I walked to the doorway and looked at the early-morning sun reflecting off a window on the Elephant Hills Hotel. I really hoped the guys doing the follow-up could pull it off and nail this bastard.

An hour later, I told the guys to stand down and get some breakfast. Still no news had come through from Dirk Bosch... We didn't know the line of flight of the terrorist group. Without that information, we didn't know where to intercept them or 'leap-frog' the follow-up team to form stop-groups.

It was gone 1030 when a message relayed from Wankie came through to us that the gook spoor had been lost – heading in a north-easterly direction towards a TTL (Tribal Trust Land) just east of Vic Falls Airport. It was reported that one set of footprints stood out from the rest. They were large – about size 12 to 14 – which confirmed what the farmer's wife had said about her assailant's size.

We stood down a short while later. I assumed our routine would return to normal – working on the camp, maybe going for a swim, but the boss had different ideas...

"I'm deploying you today," Von Stranz said as we ate a light lunch.

"Sir?" I said with a sinking heart.

"Mmm, back west of here – towards Chundu Island. I've told Sergeant Laing's guys to get straight on the vehicles that drop you off."

By then, I'd stopped chewing and merely looked at Von Stranz with my mouth half-open.

"But we've just come back from there, sir."

"Yes, but that was a week ago... we have a war on, or don't you know that, Tony?"

"Fuck off!" I thought, but merely carried on chewing. "Who's taking over the village rotation?"

'That other lieut you mentioned. Haven't met him yet... Wells?"

"Yes, sir."

❋–❋

It was good to see Phil again. What a great guy he was. I always felt calm around him. He never seemed to worry about anything. A gentleman of the old order.

"Anything to report, Phil?"

"Nothing sir, all quiet. I'll be glad to have a break."

"Know what you mean, Phil. There's only ants and ticks out here."

I watched as his guys replaced mine on the two vehicles we'd been deployed in. Prickly heat ran down my back. Something bit me on the ankle. A bloody tick was at me already!

"Kevin, you know your area. Four kays west of Chundu. Corporal Orchard... from the west end of Chundu up to Hippo Creek. My call-sign from Hippo Creek to the warden's homestead. Switch on, check your kit. It's been a holiday 'til now, but stay alert. Radio checks at 1630 and 0700 every day, okay?"

"Yes, sir."

"Good hunting..."

We walked back down the road for about a kay before heading north towards the river-front. Despite my reservations of being redeployed so soon, I actually loved the national parks; it was untouched Africa at its best. Green foliage competed with vines; creepers tumbled down from the tops of trees; elephant wallowed in the cool waters at sunset; buck leapt and danced in their hundreds; buffalo stared threateningly at you; hippo grunted under the moonlight – barging through the bush like gate-crashers at a party; bobbos barked their warnings from high above when we moved through the undergrowth. The smell of that type of Africa is so unique... dusty urine mixed with hay. Beetles scurried balls of droppings around to lay their young in. It would be a fine source of food when the grubs hatched.

There were also insidious little creatures like ticks, centipedes and scorpions. They all took great delight in sinking their fangs into young, unsuspecting flesh.

I delighted in the nights when the work of the day and heat was done – when you could lie on your back and look up at the vast expanse of stars so clear, you felt you could pluck them from the heavens... little crystalline diamonds in a limitless black velvet.

The beauty of Africa at night was tempered by the fact that both human and animal hunters were on the prowl. Lions and leopards were about... hyenas too – and a different type of nasty hyena... one that carried an AK assault rifle and trained in any one of the East European countries or Russia and China.

Because Russia and China competed for world influence, they were, in essence, enemies – even though they proclaimed brotherhood through communism. If the truth was known, they hated each other's guts.

In this sector of the Rhodesian war – in the Tangent operational area – we faced Ndebele warriors trained by the Russians. The Ndebele were direct descendants of the Zulu that broke away from Chaka, under Mzilikazi, in South Africa. They entered a land to become known as Rhodesia by the white settlers. Like their Zulu counterparts in South Africa, the Ndebele were a proud and noble people – very warlike by nature, contrasting with the Mashona from the central-north and north-east of the country (a timid, sometimes cowardly, grouping of people who would prefer to run than fight – although in some cases, they fought very well indeed).

The beauty of looking for Russian-trained guerrillas – or terrorists, as we preferred to call them, because that's all they were really – was that they followed the doctrine of structure and limited initiative the Soviet Army was well-known for. Unlike the British, American or Israeli armies, where common sense and initiative was encouraged, Russian troops only moved with the knowledge of very senior personnel. This made their chain of command slow and laborious and, in essence, it boiled down to Russian forces depending on crushing numbers to win tactical victories on the battlefield.

Because of this, we could almost guarantee that ZIPRA gooks would cross the Zambezi River in the same pre-selected areas time after time. After all, some Russian guy thousands of miles away – looking at an unfamiliar map of Africa – decided on each crossing point. This flawed thinking led to some spectacular slaughters on the Zambezi River west of Vic Falls and east of Kazungula – so much so that ZIPRA's High Command eventually decided to ship men and materiel into Botswana on a scheduled commercial ferry from Zambia, near Kazungula. They would put rifles in drums of fuel, which if opened, looked like fuel and nothing else – or they would make false-bottomed trucks and hide war materiel in there instead. Once in Botswana, they had hundreds of kilometres of unprotected border to enter the Rhodesian hinterland and commit their evil deeds.

It was against this backdrop that we constantly patrolled the known crossing points into Rhodesia. We could almost forget about the stretch of river 20 or 30 kays upstream. They just kept coming to the same crossing places time and again like brainless robots.

We'd settled into a night ambush on our third day in the bush when the heavens to the west of us lit up like a meteorite – the kwa kwa kwa of automatics spraying tracer into the air. Shooting went on for several minutes before petering out and stopping altogether – echoing slowly down the valley.

I switched my radio on to full volume, but made sure it was 'squelched', which enabled the voice of someone talking from the handset to be heard by the operator, but completely cut out any background hissing and crackles that could alert a nearby gook.

"Four Four Bravo… Four Four Alpha, over," I said into the handset. I called one more time before an adrenalin-filled voice came on the air. It was Roy Orchard's stick near Chundu.

"Contact… Contact…"

"Four Four Bravo, Four Four Alpha… What's happening, over?"

"Roger, we saw movement on the eastern end of Turtle, copied that?"

Turtle was the codename we'd given to Chundu Island. He'd seen movement at the eastern end and opened up.

"Any casualties, over?"

"Negative."

"Roger, your position's been compromised. Withdraw inland and go in my direction for one kay, and then go as far north as you can to monitor the area."

"Copied."

"Do an ammo count and make sure you're sorted out in case you bump into anyone."

"Copied that."

"I'll keep my set on all night as backup… Copied that, over?"

"Copied that… Many thanks, over."

"Well done. I'll report the incident to rear – just keep switched on. Do cross-grains at first light."

"Copied that."

I reported the incident to Von Stranz, who instructed us to do the usual cross-grain patrols at first light.

The bush takes on an ominous appearance after a contact at night. The gentle swaying motion of branches in a breeze makes it look like the tree is charging at you. Little glow-orms, or fireflies as some people call them, play hell with your nerves. At close quarters, they look like tracer zooming past your face. A twig dropping from a tree sounds like it happened underfoot.... the cry of a nocturnal animal is an enemy soldier imitating the animal before they charge to kill you with bullet and bayonet.

I thought about the oddity of gooks being on Chundu Island – or, perhaps, they were Zambian soldiers? The island did belong to them after all. It took me back a few weeks to the nights I sat listening to metal trunks being banged and clanged about in the farmer's house in Zambia – slightly east of Chundu Island. Tonight's contact confirmed without question that the island was one of many crossing points into Rhodesia. Perhaps those footprints I'd seen before the rain eliminated them was just another piece in the jigsaw puzzle? Perhaps the island was a storage and staging post for the last, brief hop onto Rhodesian soil?

It was nearly two in the morning by the time my adrenalin had dissipated enough to enable me to sleep. I set the watch and looked up at the stars for a while before tumbling into nothingness.

We were up just before first light, which was about 0530. We left our sleeping position a different way from the way we'd entered it – heading west to the boundary between Corporal Orchard and my own stick of eight men.

We paused for breakfast at 0615. Bomford was chewing a stick of grass as usual, Abbot had his idiot grin all sorted out and Kenny used his MAG as a stool while he prepared his tea and food. Breakfast usually consisted of tea, hardtack biscuits, jam and butter – although a few enterprising guys made amazing cordon bleu affairs for a couple of days before the heat destroyed the eggs and other condiments they tenderly carried with them. Some guys even brought along tinned shrimps from South Africa, which they got during their R&R. The radio crackled into life.

"Four Four Alpha, Zero Four, over."

"Go ahead," I said after swallowing a soggy biscuit.

"Roger... sunray wants you to go to the road to the south of you and standby for uplift, copied?"

"Uplift?"

"Affirmative. Your call-sign is to escort you to the road, but you are to come alone, over."

"Copied, over."

"Rv at 0900... Copied?"

"Roger, copied that. How long will I be at your loc, over?"

"Not sure... You should be back by last light, over."

I threw the handset down. My first thought was that I had cocked something up; to call me back to camp on my own was most unusual.

While we ate our breakfast, I explained our call-sign, radio channels and other necessary items to the guys before Kruger, Abbott and Duff 'Duffy' escorted me back to the dirt road running parallel with the Zambezi. The truck arrived dead on time.

"Patrol as far west as Hippo Creek, Corporal Kruger. No further."

"Sir."

"Stay switched on. Remember what you've been taught… Those were real gooks firing last night."

"I'll do my best, sir," he said, looking solemn.

"Good, see you later."

Von Stranz was waiting for me when I got back to camp about 20 minutes later. His face always looked as if it had a sarcastic smile curling up the corners of his mouth, so it was hard to tell what mood he was in. He shouted for cokes and called me into the ops room – closing the door behind him.

"Take a seat, Tony," he said, gesturing towards a chair. "I had a chat to Mike Howard from Special Branch last night. The contact with Corporal Orchard's stick has confirmed his suspicion for a long time. Chundu Island is being used as a staging post for crossings into Rhodesia."

I felt relieved that I wasn't in for a bollocking for some arbitrary infringement I had made, but his next words annoyed me.

"Com Ops has decided we must invade the island and sweep it from west to east to make sure it's free of gooks and equipment. A large stick belonging to Pete Wells's platoon will land here," he pointed at the western end of the island, "and sweep all the way east to see what he can find. Your platoon is to offer supporting fire from the Rhodesian bank."

"Good plan, sir. Just one problem…"

"What?"

"It's my guys that had the contact. It should be my platoon doing the invading."

Von Stranz looked at me in silence for long seconds before saying: "Fair enough. I merely wanted to use Pete's guys because they don't need to be brought back to base, but I see your point and agree. I'll give you a full briefing once your guys are back in camp. Make arrangements for them to come back, will you?"

"Yes, sir," I said smiling inwardly.

By 1600 two of my three sticks were back in camp. It had been decided to leave Kevin Torode where he was. I'd been itching all day to get out and find Marilyn, but duty came first.

At 1730 I had a briefing with Pete Wells and Von Stranz. It was really good to see Pete again. We sipped cokes while Von Stranz gave us the 'rundown' on the proposed op the next morning.

We would be deployed to the western end of Chundu Island by vehicle – making contact with the national parks warden on the way. His input was essential, as we needed his boat to ferry our troops over to the island. He would accompany our small convoy to the point of departure and lower the boat into the water for us.

We spent a short while discussing the operation; who would give covering fire; who the supporting troops were in case of a major contact; call-signs; and medical support – as well as air force support should it be needed.

I had entered the op with enthusiasm, but as time went by I realised the impact of what was going to happen the next morning. I was ostensibly going to get into a boat with six other men and do a mini D-Day landing in broad daylight. We had no direct intelligence about who or what was on the island... That was the purpose of my visit, after all. We didn't know if we would be met by concentrated fire by Zambian soldiers or gooks or both. I suddenly felt less enthusiastic about the whole plan, but excited nonetheless.

Once the first wave of troops was ashore, the boat would return for a second uplift. Pete's troops would act as backup in case we hit trouble. He would deploy several troops with rifles and MAGs on the Rhodesian bank to give covering fire if we got hit mid-stream. It was a mere 75 metres between the two shores.

I took a long time going to sleep that night. I went over the operation again and again in my mind to make sure all was squared away. I also had a girl with auburn hair and green eyes on my mind, and hoped and prayed that some other lucky bastard wasn't in the process of snatching her away from me.

❦—❦

I was woken at 0400 by someone tugging on my shoulder. I exchanged the warmth of my bed for the chill morning air. I dressed quickly – running over to the ablution block to brush my teeth and have a piss.

The eastern horizon was a smudge brighter when I entered the brightly-lit ops room. I was the last in. Pete was dressed and ready to go – sipping on coffee. I poured a cup for myself before going out to check on my guys. A short while later, we were ready to depart. The idea was for me to go to the warden's house to get him and the boat, while Pete led the way to the island. Von Stranz looked bleary-eyed and his hair stuck up at an angle at the back of his head.

"Good hunting and keep your head down, Tony."

"Thanks, sir. We'll do our best."

Pete and I made a few final arrangements before climbing onto our respective vehicles. It was 'all systems go'.

I followed the small convoy until I reached the national parks chalets. An air of excitement and expectation filled all of us. The road was quiet and deserted as we made our way into the dark African bush – our headlights rising and falling over humps and bumps in the road. The odd pair of eyes reflected back at us from the bush before disappearing rapidly. While I was mildly afraid, the heightened expectation and confidence in our abilities, our youth and the Rhodesian spirit pushed us forward.

When we reached the last chalet, I signalled Pete on the radio and turned right to get the warden and his boat. We bounced to a halt in our two-five[4] at the back of a building that I mistook for his house. I knocked loudly on the French door several times before a wide-eyed white male came to see what was happening – flicking the veranda light on as he peered out at us.

"Are you the warden?" I said.

"No, I'm a tourist…"

"Shit!" I cursed under my breath – turning away. "Sorry sir, my mistake."

"What's going on?" he said wide-eyed. The two of us all blacked-up with full webbing and balaclavas must have put the shits up him.

"Nothing, sir. Just checking the area."

"What for… Why?"

I ignored him and ran out to the truck – strapping myself in behind the driver.

"It's the next complex of buildings," I said, slapping him on the back. The engine roared into life and we spun out the dusty driveway, right onto the main road, along another half-kay until we saw a sign with 'Warden' printed on it. I could've kicked myself. Our timings were important to all of us.

We located the house with ease this time. The warden was waiting and ready – a large boat and trailer anchored to the back of his green Land Rover.

"Thought I'd missed the fun when the others drove by," he said with a smile. He was a handsome guy – about 30 years old.

"No such luck. Ready to go?"

---

4   Two-five: Yet another type of troop-carrying vehicle, a German Unimog capable of carrying a 2.5 tonne load – hence the nickname of 'two-five'. Despite being a slightly wobbly and unstable vehicle, it was excellent for crossing rivers deep enough for the driver to be up to his chest in water – and could climb amazingly steep hills. The mine-proofing was very similar to the four-five, and some specialist units converted it into an armoured troop-carrier or mortar-tube platform.

He nodded, got into the cab of his vehicle with a couple of black rangers and fell in behind us. The sky was getting lighter by the minute behind us, but it was still relatively dark ahead. It was that twilight time when dawn attacks are normally carried out; when one bush looks like two; when the rods and cones of your retina are fighting for superiority in your eyesight. It is a time when optical illusions and numbed brains combine to enhance the death and destruction of the enemy.

We bounced along the road, over the now-familiar Hippo Creek causeway, through the saddle of a small ridge and then down towards the drop-off point west of Chundu Island. We could just make out the river and island from the slightly elevated position as we went over the saddle. The river looked like a silver snake with a golden-pink head cast by the sunrise to the east. Palm trees stood out in stark contrast along its length – as far as the eye could see. Birds were calling out now and the odd flick of white rump from a buck could be seen heading toward the river for a drink – a drink that would have to last the whole day as it browsed on grass further inland.

It was a little after 0530 when we located the spot we needed to launch the boat into the river – situated just west of the island. A small beach with a gently sloping bank provided the perfect place to embark.

I put the guys in all-round defence while the boat was being unloaded. Pete and I chatted briefly before he moved east to drop off the guys who would offer us fire support if we needed it.

The moment of truth had arrived: Would it go okay? Would I cock it up? Was death waiting for me less than a hundred metres away?

I felt a degree of trepidation as I climbed into the small craft. 'Maximum passengers 8' was stamped on the gunwale; there were nine of us – including the warden. Dark water sped by at an alarming rate in a gentle sigh.

Willing hands pushed the boat backwards into the water, which caught it instantly – spinning us around like a toy. For one brief instant, I thought we were going to capsize. So much for the Rhodesian Navy exerting its authority! Fortunately, the motor fired first go. The warden quickly brought the craft under control – heading diagonally north-east towards a sandy strip of beach on the south side of the island, at the western tip of it. We shot forward at an alarming rate – propelled forward by the rush of water. I glanced at the guys behind me. Abbott had his idiotic grin sorted out once again, Max's glasses reflected the rising sun and Roy Orchard grinned – white teeth in a blackened face… Teeth I will always remember, with that small chip between the two front ones. The island looked dark and forbidding, with massive trees towering above us – covered in thicker undergrowth than I first imagined.

"Make sure your weapons are cocked and off safe," I shouted back at the guys. I know it was a risk to leave the boat with cocked weapons, but a rapid response to gook fire was more important than a possible accidental discharge.

We sped quickly past the large tree where I'd seen those footprints a while back – just catching a glimpse of Pete giving me a thumbs-up. A long row of guys lay waiting to offer us fire support if needed.

"Four Six Alpha, Four Four Alpha... radio check," I said into the handset.

"Got you fives. Good hunting," Pete replied.

The gap to the beach narrowed. I would be the first off and the first up the sandy embankment ahead. What was waiting at the top of it?

The boat hit the beach with the sound of plastic sliding on sand. We were off like a shot – running for the bottom of the embankment, spreading out. I quickly checked the guys as the boat engine revved – pulling the craft offshore, going back for the second wave of men.

I made for the top of the steeply sloping sand, but found it soft and heavy-going. No matter how much I tried to make headway, I just broke the sand down and wheelied in one spot. A large pair of hands suddenly latched onto my backside – propelling me forward. My heart was pounding away – adrenalin shooting into my system in big gobs. I'd reached the crest of the sandbank – pausing briefly to scan the interior of the island immediately in front of me. It was devoid of vegetation – almost parade-ground bare, the sandy soil dappled in shadows.

I pulled up the guy behind me and moved slowly forward – crouching behind the trunk of a large tree, while the rest of my team clambered up the sandy bank. My breathing was a bit more controlled now and the fuzziness and disorientation of the first few seconds of the adrenalin rush was beginning to subside.

"Switch on and spread out!" I hissed to the guys, "Extended line..."

We moved slowly forward from cover to cover – trying to look at as much as possible of everything. Unusual root structures ahead were pointed out to me by Roy Orchard. They looked like grass bashas, like tables... Was this a camp? Why did it look so parade-like in its cleanliness?

"Four Six Alpha, Four Four Alpha," I said into the handset.

"Go ahead."

"Possible sighting of bashas and a camp... Heading further inland."

"Copied. The second load of your guys should be with you in a couple of ticks."

"Roger, copied that. Thanks."

I released the handset – turning to the right to tell Max where to position his MAG on the right flank; Kenny's on the left flank. We got into a good defensive position and waited for the second wave of guys to land. I looked the bush over through binos while I was waiting for them to arrive. It got progressively thicker the further east I looked, with bent and half-fallen palm trees blending in with the foliage.

Another seven guys arrived shortly after that – spreading out and lying prone at the base of trees. I shook them out in an extended line as best I could and started moving east at a slow pace. The tension was electric. We were heading for thick bush from a section of island virtually devoid of undergrowth.

One step after another – expecting at any moment for bullets to come crashing into you. Was that a head at the base of that tree? What glinted momentarily in that bush? I was tempted to move forward by spraying every bush in front of me with fire. Static hissed in my headset. Sweat stung my eyes. My hearing was acute and alert.

I looked to the left and then the right to make sure the guys were dressed correctly. I don't mean the clothes they were wearing, but correctly spaced out – alert and on the ball.

After several minutes of this, we encountered some palm trees that had bullet strikes in them. Other hardwood trees had grazes along the bark – weeping sap down to the dry earth. The angle of the cuts in several tree-trunks indicated fire had come from the Rhodesian bank. I looked for spoor, or gook doppies,[5] but couldn't see anything.

In less than 20 minutes, we reached the far end of the island. We'd seen nothing at all. I heaved a sigh of relief, but was disappointed nonetheless.

"Sir!" Abbott called from the right flank.

"Everyone, take cover," I said as I walked over to him. "What's up, Abbott?"

"Footprints leading into the water."

I looked down at perhaps three or four footprints in the soft sand. The spacing between the footfalls was long – indicating they'd been running, whoever they were. The spoor ended abruptly at the water's edge.

"That's odd," I said to Abbott.

"What, sir?"

"The spoor's been laid by our type of boot."

"So it has," Abbott said, bending down.

The whole thing was odd. A contact with the enemy was supposed to have happened, but there were no gook doppies laying around – for that matter, no doppies at all. No packs, clothing or discarded items. It was really strange.

We made a thorough search of the island, but found nothing. I reported another 'lemon' – a wasted effort – to Von Stranz and Pete by radio before the boats came to uplift us later in the morning.

---

5   Doppie: Rhodesian slang for spent cartridge cases. The expression probably originated in South Africa and was adopted via our Afrikaans-speaking soldiers.

I wondered about that incident for a long time afterwards. Were the men that Roy engaged Selous Scouts or SAS? It was, after all, a perfect place for them to lie up before crossing over into Zambia on special ops. Was the little invasion of the island a mere charade or a cover-up for something else? I'll never know.

Chapter Six

"How did you find where I live?" Marilyn said, opening the front door to her house.

"Fred... Met him by the pool at the hotel."

"Come in," she said, smiling.

It was a beautiful clear morning – the blue sky forming a lovely backdrop to the flowers and bougainvilleas that shrouded the front door.

"I didn't recognise you with your clothes on, Tony..."

"I can easily rectify that."

"Cheeky bugger!" her nose wrinkled when she smiled. "Tea?"

"Coffee please. Milk and one sugar."

She turned towards a passage which led to the kitchen. I gave the lounge a once-over as I followed her inside. The place was a bit threadbare, but it was clean and tidy. A few of those woman's touches were spread here and there... Magazines on the coffee table, flowers in a vase, some paintings... Family photos... The familiar smell of beeswax floor polish...

"Have you eaten yet?"

"Yes, thanks. And you?"

"I'll just pop some toast on. So, what brings you here?"

She faced away from me as she talked – her body covered in a silky red dressing gown. The colour brought life to her hair, which had been piled up in that impossible way only a woman can achieve.

"I decided to pick up where we left off the other day."

"I'm glad," she said, popping a slice of bread in the toaster. The water boiled and she passed me my coffee. Her gown slipped open slightly – revealing ample, pleasant breasts.

"How come you've got time off?"

"We get a day or so every two weeks. The boss figures I need a rest."

"Rest?"

"Mmm.... The bush wears you down."

She sipped her tea – plopping butter and marmalade on her toast.

"Were you involved in that farm attack down the road?"

"No, well, almost. After I left you at the hotel, we were put on standby to help do a follow-up, but the gook spoor disappeared."

I looked at the delight she had chewing the toast – revealing white teeth as she bit into it.

"What happened?"

"The farmer got killed by gooks – about eight of them. The wife escaped into the bush, thank God."

"It's put the shits up the people in the village, you know – me included."

"You'll be okay here."

"Fred knew them... Well, not that close, but sort of acquaintances. They did a bit of gambling now and again when they were up here."

"It's gonna kill tourism when news of this gets out."

"You think so?" she said, licking crumbs off her fingers.

"No doubt about it."

"Let's finish our coffee in the lounge."

We walked back to the lounge and sat on chairs opposite each other. She hooked her feet up under her and sort of curled up like a cat – holding her steaming mug in both hands.

"Have you got the whole day free?"

"Yes. And you?"

"Mmm... Up until the casino opens at 8:00 p.m. Well, we have to get there by 7:30 to sort out the tables."

"Have you got any plans?" I asked.

"None that don't include you." Her eyes studied mine over the rim of her cup. I knew yet again that we would be lovers.

"Tell you what, Mally. I've had a sort of disjointed introduction to the village. Why don't we do a tour and then have lunch somewhere?"

"Sounds great... and finish it off with a booze cruise?!"

"Fantastic, let's do it."

She put her cup down on a side table and hopped up.

"Give me 10 minutes... Did you bring your costume?"

"Yes."

We locked the place up before hopping into her little black Morris Minor. The feeling of freedom, being out of uniform and sitting next to a gorgeous woman is hard to describe.

"Where to?" I asked.

"Swim at Vic Falls Hotel and then lunch by the pool at either Elephant Hills or the A'Zambezi?"

"Agreed," I said.

I studied her brown legs out of the corner of my eye and that oh-so-beautiful pubic mound where her shorts were pulled tight in the crutch. A white shirt tied in a knot over her belly-button finished it off. Well, not quite. The high-heeled shoes did it. Oh my word, she's beautiful...

She knew I was gawping at her, so she flashed a smile at me – her eyes hidden behind big sunglasses.

"Like what you see?" she said suddenly.

I felt a hot rush into my neck and face.

"Yes... Very much."

We walked next to each other down to the rectangular-shaped pool at Vic Falls Hotel – touching, but not quite touching. I desperately wanted to grab her hand to show the whole world that she was mine. The feeling was electrifying.

It was different seeing the hotel in daylight for the first time. What a truly beautiful old colonial building with high, shuttered windows and fans spinning slowly in every room and hallway. The high ceilings allowed the heat of the day to be drawn up and swirled away – leaving you cool and refreshed even on the hottest of days.

We ordered ginger squares from a waiter and headed for deckchairs next to the water. In a single movement, Marilyn transformed herself from a scantily-dressed woman to near-naked. I sensed other men turning to look at her. How the hell could a man give this angel up? She left her high-heeled shoes on, which only added to the incredible sensuality she generated, and sat on the deckchair.

"This is nice," she said, scooping her sunglasses to the top of her head.

"Brilliant, just brilliant, Mally... Beats the crap out of playing soldiers."

"Doesn't it scare you? It must be awful trying to catch people who are out to kill you?"

"I'm happy to say I haven't had any experience meeting them face-to-face yet. I guess if I was a Selous Scout or in the SAS or RLI I would know, but for now I'm happy to be a civvy soldier."

I stripped down to my costume and lay back on the deckchair. I was thrilled when she ran her eyes over my body.

"Like what you see?" I mocked.

"It's kept you in shape... the army."

"Thanks. What's your excuse, then?"

"Not much, really. I just watch what I eat and swim and walk whenever I can. I like tennis too."

"You'll have to teach me sometime."

The drinks arrived, and the 'cool drink' with the hidden punch filled me with fire – melting some of my shyness away. I lay back and looked at her lovely form – the full lips that she licked every now and again; the breasts that rose and fell with each breath – slippery from suntan cream.

I leapt up... and in one move pulled her shoes off, and shrieking with laughter we jumped into the pool – coming up in a burst of bubbles to flick water at each other.

"You bugger, you!" she spat, playfully, "I was just nodding off!"

"None of that while I'm around. Time's too short!"

We swam to the deep end, and then raced to the shallow end. When she stood up, I went underwater and blew bubbles into her belly-button. She folded in half and let out a deep, sensual giggle.

"My God, what are you trying to do to me?" Her nipples became proud and erect behind the white material.

I pulled her towards me... and that feeling that surpasses all description filled my body as her skin touched mine – the shape of her blending perfectly with me. You know, some people you can hold; others just seem to melt into your profile. She melted.

I stared into her green eyes. Her hair was slicked back and little rivulets of water ran down her face to disappear in the cleavage of her breasts. The sounds around us faded away. Our faces came closer together until my lips barely touched hers. She pulled me near to kiss her deeply, but I gently resisted – choosing to kiss the side of her neck, gently sucking the skin there and running my tongue over it... tasting that sweet saltiness of her.

"Tony," she said, huskily. Her body gave a little shiver. "Tony..."

I looked up at her. Her cheeks had reddened and her breathing was just that little faster. I wanted her so bad, but I knew the excitement of the chase – the anticipation of things to come – was far more exciting than the conquest itself. That would come later. I wanted to continue this exquisite feeling of desire a bit longer. I kissed her longingly on the lips.

"Lunch..."

"You bastard!" she spat, and punched me on the shoulder with her fist. She flicked herself backwards and did a few lengths of the pool – no doubt to cool her ardour.

There was no reason to hide our feelings for each other now, and we walked hand-in-hand to the pool deck when we arrived at the Elephant Hills Hotel.

The view below us was spectacular. The silver thread of the river ran beyond thick trees and palm-lined fringes. The golf course in the foreground encroached upon the wilderness – and here and there, antelope munched grass alongside ever-industrious bush pig. Golfers hacked away at little white balls.

The large thatched roof of the A'Zambezi Hotel was clearly visible to our left (or west), and to the right, the spray from the Falls towered up into the air – a perfect rainbow crowning the top. Over the river, in Zambia, little spirals of smoke curled up into the air. The green smudge of the far escarpment clashed with the blue of the sky.

"This is a beautiful country, Tony."

"God's own."

I thought about that for a minute. Rhodesia was certainly one of the most beautiful countries in Africa – if not the world. Wide open savannah spaces gave way to jungle in the eastern Highlands, which in turn gave way to pristine mountains – the rivers bursting with trout. In the north-west was Kariba – the second biggest man-made dam on earth, second only to the Aswan in Egypt. Its banks thronged with an incredible diversity of wildlife, which was the source of its main industry… tourism. Hotels had mushroomed along the shores of a dam that looked like an ocean – its waters fading unbroken to the distant horizon.

And here, to the west, Victoria Falls – one of the world's Seven Wonders… surrounded by thousands of square kilometres of wilderness. What a place to fall in love in – and to fight a war. My heart felt heavy and full all at the same time. I knew both of them – my country and Marilyn, the two loves of my life at that moment in time – were delicate and vulnerable.

I felt slightly melancholy when I ate my meal in silence next to Marilyn.

"Why so quiet, Tony?"

I paused before answering.

"I just have this feeling that it's all changing, this country… I just feel sad about the thought of that, you know? The way countries to the north just collapsed. I couldn't handle that happening here. I would hate to leave Rhodesia."

"I know how you feel. The decay that sets in… Everything just falls to pieces."

"I can't believe the Brits and other countries are enforcing sanctions against us. Do you know how few countries ever get sanctioned – especially former Commonwealth ones?"

"Tell me about it."

"Would you go back to South Africa if things fell to bits here?"

"Maybe. I love this place so much. We'll see how it goes."

I decided to change the subject because I knew I was heading for a bout of depression, so we chatted about our pasts – who we'd loved, where we had been. I told her about my years of working my way around the world and of Jess. The thought of her didn't bring the ache it used to.

Marilyn told me about her past too – where she had been born, her choice of music, her school days and her failed marriage. We had a lot in common. I felt comfortable in her presence – like we'd known each other for years instead of days. You know, that feeling of putting on old slippers. Familiar.

I looked at her when she stopped talking. I looked at all of her – her profile as she looked at the river… her lips, her hair and the brown skin… the long legs, from tight hot-pants to high-heeled shoes – a little golden chain around her ankle. I was terribly afraid this beautiful woman would be lost to me one day; that she wouldn't care for me the way I was beginning to care for her; that she would turn on me like Jess did, someday. I felt jealous about that – jealous of a person who wasn't even my lover yet.

We drove in silence towards the tar road that led to the river's edge to board the evening sundowner cruise, or 'booze cruise' as it was more commonly known.

A tour bus full of tourists emptied its cargo under bowed palm trees and plonk-plonked their way across a wooden gangway to the double-decker boat. Waiters busied themselves at the back of the boat, while the helmsman leaned out of the little cockpit, smoking a cigarette. A white female tour guide escorted her guests to their seats.

Marilyn and I climbed a steel staircase to sit on the open deck. There was nothing between us and the river except a metal railing. Tables around us quickly filled up. We ordered another 'cool drink' with a sting in its tail.

This was the first time I'd seen the river up-close in daylight. What a lovely place it was. The river flowed swiftly beneath arched hardwood branches – bobbing up and down thick reeds as it sped by. The river split in two at this departure point, with an island belonging to Zambia about 100 metres away. On the other side of the island, the river widened to about 200 metres before it got lost in a myriad of small islets, sandbanks and reeds. Monkeys gibbered and barked away in the trees above, while countless birds added to the general cacophony of noise. Hippos grunted deep uh-uh-uhs upstream from us.

"This is lovely," Marilyn said, looking back at me from the railing. I walked over to her and wrapped my arms around her waist from behind. She felt so warm – and the smell of her hair was divine. Her head tilted back to rest on my shoulder.

There was no need to say anything. Silence was the perfect message as we stood there looking into the sunset. The boat pulled away from the shore – and as it did, so a breeze picked up from the boat making headway upstream.

We chugged past the A'Zambezi Hotel on our left. The hotel was shaped like a quarter-moon – a crescent – with either tip almost touching the river. It had one of the largest thatched roofs in Africa. A colourful pool crammed with kids and adults alike nestled in the centre.

And then the river became very wide – almost a kilometre at this point. Over on the Zambian side was a booze cruise boat just like ours – no doubt crammed with tourists from the very same countries as our boat. It was hard to believe our two countries were at war – well, a sort of phoney war like the Allies and Germans experienced in 1939 and early 1940.

Although Zambia had not formally declared war on Rhodesia, they supported and harboured our enemy nonetheless – and as such, their troops were fair game to any of our security forces if they chose to interfere.

"Look at that," Mally said, pointing as some very large crocs sliding into the water.

"Gook recyclers," I said. She giggled and rested her hands on mine.

The national parks safari lodges came and went, and then the island of Kandahar came into view. In a few years gone by, the booze cruise would stop there for people to have lunch, tea or a sundowner – with the resident troop of monkeys getting more of the food than the paying guests!

I knew the bank to our left (or south) had soldiers along it – watching us at this very moment. I searched every bush and cluster of grass to see if anyone was shirking their duty, but nothing was visible at all. That was good. I knew that perhaps one of Phil Laing's men or Pete Wells's men was keeping an eye on us.

We chanced upon a large herd of elephant drinking in the shallows. The captain reduced the revs of the boat's engines so that we remained virtually static in the water to get a close-up view. This was top-dollar for the tourists, and the boat took a distinct list to the port as they crowded the railing – snapping photograph after photograph. A big bull sniffed the air with his trunk, flapped his ears and shook the dust off his head... A sort of 'bugger off, or I'll sort you out' motion. The youngsters gathered around the matriarch for guidance and protection, or generally made an ass of themselves trying to get eaten by crocodiles. What magnificent creatures elephants are; their characteristics and gregarious nature are so human, you could almost mistake them for distant cousins.

I felt so good. My heart, body and soul felt warm and content – and the sting in the tail of the ginger square was just beginning to bite. I kissed Mally on the nape of her neck – sending a shiver down her spine.

"Bloody hell, Tony. You know which buttons to press..."

We reached the end of our journey upstream, and now it was time to go back. I felt elated, but sad that this warm sunny moment in my life was ending. These moments of ecstasy are so rare in life; you want them to go on forever.

The engines were throttled back and the boat more or less took itself downstream in total silence bar the sigh of the water on the hull. The wind too had died as we no longer made headway into it. I sat – pulling Mally down on my lap. She draped her arm around my neck and nestled her head against the side of mine. The sun – a large, pinky-orange glow – slipped towards the horizon behind us, and as its enveloping rays suddenly disappeared, so the air became chilly. Mally snuggled a little closer into me. I traced invisible figures on her forearm with my fingers.

"Mmm, I feel so whole and content, Tony. It's been a long time..."

The cruise came to an end, and we were the last to depart – sitting on our chair as the others chatted and laughed their tipsy laughs. We wanted to postpone the end of this moment just a few seconds longer.

We drove in silence back towards Mally's house. I had the hope and expectation of things to come. I wanted her so very bad. I suspected that she was feeling the same way.

The car turned into her driveway and she sat staring ahead for a long time after turning the ignition off – as if fighting an inner battle.

"It's okay, Mal. It can wait. There's no pressure…"

She turned to me – pulling me close and kissing me deeply; big salty tears running down her face. We hugged a long time.

"You're amazing. I've never met anyone like you… so sensitive…"

"It's okay, really. I know you're mine and that's all that counts."

She kissed me again.

"I have to get ready for work, Tony. Will I see you tonight at the casino?"

"Afraid not. I'm the duty officer tonight and I go back to the bush tomorrow."

"You're joking?"

"Nope."

"Why didn't you tell me? We could've come back earlier… missed the booze cruise. 'How long will you be gone for?"

"Two weeks – maybe more."

"Tony, I didn't know. What the hell will I do for two weeks without you?"

"It'll be fine. You better get ready, babe."

We kissed each other for a long time, and then I got out the car and walked towards the gate. I turned only once to look back at her. She was still sitting in the car.

Day three back on patrol – and I was hot and irritable. It was becoming a nightmare being based in a tourist resort. Nearly all of us had struck up a relationship with a female tourist or a local resident of the village, and here we sat among ticks and baboons. It made all of us sour. It's not like we were regulars posted to Grand Reef Fireforce base.

Thank God Von Stranz had agreed to a 10-day turnaround rather than the normal 21 days. I only had seven days to go and I couldn't stop thinking of Marilyn. The thought that some other guy was possibly chatting her up made me feel nauseous from frustration.

I sat back against the trunk of a tree and swished a few mopanie flies away from my eyes. In fact, they weren't flies, but tiny little bees twice the size of the roller on a ball-point pen. They made the most delicious honey. Their tactic of collecting moisture was to invade your eyes, nose, ears or forearms in their thousands. You dare not kill one of them, because the scent would bring millions more to the funeral! The whine of their wings could literally drive you insane.

"For fuck's sake!" Max said, swiping at the evasive little bastards. "Ticks and elephant shit!"

I bent forward for the hundredth time in three days to scrape a red ring of ticks off my legs, where they'd gathered between my socks and the elastic band of my 'combat trousers, long'. It was great fun watching them squiggle in pain when I cooked them under a small magnifying glass I carried.

"Four Four Alpha, Zero Four."

"Go ahead," I said into the handset.

"Roger, sunray wants you to move forward at 1700 to the following locstat. Ready to copy?"

"Standby." I grabbed my pencil and notepad. "Go ahead."

The voice read off the co-ordinates in code. I repeated them for confirmation.

"What am I supposed to do there, over?"

"Sunray's had some feedback that there's movement in that area, copied?"

"Four Four Alpha, copied that. Anything else?"

"Negative, just report back on anything you see there."

"Copied."

"Zero Four out."

I took out the codes for the day and read one letter of the alphabet against another to convert it to its true meaning. The co-ordinates pointed to an area about two kilometres away on the riverfront near some rapids – just short of Hippo Creek on the way back to Vic Falls. This placed us about five kilometres west of the last national parks chalet – almost within view of the booze cruise. At least we didn't have to hump too far.

I waited until 1600 before setting out in an easterly direction. The bush was thick with greenery now, and a lot of the animals that may have come down to the river to drink were staying inland. There wasn't that density of animal spoor that we'd encountered when we first arrived.

When we were about 300 metres from our observation point, I made the guys space themselves out – and walking slowly, in a slightly crouched position, we moved down a gulley towards a concentration of trees and shrubs near the waterfront. I left the guys about 30 metres from the water's edge and crawled forward with Roy to look at the opposite bank through my binoculars. There was little to see apart from an African village with smoke curling lazily into the air and the white flicker of water tumbling over rocks in mid-stream rapids.

"What's the point of this?" I said to Roy. He shrugged his shoulders after looking through the binoculars himself.

"No action out there, sir."

The sun was settling rapidly in the west, and I knew that the African twilight would last only 30 minutes or so before it was totally black. Maybe another hour of daylight was left.

"Crawl back and tell the guys to make grub. I need a volunteer to cook for me while I stay here."

"No problem, sir."

Roy slid silently away and I faced the front once more. Static hissed in my radio handset. There was a big storm brewing out there somewhere.

I raised the binos one more time and swept the river from left to right. Nothing. My head ached dully and I had slight difficulty focusing my eyes. After a while, Roy appeared next to me with a mug of tea.

"Take a break in the ditch and I'll keep tabs for you, sir."

"Thanks," I said, gratefully accepting the mug. I felt awful.

I had no sooner started sipping the hot, sweet liquid when Roy hissed at me to come forward again. I leopard-crawled up to him.

"What is it?"

"Zambian soldiers – two of them."

I took the binos from Roy and looked in the general direction of some rocks and a sandy beach on the other side of the river. I froze. A Zambian soldier with an AK slung over his shoulder was looking at us through his own field glasses.

"Freeze, Roy. The bugger's looking us over…"

We kept as immobile as possible – and after a moment or two, the enemy soldier lost interest and chatted to his comrade, who was filling up water canteens. They seemed to be in high spirits and laughed and joked with each other.

What the hell was this all about? Why the order to come here? And why do we suddenly see Zambian soldiers for the first time after two months of patrolling in this area?

The two men strolled up a sandy bank carrying several bottles of water – and after a brief glimpse in our direction, they disappeared from view. The binos suddenly felt heavy, so I lowered them onto a large, dead palm leaf. My ears buzzed, and for the first time I was aware of sweating – even though the air was cool.

I heard it before I saw it… a swoosh-fizzz and then a massive explosion to our right. I just about crapped in my pants – and for a few brief seconds, hadn't a clue what to do.

"That was an RPG!" Roy spluttered in disbelief. A rocket-propelled grenade had just been fired at us – deadly accurate over the 400 metres that separated the two countries and equipped with a warhead that could cut through 30 centimetres of steel meant we were in big shit. A sound like tearing paper rasped across the water. We were being shot at big-time by multiple small arms fire! Bullets cracked overhead. I lay on my back – looking up at the sky. Another steam-train… swoosh… bang! This time, inland – behind us.

"Get back and bring the guys here – just their weapons and ammo… Leave the packs."

Roy slithered off as if a weasel was after his ass. We would be much safer here in the ditch. The tearing paper sound and the cracks overhead went on and on, but even in that twitching shocked state, I knew the rounds were high and off the mark.

Roy was gone only a few seconds before his fear-filled face appeared through the grass once again. Six other guys slid into the depression after him. Max arrived half on his side and half on his back – cradling the MAG and dragging belts of ammo behind him.

If we didn't suppress the fire coming at us, someone was going to get injured – or worse.

"Roy! Get Max to the side of that tree!" I shouted, and pointed at the same time. "Tell him to spray the other side to the left and right of that clompie of rocks!"

A third RPG 7 detonated behind us yet again. There was no let-up in the volume of small arms fire.

"The rest of you, spread out as much as you can. Keep low and take steady shots at likely places of concealment. Don't waste your ammo!" They nodded and belly-crawled into various firing positions. I inched my head above the parapet of earth and grass – looking intently at the other side. There was little to see…. Maybe the odd faint wisp of smoke.

Max's machine-gun opened up with a throaty roar – shortly followed by individual rifle shots from Roy and the six others. I followed the odd bit of tracer to the other side. It was low – too low!

"Adjust your sights to 400 metres!' I screamed at Max and the others. I had to repeat the order until all had complied. The guys kept up a steady stream of fire while I tried to listen to the radio handset, but it was impossible to hear anything. Instead, I depressed the handset and shouted what was happening into it and then threw it down. It was payback time. I crawled forward a few feet, set my sights to 400 metres and placed careful aimed shots into likely hiding places. One magazine of 20 rounds went at spaced intervals, and then another. I knew our aim was more accurate and must be having an effect.

"Hold your fire!" I bellowed – and then again until the shots died away. There was complete silence. Not a bird, not a cricket to be heard – only the faint tumble of water over rocks. I poked my head up again and looked through my binos. I couldn't see any evidence of anyone over there. There were no neon signs flashing 'here I am!'

"Four Four Alpha, Sunray Zero Four."

It was the boss.

"Go ahead, over."

"What's going on?"

"We've just been fired at from the other side, over."

"Confirm you're at the locstat given to you before lunch, over."

"That's affirmative."

"Why have you been compromised?"

"No idea. We entered the area as clandestinely as possible, over."

"Any casualties?"

"Negative, but the fire we took was heavy. Small arms and RPGs, over."

"Is it safe to vacate the area?"

"Negative, maybe after last light."

His next sentence was cut off by another express train and loud explosion.

"Open fire!"

The deafening crash started up again. A pile of doppies piled up under Max's gun. I felt thick-headed – as if everything was happening under a cotton-wool blanket. Just as I took aim with my rifle, I caught a glint in the sky and paused to look at it. There was definitely an aircraft up there. I knew Livingstone airport was only a stone's throw away. Maybe a plane was coming in to land? I picked up my binos and swept the orange sky to see what was happening. At first, I saw nothing – and then I caught a blurred image that quickly focused. My heart fluttered and I went stone-cold. I will never forget that feeling as long as I live...

There, in the cyclops vision of my binoculars, was a silver Zambian Air Force jet banking to the west – its nose facing towards us before the turn commenced. The underbelly flashed orange as the dying sun reflected off it – emphasising bright red rockets under the wings.

Real intense fear coursed through my veins. Now I knew what gooks felt like moments before they died at the hands of our ever-efficient Hawker Hunter pilots. I wasn't sure what to do. In both cases, running could mean death. I kept the aircraft firmly focused while I shouted at Roy.

"There's a bloody Zambian Air Force jet up there!"

The aircraft continued to turn in lazy circles as the cacophony of noise beat against my eardrums. What the hell do I do? Air to ground missiles would tear us to shreds – let alone 30mm cannon fire! I decided it was too risky to stay there.

"Leave me two of your magazines and get the guys out of here. Head east towards Hippo Creek and wait on the dirt road to town."

Roy paused to say something, but closed his mouth when he saw the look on my face. He dug the last two magazines out of his webbing and tossed them next to me. I grabbed them and crawled into the ditch. Roy tapped the guys one after the other on their shoulders and shouted at them to follow him.

I lay on my side and ejected all the rounds from Roy's two magazines – picking out the red-tipped tracer bullets and then putting them back into one magazine. Tracer bullets were designed to light up at night when you fired them, so that you could see whether your aim was directed onto a target or not. We had red tracer – a basic NATO colour made from a mixture of strontium and magnesium perchlorate, while the gooks had green tracer made from barium perchlorate. The green was predominantly for light arms, while white was reserved for heavier calibre weapons like the 12.7mm and 14.5mm anti-aircraft guns. I figured that the least I could do is set one of the huts in the nearby village on fire to create a smokescreen for our escape.

I crawled forward and took deliberate and careful aim at the thatched roof of the closest hut over the river. One round after another arced slightly until it disappeared into the thatch, with the odd bullet flicking out the burning-red magnesium in a pathetic fizzle. I hoped one of those fizzles would land in dry thatch.

I was almost out of tracer rounds when I noticed a small yellow tongue of flame lick up from the apex of the roof. In less than 30 seconds, it became a boiling inferno – orange and red sparks leaping into the air. The darkening bush around the hut appeared to dance as the light bounced off it. Smoke curled down in a vortex and headed upstream (or west) at a lazy speed. I couldn't have wished for a better effect if I'd tried. Not only were the enemy infantry cut off from view, but the aircraft would have a hard time seeing us if it dived for the attack.

I decided that discretion was the better part of valour and crept away as rapidly as I could.

❧—❧

It's hard to describe what the bush feels like at night when you've been in action. Things look hostile, alien and frightening. Every shadow and tree looks like an enemy poised to strike. I met up with the guys about 400 metres down the road. The sky to the north was aglow from the fire I'd started – reflecting orange and yellow off lowering clouds.

"Where to now, sir?" Roy whispered in my ear. I felt like shit.

"We'll go east for about half a kay and then creep back to the riverfront to see what's happening."

My groin hurt like hell and I sort of staggered along on the damp track. I found a distinct animal path leading to the left and followed it until we reached a slight depression under a big leafy tree – not too far from the dark, swirling waters of the river. I took out my binos and looked at the glowing remains of the hut that the tracer had set on fire. It was satisfying to see that a couple of other huts had caught alight also. I put the guys in all-round defence and slumped onto the ground. Should I radio the boss, or keep radio silence?

I decided to leave it and lay on my back – looking up at the stars through gaps in the cloud. What beautiful big displays of crystalline stars you get in Africa. There is relatively little city or atmospheric glow in the tropics, which makes the stars feel so close that you can reach out and touch them.

"Coffee, sir?" Roy said.

"Sure. In the dining room or the lounge?"

"You know I carry a small thermos flask, sir. It's still got coffee from lunchtime."

"You should join the hotel industry. You're a born manager."

"Funny you should say that." His smile produced white teeth against the black of his face.

A hot mug of sweet coffee was thrust into my hands. At that point, I couldn't give a fuck if gooks had the most sensitive nostrils in all of creation... the coffee was fantastic.

By 1030 I felt nothing more was going to happen and pondered if we should sleep here or move to a new place. I decided to stay put.

Chapter Seven

The phosphorescent lights hurt my eyes. There was a strong smell of disinfectant. I tried turning to look at my surroundings, but my head and eyeballs hurt like hell. My balls ached like hell too. A mature-looking nurse approached me – her shoes squeaking on the polished floor.

"Awake at last, young man. How do you feel?"

My answer was a croak, which sent spasms of pain into my head. The nurse held my forearm and took my pulse before propping my head up slightly to give me some pills and a sip of water.

"Do you know where you are?"

I moved my head from side to side just once.

"You're in Vic Falls Clinic. You've got a rather nasty dose of tick bite fever. Your war is over for a week or two."

Recent memories of tumbling into darkness… being lifted onto a vehicle… concerned faces looking down at me forced their way into my throbbing brain.

"You have a visitor," the nurse said matter-of-factly. "Five minutes – no more."

I tried to see who it was – half-expecting Von Stranz coming to give me a rev for not taking tick fever tablets. Instead, green beautiful eyes came into focus.

"Tony," she said simply – stroking my forehead. The smell of her was like a tonic.

"Mally," I whispered hoarsely, "how…?"

"Fred knows everything. He chats to officers and sergeants all the time."

"It's so good to see you. I feel like death, though."

"I'm sorry to say, you look like it." Her lips creased into a smile, but her eyes remained concerned. "I've brought some fruit."

"That's sweet of you. How've you been?"

"Fine… Well, worried when I heard all the shooting yesterday."

"Yesterday?"

"You've been out cold for over 24 hours."

I swallowed and tried to sit up, but the pain was too intense. Some stupid little prick of an insect had done this to me. I would burn out the whole shitty national park the next time I went on patrol there, which is precisely what I did in the weeks that followed.

I so wanted her to stay, but I felt like a ton of lead was pushing down on my body.

"I'll pop back again when you're better. The matron says you'll be in bed for at least two or three days, and will have to rest for another week or so after that."

"Thanks for coming," I whispered. "Just lovely to see you…"

Mally gave my forearm a squeeze and bent over to kiss my forehead. It was lovely being enveloped by her hair, which fell either side of my face.

The next morning, I felt a bit better. Von Stranz came in to see me.

"How's the warmonger today?"

"Knackered, sir."

"I should court-martial you for not protecting government property."

I smiled – knowing he was referring to me.

"What have I missed, sir?"

"Mmm – a couple of good things," he said, sitting on the edge of the bed. "We now know the gook that killed Cummings, the farmer, is a zot[1] called Albert Ncube."

He pronounced the surname with the correct clicking sound of the tongue against the roof of the mouth. The 'n' was almost silent and the 'c' sounded like 'tch'…

"Someone rat on him?"

"Yes, one of the farm labourers; he'd seen Ncube in Bulawayo. Bit of a shit-stirrer – a bad bugger… caused a really bad fight in a beer hall."

"That's good news, isn't it? That we know him? The cops must have a picture of him?"

"Indeed they have. They're sending one up this afternoon. It won't be long before the whole of Matabeleland has him on their shop windows."

I knew the post office had 'wanted' lists pinned on their walls, with the relevant reward offer under the photograph of the culprit. In a society where most people were poor, a handsome reward often turned brother against brother. The Rhodesian police and the CIO (or Central Intelligence Organisation) had a long list of informants that provided excellent intelligence for our security forces.

"What else, sir? What happened on the river the other day?"

"I was going to ask you the same thing. How did the Zambians see you?"

"Haven't a clue. We were as clandestine as possible."

"Mmm… well, I admit it was a risk deploying you in daylight. Our spies reckon an entire company of Zambian troops were having a go at you."

"And the aircraft? I nearly shat myself."

"We had a couple of Hunters on standby."

"By which time, I would've been breathing through my ribs, no doubt."

---

1   Zot: Derogatory slang for a black person. Don't worry… They had plenty for us too!

"We're not sure why the punch-up started," Von Stranz said with a wry smile. "Maybe it was a decoy for a crossing. Who knows?"

"There's an element of truth in that. I think I saw gook spoor out there before rain washed them away."

"Mmm..."

"So the war's starting for real up here, sir?"

"Looks like that... Anyway Tony, I have to go. That old battle-axe of a matron will cut my balls off if I stay any longer. You get better. I'll stick you on light duties in the camp until the doc gives you the all-clear, but do this again, and you'll swing..." He patted me once on the leg and left the ward.

I stared at a block of flats out the window for a long time before eventually dozing off.

Two days later, I was well enough to go back to camp, but I felt weak and unsteady when I walked. I had to bow my legs slightly to prevent my thighs rubbing on glands located near my testicles. I slept a lot and when I was awake, I did some radio watch and ordered the rations for the camp from Bulawayo. Marilyn had come to see me twice a day – and I realised, not for the first time, that I was falling in love with her.

Pete Wells's platoon had replaced Phil Laing's. It was really good to see him again. I always felt reassured around the guy; he was like a big brother to me. Kevin Torode ran my platoon while I was ill, and that worried me a bit. I never really had much faith in the guy as he was a hot-headed bugger with a bad attitude.

The rains had started in earnest now – and most afternoons, white clouds would build up into high cumulus before joining together, turning as black as tar. The rain that poured out of them wasn't the pitter-patter of cooler climates; rather, it came in sheets and torrents – flooding the parking area in seconds. Large bolts of lightning crashed and echoed down the valley. Flying ants fluttered around lightbulbs at night and a haze of mosquitoes zeroed in on all exposed flesh.

A squadron of armoured cars – packing 90mm cannons, plus two old English-manufactured ferret-armoured reconnaissance vehicles – had joined us in the camp. They'd strung large canvas sheets between the long-barrelled vehicles to give a bit of shelter from the rain, which poured off in sheets and waterfalls at the height of each storm.

While their presence was most welcome, it added to the growing feeling in the village that the war was closing in on us. Not only were we operating with two of the three platoons in our company at Vic Falls, we now had the armoured car squadron, which was soon followed by a troop of Grey's Scouts (horse-mounted infantry – a type of local cavalry). Even the police sent in a company of 'Black Boots' – so-called because their regulation boots were black (unlike ours, which were brown). These weren't 'Mr. Plods' that did the beat in cities, but were well-trained and often well-led counter-insurgency troops.

The increase in troops and the closing weather under darkening skies – plus the fact that we were one of the most isolated villages in the whole country – continued to put psychological pressure on all of us… We were vulnerable and alone.

After three days back in camp, I was given permission to take the day off and I spent it with Marilyn. We went for a drive in her little Morris – down past the large baobab tree to the parking area just above the awesome drop of the Falls. We walked hand-in-hand from there to Livingstone's statue, and then left down steep concrete steps to the 'Devil's Cataract', where the viewing point was halfway down the waterfall. The cataract accounted for about one third of the entire flow of water over the Falls. The volume of water was amazing… dark green and foamy white – twisting, turning and splattering apart on the rocks 150 feet below. Such massive quantities of water in a confined space was sufficient to force the spray upwards in a jet stream. In April, the spray could be thrust 1,500 feet above the forest that had formed beneath the continual mist. Anything you threw over the edge of the Falls would actually go upwards for a few seconds before gravity took hold and pulled the object down again. Mally and I stood close together – enthralled by the majesty of the place. She felt so warm and soft. Spray enveloped us like a shroud as we kissed. I felt totally lost inside her arms… Nothing mattered; everything was alright.

We walked in silence through the rainforest towards the next viewing point. The water never stopped falling here, year in and year out. The fine spray would go up and up, condense and fall back in a gentle rain that continued almost permanently. Plants, vines and creepers abounded – all fighting for daylight far above the canopy of trees. It was cool in here after the heat of the day. Mally's nipples stuck out of her thin cotton top like two small volcanoes. We kicked our shoes off – treasuring the freedom of being totally drenched from head to foot.

Barely a word passed between us while we walked the full two kilometre length of the Falls. I liked that. It showed sensitivity to the moment and it also meant we were totally happy in each other's company. We left the rainforest about halfway along the Falls – entering a treeless grassy area that led to the bridge over into Zambia. The water to our left was a boiling white sheet plummeting into the gorge below.

We continued along a slippery stone-chip path until we reached the northernmost section of the Falls on the Rhodesian side. If you looked at the Falls from the air, they ran north-south, with the broad face of the Falls facing almost due east. The water that landed in the churning gorge below travelled north, and then sharp-east at the viewing point we'd now reached. Our opposite numbers in Zambia waved at us, and we waved back. All that separated us was a 300 metre gap and a drop of approximately 300 feet. It was so hard to believe our enemy stood there waving at us!

To our right was a beautiful sight indeed. The massive silver-grey steel girders of the Victoria Falls Bridge arched above our heads and disappeared into the brush on the Zambian side. At our end, a white Rhodesian soldier paced back and forth with a rifle slung over his shoulder – and on the other side, a Zambian soldier had his upper body draped over the railing… No helmet, no rifle – just a happy guy enjoying the sunshine. Seeing those arseholes took some of the fear out of not knowing what they looked like.

"Why don't we pop in and have some tea with Fred?" Mally said, looking up at me.

"That's a great idea. I really like Fred."

We walked slowly back to the car – remaining quiet and lost in our own thoughts. It was boiling-hot in the little black excuse of a car.

Mally took the wheel – accelerating back the way we had come; past the baobab tree and its surrounding thick bush. I eyed the trees and grass with mild discomfort, I knew in my heart there was no barrier – like a fence or whatever – all the way to the border with Botswana. The village was totally open and vulnerable to any form of attack. I vowed that I would bring a handgun with me on all future trips like this one.

We turned right just past Peters Motel on the outskirts of town, down a leafy tarred road that led to the airport, and then right again down a crescent that bordered the wild African bush. Once more, I had this gnawing feeling in my gut that the village was a virgin waiting to be spoiled. Any gook with half a brain could do incredible damage to this place.

Fred lived in a really nice modern home with beautifully manicured lawns and flower-beds bursting with all sorts of tropical plants – each one spoiling for best presentation. An orange-coloured bougainvillea (my favourite of all creepers) had draped itself over his car port – offering a bit of shade to his old tinny Datsun.

Fred, his wife and two well-rounded little girls came out to greet us – the usual smile on Fred's merry face was bigger than ever.

"Visitors!" he beamed. "What a pleasant surprise!"

He introduced us to his wife and kids, and then escorted us inside. Good old Fred – he never stopped talking and always laughed at his own jokes. He looked like a fat Mexican, really.

"What will you have? Tea? Coffee? Booze? Sit, sit… Move those books there," he gesticulated to his wife. "Oh, to hell with tea. It's sundowner time. Beer anyone?"

"Please," Mally and I said simultaneously before smiling at each other.

"Doll, get us three beers will you?" Fred said, looking up at his wife.

I felt mildly embarrassed. Fred should be the gent and do the beers, but his wife just smiled broadly and headed for the kitchen. Mally followed her to give a hand. I sort of figured Fred's wife was one of those unusual females that just liked serving people and never complained. As I got to know her in the months and years ahead, I was proved totally right. She was a gem.

I felt so at ease in Fred's place. It was like coming home. Indeed, it was a home. I'd been drifting around the world for nearly three years, shoved into the army and thrust into the bush. Our base camp was pretty raw too. I'd forgotten how exquisite a home environment was. To sit on a loo; to feel a carpet under your feet; to see a stereo or television in the corner… a bookshelf; the dining room table ready for the evening meal; the cook dressed in white, smiling… Smells of food coming from the kitchen.

Fred's kids sat on the carpet smiling up at me in a sort of dumb way…Visitors must be rare indeed!

"Shoo! Stop staring you two and go and have a bath… Go on," Fred admonished gently.

They got up and waddled past Fred – stopping to kiss him on the cheek, while he playfully smacked them on the bum.

"Kids, I love them," he said, beaming at me. "How'z things with you, Tony?"

"Good. I feel much better, thanks."

"Mmm… You got tick bite fever, not so?"

"Yes. Horrible little bastards."

"And the army? I see more guys at the casino than ever before."

"I was just thinking that myself, Fred. Things seem to be hotting up."

"That scene the other day… the bangs… all that firing… It scared the shit out of 'the wife'."

I can't remember 'the wife's' name anymore; she was always 'the wife' to Fred.

"I came home to see if she and the kids were okay… I tell you Tony, we could see everything from here. It was like bloody Guy Fawkes man!" Fred's eyes always popped out of his head when he looked serious or wanted to emphasise a point. They stood out on stalks now.

The ladies came back from the kitchen and Mally handed me an ice-cold Castle in a tall glass. It looked like liquid gold and tasted like heaven… Ahh, that first swig of cold beer on a hot day!

"Cheers," I said, as all responded in like manner.

The sun was setting in the west now – and golds and oranges and purples filled the whole lounge. I felt relaxed and at peace. I shouldn't have had booze because of my antibiotics, but what the hell? Wonderful smells of food drifted in from the kitchen.

"Would you like to stay for dinner?" 'The wife' said. I looked at Mally and we both nodded.

"Yes please... Thank you."

"Doll, I was just talking to Tony about all the shooting the other evening. Tell him doll..."

"Yeees, hey!" she said in that exaggerated way so typical of Rhodesian and South African accents, "I nearly crapped in my pants when all that nonsense went on!"

I chuckled and eased back a bit more in my chair – holding Mally's hand. Her belly wobbled from suppressed laughter.

"The kids (pronounced 'kuds') almost shat themselves too!"

I burst out laughing then – and so did Mally. We nestled into each other's neck and kissed quickly. I guess she was lapping this up, also.

"I tell you," 'the wife' repeated, "it's just not cricket, what they did. The 'kuds' nearly shat themselves!" Her eyes also stood out on stalks!

Mally and I collapsed with laughter, while Fred looked on with popping eyes... 'the wife' smiling behind cupped hands. She must have thought we were idiots laughing at her misfortune, but we just couldn't help it. That accent – and the look on Fred's face – was hysterical! It was so good to laugh; really, it does something wonderful inside you.

"Sorry... I just found it funny, everyone shitting themselves. I shat myself too, I can tell you!" I wiped a tear from the corner of my eye and took a swig of beer.

"Yeees, doll. Tony was involved in all that. Tell her, Tony!"

"I can't say much really, but yes... I was involved."

"What was it all about?" Fred said.

What could I say? I couldn't tell them anything, really.

"We had a bit of a punch-up with the Zambians, that's all."

"You make a bad liar," Fred said – looking serious now.

The cook saved me by announcing that supper was ready. We went through to the dining room, while 'the wife' called the 'kuds' from their bedroom. It was a lovely dinner – honey-glazed pork chops in breadcrumbs with piles of mash, peas and veggies.

"I grow the veggies myself," Fred said, "out the back garden. I'll show you after dinner. I also want to show you something I've built."

"Yeees, Fred's built..."

"Shhhh doll," Fred said, holding 'the wife's' forearm. "It's a surprise..."

I relished the moment and ate the food with gusto. I hadn't tasted anything so delicious in months, if not years.

"You've got a good cook," Mally said.

"Mmm... yes. Took a long time to train him, but he's gud now..."

I thought about the traditional cook that most Rhodesian households had. Invariably, the cook was a man, for Rhodesian households rarely employed a female cook – not like across the border in South Africa, where females did everything… Here, it was the male cook; the male houseboy. It took me many years to learn how derogatory that word must have been to those men – and all who heard I had a houseboy when I travelled overseas took the piss out of me and insulted me. One old bastard refused to sit next to me on a coach tour through Betwys-y-Coed in Wales when he heard I was from Rhodesia.

"Where's your gun?" he would spit when I got back on the coach. "How many blacks have you killed today?"

It would've been useless trying to explain to him the unique relationship we had with our houseboys. Many of them were like family to us – and were treated as such. I loved our houseboy, Sampson. I would sit with him and eat sadza – a stiff porridge made from maize meal, which you dipped into gravy (made with meat) in an old pot. To this day, I have cherished the aroma of that slightly-burnt meat smell from a kia – an African's house.

Our houseboys often ate the same food we did; their kids got free education, free medical and they generally lived a good life. Yes, they were servants – a noble profession indeed… 'in the service' as they say in the UK, but this did not make them slaves. Why were we looked upon as slave owners and cruel when the lords and titled people in England and elsewhere had servants also? Why the hell were we bad because we were white and the servants black? We never forced them to work for us! They came in droves seeking us out to employ them! But no, the whole world thought we were racists and slave-drivers… fucking idiots!

"You okay, babe?" Mally said, sensing my mood change. Booze does that to me – happy one second and moody the next.

"Mmm…"

We finished our meal about half an hour later, and while the two women went to the lounge to have coffee, Fred took me out the back door. He flicked on a powerful security light.

"Veggies," he said, pointing and looking back at me.

"Good crop, Fred."

It certainly was a good crop. There were few water restrictions being so close to one of the biggest rivers in Africa. Beans climbed wooden scaffolds in a similar manner to rows of tomato shrubs that bulged with red fruit, for a tomato is a fruit – not a vegetable. Cabbages exploded in all directions – as well as carrots, onions, lettuce, spinach and rhubarb. I followed him to a small building that still smelled of raw mortar and plaster. A couple of scaffold planks on trestles had a builder's bucket and a trowel on it.

"My bunker," Fred said, flicking on a torch.

"Bunker? You're joking?"

"Dead serious… Come take a look."

We went down about six steps into a spacious room that smelled slightly mouldy from moisture evaporating out of the plaster. It was a solid, well-built structure with a concrete roof.

"What's it for?" I said, my voice echoing slightly.

"Let's get serious for a moment, Tony." Fred's eyes bulged even more in the shadow of the torchlight.

"The shit is going to hit the fan here, Tony… Come here a minute…" He led me by the forearm back up the steps. "Let's walk a bit…"

We turned left at the back door of the house, and then right towards the main gate. It was really dark now – and the only light was from a street lamp.

"Look at that, Tony."

I looked, but wasn't sure what he meant. He paused before speaking.

"Bush, Tony… We are 50 metres from the African bush. We don't feel safe here; we don't feel protected at all."

I saw what he meant. His garden ended at a one-and-a-half metre-high fence. The road ran past the front gate, and then there was nothing but hundreds and hundreds of kilometres of bush. There were virtually no settlements west of here all the way to the Atlantic Ocean on the west coast of Africa.

"What's to stop a gook coming up to my window and revving the place, Tony? I tell you, that punch-up that you were involved in scared the hell out of me. My gut was in my mouth all the way home from the casino. I never felt so scared in my life. I pictured my kids disembowelled and my wife raped and hacked to pieces…"

"But you haven't had time to build that bunker since my punch-up… What do you know that I don't, Fred?"

He paused a long time before talking.

"I see a lot of people in the casino, as you know."

"Yes?"

"Cops, army, CIO… the whole 'bang-tooty'. I keep my ears open – and I don't like what I'm hearing."

"Such as?"

"There's going to be a big push on the village, Tony – either from inland or from Zambia… Some guys even reckon a conventional assault across the river or bridge."

"That's news to me. I certainly haven't heard that one."

"What's to stop them mortaring us, or even shelling us, from Zambia? I got the idea of the bunker from the Air Rhodesia crowd. They've been building a huge bunker at their block of flats for the last six weeks."

"You're joking?"

"I'm not," he said, shaking his head. "Dead serious."

I thought for a while… an extra platoon of troops… armoured cars, Grey's Scouts…. 'Black Boots', and lately, rumours of artillery coming up here… A whole company of Zambian troops engaging me. Just a few weeks previously, over a thousand gooks were killed during a Selous Scout raid at Nyadzonga-pungwe in Mozambique. Perhaps the war was hotting up on both fronts? Fred's words were beginning to make sense.

"It seems Angola may even be lending or supplying tanks to either Zambia or ZIPRA."

I looked at the bush again and felt that same gnawing pit of fear I'd experienced earlier in the day. Things were closing in – ready to go 'bang'.

"You need a higher fence," I said.

"Already ordered by the casino. Should be fitted in a week or two."

"And what will you do Fred, if you're at home and the gooks attack? How are you going to defend yourself against a dozen or so men armed with AKs? Why don't you clear the kids out, at least?"

"I've been thinking of that – thinking maybe they should go to Bulawayo… but 'the wife' wouldn't have it; it would be the end of us here."

We walked back to the house. It was a sultry hot evening with crickets screeching their lungs out – lightning flickered in high clouds to the north-east. There was definitely a feeling of tension creeping over the village.

"Anyway Tony, the bunker and all that, well… that's just there to keep us alive long enough until the army reacts. I'm no hero."

"What weapon have you got?"

"A 9mm Browning and a Sten Gun."

"Ammo?"

"Not much… not much at all. Maybe 30 rounds."

"I'll speak to the boss," I said.

We walked back to the lounge swatting flying ants as we went. 'The wife' and two girls were laughing and pointing at the television. Fred's mood became jovial immediately.

"You gotta see this," he said. "It's a typical Friday night in Zambia. The TV crew are pissed!"

"You get TV from Zambia?"

"Yes – and Rhodesia makes us pay bloody TV licenses! Can you believe it?"

I sat on the arm of the chair that Mally was on and looked at the TV presenter reading the news.

"There it goes!" Fred and his family shrieked with laughter.

As I watched, the presenter's face started to move off the screen and then slide to the top so that only a portion of the neck could be seen, with the lower jaw doing the talking.

"What's going on?" Mally said, bursting into laughter with the rest of them.

"The guy behind the camera's pissed – pissed as a fart!" Fred hollered with laughter, slapping his thigh.

I started to chuckle at first, and then a deep belly-laugh came up and out of me – ending in a high-pitched giggle that I'm known for. The girls looked at me and laughed even more. Mally and Fred were doubled up and it went on and on until our jaws ached and stomachs hurt.

It was really good to laugh like that. Laughter is the best medicine.

The four vehicles of my platoon kicked up columns of dust as we headed east away from the village. Von Stranz had me checked out by a doctor in Wankie, who declared me fit for duty. The days of rest with Mally had been therapeutic and healing.

We headed east along a good dirt road towards one of our company's sub-base camps called Jambezi – situated 40 to 50 kilometres east of the village and about 15 to 20 kilometres south of the Zambezi River. The country to the north of the road we drove on was mainly open bush – full of nothing but ticks, snakes and trees. The country to the south, on the other hand, was full of African settlements – Tribal Trust Lands (or TTLs, as we called them). These areas had been set aside solely for the black people of Rhodesia, but naturally, was a major bone of contention for them as they felt they'd lost the freedom to live where they wanted in their own country. In essence, it was the major cause for them to rise up against white rule.

Jambezi was the main base for the eastern part of 4 Indep's sphere of operations. Our eastern boundary was the Matetsi River – and beyond that, 1 Indep took over – or on occasion, a few RAR companies. The thought struck me yet again how thinly-spread our forces were. We had no real hope of ever intercepting the gooks before they hit targets further inland. Our efforts were purely cosmetic, in my opinion.

I turned to look at the vehicles behind me, and once again felt the pride of leading these young men. We certainly looked less 'fresh puss' these days with our fading webbing and slightly grubby appearance. A number of guys had made their own chest webbing, as indeed I had. The government-issued ones were useless and impractical.

Huts and villages rolled past us for kilometre after kilometre – and as usual, the over-grazed and over-shagged place was devoid of grass and full of goats and pot-bellied children staring at us.

My mind kept going back to Mally and how much I felt for her. It was gut-wrenching coming out here and leaving her behind. We had almost made it to third base with each other, but in a way, I'm glad we hadn't made love yet. The sexual tension between us was electric... fantastic.

Pete Wells was deployed at the Falls and Phil Laing was down in Wankie. I just hoped I never got rotated to Wankie. What an oven-like hellhole that place was. I'm sure it was the arsehole of the country – and someone had eaten hot curry the night before!

My daydreams came to an end when the driver pulled over and spoke to me through the cab window.

"Is this where we turn, sir?"

I looked at my map and had, thankfully, recorded the white flag stones on the journey. I cranked my head to look at the road turning sharp-left up ahead – just as it did on the map. There were also signs of heavy vehicles taking the track to the right.

"Yes, this is where we turn."

I called the vehicle commanders up on the radio and told them to keep the spacing between the vehicles and to 'switch on'. No more fucking around now.

The track that led to Jambezi was soft sand under thickly-leafed trees, with the odd village laid out in sections of sparse grass with few animals. It was lovely country, with gentle hills and the odd small stream harbouring butterflies and birds, but it was also good ambush country – and I made a mental note to come back and burn some of the bush closest to the road. We often used the tactic of licking the head of a match and then flicking it off the striker of a matchbox into the bush. The spit on the match-head would prevent the match going out before it landed in the grass; it literally dampened it so that when it did land, it ignited fully in the grass. We would drive for 20 or 30 kilometres doing this – burning out all potential ambush points along the way.

A set of buildings came into view through the trees. They were A-frame structures with asbestos roof sheets over gum poles, with vertical asbestos walls forming rooms under the sheets. There were three of them – two parallel and one at right angles. A small shop with people sauntering around was off to the left (or east) of the complex. All the buildings were behind earth-graded walls about 12 feet high – and at each corner of the rectangular-shaped camp was a large bunker with sandbags piled on top of thick wooden beams.

I led the vehicles into the complex through offset earth embankments (that would prevent bullets directly entering the camp) and came to a halt.

"De-bus!" I shouted.

Thirty-three guys – plus drivers – climbed off the trucks and dusted themselves down, chatting among themselves.

"Sergeant Torode, allocate one bunker to each of the four sticks we have and tell the guys to wait at each bunker until I check it out."

"Sir."

I turned towards the entrance of the building that was at right angles to the other two – and as I did so, a tall blonde guy stepped out into the bright sunlight – shielding his eyes from the glare. Two shorter, dark-haired men followed him – one of whom was dressed in a khaki Internal Affairs uniform with red flashes on the shoulders. INTAF, as they were known to us, were responsible for the administration of the TTLs and had their own quasi-military force which guarded various places – such as the one we were in now.

"You must be the army boys we've been expecting," the blonde said, stating the obvious.

"Lieut Ballinger," I said, unsure of his rank.

"Ian," he replied casually. "Section officer, Support Company." He turned to the shorter of the two men behind him. "This is 'Nipple'."

What a strange way to introduce someone. I knew we were quite casual as national servicemen, but I at least expected a name or rank or whatever.

"First time I've shaken hands with the front end of a tit," I said. They laughed like they'd heard it before.

"This is John Kemp, INTAF."

We shook hands. I knew so little about police ranks that I sort of deferred to Ian – although when I joined the police's PATU (or Police Anti-Terrorist Unit) as a regular instructor a couple of years later, I came to realise that a section officer was non-commissioned, which meant I outranked him. As fate would have it, Ian became one of my assistant instructors – although only on a part-time basis during his call-ups.

"Tea?" Ian said.

"Ja, please."

We walked into the cool interior of the building. One thing that I liked about asbestos is that it was good insulation against heat. It was scorching outside, but cool in here. The walls on the side elevations finished about 100 millimetres short of the asbestos roof – allowing air to blow through the structure.

Both sides of the building had sleeping bags and stretchers laid out, along with military kit-like rifles and webbing. A dining room table was situated near the door to a kitchen off to the left, with bottles of tomato sauce, knives and forks on it. On the left, near the dining room table, was a large vertically-suspended pin-board with maps on it and a table with two radios.

"How's this going to work with you guys and us up here?" I said. "Where are our boundaries?"

"Here," Ian said, using a fork to point at one of the maps. "The red line here is a tributary of the Matetsi that runs south of us. Everything south of that line is ours and everything north is yours... quite simple."

'Nipple' handed me a cup of scalding-hot tea in a steel mug. I just hoped the milk wasn't squeezed out of him – being a nipple and all.

"How long are you here for?" John said.

"Three weeks, initially. We rotate all over the place with two other platoons... Things quiet here?"

"Ja," Ian said. "Fucking boring. We never see anything."

"How many guys you got?"

"One-hundred-and-thirty – including 'Nipple' here. Sorry, that's 129-and-a-half..."

'Nipple' punched him hard on the shoulder – spilling tea all over the ops table. Yes, the cops were definitely much more casual than us!

"And you?" I said to John from INTAF.

"Twelve – plus me."

"What's your role here?"

"To guard the camp, basically."

I nodded and attempted to drink some more of the scalding-hot tea. 'Nipple' made a sandwich and gave it to me without asking if I wanted it. But it was good – pressed pig (our slang for tinned pork), tomato, lettuce and mustard.

"Mmm, good. Cheers, 'Nipple'. I better check on the guys... Ian, John, can you guys brief me later about what you know of the area?"

"Sure," Ian said, as a chunk of sandwich left his mouth. "We're not going anywhere."

No 'sir'; no fuck all – what a way to go, guys!

I walked back out into the glare and skin-drying heat to see what Kevin had organised. One of the four eight-man sticks led by Roy was standing next to a bunker by the door I exited. The guys looked longingly at my sandwich.

"Leave Max's MAG in here with all his belts of ammo. Get one box of ammo into each bunker."

"Sir."

"This is your bunker, Corporal Orchard. Your guys come here if we stand to, okay?"

"Sir."

"Make sure you bring all your webbing, guys – especially rifle grenades..."

"Sir!" times eight.

"This is Alpha bunker."

I did the rounds with Kevin to Bravo, Charlie and Delta bunkers – giving similar instructions. Bomford's MAG was put into Bravo bunker. Both Alpha and Bravo faced north, with arcs of fire facing west and east respectively, while Charlie and Delta bunkers faced south, with corresponding arcs west and east also. In other words, all 360° of the camp was covered. Kenny's MAG was positioned in Charlie bunker – facing the most ominous section of bush to the south. I only had three machine-guns in my platoon, so Delta bunker received a few extra rifle grenades. Our only two-inch mortar, which would be fired from just outside the blast wall of Alpha bunker, was given to Roy to look after.

During my rounds, I came across John Kemp's INTAF men dressed in their khaki denims and short-sleeved shirts. They looked wide-eyed at us as we passed. I spoke to one of them with sergeant's stripes on his sleeve and he came smartly to attention – the barrel of his old .303 rifle nestling under his left armpit. At least they seemed disciplined and full of spirit. That was good.

In all, we had over 50 men in the camp.

"Kevin, find out where these okies are sleeping and then put our guys wherever you can. Make sure our ammo trailer is emptied – all ammo shared equally among the four bunkers – then spread the vehicles as far apart as you can in case we get revved."

"Sir."

I'd noticed that Kevin had become more sullen and bitchy than ever before. It was only a short few weeks now until he deserted.

"Start guard duty at 1930 – one guy in Alpha bunker and one in Charlie. See if the INTAF guys do guard duty and mesh in with them."

"Sir."

"Good. Once that's done, tell the guys to get some skoff and take it easy for now. You can come listen into what the cops have to say about this area just now."

"Sir."

I found a place to settle in and washed the dust off my face in the small bathroom before establishing where we could erect our radio aerial. As it turned out, we could pull our co-ax up the main radio mast and tie it away from the steel girders with a broken broomstick. The reception with base back at Vic Falls was about strength three or four.

As soon as Kevin had finished the tasks I set him, he joined the rest of us having a coke at the ops table.

"So, tell me Ian, what's the background to this area?"

"There's little I can say, Tony. We've never really made contact with the gooks around here – a few fleeting contacts maybe, but that's all." He got up and crossed to the main map – pointing at the Matetsi River, which ran south-west to its source in the interior of the country. "The river is a natural path to follow inland to reach Wankie, and then Bulawayo. Not only do the gooks need water in this dry area, but as you can see, the river virtually points itself where they want to go. The tribal chief around here is really anti-us and I reckon he does all he can to hide gooks whenever he gets the chance. We do a lot of kraal searches, but they're pretty shifty around here."

"I reckon we should piss the locals off and draw the gooks out," I said.

"That's not a bad idea, but first, tell me who you want to piss off because I have quite a few informants around here. You could sort of rough their places up, but not as bad as the others."

"Okay," I agreed. "Where's the chief's kraal?"

"Just here," Ian said, pointing at a spot on the map. I copied off the co-ordinates.

I decided there and then that if the locals were pro-gook, that we would give them a hard time. Burn down a few huts here and there or food in storage bins; close the shop outside the keep for a week or so without notice; stop, search and irritate bus drivers and their passengers; kill some livestock; ruthlessly enforce curfew by killing a few locals – but all that could wait until tomorrow. Someone switched on a radio with Steely Dan's 'Do It Again' followed by The Doobie Brothers' 'Long Train Running'. Radio 702 from 'down south'… South Africa. The sun dipped lower – and to my pleasant surprise, beers came out of the kitchen on a tray. I selected a Lion 'bomber' – a huge bottle of potent lager – and rocked back in my chair listening to the guys chewing the fat… music washing over us. There's nothing greater on all God's Earth than a fine woman or the camaraderie of men in arms. You become like brothers with these guys. You share terror, death and life with them – and that moulds you together for life.

I felt a bit irresponsible having a beer on my first night in camp, so I put the half-finished bottle down and wandered outside – rifle in hand. Your rifle went everywhere with you in an operational area; it was closer than your wife or best friend.

I did the rounds past the three bunkers furthest from my own – stopping to chat to the guys and listen to their good-natured, youthful banter. It's amazing how guys just sort themselves out. A bivvy stretched here, a bit of canvas there – and hey presto, you have a home. Little homes sprung up all over the camp – and as the sun crept lower to the ground, so the odd fire started and gas lamps were struck. Different tunes from different radios competed with each other. I didn't really care that lamps and fires were lit. After all, the camp was surrounded by bloody great security lights that would come on when it was dark.

I completed the tour of the camp – arriving back at the bunker nearest the ops room, climbing onto the sandbags and looking west. It was one of the most stunning sights I have ever seen, and it will remain with me until I die.

The sun had half-melted into the horizon – massive and orange, with slithers shining through clouds that had been swept across it like a painter's brushstroke. In the foreground were dozens of African huts with smoke curling out of the apex of their coned, thatched roofs. The sky had turned a sort of purple above the orange glow – blending into the approaching darkness.

A sound to my left attracted my attention, and as I listened, there came the sound of men singing as they marched. African men with deep voices in perfect harmony – singing as only African men can. I figured they must be Ian's guys – and at the sound of their voices, he came and joined me on top of the sandbags. We didn't speak because the spectacle beneath us was so awesome; the sunset... the dusty glow of light and the sound of men singing as they approached the camp – saluting us as they marched past.

It was a sight so memorable, so awesome, I knew I would remember it forever, so I just sat there – savouring it and drinking in Africa... that beautiful wild mother to all of us.

The first thing I did the next day was close the trading store. Ian told me it was the only store for at least 30 kilometres – and I knew this would piss the locals off immensely. I also initiated thorough bus searches and deliberately delayed their departure times. I harassed the locals as much as I could. I set a couple of food silos alight and shot a few pigs and cows. One of our favourite methods of killing pigs was to squash them under the sump of our 'four-fives' as they wallowed in muddy pools left by the heavy rains. One of the better artists drew pigs, goats and other dead livestock on the cabs of our trucks as the toll rose higher and higher.

Patrols and ambushes in all areas were intensified – and wherever we found anything dry enough to burn, it went up in flames... straw, thatch, grass on the side of the roads. We raided the chief's kraal and searched all the huts in his compound.

On one search, we found drums of aviation fuel that had been left behind by the South African Army base about 10 kilometres away – now run-down to a few bricks and foundations. We found the drums in a compound of about 10 huts and I watched in horror as Ian kicked the teeth out of one old woman's head before burning every hut to the ground as a reprisal for having military fuel stored there. At the peak of the burning, an aircraft belonging to INTAF flew in circles over us – and we could clearly see someone taking photographs. To this day, I will never know if John reported us for messing up his quiet neighbourhood – where he was trying to win people's hearts and minds. But to me, if you have a guy by the balls, his heart and mind would surely follow.

A week later, sitting in the ops room, I was still trying to decide whether this tactic of drawing the gooks out into the open was having any effect when one of my drivers brought me some sobering news. He handed me a copy of the previous day's *Bulawayo Chronicle*. The lead page was a report on Peters Motel in Vic Falls having been severely revved by a large group of gooks. Pete Wells had been chatting to a gorgeous girl called Karen Blaauw when it happened. She lived next door to Marilyn. A salesman from Bulawayo was killed by an RPG that exploded over his head while he was being served at the open-air reception. Several other guests had been injured in the TV lounge when hundreds of rounds poured through the windows. Fortunately, a couple of off-duty police and local hunters from various regional hunting concessions had been able to return fire and foil what could have been a massacre. I bet Albert Ncube had a hand in it.

I could just picture Fred racing home to be with 'the wife' and 'kuds' – tearing along the road that bordered thousands of square kilometres of bush. I pondered about how he got home, because the attack on Peters was on the same road he would use. Hopefully, there was a back route to his house.

And what about Mally? The report said that the attack happened at about 10:00 p.m. Fortunately, she would have been at work, where Ivor Ring – the assistant manager of the casino – was a territorial soldier. The safe in the hotel was packed to the roof with hunting rifles that belonged to Don Goldin – the casino owner – so I was pretty sure Ivor got out a rifle and that Mally was okay. Well, the newspaper reported only one death, so she was bound to be alright. I wondered why we hadn't heard about the attack via our main base, but then again, they must have had their hands full that night.

The news left me with an empty feeling in my gut. Fred's prophecy that the village would take a hit rang true. I felt helpless and cut off; there were no phones out here and I couldn't ask personal questions over the radio net. I figured the cops would be less concerned about this, so I asked Ian if his radio operators at the police station could phone Fred or Mally and see if they were okay. It took four hours to get an answer, but it was positive in both cases – they were all okay.

I was pissed off by what had happened and pushed the heat up some more under the locals' bums. They looked more sullen than usual, and even the little kids had stopped waving at us.

By the end of the third week of making life hell for the locals, I decided it wasn't working and enough was enough. I would send out one last batch of patrols to intimidate people and set ambushes for curfew-breakers, and that would be the end of it.

I'd been cooped up in the hot, sticky camp for three weeks – and the only kills I'd enjoyed were buckets of flies that would swoop down and lick everything off our plates and mess tins – big fat blue things that died easily when you swatted them – so I decided to go out on deployment late in the afternoon.

It was refreshing and invigorating to travel on an open truck again – heading west to drop off guys like Hugh Bomford, Roy Orchard and Al Currie in isolated areas with a view to them moving into ambush positions after dark. From there, I turned north to the main road and then east towards a set of villages that were particularly arrogant about ignoring our curfew warnings. Locals had been seen wandering around at least half an hour after last light. I was determined to shoot a few of them.

We got dropped off about four kilometres from the cluster of villages and crept in slowly among them – stopping every now and again to listen and let our eyes adjust to the black of the night. Fires glowed and people chatted and called between huts. Lovely smells of food cooking wafted in the air – little 'kaffir' dogs barked into the night. Those shitty little animals could sense us and alerted the locals to our presence.

We shuffled slowly forward into a bowl-like depression with huts all around us – the air thick with smoke from cooking fires. I decided the ridge ahead of us would be a good place to spot a curfew-breaker, as the track beyond it led to a beer hall.

I could barely see the guys behind me as I lined them up in thick trees along the edge of the track. There was no moon at all, but a faint glow from billions of stars lit up the landscape in an eerie grey glow.

The rules of engagement stated that we mustn't ambush closer than 50 metres to a hut. This was primarily because most huts had no latrines and the bush was used as a crapper. The powers that be said a person was relieving himself or herself up to a 50-metre radius – and after that, he was a gook.

I settled down about 60 metres from the nearest hut on my left and waited. 'Nipple' had come with us to make sure we weren't culling one of his informants, and nodded vaguely when I asked him if this set of huts was okay.

Nothing but the irritating buzz and whine of mosquitoes happened for hours – and I was just reflecting on the new name for our operational area (op lemon) when I heard foot-steps and the voice of a man singing at the top of his lungs. I knew in my heart of hearts it was just a man heading home from the beer hall, and that what we were about to do was sheer murder, but it had to be done to instil discipline in the local population and deter gooks from moving at night. This was a war, after all.

My heart thumped wildly as the man approached. I raised my weapon to face in his general direction. My hands shook nervously; I was about to kill a human being. I still couldn't see him, but I could hear him as loud as daylight now. He'd stopped singing – pausing in front of us to piss.

I pulled the trigger several times – and in that instant, eight other weapons opened up. Red tracer flew away at an incredible rate – bouncing off rocks up into the black night. The area immediately around us lit up like fireworks – the din overpowering. Cordite filled my nostrils and dust hung in the air.

"Cease fire, cease fire!" I shouted after several seconds. The silence that followed the avalanche of noise was total and absolute. You could have heard a pin drop. No dogs barking, no crickets – nothing. I felt like a real piece of shit. I was almost grateful when I heard a shrill cry from in front of us.

"No power, no power!" the man screamed. "No power… Pliz!"

We walked cautiously forward – ready to 'pull him' at the slightest sign of a weapon.

"Spread out, guys!" I hissed. "You two, go that way for about 20 metres and keep your eyes open… You two, go the other way… You, watch my back. Roy, look to the front."

I was still shaking like a leaf when I approached the dark, writhing form on the ground.

"No power!" he shrieked again. "Pliz… No power!"

"Let me finish him off!" 'Nipple' spat.

I was in a quandary; what should I do? I just couldn't murder a man pleading for his life!

"Let me finish him!" 'Nipple' repeated.

"No," I said, flatly. I picked up my handset and called the guys in the trucks four kays away to come collect him. I knew it was a stupid risk moving trucks at night – risking my own men's lives. Later in the war, I had no compunction letting these guys get 'finished off', but for now, I was still too close to being human – being a civvy that loved life.

A long, plaintive wail went up from one of the huts and I could see several women running towards us with a lamp of some type lighting their way. The darkened form on the ground recognised their voices and set up a long, howling wail – the sound of which will stay with me forever.

"Shut up or I'll fucking kill you!" 'Nipple' shrieked – and kicked the almost-invisible form. The man's wails reduced to a whimper. The light of the lamp drew closer… and when it finally reached the man, I saw that he was no older than me. Strange – I was convinced he was much older by the sound of his voice. The women came forward – pleading with us and touching our ankles. I looked down at the blood-soaked figure. His white, tatty shirt was full of blood and his legs were shiny and wet with the black, sweet-smelling liquid. It was the first time I'd smelled that cloying, sweet smell that stuck in the back of your throat.

I couldn't take anymore and stepped back a pace or two – thankful I hadn't killed this innocent young man, for that's all he was. I am glad his mother could pick his head up and cradle him in her lap. I am glad that I didn't let 'Nipple' finish him off now. The relief, fear and gratitude – yes, gratitude – in the old woman's face was palpable.

Then the reality of this situation hit me like a ton of bricks. The nearest hospital was in Wankie – over 100 kilometres away – and in order to meet standard convoy safety, I had to send two vehicles with a minimum of two guys on each as escorts. That was going to piss my guys off big-time, I knew it, but what could I do? Shoot the boy and his mother, sister and aunts?

The trucks arrived and we loaded the boy on board, followed by his mother and two other local villagers – all women. There was no sign of a man anywhere. For obvious reasons, they feared getting shot. The boy was in a bad way and sort of blew a few bubbles of blood out of his nose as we lay him on top of some blankets. A lung shot. I told the guys to lay him on his side where the bullet had entered his body and cover him up.

"You can refuse to take him to Wankie," I said to the driver. "I will not charge you. It's a big risk you're taking for some floppy."

"He's only a kid," the driver said. "He needs a chance at life."

I patted him on the arm and climbed aboard a third truck that Ian had sent us at 'Nipples" request. I watched silently as the two vehicles disappeared into the night – their red tail lights taking a long time to fade behind trees and rocks. I swore I would never risk my guys like this again and that all future requests to finish off curfew-breakers would be granted.

Amazingly, that young man survived – and I sometimes think that out there somewhere is a man, roughly my age, with chunks of lead, copper metal jacket and scars in his chest that I helped put there.

Two nights later, Corporal Currie got a second curfew-breaker. I went out in the vehicle to look at the dead man. He was as stiff as a board by first light – aged about 65. The really curious thing about him was his penis, which dangled out of his pants in shreds – like a peeled banana – but still stiff as a rod. It's quite probable that a bullet had entered the head of the penis and simply split it apart like a plank of wood – remaining in that position until rigor mortis set it permanently. 'Nipple' explained that a few ladies of the night lived nearby. Maybe he was on his way to have his jollies when he was cut down.

"Bit of an over-kill, Currie," I said, counting 20 holes in the corpse – including one in the head.

"At least we hit him," he replied sarcastically.

I pursed my lips and gave a lop-sided smile. He was right, actually. How the hell we missed our curfew-beaker was a mystery – although he did fall into a slight dip in the ground where we found him. He was bloody lucky.

The next afternoon, Ian invited me to go with him to meet one of his informers at a remote rendezvous point about 12 kays east of where we were. I found this cloak-and-dagger aspect of the war quite fascinating, and agreed to go along with him. His main motive, I found out later, was to have some white-handed firepower with him. Meeting a strange black guy in the middle of nowhere with black troops really unnerved him – especially when they knew that he carried bundles of money to pay the informant.

We turned right onto the main dirt highway, sharp-left along the bend in the road and down past the compound, where we'd attempted to shoot the curfew-breaker. The bush appeared to thicken immediately after that – and 10 kays later, we pulled over to the side of the road by some large rocks.

"Now, we wait," Ian said. "There's no guarantee the bugger will come. He'll only be here if he's broke."

I looked around me – understanding what Ian said about the risk of meeting informers like this. What happens if an informer had 'turned' – and this was an ambush now?

'Nipple' and two guys went left, while another two went right. I strolled over the road by myself and faced the rear. It was thickly-wooded here, and I sat on a small rock with my rifle off safe – ready to fire.

My mind drifted back to Mally and how much I was falling for her – hoping that no-one else was trying to claim her while I was stuck out here in the middle of nowhere. How many other men throughout the country were wondering what their wives and sweethearts were up to? Well, for that matter, a few men fooled around in cushy areas like Kariba, Vic Falls and Umtali on call-up. What a waste this whole war was. I'd grown up in a country close to perfection with good schools, good hospitals, roads and an excellent police and judicial system. I knew it would never be the same again… Going to Beira in Mozambique would never happen again. We would never stay in the Estoril Hotel or any of the beach chalets there – nor the campsite ever again. We would never see old Joe the cop, who swaggered around with a handgun on his hip – nor lick twirly-topped ice-creams that had wrappers on them. I would never sit on a beach at sunset with an erection while I watched two lovers kissing nearby… It was all gone now. Beira was a tip – a slum now – run by a bunch of mindless gooks that caused the ejection of most of its white population. Was that going to happen here too? And what of support from the Allies we supported in two World Wars? No, we were racists and murderers now – no longer 'Defenders of the Realm'.

"Tony," Ian called. "We can go now."

"Didn't he come?" I said, walking back over the road.

"He did. There he goes, through the bush."

I looked at a scraggly man of about 40 walking quickly away in a north-easterly direction. He was hardly what I expected. Well, what did I expect – a guy looking like James Bond or Sherlock Holmes?

"Anything interesting, Ian?"

"Could be," he said, chewing on some grass. "He reckons gooks are moving into the area – away from the Matetsi."

"What for? There's no target around here?"

"Not even us?" he said sarcastically. "Isn't this what you've been pushing for?"

"Shit, I didn't think it was working…"

"It's the old chief – you hit a nerve there. He's losing face in front of his people… He's sort of requested a hit on us."

Shit, what had I done? It was bad enough having the inherent risk of a punch-up, but to invite it was stupid.

❦

The thud made me sit forward rapidly – spilling my tea. Everyone stopped talking.

"What was that?" Ian said.

"Landmine, for sure," 'Nipple' responded.

We sat in silence for a few seconds before the radio cracked into life. It was one of Ian's call-signs that had left 15 minutes previously for some R&R (Rest & Relaxation) back at their respective TTLs and rural homes.

"…Hit landmine… No casualties, over."

"Confirm, no casualties?" Ian repeated.

"Affirmative, affirmative… but the vehicle is fucked, over…"

I smiled inwardly. The word 'fuck' was used for everything by our black troops. 'The engine is fucked', 'the crops are fucked', 'the economy is fucked'… everything is 'fucked.'

"What's your location, over?"

"On the South Road – one kilometre past the big compound."

"Copied. Get the men in all-round defence. We'll send backup… Copied?"

"Copied."

"It's near the compound that provides labour for the sawmills," Ian said, turning to look at me. I nodded. I knew the place well. I'd walked through the forests in the area on patrol. The place was thick with massive spiders that spun webs between trees. Every time I went on patrol, I got several of them stuck on my face, which sent shivers of horror up me!

"Do you need any help, Ian?"

He thought for a second, but shook his head.

"I've got three vehicles and two sticks in camp... That should do it. Can you hang around here in case things go tits-up?"

"Sure, no problem. Kevin, put a stick on standby in case they're needed."

"Sir."

Ian reported the incident to his rear base and then left with 'Nipple' to see what was going on. They returned two hours later with one stick less.

"How'd it go, Ian?"

"Brilliant. Those slopey mine-proof vehicles... The landmine just popped the wheel off with barely a scratch on the chassis."

'Slopey' was the Rhodesian nickname for a South African. We considered them slightly inferior to us in a good-humoured sort of way – rather like the Aussies and Kiwis did each other. Ian's guys had hit a TMH46 landmine with no injuries and barely a scratch on the bodywork.

"The soft sand must have helped," Kevin said.

"I'm sure it did, but the bloody thing still landed on its side... bags of stuff all tossed around inside."

"Where are the guys – the ones going on R&R?"

"I put them on another vehicle and left a stick to guard the truck. Follow-up is pointless."

"That compound is a pain in the arse, Ian... Gook footprints heading for it always get wiped out by mujibas[2] – plus that gook suspect you found there... It's got to be a hotbed of terrs."

"I think we should do a cordon and search sometime. What say you?"

"That's fine by me. Just give me one or two days' notice and I'll make sure we have the manpower."

The days rolled by. There was, without question, an increased presence of gooks in the area. Even a few locals had reported seeing strangers at night. Apart from ambushes we set up, they knew we rarely patrolled after dark – and could, therefore, safely assume they were gooks. Finding these bastards was a bit like trying to pin the proverbial tail on a donkey.

---

2   Mujiba: Slang for a young black person – often a goat or cattle herder – who would be employed by terrorists to drive their cattle or goats over terrorist footprints (or spoor) to hide them from our trackers. They were also the local 'eyes' and 'ears' for the terrorists – and would warn them of our presence. They were irritating enough for us to want to kill them – and I'm sure a few were illuminated with a 'third eye' (or bullet to the forehead).

One afternoon when I jumped off my truck as we headed back into camp, I noticed a small group of guys gathered around something lying on the floor.

"What's up?" I said to no-one in particular. As the men parted to make way for me, I could see for myself... Two dead gooks lay sprawled out on the dust. It was the first time I'd seen our elusive enemy up-close. They were both dressed in semi-military fatigues, which surprised me. I thought they would be disguised as civvies all the time. They wore Russian chest webbing under blue denim tops, and an AK rifle lay beside both of them. One had a huge head wound, with a pile of brains plonked unceremoniously on the dusty floor.

"What happened?" I said to 'Nipple'. For a brief instant, I thought one of our call-signs had got lucky.

"Scouts," he said simply.

"Scouts?"

What the hell were the Selous Scouts doing in the area without telling us? Or maybe that's why we were told to stay south of the main boundary road a week or so ago? It made sense now.

The Selous Scouts – a highly secretive unit that operated with 'turned' terrorists – also had the nickname of 'Eskimos' because whenever they operated in an area, it became frozen to ordinary ground troops like ourselves.

I felt a bit embarrassed that we'd been in the area a month and had only shot one-and-a-half civilians...

❧—❧

Two more landmines went off in a relatively short space of time after that. A roads department vehicle went up on the same dirt track as the cop vehicle, but a bit further west. Theo Nel did the follow-up without success. The kids in the area – 'mujibas' as we called them – were brilliant herding cattle over gook spoor... the little bastards. If I had my way, I would've shot every herd boy on sight.

The second landmine proved a bit more interesting – and a bonus for us, as well. A big bull detonated a landmine by standing on it with its right front hoof – instantly turning it into tree decorations and biltong (the local name for jerky). There was nothing left of the animal forward of its hind quarters, and its intestines made an elongated thread up into a nearby tree, where the remainder of the animal hung.

A cow immediately behind the bull was also dead, but without any apparent external injuries. Perhaps it was the shockwave that killed it. A second cow wandered around with blood dripping out of its nostrils. Half of its right eye dangled down to the top jawbone. I took careful aim and shot it just in front of the ears. It dropped like a ton of rocks.

We got out our knives and cut off huge slabs of meat to take back to camp. Much to our mutual pleasure, we had a cordon bleu chef on call-up among Ian's men. He would work magic with all this beef. We concentrated on the fillets that ran down the spine – as well as the rump. A couple of legs would do well for the black troops.

"Time for a braai" I said, lobbing a leg of beef on a truck. Even if the meat was diseased, if it was properly cooked, you could eat it. Heat it up again, and you would die a painful death.

"A braai's no good without beer and sadza," Kevin said.

I decided that after deploying some guys in the afternoon, I would go and get some beers from Dekka Drum – a fishing camp and hotel about 25 kays to the east – and have a braai with the guys in camp. I would be in big shit if I got caught or ambushed, but you need to take the pressure off now and again. It was worth the risk.

The rear tail lights illuminated the guys I'd just dropped off, but within a few seconds they'd melted into the darkening scrub. We had 20-odd kilometres to go… Get the beers and return to camp. We would be back by about 8:00 p.m.

The road dipped and turned – the headlights of the truck casting a well of light ahead – outside of which very little could be seen.

As we approached the Matetsi River Bridge, I realised what a stupid risk I was taking – two almost-empty vehicles crossing our eastern boundary into an adjoining force's territory. I had no idea where friendly troops were in this area or what they would do if they spotted us tearing down the road. Were there 'Eskimos' here or SAS or what? Was a gook ambush lying in wait?

We proceeded through totally unfamiliar territory – the glint of the Zambezi River off to our left, with scraggy hills on the right. There was little, if any, civilisation here – no fires from kraals or electric lights burning… just the flicker of lightning in clouds over Zambia.

Twice I almost bent forward to tell the driver to turn around, but something kept me from doing so – and before we knew it, we came to a sign indicating Dekka Drum. It was weird driving into a tourist area all lit up, as if the war was a rumour. I shouted to the driver to enter the gate slowly because if there were signs of army personnel, we would turn back. The place was empty apart from a few civilian vehicles and a police Land Rover. We parked the trucks facing uphill, with the tail lights pointing at the dark waters of the Zambezi.

A couple of curious fishermen watched us sidle up to the bar to buy the beers, but didn't say anything.

"What about a quickie before we go, sir?" Kenny said once we'd loaded the beers. I looked at my watch. It was nearly eight already. There would be no braai tonight; it was too late.

"Just one," I said. We sat at the end of the veranda outside the pub on chairs made of plastic flex in metal frames. Flying ants swirled above our heads and little miggies and bugs went down our shirt collars. I felt totally ill-at-ease and irresponsible for being here. I urged the guys to drink quickly so we could go.

I had barely spoken when one of the 'four-fives' started to jerk and roll backwards. The handbrake must have failed, because the air cylinder that operated it always leaked. Kenny dropped his beer and leaped over the handrail of the veranda like a scalded cat. I've never seen a man run so quickly – but by the time he reached the driver's cab, the tail lights were just entering the river. I will never know how he saved that vehicle from disappearing into those dark waters, but he did... only just. It gave me a helluva fright.

"Let's go!" I shouted to the guys. We boarded the trucks and headed back the way we came. I couldn't shake the feeling that it was a warning or an omen of some kind. I had this feeling of dread all the way back to Jambezi – and if that truck had gone into the river, I would have been court-martialled, stripped of rank and imprisoned.

As we came down the escarpment on the eastern side of the Matetsi River, a bright light in the sky attracted my attention. I knew instantly that it was a flare. My blood ran cold and I wondered what the hell I'd missed. What was going on? I called the base repeatedly over the radio, but no-one answered. Another flare, a bit closer this time, arced into the air before floating slowly down on its parachute. Flashes lit the source of the flare and the odd green tracer ricocheted lazily upwards. I felt sick to my stomach because I knew Jambezi was getting a serious stonking. All my efforts to coax the gooks into attacking us was happening right in front of my eyes – and there was nothing I could do about it! I was so angry that I banged the metal of the roll cage on the truck – shouting at the driver to go faster. I knew he couldn't, of course, because all our vehicles were governed to 80 kilometres an hour.

Our truck bounced over the concrete Matetsi River Bridge and then up the other side. I caught another brief glimpse of what was happening, and then all got lost in the thick of trees in a shallow valley. It took nearly 20 minutes until we reached the turn-off to Jambezi. I was scared shitless because we could hit a mine or be ambushed by a gook stop-group, but thank God they never used this tactic for some reason.

Every bush was an enemy; every shadow was someone charging at us. It was a horrible 15 minutes driving through the thick scrub to the base camp. With hindsight, it was the most stupid and irresponsible thing I'd ever done in my life.

One of the security lights on the perimeter of the camp flickered on and off. A strong smell of dust and cordite hung in the air. An electric thrill of fear and anticipation ran down my spine.

The gate to the keep was bolted shut, and no attempt to get anyone to open it was answered. What the hell had gone on? Were they all dead? I shouted to the guys on the trucks to get off and 'switch on'. The driver blew the horn again.

The skinny form of Mike Abbott ran down the embankment of the keep with a set of keys in his hand. He was visibly shocked – white and shaking like a leaf.

"We've just been revved really badly, sir. It's gone on for ages!"

I felt shocked and alarmed. There were only four of my guys in the camp: Stu Moll, Leonard Ferguson, Kieron Robinson and Mike Abbott – plus one or two men from Intake 146 and about six INTAF guards. I hurried the trucks into the keep and quickly locked the gate – expecting to get shot to bits any second.

"Kenny, you and two guys go to Charlie bunker. You two, to Bravo!"

"Shit, I'm glad you're back, sir," Abbott said as I entered Alpha bunker.

"What the hell happened?"

"An hour or two after you took off, the sky just lit up with tracer, RPGs, mortars... Dozens of them!"

I could tell from the subdued attitude of the guys that they were in a state of shock.

"Go and do an ammo count," I said to Abbott.

I turned back into the ops room and reported the incident to the main base at Vic Falls. Von Stranz questioned me at length and I had to pretend I'd been present to give him the answers he needed.

"What were the flares for?" I said to Robinson back in the bunker.

"We needed to light the bush up and were scared shitless the INTAF guards were going to open the gate!"

I peered out at the bush on the rim of the security lights. It looked dark and ominous. I wouldn't have ventured out there if you paid me millions.

"Tell me more, Robinson."

"We were playing cards with the INTAF guys when we heard a noise at the gate. When we got to the bunker, we saw one or two guards shouting at someone. All of a sudden, firing broke out – which was quickly followed by mortars, RPGs and really heavy small arms fire. The two guards ran for their lives!"

I got as much info as I possibly could in case Von Stranz questioned me again. I was really pissed off I'd missed the attack.

There was nothing to do but wait for first light now. I did a quick tour of the camp to make sure everyone was okay, but apart from a few light injuries among the INTAF guys, all was well. I spread the guys out among the bunkers, set the guard as I saw fit and headed back to the ops room. Kevin, out in ambush, had fortunately turned his radio on to find out what all the shooting was about. I told him to stand by for uplift in the morning to come back to base camp.

Abbott came back in with the ammo count. Over 40 percent of our ammo reserves from the trailer had gone in less than two hours.

"You did a helluva lot of firing. Some of them must have a few leaks," I said.

"Yessir... It was them or us."

"Good. You'll find some beers in the truck we came back in. Give one to each guy."

"Ah, that's shit-hot, sir."

"Bring the rest in here when you've dished them out."

"Yessir."

I walked into the kitchen where our free beef – courtesy of the landmine – had been prepared by the chef, but it was useless to us now. One of the mortar shells had penetrated the kitchen tent outside and blown the tent – and our adjacent glass windowpanes – to smithereens. Large slices of sharp glass lay all over our tasty rump and fillet steaks.

"What a waste," I said to Kenny.

It was amazing that no-one had been injured. Thankfully, the chef had just run for a bunker when his kitchen dissolved behind him.

Abbott arrived shortly after that with about 10 beers. We cracked some open and glugged the golden liquid down – thankful that we were still breathing through the correct hole in our bodies.

The next morning, I organised a follow-up and commenced a sweep of the internal and external perimeter of the complex. We quickly established that roughly 50 gooks had formed an assault line running roughly north-east to south-west just beyond the store – firing south-east into the keep. Over 4,500 spent cartridges, or 'doppies' as we called them, were found lying on the ground. In addition to this, 52 mortar shell tailfins were found scattered around the immediate vicinity. I was staggered at how accurate the mortar fire had been. Over 80 percent landed within effective shrapnel range of its target in any given sector of its impact.

It slowly dawned on me that my absence had not only saved Jambezi, but probably my life also. In the first place, the gooks had no doubt been watching the keep for some time

– gathering intelligence and monitoring our movements. If I had stayed at the keep the previous evening, I would have only kept a skeleton crew with me – and knowing this, the gooks may have been encouraged to overrun the base. However, my vehicles returning to camp from Dekka Drum looked like a reaction force arriving to effect a rescue, which no doubt caused the gooks to break off the attack.

As for my life being saved – well, that was clear to see. One of the small impact craters and a tailfin from a mortar shell was found just outside the rear blast wall of the bunker I would have run to when the firing started. In all probability, the explosion would have seriously injured or even killed me.

In all, three mortar shells exploded inside the keep – with the remainder being close enough to bunkers and other targets to cause serious injury to anyone exposed to the shrapnel. It was a complete miracle that the only injuries had been light cuts on two INTAF guards.

The accurate mortar fire, however, could not be complemented by the small arms fire. Only two strikes were found in the entire camp – one in the water tower three metres above the roof of the nearest A-frame barrack block, and one in a security light. Four-thousand-five-hundred rounds to achieve that!

"You should've seen one of the INTAF guys standing up on the water tower shooting down at the gooks; it was unbelievable! He only got down when loads of tracer crept towards him," Robinson said.

At 1000 the next morning, four armoured cars and a two-five full of infantry arrived to 'show the flag'. It was important that we portrayed the attack as a failure to the local population and gook spies. The armoured cars were virtually useless in the soft sand found in the area, but just seeing them was a real morale-booster.

The arrival of the armoured cars had been preceded by the arrival of two helicopters from 7 Squadron. One of them was a troop carrier – commonly known to us as a 'G' car, while the other was a gunship, or 'K' car. The 'K' car carried a 20mm machine-gun that would've made short work of any gooks found in the open. They had already done several sweeps ahead of the small tracker force to see if they could intercept the fleeing gook column, but we all knew they had 'bomb-shelled' in the night and gone their separate ways in small numbers. No doubt, the mujibas had already run their cattle over the bulk of the gook spoor by now anyway.

The helicopters brought some plain-clothes cops along to collect the doppies and look for any other intelligence that may help them build up a profile of the attackers. The spent cartridge cases would be closely examined by ballistics experts to see if they matched cartridges of weapons from nearby operational areas. This was a valuable clue as to the movements and numbers of resident gooks in some areas. In addition, this type of evidence put a few of the bastards behind jail on more than one occasion.

❦—❦

"We've got to search that forestry commission compound," Ian said later that night when everything had settled down again. He'd been in Wankie with 'Nipple' when the attack started, and rushed back earlier in the day to see how he could help. "That's where the gooks have run to."

"We need lots of manpower for that, Ian. It's quite a specialised process – searching an urban area. It's no good going in one end and the gooks run out the other."

"What do we do, then?"

"Leave it with me. I'll chat to the boss."

After my evening meal, I radioed Von Stranz back at Vic Falls. I told him as clearly as I could about our intention to search the compound without compromising any details over the air. Luckily, he caught on quickly and told me he would come back to me by 1100 the next morning.

"We should strike while the iron's hot," Ian said. "I just know there're some gooks in that place."

"Patience, Ian. The compound's never been searched properly before. Gooks will think they can lie low there without any hassles."

"Fuckers. I hate them."

"We all do, my mate."

Ian cracked open some beers he brought back from his supply run and we all went to bed that night secure in the knowledge that we had half of Ian's company in the keep – as well as Kevin's stick. I got mildly smashed on my two beers before flopping into bed at about 2300.

Von Stranz was as good as his word. By the following afternoon, we started rehearsals for getting large numbers of men on and off vehicles in the dead of night. This technique was known as en-bussing and de-bussing and was essential to practise in daylight to iron out any mistakes that could occur when it was too dark to see clearly. I spent the best part of an hour making sure everyone knew where they were in the column, as well as who would be in front of them and behind them when they marched to the compound. Radio channels, call-signs and vehicles had to be allocated.

Once that was done, an ex-SAS sergeant by the name of Mike Kemish joined me on a recce of the compound. We decided to do the recce in broad daylight – pretending our vehicle had broken down once we reached the outskirts of the large compound. While Mike made 'repairs' on the engine, I studied the complex through binos – making notes and sketches as I went along. I did my best to determine its full size. This was essential because if I had too few men to encircle the compound, large gaps would be left open for gooks to escape through.

Our convoy of six trucks moved off the next morning at 0200. I took the lead – ensuring the vehicle I was in was the same one used in the recce the day before. If I chose a random truck to lead the way, the odometer reading could be different, which would have thrown us off our de-bus point and cocked the whole thing up.

I chose to start walking towards the compound from a drop-off point five kilometres away. I knew this was far too close, but I figured a shallow valley leading to the compound would hide any glow from our headlights, as well as engine noise.

When the odometer clicked over to '22', the driver pulled off the road – killing the engine and lights. The other five vehicles followed suit. Fifty-five men de-bussed as quietly as they could and stood silently on the other side of the dirt track. I walked down the line doing a quick head-count before returning to the head of the column to lead the way.

It was heavy-going in the thick, powdery sand – and after two kays, I was swimming in sweat. The effort was compounded by a sloped incline, so after 20 minutes or so I paused to let the machine-gunners catch their breath. There was very little light; no moon at all – only the glow from billions of stars in the Milky Way above. The dirt road disappeared ahead like a pale arrow into a dark heart. Shrubs and trees varied from pale grey to black.

For some reason, time and distance is distorted at night – and after 40 minutes of walking, I was beginning to think I'd missed the turn-off to the right or cocked the whole thing up. But just a few minutes later, there it was – the thick tyre-worn T-junction leading to the sleeping village. The air had cooled to a chill. There was complete silence bar a single dog barking a bored lament in the middle-distance. I hated those bloody dogs and took great delight watching one explode from a dum-dum bullet I'd made from one of my FN rounds a few weeks earlier in the 'torment the locals' phase of ops.

Several minutes later, I reached the point where we'd 'broken down' the day before. A few more metres towards the compound and I would start depositing men in pairs around the entire circumference of the complex. The guys had been briefed to find whatever cover they could and face inwards to meet anyone trying to run out of the dozens of huts into the nearby bush. They had also been instructed to shoot to kill.

I continued round the outer edge of the compound – dropping men off in pairs until I reached the first pair I started with. With a bit of juggling and shaking out, the guys were in position by 0415. I sat against a relatively thick tree and did a radio check. Cooling sweat sent a cold shiver up my spine. Everyone checked in. All was okay. I hadn't cocked up after all.

At 0530 – just as the eastern sky was turning apricot in colour – the sound of advancing vehicles drifted over the dense air. It took longer for them to appear than I thought it would, but when they finally heaved into sight, it was impressive. Six Eland armoured cars interspersed with eight troop-carrying vehicles ground down the road towards me. I contacted the convoy commander to make sure I wasn't mistaken for a gook and shot on the spot.

Dozens of men de-bussed when the convoy finally came to a halt. Von Stranz was in the lead, followed by some cops – two of whom wore khakis with webbing and rifles. Central Intelligence Operatives no doubt.

"Everything okay, Tony?"

"Yes, sir. Nobody's tried to make a run for it."

"Pity," he said sarcastically.

We watched the men file past us before fanning out into a sweep line. They stood there until it was light enough to see, then moved forward at a slow pace – slowly disappearing into the hotchpotch of huts and gardens.

"Where'd that lot come from, sir?"

"Oh… it's a mixture of PATU, armoured cars and Phil Laing's platoon."

"Is Phil here?"

"No. I've left him in charge for a few hours. You've been having some fun out here, hey?"

"I guess you could call it that, sir."

"Mmm… You heard about Peters Motel getting revved?"

"Yes, saw a newspaper."

"Spooks reckon it's the same bastard that killed the farmer."

Spooks… Special Branch and the CIO – the Central Intelligence Organisation; I would love to know what those guys knew about the war and what really faced the Rhodesian people. I had long-suspected that the press filled us with a lot of patriotic crap to keep our spirits up.

"Ncube attacked Peters?"

"Seems like it, but the spooks don't tell us everything."

The cordon sanitaire was a complete success, and by 1400 15 men between the ages of 16 and 45 were bundled onto the back of a truck belonging to the cops. Each one had been neatly handcuffed with white plastic packing cords that were virtually impossible to break.

Von Stranz was long gone by that time, and was no doubt swallowing a beer by a pool somewhere. He'd parted with some excellent news: we were getting 10 days' R&R when we got back to Vic Falls in a day or two. It was the best news I'd had in months.

I could relax and take it easy for a while. I'd pecked away at the local villagers' patience until they got some gooks to come give us a rev. Trust me to miss it! And as it turned out, two of the captives were gooks. They provided invaluable information about other gooks in our area. No doubt the 'Eskimos' would then move in and 'freeze' the area until more gooks were culled…. and so on and so forth.

Figure 1
Jess at my aunt's horse ranch just outside Cape Town. (Credit: Tony Ballinger)

Figure 2
Me at my aunt's horse ranch near Cape Town. (Credit: Tony Ballinger)

Figure 3
Jess with me and our mutual friend we met on the cruise back to South Africa, 1976. (Credit: Charlie Pope)

Figure 4 A photo taken just after a gruelling battle march at the School of Infantry, 1976. The author is standing, with cap on. (Credit: Charlie Pope)

Figure 5 Weapons demo: Passing out ceremony for friends and relatives, School of Infantry, 1976. I loved the MAG and am seen here fondling it lovingly! (Credit: Tony Ballinger)

Figure 6 Officer selection course, Intake 152, School of Infantry, 1976. (Credit: Tony Ballinger)

Figure 7 Theo Nel, soldier par excellence, in pensive mood during an LTU course.
(Credit: Alan Currie)

Figure 8
This photo was
taken in my
mom's garden
just before
deploying to 4
Indep. In the
background is
my brother's car,
which I used
to take Jess to
Mazoe Dam.
(Credit: Tony
Ballinger)

Figure 9 The police station at Vic Falls. You can see the tent where we were based up until such time as National Parks gave us the buildings, which became Vic Falls Barracks. (Credit: David Gates)

Figure 10 A typical defensive bunker at our Vic Falls base. (Credit: David Gates)

Figure 11 A civilian truck destroyed by a ZIPRA landmine just south of Vic Falls, near the railway line. (Credit: David Gates)

Figure 12 The author sitting in a landmine crater not far from where the white truck was blown up. (Credit: David Gates)

Figure 13 A train sabotaged while crossing the Matetsi River Bridge, south-east of Vic Falls. (Credit: Charlie Pope)

Figure 14 The locomotive narrowly missed being blown up when the Matetsi River Bridge was attacked by gooks (circa 1977). (Credit: Charlie Pope)

Figure 15 Another view of the train sabotaged while crossing the Matetsi River Bridge. (Credit: Charlie Pope)

Figure 16 An actual photograph taken during the hunt for Albert Ncube. (Credit: Alan Currie)

Figure 17 Punch-up with the Zambian Army at Kazungula. Just above the wooden post in the foreground is a bunker on the Zambian shoreline, which we neutralised with our Eland's 90mm gun. To the right is the Zambian customs post. (Credit: Alan Currie)

Figure 18 Smoke rises from the Zambian shoreline after our mortars silenced an enemy 12.7mm heavy machine-gun. (Credit: Alan Currie)

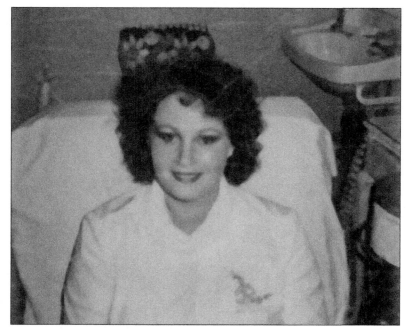

Figure 19 Marilyn: the girl with green eyes and auburn hair.
(Credit: Tony Ballinger)

Figure 20 Dave Kruger KIA – one of the author's buddies from school.
(Credit: Hugh Bomford)

Figure 21 Roy Orchard KIA.
What a superb guy you were, Roy.
(Credit: Hugh Bomford)

Figure 22 After hitting a landmine outside Jambezi Keep. Left to right:
Hugh Bomford, author and Graham Duff. (Credit: Al Currie)

Figure 23 Elephant Hills is seen burning down from a Strela strike gone wrong in this unique photograph. (Credit: John Moore)

Figure 24 The still-smouldering ruins of the Elephant Hills Hotel. (Credit: Ian Gates)

Figure 25 Elephant Hills still smouldering after its spectacular destruction. I watched it burn down from the hill at the back of the hotel. (Credit: Ian Gates)

Figure 26 The inside of the Elephant Hills Hotel was extremely luxurious, with each suite having a commanding view of the Gary Player-designed golf course and the Zambezi River and some even had a view of the magnificent Victoria Falls in the distance. (Credit: Ian Gates)

Figure 27
Life ticks on at
the devastated
hotel. (Credit:
Ian Gates)

Figure 28
Ever-
resourceful
Rhodesians
kept the bar,
squash courts
and one
swimming pool
operating at
Elephant Hills
for at least two
years after it
was destroyed.
(Credit: Ian
Gates)

Figure 29 All that remained of the glorious Elephant Hills Hotel after the roof caught fire from a stray Strela missile. (Credit: Ian Gates)

Figure 30 1 and 4 Indep's Vic Falls Barracks, post-independent Zimbabwe. (Credit: Ian Gates)

Chapter Eight

I was free again! It was like coming out of prison. To wear civilian clothes and act normal was an amazing feeling. Apart from a weekend or two during training, this was my first leave in nearly 10 months.

The last two days at Jambezi were really quiet. I suspect word got around about the arrests at the compound. Gook commanders would know two of their guys had been collared. It was time for them to lie low and see what would happen.

I used the time to catch up on some much-needed admin, to write reports and check kit and ammo returns. The 3,000 rounds of ammo the guys used to defend Jambezi had been replaced when Kemish came to join us.

I walked out the back of the base camp at Vic Falls late in the afternoon after sorting out my guys' train passes. Ten days of sleeping late, swimming and doing precisely what I wanted to do lay ahead. I hadn't read a book or watched a movie in months.

The back of the camp butted onto some houses. One road back and to the right was Mally's place. I felt nervous as I headed for her gate – hoping and praying she was at home; hoping and praying that some other guy's car wasn't parked there. I hadn't seen her for a month.

I was in luck. Her car was in the driveway on its own. Stone ballast crunched under my shoes as I walked up to her front door. My heart was hammering away inside my chest. My mouth dry.

"Tony!" Mally shrieked when the door opened. She jumped into my arms and wrapped her legs around my waist. It was a far nicer reception than I expected. Her smell and softness enveloped me. We stood like that for a long time before she pulled away and kissed me on the lips – leading me inside by the hand.

"I've missed you so much, Mal…"

"Me too. You have no idea… Gee, it's good to see you." She drew back and ran her eyes over me. "You've lost so much weight!"

"Army rations. Hard to swallow."

"Hungry? Want something to eat?"

"No, I'm fine. A drink perhaps."

"Wine?"

"Mmm... lovely. Red, if possible."

I watched her walk down the passage to the kitchen. I really needed her badly!

The lounge had lost that threadbare look. It had been freshly painted and new curtains rustled in the warm breeze. Paintings and pictures were dotted around the walls. Good second-hand furniture with a stereo and TV, a thick carpet... coffee table with magazines.

"You've done a good job here," I said, as she handed me my wine. We sat on the couch next to each other – not quite touching. It was electric.

"Fred gave a hand with the painting. I had the furniture shipped from Salisbury. Cost a bloody fortune... So how've you been?"

"Okay. Just glad to be a civvy for a while."

"How long?"

"Ten days."

We sipped our wine. The earthy liquid warmed and relaxed me – stirring my manhood. I stared like an idiot at her beautiful eyes.

"I heard from Von Stranz that the keep you stayed in got attacked?"

"Trust him to give away confidential info."

"A couple glasses of booze loosens tongues."

I knew what she meant. I was beginning to feel very loose myself. My mind was surging with things to say to her; to share the thoughts and passions that had been building up in me for weeks and weeks. I sensed she knew what was going on inside me.

"Peters Motel got revved," I said stupidly. "Where were you when it happened?"

"At work. It was really scary, you know... All those explosions, the sound of so much firing."

"Mmm, the gook that killed the farmer... Ncube... he led led the attack – or so the fuzz reckon."

"You better get him then... Finish him off."

She made it sound like a game – cops and robbers or something. How could you explain any of it to people who hadn't been involved?

"Where will you stay, during your leave?"

"I hadn't thought about that. I've got a subsidised air ticket back to Salisbury... My folks have been bugging me to go see them."

"Go to Salisbury? You've just got back for the first time in a month..."

I wasn't sure, but her eyes looked moist.

"I suppose I could split the time with five days here. I could sleep in my quarters, then five days home with the folks."

Mally went silent – focusing on nothing in particular out the window. She seemed to be going over something in her head. I suddenly felt very tired. I rested my head against the back of the chair – closing my eyes.

Her lips brushed against mine – ever so tender and sensual. I kept my eyes closed – relishing the smell and feel of her, tasting her sweetness. We kissed deeply. I picked her up in one easy move – carrying her towards the bedroom.

"Tony…" she said softly, but I didn't want to hear any words from her. I didn't want her to object or talk me out of this. There was nothing on earth that would stop me now.

Our lovemaking was deep and urgent – full of exploration and wonder – hot breath on flushed faces… a feeling of leaving one's body, floating high.

We cuddled for ages after that without saying anything – lost in our own thoughts. Thunder rumbled in the distance; sunlight danced on the window sill. I think I was asleep when she said it, so I asked her to repeat herself.

"No need to go to Salisbury anymore. You can stay right here with me."

I smiled and cuddled back into her before falling into a deep, restful sleep.

The next few days were amazing. Mally and I would sleep in late after her evening shift at work. The start of each day was a leisurely ritual of waking slowly, making love, eating breakfast in bed and making love some more. She was an incredibly passionate and loving person – responsive and warm… a good communicator, which to me, mattered more than anything. I cannot stand thick women.

Fred was good enough to give her a few days off, so we spent them visiting the curio shops, going on booze cruises, playing tennis, visiting the croc farm, dancing and gambling at the Elephant Hills Casino. Unfortunately, Mally couldn't gamble at the tables because she was a croupier at a competing casino, but we had many laughs playing on the one-armed bandits. Sunset was my favourite time of the day – the heat subsiding; golden rays casting long shadows over the golf course; pig trenching up sweet roots on the golf cause-ways; elephant, buck and eland drinking from water traps. And there, beyond the silver palm-lined river, lay Zambia – often covered in smoke from small fires. I was starting to think I could make this place home.

"Penny for your thoughts," Mally said, as she sipped a ginger square.

"I was just thinking I could live here."

"How much time left in the army?"

"About a year…"

"A year? As long as that?"

"It'll pass quickly enough."

"I'll worry when you go back to the bush."

"No need. It's not exactly Stalingrad."

"What would you do if you decided to settle here? Do you have any training or qualifications?"

"Not really. I wouldn't have a clue, really. I worked in a bank for a year. Maybe I could get a job as a teller or something."

"You, a banker? Give me a break. You'd be bored stiff."

"Well, maybe I'll become a hunter. Who knows... I have no idea, actually."

I felt mildly depressed that it would be hard to find work in the village. I hadn't studied for anything. Life was too good for that.

We often went down to the Falls or walked along the riverbank close to the lip of the Falls. It sort of became our special place and we would often just sit in silence and enjoy the splendours of nature.

The rains had started in earnest – and although it poured down every night, the river was still at its lowest point. This was because the main catchment area was in Zambia and it would take a month or two before the deluge of water reached us – about March or April – when the spray from the Falls was thrust hundreds of feet up into the air. Every window in the village would vibrate from the 500 million litres per minute pouring into the chasm of the Falls.

And, of course, we visited Fred and 'the wife' – laughing each time there was a cock-up on Zambian TV.

Although I didn't know it then, the Rhodesia I loved only had three years and five months of life left, but these were wonderful – if not scary and traumatic – times. The war and sanctions had pulled our whole population together. We fought together, laughed together and, in many cases, died together. Managers of factories 'made a plan' to overcome sanctions – and because of their thriftiness and wisdom, our local industries not only remained viable, but grew and thrived. Products that had been imported for decades were now made at home. An incredible pride in our flag, nation and principles ebbed through every person that thought the way we did. In our naïve way, we truly believed we were a bastion of good against evil – the last stand of good governance and Christian principles in a dark and troubled continent. We were young and proud to be Rhodesians – to be 'Rhodies'.

One of the things I enjoyed most about Mally was that we could talk in-depth on all these topics – and many others. She had a wicked sense of humour and, as I very quickly discovered, a stubborn nature – but she would become soft and loving when the moment arose. I knew that I was madly in love with this girl… I would never let her slip through my fingers.

Our favourite moments together were spent by the swimming pools of various hotels. We would suntan on deckchairs, eat when we wanted to, or just read a magazine or news-paper, or just doze and chat – whatever we wanted to do; such freedom, such idyllic days of youth. The thought of growing old or dying was outrageous.

Another favourite time, which indented deep memories in my mind, was spent lying in Mally's double-bed listening to the raging tropical storm outside. We would switch the light off and open the curtains – lying there mesmerised by the display of lightning and deafened by the avalanche of water on the corrugated iron roof above us. We felt warm and safe in each other's arms.

I must admit though, that each crash of thunder made me think a bomb had gone off or a landmine in the adjacent valley. My mind would often turn to the poor buggers less than five kays away shitting off in these storms – knowing the terror of sleeping in the open with lightning zapping all around you.

❦

It was during a walk into town to buy a newspaper when I first heard about Pete Wells. Von Stranz pulled over to the side of the road in his Land Rover and spoke to me above the idle of the engine.

"Tony!"

"Morning, sir." I hope and prayed the bugger wasn't going to recall me back to camp for some reason.

"You hear about Pete Wells?"

"No, sir."

My heart missed a beat. I hoped the news wasn't bad.

"He's in hospital in Wankie. Him and two of his guys were shot up in an ambush."

"No…" I said with a sinking heart. "Where?"

"That cut-line near the national parks boundary, on the left going out to the airport." I thought for a while until I could picture it in my mind.

"I know the place… Is he bad?"

"He's lost a big chunk of his right leg. Corporal Brown isn't too bad, but Rootman is critical; got it in the chest, I think."

"Tex Brown, sir?"

"Yes, that's him."

I couldn't believe it! Pete shot up! I remembered Tex from a party in Highlands, Salisbury. He was a wild guy – full of life. I only vaguely knew Rootman.

"I can't believe it," I said.

"What happened?"

"Apparently, they'd just settled into ambush when a group of gooks coming down the cut-line heard them and opened fire. They tried to hit back as much as possible, but their casualties prevented it."

"Shit, that's awful sir, but thanks for letting me know. You say they're in Wankie?"

"Yes, the civvy hospital. Pete may lose his leg; it's touch and go."

"Shit," I said again, looking at my feet. I felt guilty I was on leave, while Pete and the other two lay in pieces in hospital. The news dampened the rest of my R&R.

I don't remember buying the newspaper or the walk back to Mally's place. My mind was a jumble of thoughts and emotions.

❧—❦

I sat bolt-upright in bed. Did I hear it, or didn't I? Was it thunder? My heart skipped a beat. Rain poured steadily onto the roof, but not in the usual torrent.

"What's wrong?" Mally said, sitting up.

"Let's listen…"

I strained my ears – turning my head sideways to try a different angle of approach to the sound. A loud kwa-thoom was preceded by a bright blue flash reflected off the trees next door.

"It's just thunder."

"Like hell it is. I know that sound anywhere!" I leapt from the bed in one go and ran to the back door – opening it. Water cascaded off a blocked gutter – splashing my feet. I stood there – stark-naked – listening.

"What is it?"

"Shh," I said, just as another bang and echo rolled down the valley. I saw the green tracer arcing overhead a few seconds before the kwa-kwa-kwa sound of communist weapons reached me.

"Tony, oh my God!" Mally shrieked – holding onto my arm. Bright flashes preceded deafening explosions, which echoed down the valley at spaced intervals after that. It could be an RPG, but this sounded much heavier.

"Get my rifle," I hissed at Mally.

The white of her bum disappeared into the darkness. Her face was alive with fear when she handed the weapon to me. I cocked the rifle and stood there like a complete idiot looking down the driveway. Mally held onto me and I noticed she was shaking and wobbling as much as I was.

"It's Peters Motel again," I said simply.

"Not again. How can those bastards just get away with it all the time?"

"There's a lot of bush out there – far too much for us to watch."

It occurred to me that Mally's house was more or less in line of an over-shoot of any projectile the gooks were firing. A shiver of fear ran up my spine.

"Mally, go back to the bedroom and get on the floor by the air-conditioner. Pull the mattress over you."

"What about you?" Her eyes were big white balls in the dim light.

"I'll keep watch."

"I don't want to be alone…."

"Just go, dammit!" I snapped. "There's no point me lying under a bed if there's gooks in the village. Now go!"

She took off quickly – her white bum disappearing once more. The neighbour came out his back door.

"It's Peters," Frikkie said simply. He didn't seem to worry I was stark-naked. I didn't worry that he was in underpants. We both stood there, cradling our FNs, watching the fireworks.

"For fuck's sake, poor old George and Rowina – twice in a few weeks." Frikkie took a big swig from his beer bottle. I swallowed a large gulp when he offered it to me. The alcohol steadied my nerves somewhat.

"It's gonna kill business. Man, this is bad…"

Never mind that people were probably dying. As I got to know Frikkie better over the years, I came to know him as a pessimist – griping that things are bad… bad man, bad…

Green tracer was whizzing by at tree-top level – and I knew from my training that none of the weapon reports were from a NATO origin; in other words, no-one was firing back. Those poor bastards were taking the full heat of the attack on their own!

I was just starting to get angry when I heard the sound of high-revving, but slow-moving vehicles; only armoured cars sounded like that. I was appalled at how long it had taken them to react, and equally appalled that a permanent presence had not been maintained at the motel.

"The whole village is a sitting duck," Frikkie said, before taking another long draught from his beer. "We need a bloody security fence with checkpoints to stop this. It's bad for business…"

The firing decreased – and then stopped abruptly. It would be highly unlikely that any of the gooks would be caught. You're asking for trouble trying to look for gooks at night unless you are trained or equipped for it. So in the end, all the reaction force could do was offer a presence – a reassurance for the patrons of the motel... some of whom may have literally crapped in their pants from fear.

"My name's Tony, by the way," I said, extending my hand.

"Frikkie Blauw."

"I've seen you in the casino before..."

"Mmm... Security manager." He looked at his empty beer bottle. "Time for a top-up."

To an outsider, it would be hard to believe that two men – one naked and the other dressed only in underpants – had chatted so easily with each other. Fear sort of makes you do stupid things. I was wet and chilled to the bone. Mally was still under the mattress when I found her.

"It's okay now, babe."

Her eyes were wide with fear and she was shaking like a leaf. I pulled the mattress off her, rearranged the blankets and pulled her close to me. We shivered together for a while until the warmth of our bodies under the blankets warmed us up.

"What happened?"

"Peters got it again – poor buggers."

"What's to stop them hitting somewhere else next time?"

"Not much. We have far too few troops here."

"And what would have happened tonight if two or more groups attacked simultaneously?"

"We would be in the shit."

"I dunno..."

"Dunno what?"

"If it's worth staying here?"

My heart went cold. The thought of Mally leaving the Falls made me feel ill... desperate.

"It'll be okay. Things will get better. The brass will have to do something."

"I hope so, 'cos if it carries on like this, I won't stay."

"You'd leave me?"

"I wouldn't be leaving you; I'd be leaving the village. That wouldn't be the end of us."

"A whole year... I couldn't go that long without seeing you."

I felt jealous and afraid. Would she find someone else? Sensing my anxiety, she kissed me – slow and longingly on the mouth.

I rolled her onto her back and entered her... just lying on top of her – kissing... not moving. I wanted to be a part of her being – to belong to her totally.

The next morning we, like half the village, took a drive to Peters Motel to see what had happened. There was only one lightly-armed policeman on duty, so we drove into the complex and parked under a large, spreading tree.

I was surprised to see the swimming pool crammed with kids and adults as if nothing had happened the night before. As it turned out though, most of them were locals and were using the motel facilities as an excuse to poke around and look at the damage.

Mally and I didn't bother being so deceptive and simply walked to the left (or south) of the reception and bar area. We passed one row of terraced chalets before seeing any damage. A tree with a 500mm girth had been cut clean in half, with the branches resting on the crumpled metal roof of one of the chalets. The pre-cast concrete boundary wall had two or three large holes in it. One section of panelling had almost vaporised. Just beyond the axed tree were two badly-damaged chalets. Both had walls with big holes in them. Glass lay everywhere. Someone's toothbrush and toothpaste leaned at a dizzy angle on a shelf in one of the bathrooms.

"Anyone get hurt?" Mally said.

"Who knows? Probably not, or else the cops would have ringed the place off."

Just then, George – the owner of the motel – and a policeman exited one of the damaged buildings. I recognised the cop from when we were based at the police station.

"Morning. Any casualties?"

"None," the cop said. He turned to shake hands with George and then faced us once more. "It's hard to believe, isn't it?"

"Yes, it is… This is Marilyn by the way, my girlfriend."

"You're a croupier at the Casino Hotel, aren't you?"

"For my sins…"

"It's a miracle. Both chalets had guests booked into them, but they were gambling at Elephant Hills when the attack started."

"That," I said, pointing to all the damage, "wasn't done by an RPG. What the hell did they use?"

"We're not sure, probably a B-10. There's small wheel-marks on the ground – down there, by the cut-line." He pointed to our left. An overhead power line ran along a cleared section of bush in the cut-line. I knew a B-10 was an anti-tank weapon. It had simply been fired along the cut-line.

"What's a B-10?" Mally said.

"An anti-tank weapon."

"Anti-tank? Isn't that a big thing?"

"Not really, it's like a long pole. They load it from the back and can pull it along on a set of small wheels."

"So they just drag this thing in from nowhere and blow up a motel?"

I looked at the cop, who merely turned up the corners of his mouth – shifting the weight on his feet.

"I've got to go," he said, "forensics will be here soon. Don't touch anything, okay?"

"Sure... Cheers."

Mally turned to face me – bent slightly forward.

"A bloody anti-tank weapon! And no guards here from the last attack? That's pretty slack, isn't it?"

"Tell me about it. I was in the bush, remember?"

"I'm not having a go at you, Tony, but surely..."

"I agree. Something will be done about it, that's for sure."

We ambled around for a while looking at the damage before going back to the pool to have a ginger square each.

I had only been back in base a day when the phone rang in the ops room.

"It's for you, sir," the radio operator said.

"Hello?"

"Von Stranz here, Tony. I'm at the cop station. Get a vehicle and come join me at Peters Motel."

"Sir."

The phone went dead. I stood there for a moment or two – cradling the receiver in my hand. What was this all about, then? I picked up my rifle and called for a driver. Five minutes later, I passed the cop shop and headed up the hill towards Peters Motel. I was waved down by a small gathering of men in camouflage standing around a grey police vehicle to the left of the motel gate. I saluted Von Stranz.

"We're here to go through the attacks on the motel with the cops... and their lead witness," he said, smiling.

"Lead witness?"

"Yes, Albert Ncube. He's in the van."

I turned to look at the van just as a tall, ragged man stood up from the cramped area in the back of the vehicle. His hair was matted and unkempt and he had a raggedy beard running down to his chin. Although he was thin, you could see he was a powerful man. I ran my eyes downwards to the feet, and there they were – big long feet... size 12 to 14 at least; the very feet that had generated all those footprints on the follow-up from the farmer's house. I ran my eyes up to his face – catching my breath involuntary us our gaze met. I have never seen a look of such intense hatred in anyone in my entire life. He looked unwaveringly at me out of yellow eyes – eyes like that of a leopard. He continued to stare at me – and to my shame, I was the first to look away.

"How? Where?" I said, facing Von Stranz.

"Bulawayo – four nights ago. He was on R&R – probably trying to find out about his wife and kids. CIO took them after the farmer was killed."

"I remember."

"He's the brains behind everything up here – Pete Wells's ambush; the farmer; and both attacks on Peters Motel."

"How can they prove that?"

"Ballistics – plus a couple of chats late into the night."

"He's the boss, then?"

"Yes. He's a section commander."

I turned to look at Ncube once more. He had turned his face to the south – just staring at nothing but empty bush. I wondered what thoughts were going through his head? It was hard to tell his age, but he wasn't much older than me.

I played no part in the investigation, really. I simply walked behind the cops – listening to what they were told through an interpreter. Two plain-clothes detectives made notes wherever they went – obviously Special Branch boys.

A few more doppies and a propellant charge for an RPG were found under a nearby bush. This is where they had stood – line abreast – firing into Peters Motel when I was out at Jambezi. At that point in time, there was no pre-cast concrete wall facing the main road, so they chose this vantage point to attack. One man had been killed, and a few others cut by flying glass. Thank God they were such useless shots – generally speaking, that is.

After gathering as much evidence as possible on the first attack, we moved into the complex and listened to the description of the second attack – the one I had witnessed from Mally's house. Ncube concurred that a B-10 had been used, but said he had no idea where it went as another section had joined his in the attack. Well, that was for the cops to sort out anyway. Ncube did not give up any information willingly and spoke begrudgingly throughout the whole process.

By noon, I asked for permission to return to camp as we were set to deploy the following morning. I drove back in silence. It was weird meeting Ncube. I didn't hate him as a person; I just hated what he stood for and how he was going about getting it. It didn't take a genius to realise that if we lost the war, that bastard would be on the side of those in control – and that sent shivers up my spine!

I spent the rest of the afternoon preparing to relieve Phil's platoon out in the bush the next day. It was his turn for R&R, the lucky bastard. I was so missing my recent experience of being with Mally as a civvy that I would have killed to take Phil's place.

As I wasn't duty officer that night, I was able to go see Mally at the casino.

"Look who it is," Fred said when I walked through the door. A couple of new croupiers had started since my last visit. I looked them over quickly. They smiled back.

"Good to see you, Fred," I said, shaking his hand, "I'm amazed you're so busy with all the excitement that's been going on."

I bent over a corner of the roulette table and kissed Mally on the lips – winking at her.

"The human race is insane. Some people leave because of the attacks, but even more replace them. What'll you have to drink?"

"Whisky, please."

"I heard they used an anti-tank gun on Peters?"

I looked at Mally, but she shook her head.

"What don't you know, Fred?"

"Not much," he said, laughing his Mexican laugh. "I am a police reservist, you know."

"It's a bit hairy really, Fred. We just don't know where they'll strike next."

"Maybe so, but I hear you've got their boss man – old Albert."

Once more I looked at Mally, but she only smiled back at me. One of the other croupiers stood close alongside her. She was gorgeous. When I looked back at Mally's eyes, they said: "touch her, and I'll kill you!" It was my turn to smile…

"Fred, you know man, you need to keep all these things you hear to yourself."

"Balls, Tony. This village is worse than a soap opera. I reckon even the munts[1] on reception are terrs. They all know what's going on."

"Even so, we need to be a bit discreet, okay?"

"You're the boss!"

I sat on a chair and watched Mally deal. She really was good. The place was just about full – the air thick with smoke and loud voices. Donna Summer did her best over a poor stereo system to bring a mellow mood to the place.

It was gone two in the morning when the doors finally closed. We'd been invited to a party at the hotel manager's house – located about five houses down from Mally's. Robin Ellis's place was packed when we arrived there. Croupiers from both casinos danced to the Hues

---

1   Munts/Muntu (the single 'u' would be pronounced 'oo' quickly, and the 'tu' would be pronounced 'two'): Although loosely derived from the Mashona word 'person', it became bastardised into a mild insult: "You bloody munts get a move on!" for example.

Corporation's '*Rock the Boat*' or sat around on chairs. Some were eating or standing in small groups chatting. I had never seen so many beautiful women in one place for a long time. I felt Mally's grip tighten on my hand as she pulled me closer into her. I kissed her to reassure her. After getting a couple of drinks, I pulled her outside.

The moon was as bright as a street lamp and the sounds and sights of people having a good time was a total contradiction with the war going on around us. It brought back a conversation with my dad, who was in the Royal Air Force during the Second World War. He had told me how hard people partied just to forget, for a brief minute, that there was a war on. I guess this was a little of the same.

We danced a long while before I felt it was time for me to go. I had desperately wanted to spend my last few hours making love with Mally, but somehow this was just as nice – holding her in my arms, turning slowly to the music and kissing. She moulded so perfectly into me; it's like we were one.

"I have to go," I said, with a heavy heart.

"So soon?" she said, looking up at me.

"We're deploying in a few hours' time. I need to get some sleep."

"Come back to my place…"

"I can't. I was supposed to be back at midnight. I don't want to push my luck."

"I'll take you."

"Not to worry. You stay and enjoy yourself. I'll walk back."

"Sure?"

"Yes. Take care of yourself."

"You too, Tony. Please take care… I love you."

"I love you too."

I bent over and kissed her for a long time on the lips. She held me tight like she didn't want me to go. Her eyes were moist when I looked into them.

It was a lovely warm night as I walked back to camp – the moon a bright silver-grey in the starlit sky. My mind raced with thoughts as I strolled along – the sounds of people laughing and Carlos Santana's '*Black Magic Woman*' fading behind me. My heart felt so heavy. The end of my interlude had arrived; it was time to face reality once again.

"Wake up!" Von Stranz said forcefully. "Get up!"

I looked at my watch. I was paralysed with disorientation for a few seconds. It was only 0645. I didn't have to get up for another 15 minutes.

"Sir?"

"Get up, Tony. Ncube's escaped from prison. I want your platoon to form a stop-group."

I bolted upright – pulling on my camo denims, combat shirt, boots and webbing. I ran over to the ablution block, relieved myself and quickly brushed my teeth. The whole camp was a hive of activity. I found Von Stranz in the ops room.

"Tom, order sandwiches and coffee for us, will you?" Von Stranz said to the radio operator.

"Sir!"

"Sorry for the rude awakening, Tony. Take a seat."

I sat opposite the large wall map. Kevin Torode joined us. It was a crisp clear morning – fresh air, birds singing. Men were running everywhere outside.

"Ncube broke out of camp half an hour ago when someone came to feed him."

"You're joking, sir?"

"Afraid not. A stick of PATU and trackers are already hot on his heels – heading west."

"Sounds like an inside job…"

"You're probably right," Von Stranz said, tying up his boot laces.

"Why west? He's bound to get caught out there?"

"Just what I thought. I smell a rat in the whole thing."

"What should we do?"

"Okay," Von Stranz said, picking up a pointer, "I want you to break your guys up into sticks of four and patrol about two to three kilometres ahead of the PATU stick on the main road. Six or seven sticks must walk along the road – separated by about a hundred metres or so. The remaining sticks must remain mobile – driving ahead of the walking column and then returning to the tail of the column. Make as much noise as possible with the vehicles."

"Why?"

"At the moment, Ncube's tracks are north of the main road to Kazungula. If we can prevent him turning south, we have a really good chance of catching him. We have armoured cars by the river… here and here," he pointed at the map, "a PATU stick here and two of Phil Laing's sticks here and here. Hopefully, he will hear your vehicles and stay north of the road. If he turns south, we've lost him."

"How will I know where the follow-up team is?"

"I'll be with the cops. I'll relay their progress every half an hour."

The sandwiches arrived shortly after that and we devoured the tasty bacon and eggs while we scribbled down more details on notepads. Police call-signs from Kazungula would operate west of where the tar road turned sharp-north – about 10 kays east of Kazungula itself – but that was 65 kilometres away. If we didn't catch him before then, he would be long-gone.

I was just preparing to leave camp when the company commander, Martin Pearce, arrived in his Peugeot staff car. He merely nodded at my salute and rushed into the ops room.

"Let's go!" I said to the driver.

We took off in four vehicles. I'd divided the guys as best as possible. There were only six radios in my platoon, so each alternate stick had one. This was not ideal at all, but I banked on Ncube being alone and unarmed. He shouldn't present a problem.

The trucks accelerated up the hill past Peters Motel before slowing down and turning right (or west) towards Kazungula 65 kilometres away. It was a beautiful day, with a promise of lots of heat later. There was already a bit of humidity in the atmosphere, but thankfully, no clouds so far. Only a few early-bird tourists on bicycles waved at us as we surged past.

I took out my map and looked at the co-ordinates provided by Von Stranz for the start of my deployment. The first stick would have to be dropped about three kays west of the dirt track I drove down that very first night of deployment so long ago. A stop-group of 'Black Boots' were already forming up for deployment down the track as we sped past them.

The object of tracking a person in the bush is to determine his rough line of flight and then send groups of men ahead of him to try and intercept him. This is called 'leap-frog-ging'. The 'Black Boots' were the first line of interception. If Ncube turned north of them, he would hopefully hit one of Phil's sticks that were doing cross-grain patrols to and from the riverfront to the edge of the escarpment.

It was imperative that we caught him as soon as possible. Every hour that passed would improve his chances and reduce ours. He had a strip of land 65 kilometres long by approximately eight kilometres wide to get lost in. That's roughly 500 square kilometres to avoid a search force of no more than a hundred men.

I recalled the look in Ncube's eyes and knew this was a determined bastard – full of hate. He would be a tough nut to catch. Vic Falls better be prepared to get revved again.

I dropped off the first stick on the left-hand side of the road – instructing them to search all culverts and soft, sandy patches for footprints – or indeed, signs of footprints being rubbed out.

When they were about a hundred metres behind us, I dropped off the second stick on the right-hand side of the road – giving them similar instructions. Thereafter, the sticks alternated from one side of the road to the other.

By the time I'd dropped off the remaining men, Von Stranz had radioed the location of the stick doing the actual follow-up through to me. They were roughly four kilometres east of my tail-end call-sign, still heading west.

Ncube's hour-long head-start would put him anywhere between four and eight kilometres ahead of the tracker team depending on his level of fitness, firmness of soil underfoot and injuries. I figured I would keep my guys at the minimum distance ahead of the tracker team rather than the maximum distance because I knew the soil in the area was very soft and tiring to walk in. Anyway, the whole thing was a guessing game.

I instructed Kevin's vehicle and one other to race ahead for about two kilometres and then turn back to the tail of the advancing column, while the other one started at the tail of the column and then went forward. I proposed to make as much noise with the engines as possible to keep Ncube inland, where more stop-groups were being leap-frogged into position.

A helicopter belonging to 7 Squadron buzzed over the trees to the north of us, while a small fixed-wing PRAW plane circled overhead to relay communications. PRAW (or Police Reserve Air Wing) pilots played a valuable role supporting ground troops in various roles – principally in communications relay, but sometimes as casevac pilots or even attacking gooks with weapons fired from their aircraft.

After an hour of our attempts to keep Ncube hedged in, his tracks just vanished into thin air. Everything ground to a halt. I told my men to spread out along the road and keep their eyes peeled. A couple of truckloads of guys zoomed past in a westerly direction – no doubt to be dropped off as stop-groups somewhere.

The sun rose into the sky until just short of its zenith, the tar road turned into a shimmering, dancing mirage. It was becoming harder to see each stick from the next because of this.

The order came to progress some more. His tracks had been found 40 metres past a rocky outcrop. We were still in the right place – or so I figured. I made two sticks sitting on the trucks swap with another two, and did this for most of the day – always ensuring each guy had a chance to have a rest and drink from the water tanks on the truck.

Lunch came and went. By early afternoon, thick black clouds had started to gather in the north-east over Zambia. Our elevated position above the valley showed it was a humdinger of a storm in the making. I just could not believe that this bastard of a murderer could get away because of the weather. The temperature dropped noticeably and the wind picked up, but we kept going.

We must have been a good 25 kilometres west of the village when Ncube's tracks disappeared once more. This time, however, they were not found again. They had simply vanished, close to the river. It coincided with the arrival of the storm, but speculation about his disappearance raged for many weeks after that. Did fishermen from Zambia pick him up? Did he have a boat or dinghy stashed from some previous crossing? Stop-groups and the follow-up stick were so close to him, they were sure he would be bagged – but no-one will ever know how he got away. I remain convinced to this day that he'd been turned to our cause and was deliberately released. How else could he walk out of a jail where he was in chains 24 hours a day?

We didn't know this, of course, so I was instructed to leave some men on the road as stop-groups while others went inland down tracks and paths to see if we could locate his spoor. I decided to do some cross-grain patrols myself, but it was a hopeless exercise because it didn't stop raining the whole day. Indeed, the storm that hit us was the most ferocious and hard-hitting I had ever been through in my life – worse than a cyclone I had experienced in Thailand two years earlier. It was in this very storm that Kevin Torode got separated from his men and remained lost for the next 24 hours. He deserted a short while later by faking a letter from a sick relative in the UK. He was even given company funds to help with his air ticket, the bastard.

By sunset, I was knackered and freezing-cold from the driving rain. We'd reached the sharp bend north in the road, near a roads department base camp. This was our boundary with the cops from Kazungula; we could go no further west. I tried to radio Von Stranz, but Major Pearce answered the call. He instructed me to take two sticks to the police camp at Kazungula and wait for further instructions. The remainder of my guys would stay on patrol.

The tar road ended at the roads department camp – after which it became a good, wide dirt road – or should I say, mud road. We passed several sticks of PATU standing at the junction of the two roads. We waved at each other as we drove by.

I'd never seen this part of Rhodesia before. It was wild, wooded country with few, if any, people living in it. In fact, hardly any humanity existed between here and the Atlantic Ocean to the west – hundreds of kilometres away. The main economic activity in the area came from hunting concessions and a border post with Botswana. It was at this very point that four countries met: the Caprivi Strip of South West Africa, Botswana, Zambia and Rhodesia. The main Rhodesian police camp I was heading for was about eight kilometres east of the border post – built right up against the majestic Zambezi River.

My truck paused at the gate of the police camp, while a smartly-dressed guard slithered his way through the mud to open it.

I was impressed with the camp. It must have been an idyllic posting in peaceful days gone by. Built on a green, grassy slope that ended in the river, the camp was big and modern. Rows of staff quarters filed off to my left. They were modern A-frame buildings not more than 10 years old. A large communications tower came next, and then the actual police station itself – a small charge office, holding cells and car park under a large tree with one or two grey police Land Rovers parked there. Beyond that were several more large buildings. A white policeman walked out of the charge office – hands on hips.

"Been having fun?" he said, looking at our wet and bedraggled bodies.

"If that's what you want to call it... I'm Lieut Ballinger, Tony."

"Steve," he said, shaking my hand. He turned and shouted at an African constable. "Tell your guys to follow him. They can shower and find a place to doss for the night."

I told the guys what to do and then followed Steve into his small ops room. A radio operator looked up at me out of mild curiosity before carrying on with his newspaper reading.

"Tea?"

"Please. I'd kill for some."

He poured a cup of strong, sweet tea into a metal cup before handing it to me. I felt a bit warmer in the ops room, although the rain had started again. A large map covered one wall. Little red, green and yellow stickers were stuck into it near where Ncube vanished.

"That was a helluva storm," I said.

"Just about washed the camp into the river."

"Your bum's in the jam being posted here, hey?"

"Couldn't be better. Great fishing..."

"Any news about how Ncube escaped from jail?"

"No," Steve said, as he sipped his tea, "reckon it was an inside job."

"That's what I thought. Question is: who let him out? Sympathisers or Special Branch?"

Steve gave me an odd look, but didn't say anything. He sipped his tea a couple more times.

"Not a complete waste of time," he said, standing up to tap the map with his finger. "Our guys caught a gook here."

I looked at the spot he was pointing at. I had gone through there several hours earlier. It's quite possible the gook had watched me walk right past him.

"That's a bit odd," I said.

"What?"

"Ncube heads west towards who knows what from Vic Falls, disappears into thin air and then some random gook gets picked up in the middle of nowhere. Think Ncube knew something we don't?"

"Who knows? Fancy a drink?"

"Sure, but I'm broke."

"No probs. We have a canteen fund for guys like you."

I followed him out the back of the ops room, down a passage to a dining area and then on to a well-appointed pub. Several men in uniform were drawing on beers as if there wasn't a war on. Music played quietly in the background.

"Life's tough for the fuzz," I said sarcastically. Steve just chortled.

"What'll it be?"

"Pilsner please… Cheers."

A cheerful black barman poured the beers. We took them outside to the veranda – swiping raindrops off metal chairs before we sat on them. The sun was just about gone now, but it was still light enough to see the river about 60 metres away. A short jetty had two speedboats anchored alongside it – a fuel pump at one end.

"Have you guys been hit yet?" I said, sipping my beer.

"No, but it's only a matter of time."

"How long have you been stationed here?"

"Four years… And you? Doing your NS?"

"Yes, about a year to go."

"Things are hotting up, that's for sure. The intake before you were bored stiff – nothing much happened with them."

"Where're you from originally?"

"Gwelo… And you?"

"Salisbury."

"Bambazonke!"

I smiled and studied Steve out the corner of my eye. His thinning blonde hair did not detract from his good looks. His face was tanned and lean – about 35 years old, I would guess. I also guessed he was a bit of a pisscat – a bit wild maybe… My type of guy! Maybe he'd gone 'bush' being based all the way out here?

"I figure you've been chasing old Albert all day, but why've you come here?"

"No idea, Steve. My boss told me to wait here until he made contact."

"Cheers then," he said, holding up his glass.

"Cheers mate…"

The one drink led to two and three – eventually finishing after six of them. The rest of my guys had showered and made themselves look as presentable as possible. I forgot about rank and just had a good laugh with them. Max, my MAG gunner with the look-alike 'Smiling Shit' glasses, turned out to be a complete pisscat. It was fantastic sitting there, talking very little – just listening to their good-natured, youthful banter. I hadn't even given guard duty a thought – and for once, didn't give a toss.

The walls of the pub were covered in badges and insignia from various military units – as well as banknotes from many different countries. I was particularly intrigued by a painting depicting a fire force operation, with little helicopters circling over brown and yellow bush – small insect-like figures moving through tall grass below… Some of the bush was on fire – a Lynx aircraft circled in the distance. The Moody Blues fined-tuned the atmosphere with their haunting music.

I remembered seeing early Vietnam movies where soldiers did the same thing we were doing – just having a good time, chewing the fat and remembering that the war wasn't everything. We were human beings after all. I loved the atmosphere in the pub that night – the music, the humour… our youth, being in uniform together – the camaraderie that cannot be felt or experienced at civilian gatherings.

I went to bed at about 11:30 p.m. – pissed, but immensely content. I had no idea at that stage that Kevin Torode was lost out in the bush all alone – nor did I care. I just followed Steve blindly to an immaculately-kept room with crisp, clean sheets on a solitary bed. I flopped onto it and fell into a totally dead sleep.

❦

A steward woke me up at 0700 with a cup of coffee and a smile. The sun beaming through the curtains was bright and crisp – as is normal after a rainstorm in Africa. I enjoyed the shower that followed, but felt dirty again putting on day-old, mud-caked clothes.

A lavish breakfast of bacon and eggs awaited me, which was surprising. Very few military or police units would have sufficient rations to splash out on unexpected guests, but I ate with the gusto of a young, hungry man. Strong coffee washed the meal down.

I was surprised to see the guys up and about, cleaning their rifles. They looked relaxed and refreshed – apart from Max, who was coaxing a huge hangover.

"You missed the action last night, sir."

"Action?"

"Some chicks from customs and immigration came to the pub after you left…"

A couple of the guys cat-whistled and made male masturbation motions.

"In your dreams…"

"Serious, sir," Max went on, "you missed your chance last night."

"Sure, grab a granny night. You've still got her false teeth on your knob…"

They laughed and threw things at Max.

"The major will be here just now, sir."

"So early?" I said, looking at my watch; must be important.

I walked over to the ops room. Steve was talking on the phone, but gave me the thumbs-up when he saw me. He was wearing regulation khaki shorts and shirt with a handgun strapped to his right hip.

"That was Mike Howard back at Vic Falls. No sign of Ncube... Just vanished into thin air. Got one gook as you know, and guess what?"

"Do tell..."

"Your sergeant went missing yesterday."

"Missing?"

"Got separated from his patrol in that storm."

"Idiot," I said, shaking my head. "How the hell do you get separated from guys you're leading?"

Steve chortled and swigged some coffee down. The sound of vehicles coming into the camp made me look out the window. It was the major in a two-five with an escort. I walked outside to meet him.

"Morning, sir," I said, standing to attention.

"Morning, Ballinger. Had a good rest?"

"Yes, sir. The cops live like kings here."

Steve gave me a discreet middle finger before casually saluting the major. Typical cop.

"I figured I could use you to fly the flag while you're down this way," Pearce said. "We haven't done any patrolling along the border with Botswana for a long time."

"Sir."

I was really chuffed. 'Flying the flag' just meant riding around on vehicles to show a presence. This would be a piece of piss.

"I've got a 60mm mortar and two cases of ammo to take with you."

"We seem to fly the flag a lot after screwing up, sir."

He gave me a caustic look, then smiled thinly. Pearce was a bit of a softy, really.

"That's why we show the flag, Ballinger..."

"Sir."

Two guys offloaded the weapon and its ammo. I hadn't seen a mortar apart from some basic and rudimentary training at Katanga. I knew the safest place to be if I fired that thing was the target! Pearce pulled out a map and spread it on the bonnet of a nearby Land Rover.

"This is where we are," he said, stabbing his finger at the map. "I want you to hover around the border post for a day – let the Botswana Defence Force see you. Let truck drivers and civvies going through the border post see you. I want word to get around that we have a presence in the area. I don't want any more lone gooks wandering around here like it's a bloody holiday camp."

"Yes, sir."

"Once you've done that, I want you to drive along the border fence as far as Pandamatenga and then come back to Kazungula."

"We've only got one vehicle, sir."

"I know. Some armoured cars will be along shortly. You'll be the infantry escort. It's nothing highbrow – just a local show of force."

"What do we do when we get back to Kazungula?"

"Stay here at the police camp until I make contact. You must report in every morning and evening at 0700 and 1700 respectively."

He went on for a short while reminding me about our call-signs, radio frequencies and boundaries. Rations, batteries, jerry-cans of diesel and boxes of ball ammo were loaded into our four-five.

We had barely finished chatting when the familiar sound of armoured car engines carried over the morning air to us.

"It's not exactly the American 4th Armoured," I said to Pearce as a single Eland and a tired old Ferret pulled into view. I pursed my lips and chuckled inwardly. Showing 'the flag' with that lot might bring more contempt than respect. The vehicles pulled up in front of us. A thick-set sergeant called Dave that I'd met earlier saluted both of us and hopped onto the gravel.

"Morning, sirs."

"Morning, sarn't. I've briefed Lieut Ballinger about your task. You can carry on whenever you're ready."

"Sir."

"I hear the cops here have a good pub," Pearce said, looking at me, "I think I'll try an orange squash before heading back."

We stood to attention as he walked off with Steve. I was sure a bit more of the cops' boozers fund was about to take another dent.

"One of the Elands broke down on the way here," Dave said to me. "I've left the infantry with them for protection."

"I thought we were supposed to be your infantry?"

"Yes, yours plus ours."

"Nice of Pearce to brief me on that one. Do you know the score; what our task is?"

"Yes, sir."

"Good. We may as well get away before the war changes Pearce's mind. Not too many cushy numbers come along like this one."

"Agreed. You follow us, sir?"

"Yes. Let's head for the border post for a while as instructed."

We checked our radio sets quickly before I shouted at the guys to mount up. The Eland fired up – turning in a slow circle on the grass near the charge office. We followed the Eland and the Ferret followed us. The commander of the Ferret was a blonde guy with a big hooked nose. I figured he would make a good pirate looking like that.

Our little convoy bounced through the front gate of the camp – turning right. The ground had a slight downhill slope to it and before long we were gliding effortlessly downhill towards the border post. There was no civilisation at all here – a panoramic view went down to the river on our right and a gentle valley to the left. The sun shone brightly – and already, tendrils of dust were kicking up behind the Eland as the well-drained dirt road dissipated rainwater from the day before.

The short drive gave me a chance to think about Mally and Ncube and Torode, the stupid shit. I just hoped I wasn't out for another month from base camp. I had fallen deeply for Mally and I wanted to be with her all the time now. Up to the point of meeting her I didn't really care about myself, but now that she was in my life, I felt a bit more hesitant about taking risks. I knew now how guys with wives and kids felt when their call-ups came around, or regulars who were away for months at a time on occasions. It was hard-going for all of us to be away from family and loved ones.

It wasn't long before we reached the border post with Botswana. There wasn't much to write home about. Two buildings behind a tall fence on the right-hand side of the road said it all. A little further on was a boom and guard post for an immigration official – and beyond that, a few buildings on the Botswana side under tall trees. A single, uniformed sentry from the Botswana defence forces paused in mid-stride, raised field glasses to his eyes and looked at us. Two more soldiers appeared as if by magic.

"We've impressed the locals," I said to Dave over the radio.

"Affirmative, that we have," came the metallic reply.

I told the drivers to park under some trees and put the guys in a semblance of all-round defence before strolling over to the immigration building. I waved cheerfully at the Botswana soldiers, but they didn't respond.

Dave, Corporal Kruger and I entered the typically dusty and hot front office area. Kruger nodded at two youngish white women who he recognised from the night before. The place was crammed with humanity… Babies crying on the back of women; the smell of rural humanity, flies and heat.

"Charming," I said, leaving the building. "This is gonna bore me to death."

I suddenly felt deflated and depressed about our mission. There wasn't going to be anything exciting and romantic about showing the flag; it would just be boring and hot and full of flies.

"Why don't we check out the bunker down by the river?" Dave said.

"Bunker?"

"I've been there before. I think the slopies built it when they were up here in the late '60s or whenever."

I thought about it for a minute. It didn't really breach our orders. Showing the flag north of the border post was just as good as showing it south.

"Okay, Dave. Lead the way."

We crossed back to our vehicles and climbed aboard one more time. Dave led the way around the back of the immigration buildings and then sharp-right (or north) down a sandy causeway that was surrounded by swamp on both sides. Large lizards scurried off the road as we approached. The bush here was non-existent because of swamp either side of the road – and only a few short trees lined the riverbank up ahead. We initially stopped to look at a bunker on the right-hand side of the road, but the view over the river was obscured by two trees – and, in any case, it was full of angry hornets. Abbott, forever the clown, came running out of the place swatting the large insects as they tried to sting him – much to the amusement of the others, of course! I enjoyed the way guys always took the piss out of someone else's misfortune.

We came to a run-down security fence and then a clearing at the back of another bunker – situated right on the riverbank itself – with a clear and commanding view of Zambia's immigration building on the other side of the 3-400 metre-wide river. This looked like a good place for a nap before moving on. I didn't realise it then, but the fence just off to our left was the border with Botswana.

Dave parked his Eland behind the bunker, while the commander of the Ferret parked upstream of a big tree on the bank of the river to our right. Our vehicle was parked next to the Eland.

I ordered the guys into the bunker. Dave opened the side hatch of the Eland and just sat there. The commander of the Ferret lit up a fag – resting his hand on a Browning machine-gun. It was cool and damp inside the bunker. I picked up my binos and studied the other side of the river – over in Zambia.

A long, flat-topped ferry with what looked like an engine on the side of it was moored on the far shore – anchored to a jetty of some sort. To the right of the ferry was a concrete ramp running into the Zambezi River – at the head of which stood the small Zambian customs and immigration building.

Along the shore to the left – or west of the ferry – was a well-concealed military bunker. Long reeds from the river obscured most of it, but it was plainly a military installation. Even as I watched, a couple of Zambian soldiers put on helmets and looked at us through binoculars. I looked at the river for a long while before losing interest. I strolled outside into the sunshine and studied a 15 metre steel communication tower set inland behind the Ferret. It offered an excellent viewing platform, so like a complete idiot, I climbed it. Corporal 'Gommo' Hill climbed with me. 'Gommo' sort of looked like a bobbo – a baboon – and could climb like one too. 'Gommo' and another guy called 'Mabrook' were renowned for their lack of hygiene. A joke circulated later in the war that when 'Mabrook' was taken by a croc, he gave the thing food poisoning – but I think 'Mabrook' came off second-best by the look of him when I saw him in Wankie Hospital. He was full of lacerations and teeth marks. However, both 'Mabrook' and 'Gommo' were beaten to the smelliest goalpost by 'Boots'... I can't remember his real name now, but he could literally empty an entire barrack block when his boots came off!

The view from the top of the tower was good. I could see over the Zambian bunker into the middle-distance. There was quite clearly a tented Zambian Army camp there with vehicles under a cluster of thorn trees. To the right of the Zambian customs building was a large steel water tank on a tower – and further right, a complex of brick buildings under asbestos-cement roof sheets obscured by more thorn trees. I had a good, long look at the Zambian bunker and its small complex of tents and vehicles before climbing down from the tower. My little observation stunt had apparently annoyed the Zambians, because suddenly, more had appeared around their bunker – helmets on, binos raised. Some even stood on the roof of their bunker to get a better look at us. For that matter, so had a couple of my guys on our side.

A few insults were traded at that point. Sound carried clearly across the dense air hovering above the cool waters of the river. We were accused of being children in uniforms; of being racists and Ian Smith's 'dogs'. We insulted their country and President Kaunda and told them their womenfolk were better soldiers than they were. All insults were exchanged in surprisingly good English. Well, Zambia was yet another former Brit colony after all...

We could sense the Zambian soldiers were getting annoyed with us, so we mocked them even more. Rifles started to appear – and those without helmets put them on.

I decided to up the ante and put the shits up the goons looking at us. Just behind our four-five was a length of black piping that could easily be mistaken for an anti-tank gun. I called four guys out of the bunker to pick it up and put it in a small depression that must have been a mortar pit once upon a time. A few of the Zambians climbed down from their bunker, while one continued to study us closely through binoculars.

"Dave, any chance of giving us some of your 90 mil shells?"

"What for, Sir?" Dave said wide-eyed. "You can't be serious?"

"I just want to wind them up a bit, Dave."

"I dunno, sir..."

"Come on, I'll take full responsibility. They can't mock good old Smithy like that."

Dave pursed his lips and disappeared inside the armoured car for a few seconds before returning with a long 90mm round from his main gun. The brass case glinted in the sunlight as he handed it to one of my guys – then another one and another one.

The Zambians had all disappeared now. My guys were chuckling away like a bunch of idiots – egging me on. The commander of the Ferret had a wide grin under his hooked nose.

"Guys, listen in. Pretend to run for cover… 'Fergie', make it look as if we're loading a round down the tube."

There was total silence; you could have heard a pin drop. At that point, I honestly thought it would just wind the Zambians up for a bit of a laugh, but the shots that cracked overhead changed the end-game in a heartbeat.

"For fuck's sake… Take cover!" I screamed in horror. "Set your sights to 300 metres. Fire at will!"

A brief pause of sight-adjusting was swallowed up by the throaty roar of Max's MAG and six rifles. I retraced my steps and legged it to the back of the truck – yanking two boxes of ball ammo into the bunker. Doppies piled up underneath the machine-gun, while others from rifles bounced off the next guy's head. I followed our tracer towards the Zambian bunker. It was smack-on. I noticed that Dave's armoured cars were silent.

"What's going on?" I mouthed to him above the uproar. He mimed that he wasn't allowed to use the Eland's main weapon. I went to the front of the bunker and decided to have a go myself. I adjusted my sights to 300 metres and took careful aim at the slit in the front of the Zambians' bunker – loosing off 40 rounds in spaced, aimed shots. Max's gun was eating the ammo up at a heck of a rate. I slapped him on the shoulder. He looked at me – eyes wide with a mixture of fear and excitement.

"Short, well-aimed bursts, Max!"

He nodded and licked the sweat off his lips before doing what I told him to do. 'Fergie' and one other guy started breaking open the wooden ammo boxes by picking them up and crashing them back onto the ground. They reloaded empty magazines other guys were dropping on the floor. In what seemed a few seconds, some of them had used up all 140 rounds they carried.

"Slow down your rate of fire!" I shouted in a brief lull. "Take better aim!"

I popped my head over the rim of the bunker. Even above the racket of all that weapons fire, I felt – rather than heard – enemy rounds hitting the corrugated iron sheets lining the front of our concrete bunker. That was truly hairy! Bullets aimed at us were landing only two feet below their intended target. There had to be another enemy bunker over there; the rate of fire we were pumping into the one we could see would definitely reduce or stop any return fire – and here we were, getting hit! I felt really concerned for my guys now. If small arms could hit us, so could something bigger. I kicked myself for starting this firefight, like some bloody kid. If one of my men got hurt, I would never forgive myself.

Dave must have said something to the commander of the Ferret by radio because all of a sudden, the blonde with the hooked nose popped up and opened fire with the car's Browning. Flames and smoke curled out the end of the barrel as he let off a 10-second rip.

A loud explosion went off behind us – maybe 50 metres back – then another one and another one. I felt a flutter of fear rise up within me. If my guys were scared, they didn't show it; they just hammered away with their weapons.

I sheltered my head behind the one corner column that supported the roof of the bunker. It was made of solid concrete and would afford me a bit of protection from rounds coming towards us. I fired off a third magazine before bending down to reload.

Just as I raised my head to fire again, I noticed a flash to the right on the Zambian shoreline near a big thorn tree. White tracer, clearly visible in broad daylight, cracked over the top of the Ferret – neatly cutting a few small branches off. 'Hook nose' disappeared liked greased lightning into the interior of the armoured car. It was a stroke of luck. Just as the cupola lid to his turret slammed shut, there was a loud explosion in the tree above him. A large section of the tree swayed for a brief moment before crashing on top of the Ferret.

This was getting serious now. They were firing RPGs, mortars and possibly a 12.7mm anti-aircraft gun at us. I knew a round of that calibre would go through both sides of the ancient armoured car like the proverbial hot knife through butter. Hell, the guys in there would be lucky if their armour stopped an AK round. We were losing – and I had to do something about it. 'Hook nose' and his mates were in real danger of being killed.

Getting hold of the mortar tube and setting it up under fire was a risk I wasn't willing to take. There was only one alternative: getting Dave to use the 90mm main gun of his armoured car on the Zambian bunker and any other likely targets. I told the guys to cease fire while I talked to him on the radio. Our ceasefire merely encouraged the Zambians to fire even more rounds at us.

"Can you fire on their bunker?" I repeated to Dave.

"You mean my main gun?"

"Affirmative. The situation warrants it."

"I'll have to get permission from my rear base."

I knew that anyway. Rhodesia officially didn't have any armoured cars. Their existence was denied by our government to prevent embarrassing South Africa, who supplied them to us. Using them meant getting special permission from 'higher up'.

"Get the permission – and when you do, take out that bloody bunker for starters!"

"With pleasure, sir."

I let our guys start firing again. Doppies tumbled into a growing pile of brass. A surprisingly short space of time elapsed before Dave started the Eland's engine up. As he manoeuvred into position, he opened his side door and gave me a thumbs-up with a big, cheesy grin all over his face. He indicated to me to put my hands over my ears when he fired. I returned the thumbs-up.

The rate of small arms fire coming at us dropped noticeably when the Eland's long barrel swivelled to face the opposite shore, but the 12.7 opened up again. I prayed and prayed that the operator of that impressive weapon was a lousy shot, or else Dave and his crew would be turned into Swiss cheese. Mortar shells exploded with a 'ca-rump' behind us – thankfully still far away.

I could tell by the small adjustments to the Eland's barrel that the gun was laid on target and ready to fire. I screamed at my guys to cease fire, get down and cover their eardrums. The end of the 90mm gun barrel was directly in line with the edge of our bunker – and at that very close range, the shockwave from the speeding projectile could do our eardrums some nasty damage.

I felt, rather than heard, the weapon fire. All eight of us poked our heads above the lip of the bunker to see a cloud of dust and smoke rising behind the Zambian bunker. Dave had missed. A small adjustment to the trajectory was made, and down we went again. When we looked up a second time, the bunker was spewing dust and smoke out if its slit trench. Two more rounds followed in quick succession. I was impressed by the speed of the round. Dave had barely fired when it reached inside the bunker 300 metres away. A small white plug of some type skidded over the water after each shot was fired.

"Next target at three o'clock, Dave… base of big tree… seen?"

"Seen."

Final adjustments to the barrel's elevation before two rounds sped off to their destination… A satisfying kwa-thump rolled down the valley a few seconds after each explosion. We jumped up and down yelling our approval. This was more like it!

Only five rounds had been fired, but already the wind had been taken out of the Zambian sails. A total silence fell over the land – and not even a bird chirped. Smoke and dust drifted west. Dave reversed the Eland behind the bunker one more time.

"Is everyone okay?" I said.

"Yes, sir! That was shit-hot, sir!"

"Fantastic!"

My body was still quivering from the adrenalin rush, but I had to act and think.

"Everyone, fill up your magazines with ammo. Abbott, you and 'Gommo' get the mortar off the truck and stick it inside that slit trench, there. Put the ammo just behind it in that depression," I said, pointing.

"Yes, sir."

I could hear Dave talking to someone on the radio. He wasn't on my radio net because nothing came out of my handset. I got hold of Major Pearce back at Vic Falls to tell him what had happened. He sounded casual about the report – well, he would be casual wouldn't he? He wasn't the one getting stonked! He instructed me to pull out when I felt it was safe to do so, then go back to the police camp.

"Sir," Dave said, leaning out of the armoured car.

"Yes? What's up?"

"We've been told to pull back to the customs post. Comops is having a fit in case this escalates any further."

"Typical – just when we needed you the most."

"I'm sorry about that, sir…"

"It's not your fault, Dave. Are you able to help us if we get into trouble?"

"Affirmative."

"Okay, good. That was excellent. Well done to your guys… We'll cover you if they open up again."

"Cheers, sir."

He slammed the 15mm steel door shut and started the engine. The Ferret puffed a few rings of smoke from its exhaust pipe before exiting its position very smartly indeed. Dave's car followed shortly thereafter, until we could hear their engines no more. I felt totally alone and exposed.

"Let's set up the mortar," I said to 'Fergie' and 'Gommo'. In less than a minute, the tube was resting on its bipod. It was pointless connecting the site or going any further because I had no plotting board, map or marker pole for the sight. I figured if we got stonked again, I would just lob a few bombs in the general direction of Zambia and hope for the best.

Things settled down after that. The guys had replenished their magazines, but there was no more ball ammo if we needed it. We had used one of the two boxes in the firefight, and the remainder went into our magazines and Max's ammo belts. Four guys broke open cardboard packets to help Max reload the gun's belts.

I picked up my binos and studied the other side. A little red car with two white civilians arrived at the customs post on the other side of the river. The one passenger was a female – and a rather attractive one at that. They disappeared into the building, but didn't come out again. I hoped they were okay because those Zambian idiots could get all bellicose after a licking. When Rhodesian forces hammered bases in Zambia, the white population there got beaten up and knocked about a bit – I guess because they were white and no other reason… a bit of payback.

Fifteen minutes later, while the white couple were still in the building, an ambulance arrived. It was not a civilian ambulance. Rather, it had that olive-green drabness about it with a large white circle and red cross superimposed on it.

"Check this out," I said to no-one in particular. Seven heads popped up to have a look.

A pair of orderlies walked around to the back of the ambulance and pulled out a stretcher. I followed their progress down a path that ran along the edge of the river – disappearing now and again behind shrubs and reeds. The stretcher-bearers paused at a spot that looked blacker than normal against the background. It was another bunker – smaller than the one Dave hit, but a bunker nonetheless. The orderlies had done me a favour by stopping to talk to someone there. I made a mental note of where it was.

A short while later, the orderlies returned to the ambulance. A prone, lifeless-looking body lay slumped on the stretcher. He was loaded with some difficulty into the back of the vehicle before they went back for a second and third casualty. A Zambian soldier, meanwhile, was poking his head around the corner of the customs building and looking at me through binoculars. I was tempted to shoot him – and knowing my skill with a rifle, would probably have got the bastard. The ambulance pulled away in a cloud of blue smoke that drifted slowly upwards. All was quiet again.

"Looks like a few are leaking," Abbott said with a sadistic smile.

"Mmm," was all I could manage as I continued to look through the binos. "Max…"

"Sir?"

"You see that large thorn tree about 50 metres to the right of the main bunker?"

"Yes, sir."

"Go diagonally down to the right – just above the water. There's like a dark patch there?"

"Seen, sir."

"That's another bunker. If the shit hits the fan again, I want you to empty a belt in there."

"Sir."

"Then slowly sweep the reeds left and right of the main bunker."

"Sir."

It was now mid-afternoon – and I expected that was the end of it. What I didn't know at that point was that we had killed a few of the Zambians and injured 17 others – some lightly, others quite severely. The Zambians took exception to what we did, and over the months and years that followed, Kazungula turned into an ongoing mini conventional war. The SAS had to be called in to lay mines in Zambia and 105mm Howitzers were deployed to crush opposition there. Rumours swirled that a battalion of Zambian troops were moved to the area with Stalin Organs. Whether that was just a rumour or not, I will never know.

The police camp, several months later, received serious damage from heavy mortars fired from Zambia – with one shell landing square on top of an Eland armoured car parked there for the night.

It started again at about 1600 with a single rifle shot cracking over our bunker. I told the guys to open fire before physically pulling 'Gommo' out the bunker to assist me with the mortar. My knowledge of the weapon was pathetic, but I knew enough about the correct charge to use and how to elevate and rotate it. That was good enough for me.

"Room for one more, sir?" Abbott said, imitating a local deodorant advert.

"Abbot... Just get in the trench!"

I checked the charge on the first shell, rotated the fuse head to make it live, got the guys to position the mortar as I wanted it and slid the round down the tube. The shell left the barrel with a satisfying ka-thoonk – accelerating high into the air before being defeated by the pull of gravity to come racing down on its target. On this occasion, a croc and a hippo got the shit scared out of them.

"Add 25 metres," I said to myself. "Drop the barrel slightly, guys!"

My target was the immediate vicinity of the main bunker, and then the vehicles and tents behind it. I watched the shell arc into the air and explode with a satisfying ca-rump just beyond the bunker. I eased back on the tube just a fraction and dropped two more shells down it in quick succession. Smoke and dust shrouded the bunker.

"Swivel the tube slightly that way," I said, indicating to the left. I kept one of the charges on each of the next 10 shells and dropped them with satisfying accuracy around the nest of vehicles and tents. Smoke started a lazy spiral upwards into the air.

Maybe I did a stupid thing then, but I decided to hit the ferry with a couple of mortar rounds. They were near-misses though, and spouts of water leapt into the air. Anyway, the SAS finished off the ferry sometime later when it was discovered it was being used to move ZIPRA gooks in and out of Zambia and into Botswana.

"Three o'clock right, 'Gommo'!" He swivelled it to the right. I added one more charge. The target was the base of the tree where the 12.7 had been firing from. The first two rounds were wide of the mark – landing among buildings in the middle-distance. The next six rounds were spot-on-target – and once more, a faint spiral of smoke curled upwards. The bush near the tents and vehicles had caught alight beautifully by this stage – and snarling, twisting orange flames leapt into the air.

I had no conscious thought about bullets coming back at us, but it didn't bother me. My nerves had settled and I was having a fantastic time. I did notice a strange smell though, and in the heat of the battle, noticed 'Boots' standing in the slit trench near me – popping off magazine after magazine into enemy territory.

"Don't hit that red car, 'Boots'! It's not their fault they're in this war!"

Those poor bloody white civvies must be shitting themselves – and who knows what the Zambians would do to them afterwards?

Our fire was steady and constant, but in one brief pause I noticed that nothing was coming back at us. The mortars, which scared the shit out of me, had stopped – so had the 12.7 and the odd RPG7 – but I didn't give a shit. They started the serious part of this, and I was darn well going to end it.

I checked the ammo boxes and saw at least another 15 shells in them. I turned the tube back to the main army camp I'd seen from the tower earlier in the day and dropped the lot in a wide arc around the area. As the last shell flew into the air, so I picked up my rifle and headed back for the bunker. In so doing, I kicked off the edge of the slit trench where a nest of hornets were camped. They took off in an angry mob – zipping this way and that until 'Boots', Abbott, 'Gommo' and I were running in circles trying to swat them off us. To hell with bombs and bullets; this was serious shit! One big bastard zeroed in on me and machine-gunned my top lip. The pain was excruciating and my eyes poured buckets of tears. I was blinded by water pouring out my eyes – and a few seconds later, I couldn't speak as my top lip swelled up like a balloon. I'll never forget the look on Al Currie's face when I staggered back into the bunker. He must've thought I'd been hit – the first casualty of the punch-up! Not bad results really – 17 Zambian casualties versus one seriously swollen lip!

The sun sank into the western horizon in an orange and pink glow, with smoke forming around it like a halo. Yellow, angry flames leapt into the air – reflecting off the darkening river. The sky to the east, just above the distant escarpment, was purple bordering on black; total silence – apart from the crackle of flames. The entire opposite bank was alight now.

"Start preparing to leave, guys," I said with a lisp. Max cackled.

"Got yourself a harelip there, sir."

"Thuck off, Maxth," I slobbered. The pain was unbearable.

We packed in silence in the growing dark. I radioed Dave that we were coming back to the customs post. I knew our truck would be a target if we tried to drive out with the headlights on. Even the brake lights would be visible.

"Kenny."

"Sir?"

"Get some of those cardboard ammo boxes and put them over the brake lights."

"Yes, sir."

"Listen in," I said to all of them. I could hardly see their faces now. "Get the mortar back on the truck – plus any personal kit – and then walk out the gate until you're about 200 metres back. Wait for me there. Who's got the keys to the truck?"

"I have," said Kenny, handing them to me.

"Right. Sort yourselves out and get going. You're in charge, Corporal Kruger."

"Yes, sir."

They fumbled around for a while putting stuff quietly onto the back of the truck before marching in a single column out the gate. I counted slowly to 60 before climbing into the cab. It was now or never. If the Zambians heard the truck start, they could light me up like a Christmas tree. I flicked the ignition switch and the engine idled over straight away. Selecting reverse gear, I eased the clutch out – pointing the bum of the truck at the river. The reverse light and brake lights were hidden behind the empty cardboard boxes our bullets were normally packaged in. I kept the headlights off, and peering out the side window of the cab to overcome the dashboard glare, rolled the vehicle slowly out the gate at minimum revs. My heart was in my throat, but nothing happened.

I picked up the guys a short distance down the road and drove for about another hundred metres before turning on the headlamps. I was glad I switched them on because we were heading straight for the swamp. That bloody river was determined to swallow one of my trucks!

Dave was standing by his armoured car when we got back to the customs building – hands on hips. My lip had swollen to four times its normal size by this point.

"You stirred up more shit, hey sir?"

"Not thliss thym," I dribbled.

"What the hell happened to your lip?"

"Thucking thornet... thla thucking thing!"

"Ouch! That looks einaar!"

We got into convoy formation and prepared to head back to the police camp eight kays away. A startled guard, looking after the immigration buildings, stared wide-eyed at this weird bunch of white men – one of whom spoke with a swollen lip and waved us on our way as if he could stop us doing whatever we wanted to do, the thsupid thucker!

The whole police camp came out to greet us when we rolled to a standstill in front of the brightly-lit charge office. I found the lights such a contradiction to what I'd just experienced.

"Warmongers," Steve joked as we jumped down from the vehicles.

"Unplanned and unprovoked, of course..."

"Anyone hurt?"

"Not on our side, but saw a few with leaks getting loaded into an ambulance."

"Good stuff. We need to celebrate."

I told Kruger to sort the guys out and make some grub. Steve gave me an anti-histamine tablet from a first aid box to bring the swelling down in my lip.

The cook made Steve and I steak and egg rolls, which we carried through to the veranda. Although I was a fool provoking the attack, I felt relieved no-one was hurt and sort of unwound like a clock spring after a couple of beers. It left me feeling totally drained.

"So, tell me what happened," Steve said. I told him most of the story – not quite sure if he would react as a cop or an acquaintance. Dave made eye-contact and smiled slightly when I left out the fact that I provoked the whole incident.

I enjoyed sitting and relaxing after the day's activities – wondering for the tenth time when this brightly-lit oasis would be wiped off the face of the Earth.

Around 2200 that night, the sounds of heavy thuds and explosions reached us from the west, in the direction of the bunker. We stared at each other in silence. My heartbeat accelerated.

"Let's have a look," Steve said, springing up.

I followed him back through the pub, out past the charge office and as far as the high communications tower. Without breaking his stride, he tossed his beer bottle away and started climbing rapidly up the access ladder – confirmation Steve had gone totally bush-happy.

"Come on!" he yelled down to me. All I could see was the white soles of his shoes.

I took a long swig from my beer before tossing the bottle on the grass nearby. I hated heights at the best of times. I took a firm grip of the cool metal rungs and went up one cautious step after the other. A gentle easterly breeze got stronger the higher I went. We stopped at an intermediary platform about 40 feet up. We didn't need to go any higher.

The sky to the west was a dull-orange glow, with clouds of smoke lit from within like a cauldron. Several heavy ka-dooms and thuds followed each other in slow, measured gaps.

"Looks like my little trick worked, Steve."

"Trick?"

"I stuck cardboard boxes over the back lights of the truck when I drove it away from the bunker. They probably think we're still there."

"Well, someone's getting it. I hope a few over-shoot and land in Botswana."

"Mmm..."

We sort of 'hung' there in silence for a few minutes – listening to the hammering an empty bunker was getting.

"I've got an idea," Steve said suddenly. "Let's give them a rev from the river."

"No Steve. I've had enough for the day, honestly."

"Come on, man. They have an army camp right on the river about two kays west of here. Their officers' quarters face the water… Just a quick rev into the windows."

I knew it was the alcohol talking. I also knew it was the alcohol listening.

"C'mon, man. Let's give the fuckers a rev!"

"What the hell. Why not?"

We reached the bottom of the tower a lot quicker than we went up. I told the guys our plan. I was surprised that most said it was a daft idea – should leave it well alone. Max volunteered his MAG, but it was virtually out of ammo.

"You leave that with me," Steve said. He disappeared into the night – returning several minutes later with four belts of MAG ammo. "Compliments, Intake 146!"

I picked up my rifle, checked the ammo and the three of us walked down to the jetty. We hopped into the left of two boats. Max unfolded the legs of the MAG and rested it on the engine cowling. The boat had an internal jet-wash engine that sucked water in before forcing it out a back nozzle, under pressure.

A single twist of the key made the powerful motor kick into life. Steve untied the bow lines, while I did the others at the back. The water was dark and swift-flowing; the shore opposite us a black smudge against a pale sky. I felt foolish and irresponsible – knowing full well I would get court-martialled for this if something went wrong – but I was also excited.

Steve nudged the accelerator forward – spinning the steering wheel to the left. The current caught the head of the boat, trying to push it to the right. He accelerated slowly until the throttle was fully open, and we were zooming along at an impressive speed. White spray hissed past us on either side, but up ahead, the water was smooth and dark – reflecting the stars to perfection. It made me feel like we were soaring through the heavens rather than riding in a boat.

Our journey west continued for about six minutes. I enjoyed the sensation of power and speed – the openness and freedom. The boat seemed to follow its own path down the silver stretch of water – blackened banks of bush sweeping by. Suddenly, Steve decelerated until we were just keeping our head against the flow of the river.

"That's the army camp there," Steve said, pointing to the right. A complex of buildings nestling among thorn trees was clearly visible under the starlight – even though it was in total darkness. Zambian soldiers based there must have decided to keep a blackout because of events earlier in the day.

"Max, get ready to fire," I said. I cocked my own weapon in readiness. "Steve, turn the boat so that Max's gun can come to bear."

Steve spun the wheel – keeping the boat heading diagonally towards the Rhodesian bank.

"When I open fire, put all your ammo into the large windows there…"

I picked up my rifle and aimed down the top of the barrel. It was impossible to see through the sights. With adrenalin racing through me, I pulled the trigger. A small flash erupted in front of me – and then another and another and another…

Max's weapon tore into the night. The end of the barrel glowed and flashed as 600 rounds per minute left the barrel – an impressive sight – with so much red tracer streaming away from us like scalded cats. Tracer entered the building – dying instantly as it ploughed into brick and plaster. A few tracer cartwheeled up into the sky. I emptied three magazines one after the other – and then, it was all over… in less than 30 seconds.

"Let's get out of here, Steve! Go, go, go!"

Steve floored the accelerator. The bow rose up sharply – dropping a few seconds later as the boat planed out. Max and I pulled ourselves up from the side of the engine where we'd landed during the acceleration. All three of us were laughing from the release of tension and fear.

Steve banked the boat left and then sharp-right until we were racing away downstream – our wake a white froth against the blackened waters of the river. Not a single shot had been fired back at us.

I learned some time later from Steve that we'd succeeded in smashing the new plate-glass windows belonging to the Zambian Army officers' mess during our little escapade. Who knows, perhaps that was the real reason for them turning Kazungula into a classical war zone for the next three years…

We spent the next couple of days based up at the Police Station in case we had to react to retaliation from Zambia. Dave's other two armoured cars had joined us. We spent most of the time fishing. The downside was we had to pay for our beers now! On the afternoon of the third day, I received a message to return to Vic Falls the following morning to link up with the balance of my platoon. It was time for re-deployment.

I enjoyed that last night at Kazungula police station. There were a lot of us in camp and it was like a big party. We braaied meat bought from town on a police resupply run and had our share of beers too. It was one of those nights of camaraderie that you don't forget – a brief time to feel young and free and forget about the troubles the adults of the world had led us into. The stars twinkled in the sky – a warm breeze enveloped us; crickets screeched in the bush. How I loved this life – and how I loved my country. They say that once you get Africa under your skin, you will never forget about her. The image of the guys around the fire that night will stick with me forever. It was the last time I saw the police camp or its bush-happy OC. I heard some time later that Steve went totally off the wall and had to be discharged from the police.

Our small convoy arrived back in camp at 0800 the next morning. The remainder of the platoon had just eaten breakfast. A very embarrassed and sulky-looking Torode sat in the canteen drinking a cup of coffee. I didn't really know what to say, so I ignored him. I ordered a bacon sandwich from the cook before giving Pearce and Von Stranz a de-brief. My statement about how the fighting started didn't seem all that convincing in the light of day. Both of them tried to suppress a smile.

"We'll have to call you 'Bomber Ballinger' from now on," Pearce said.

"Yes, sir," I said in embarrassment.

"Sort your guys out to return to Jambezi tomorrow. Pete should've deployed there, but he's in hospital, as you know…"

My heart sank. I really didn't want to go back to that keep so soon. The turnaround was at least three weeks there. Mally was only 200 metres away and I had to go back to Jambezi. I felt depressed.

"How's Pete and the others doing, sir?" I said, changing the subject.

"Not sure, really. Captain Von Stranz will be popping down to see them in an hour or two."

"Is there a chance I could come along, sir? Pete and I have been together since Llewellin."

"I suppose that'll be okay," Von Stranz said, after a pause. "You can stay at the officers' mess at 4 Indep. Get Sarn't Torode to start issuing stores and ammo today. You can deploy tomorrow afternoon."

"Thanks, sir. Do you need me for anything else?"

They both shook their heads. I gulped down the dregs of my coffee before finding Torode to brief him.

"You know what to do, Kevin. Full ammo count, fuel and rations for the first week. Batteries and radio checks. I'll look all over with you first thing tomorrow."

He nodded and looked at the floor. I felt uncomfortable in his presence, so I went outside and had a chat with the rest of the guys in the platoon. I liked every single one of them. We were all just kids really, and I found it hard to be an officer around them. I just wanted to be their mates. Now I knew what 'The Smiling Shit' meant when he said I was too familiar with my subordinates, but I knew in my heart they would follow me anywhere because I was no chicken-shit.

I was halfway through a joke Corporal Orchard was telling the guys when I realised I could sneak out of camp for half an hour and see Mally. My heart raced at the thought of it. I waited in suspense for the end of Roy's joke and then ambled away towards the far end of the camp. I turned once to make sure no-one was looking and took off like a rabbit trying to escape the pot. I reached her front door breathless, but relieved she was in.

"Tony!" she said, leaping into my arms – wrapping her legs around my back. I held her tight against me. Oh, the smell of her as we kissed.

"I've missed you!"

"Me too. Come in… How long are you in town for?"

"Less than an hour."

"You're joking?" she said, pulling back from me – her smile fading.

"I'm dead serious. I have to be back in camp in about 30 minutes. I'm going down to Wankie for the night to see Pete Wells and the other guys."

Seeing Mally in the flesh made me angry with myself. I could've spent the night here with her, but I needed to see Pete.

"We better not waste any time then," she said, taking me by the hand.

We went through to the bedroom. It was cool and fresh-smelling in there. I took in her dressing table with all those ladies' things all over it – lipstick, make-up, jewellery… Shoes kicked under it.

"It takes ages to get my boots off…"

"No need," she said, kissing me. She pushed me gently backwards – undoing my shirt as she did so. The smell and warmth of her was divine – so sensual after the fear and adrenalin of the last few days.

Our lovemaking was intense, yet tender – deep needs were met and satisfied in the mystery that sex is.

"I have to go," I said a while later. I wasn't sure if I'd fallen asleep or not.

"I love you Tony," Mally said in a sleepy voice.

"I love you too. More than you'll ever know…"

I got off the bed and walked through to the bathroom to wash myself off – taking a hot cloth back to her.

"Got time for coffee?"

I looked at my watch.

"No," I said, shaking my head. "I'd love to, believe me."

"Okay babe. I'm gonna catch a nap for a while… Miss you already."

"I miss you too," I said, kissing her forehead tenderly.

❧—❦

The ride down to Wankie passed in a bit of a blur. The polite conversation between Von Stranz and I ended about 20 minutes into the 90-minute journey. I was glad because it gave me time to reflect on my life, on Mally and my time here at Vic Falls. I realised I had fallen totally and utterly for her, I wanted to be with her every minute of the day. It was sheer agony being apart from her. I loved the Falls too – no wonder it was one of the world's Seven Wonders. I wanted to be a part of the place; to build a life there, perhaps… Young, immature thoughts and hopes in a dying land?

The beautiful tall trees that lined the road south-east of Vic Falls soon gave way to the rugged, dark-green hills that led to Wankie. The heat increased the more we descended towards the mining town. I could smell the coalfields long before the village came into view. We bounced over the expansion joints of a bridge near 1 Indep and we were suddenly in Wankie. I sat upright and withdrew from my reverie.

"What a shithole, sir," I said. Von Stranz smiled and nodded, but didn't say anything. I guess he'd been lost with his thoughts, also. Four kays later, we passed the turn-off to the village, with the big railway steam engine mounted on green grass as a permanent display, then round the corner to the turn-off to the Baobab Hotel up on the hill – the place Pete and I had had a drink together four months earlier when we first arrived at 4 Indep. I felt depressed.

"I just have to drop an envelope off at the base; then we can go see Pete," Von Stranz said.

It was weird driving into the camp again. I sort of looked at it through different eyes now. It was no longer intimidating. A guard saluted as we drove through the gates. We turned left and wound our way up the hill to the admin block where I had first seen Major Pearce so long ago. I waited while he dropped the envelope off and then we retraced our route to the big steam engine before turning left up a small incline towards the village. The road was lined by flamboyant trees that were in full bloom. It was a pretty village – colonial in design. All the buildings had big verandas and roofs covered in corrugated iron.

The hospital was a relatively modern, sprawling single-storey complex set among neat lawns and colourful gardens. Cannas and bougainvilleas competed to be the most colourful. I hate hospitals with a passion, and I recoiled as the smell of anaesthetic and disinfectants entered my nostrils. I didn't know what to expect and walked down the corridor in trepidation. The sight that greeted my eyes was far from what I expected. I heard a screech and a yelp, followed by peals of laughter.

Pete was rushing hell-for-leather in a wheelchair towards us – his face set in a wide smile, arms spinning away. Close behind him was Tex Brown. They were having a wheelchair race! I felt instantly relieved as images of torn limbs and wires attached to bodies fled my mind.

"Pete!" I said, as he zoomed by. He just smiled wider before continuing around a corner – soon disappearing from sight. He returned a short while later, breathless but ecstatic.

"Another beer Tex owes me!" he said, shaking my hand. "Good to see you, Tony!"

Pete's right leg was stretched stiffly out ahead of him wrapped in blood-stained plaster. He looked a bit pale and had lost some weight, but was still full of crap. I greeted Tex Brown and shook his hand before he wheeled himself down the passage.

"That's three beers, Tex!" Pete called after him. All he got was a disrespectful middle finger in return.

Von Stranz, Pete and I went a short way down the hall before turning left into a well-lit and airy ward with one other person in it. Several empty beds separated the two occupants.

"Matron will kill me if we get caught doing that," Pete said, as he hobbled back to his bed before launching himself onto it. A shadow of pain crossed his high brow.

"What's the latest on the leg?" Von Stranz said.

"Touch and go for an amputation… Specialists wanted it off, but the doc here's fantastic. He refused and said he could save it. I had an op a week ago to try and join the bones together. He took some bone out my hip; hurt more than the bullet. We're just waiting now to see if they mend strong enough for me to walk on."

"I'm sure they will," I said, stupidly. "What happened that night, Pete?"

A look of pain crossed Pete's eyes, but it wasn't pain from the wound. He shook his head and looked out the window.

"It was a cock-up."

"What do you mean?"

There was a long pause before he replied – as if he was fighting an inner battle.

"We'd gone walkabout earlier in the night. Tex can speak Shona and he'd heard gooks were about, so we set up an ambush on the cut-line. We'd barely settled into our pozzie when I saw a gook walking towards me – maybe a bit further than the door there… I was the one who had to initiate the contact; my weapon wasn't cocked. I had someone else's weapon – a shitty Bren gun, you know? I tried to cock it…" His voice trailed off.

"And they heard you?"

Pete nodded – looking far away. He was obviously beating himself up for getting two other men injured.

"He opened fire from me to you; it was that close, Tony. A big orange ball of flame erupted in my face. I was sitting up. I have no idea how I didn't die. The bullets the gook fired were armour-piercing. One bounced off my shattered leg, smashed the stock of the Bren gun and ended up in my gut – almost taking my little finger off in the process."

A long silence fell between us.

"It could've happened to anyone, Pete. You're human," I said. Von Stranz nodded in agreement.

"You can make all the excuses you like. I cocked it up. I spent so much time making sure my guys were jacked up, I forgot to look at myself."

"Don't blame yourself. You're a good soldier and an even better leader. No-one respects you any less."

After a long pause, Pete said: "A perfect kill turned into a perfect cock-up."

I felt awful for Pete. I knew how hard he tried. I knew he cared for his guys and drove them hard to protect them. Things had to be 'just so' with him – and despite this, fate crept in through the back door. I respected and admired him no less.

"How's Tex and Rootman?" I said at length.

"You saw Tex. He's doing well, but I'm really worried about Rootman, though. He got it in the liver and lung. It's touch and go, still."

"Where's he now?"

"Down there in intensive care," he gestured with his hand. "I hear that Ncube escaped?"

"Mmm, unbelievable. Must have been an inside job."

Von Stranz looked silently at me. I wonder what he knew?

"And you helped in the follow-up?"

"Ja. The guy just disappeared into thin air halfway to Kazungula."

"And you've been toying with the Zambians?"

"News travels fast, hey? We gave a few some leaks."

"Good kit, Tony. Just wish you'd nailed Ncube."

"His time will come."

Another silence broke the flow of conversation. I suspected that Pete felt really rotten about his ambush going sour, or maybe he was just plain tired?

"I'll pop in to see Rootman," I said, standing up. I shook Pete's hand and left him there with Von Stranz.

I walked down the corridor until I came to a reception desk for the intensive care ward. I asked where Rifleman Rootman was and if it would be okay to visit him. The duty nurse checked it with the matron, who okayed it, with the proviso that it was a short visit.

I walked slowly up to Rootman's bed. The hospital didn't really have an intensive care ward. It surprised me he hadn't been sent on to Salisbury. I didn't know Rootman at all – he was one of Pete's guys, after all. His chest was tightly bandaged, with blood seeping through it. A small mechanical pump beneath his bed sucked excess blood from his damaged lung. He opened his eyes when he sensed my presence.

"Hello, sir," he said weakly.

"Hello Rootman. How're you doing?"

"Getting there, sir."

I felt tears well up in my eyes. They were tears of anger – as well as compassion. To me, the war had just been a game to date, but seeing Rootman lying there struggling to breathe with pipes coming out of him was too much. He was the epitome of everything I hated about hospitals.

"Have you seen your folks? Got everything you need?"

"Yes, sir," he said, shutting his eyes, and then suddenly: "am I going to die, sir?" The comment caught me off-balance.

"No, the doc says you're doing very well," I lied.

"Good, I don't want to die, sir."

I got all choked-up then. I didn't know what to say. What could I say? That he looked like shit and I thought he wouldn't see the week out? That he was as pale as a corpse?

"You'll be back in time to put Ncube in his grave. Just rest and get better."

"Yes sir… Thanks for coming."

"It's the least I could do." I squeezed his forearm. He smiled through cracked lips – eyes still shut.

I felt heavy-hearted and depressed as I walked down the corridor back to Pete's ward. I paused to let the tears and emotion leave me before I went in to see him again, but he was asleep already, so Von Stranz and I drove back to 4 Indep in silence – alone with our own thoughts.

It had all been a game up to this point. Now, my innocence was dead in the wink of an eye. Something changed in me then. Maybe I grew up in that moment? I knew I could never treat the lives of my men lightly or superficially ever again. From then on, I would act my age and rank.

🌿—🌿

It felt like we'd left Jambezi the day before – and now we were on our way back there again. News had trickled through to us that two groups of terrs had attacked Jambezi the night I went to Dekka Drum to get beers. One group of 30 came south from a hideout in the vast expanse of uninhabited bush north of the main dirt road and the Zambezi River, while another group of 20 moved north-west from a camp near the Matetsi River. It transpired that nearly 50 gooks had hit the camp that night. I was convinced they had spies among us to choose the night of attack. How did they know so few guys were there when they attacked? From that day on, I looked upon the Internal Affairs guards with a great deal of suspicion and mistrust.

We took a different route to Jambezi this time. We went further south-east along the tar road, past the airport, until we reached a secondary road and turned left (or east). The area was heavily-inhabited and no doubt was the source of succour for the likes of Ncube and his band of merry thugs. I was surprised that protected villages hadn't been erected in the area to cut off food and other supplies the terrorists needed from the local population. The principle behind the protected village was to make the rural peasants sleep in huts behind barbed wire at night. Generally speaking, gooks got fed at night. Take away their food, and you force them out into the open where they might make mistakes. It also denied gooks the luxury of having R&R and sex with local women. The system was used very effectively by the British in Malaya.

We bought huge watermelons just before the turn-off to the keep, while the locals 'twisted their torsos' to look at us. They portrayed an indifferent attitude towards us and were quite happy to get our coins in exchange for their delicious fruit. The African peasants, in general, did not show hate towards us.

Taking an alternate route to the base wasn't the only thing that had changed. I had changed. I was different. This wasn't cops and robbers anymore. People got hurt and killed in this business. The thought of it made me mildly depressed. I wasn't as keen to get to the keep as I was the first time round. I knew the loss of my innocence and naivety would bring the weight of responsibility down on my shoulders. I was directly responsible for the welfare of 33 young human beings in the prime of their life. I did not want to see any Rootmans among my men.

It was quite weird driving into the compound – towards sunset. The place hadn't changed at all – like time had stood still. Ian and 'Nipple' strolled out to greet us like they did that first time so long ago. We slapped each other's backs and shook hands. I told them we had watermelons, beers and cokes – as well as a few newspapers and magazines. They were chuffed. I told Kevin to position the guys exactly as we did the last time – roughly eight men to a bunker. Ammo must be removed from the trailer and distributed equally in each position. Men must sleep closer to their allotted bunker and head straight for it in the event of an attack. Communications between each stick leader was essential – and for that reason, a radio was kept inside the blast wall of each bunker all the time.

"It's good to see you," Ian said. "Come to stir up some shit again?"

"Not this time," I said, shaking my head. "Just routine patrols and ambushes."

"Why? It worked last time."

"That's why it won't work again, Ian. Anyway… I've had a change of heart." He pursed his lips and shrugged. "What's happened since we left?"

"Nothing. Things have gone dead since the Scouts killed some of the gooks that attacked us."

"Mmm… Let's have a beer and in an hour or so I want to try standing to without warning the guys."

Ian looked out the corner of his eye at 'Nipple' as if to say: "What's crawled up his ass?"

I sat at the cheap formica dining table under the glare of the naked lightbulb. It was hot and oppressive in there, but at least we could sit with a light on. The golden beer took some of the edge off – perhaps it wasn't so bad, after all.

"I've been thinking, Ian. This place looks like a bloody spaceship at night with all these lights on. I'm convinced the gooks' mortar fire was so accurate the last time because they had a point of reference to aim at. In future, if we get attacked I want the generator killed."

"But we need the security lights to see them coming."

"Those guys haven't got the balls to assault this place, Ian. I'm telling you, the lights are counter-productive – especially under mortar fire."

"Perhaps…"

"Okay, I'll compromise. If they attack with mortars, the lights go off until they stop stonking us. They can't move infantry forward while they're bombing us; then, we'll turn them back on to blind any gooks on the ground… Agreed?"

"Agreed," Ian said at length. I didn't really care whether he agreed or not. The army had priority in situations like this anyway.

I made some supper out of 'pressed pig' and biscuits before easing back in my chair to chat to the guys for a while. An hour later, when it was pitch-black, I walked out to the bunker nearest me and fired a full magazine of bullets over the camp's buildings. Tracer sped off into the inky blackness of night. The camp exploded into life as guys scrambled to and fro – cursing and slipping on the stony soil. It was a complete cock-up. Some guys arrived inside bunkers without webbing or ended up going to the wrong place altogether. I spent the next half-hour re-organising everything – and an hour later, repeated the exercise. Things had improved noticeably.

After the guard was set, I climbed on top of Alpha bunker and had a quiet drink with Kevin, 'Nipple' and Ian. The bush looked dark and sinister outside the halo of light cast by the security lamps. Was there somebody watching us out there? Were we going to get revved again? I became silent as the others spoke in quiet undertones – looking up at the millions of stars twinkling in the Milky Way overhead. How puny we were compared with its majesty. I figured the Creator of all of that must be looking down at His creation – a creation gone bad – and wept.

I definitely didn't want to start a war again. The injured guys I'd seen – plus the stonking we received at Kazungula – had tempered me a lot. I decided on routine patrols, cordon and searches, and ambushes – and nothing else. The rains had ended early, and already the green grass – what there was of it in the over-shagged TTL – was turning yellow already.

The days turned into weeks – and with every passing hour, my frustration and irritation mounted to the point where I wanted to explode. I was trying to do everything by the book and I also missed Mally like crazy. I just couldn't bear to be out of her company anymore. My initial indifference to being drafted into the army was turning into resentment. I was, after all, a civilian in uniform.

Any person who has served in the military will tell you that war is 96 percent 'wait and see' and four percent blind fear and terror. About two weeks into the camp, the pendulum swung towards the four percent.

It started with a curfew-breaker that Kevin Torode shot. I was out of camp when the body was dumped unceremoniously into the keep for SB to have a look at. The sight that greeted me made me want to vomit and added to my growing distaste for the waste of human life.

The man, probably in his mid-forties, was lying on his back – arms spread-eagled. He had been hit in the chest and head. The back half of his skull was missing and chickens that normally had the run of the keep before ending up in a pot, were picking at his brains. I didn't know whether to laugh or cry, so I just stared like everyone else. It put me off chicken for months.

I had a sneaky suspicion that this was the 'straw that broke the camel's back' for Torode. He became sullen and long-faced. He disappeared for good during our next R&R.

A few days later, a Coca-Cola truck heading for the African store about 20 kays west of us hit a landmine. Ian's guys reacted to the incident and commenced a follow-up. I arrived after the driver's body had been removed from the cab – what was left of him that is.

It didn't take a genius to realise that the vehicle hit a mine on our new route into Jambezi, which meant the gooks were onto us – watching us day and night no doubt. The upside of the incident was a hefty supply of cokes and Fanta orange for weeks to come – having been liberated from the truck as 'evidence' by Ian and 'Nipple'.

I think boredom more than anything persuaded me, in the third week of the camp, to start putting pressure on peasants around the keep one more time. I did this initially by ambushing kraals near the chief's village – deliberately letting them know we were in the area… harassing them. We, as national servicemen, didn't have the training, knowledge or sophistication of integrating with gooks like the Selous Scouts did; to call in Fireforce for a major kill. We could only beat around the bush so to speak, in the vain hope that we would get a response or have a contact. It was a hopeless task really, and I think our armed forces lost a lot of valuable opportunities and manpower by not specialising our training. We had extremely able and talented soldiers in our Indep companies like Theo Nel, BCR, who went on to join the RLI and pass his Selous Scout selection course at the end of the war. There were lots like him – tough, talented soldiers fucking about in the bush trying to kill gooks who laughed their cocks off at our vain attempts to find them.

In my opinion, all Indep soldiers who passed the requisite selection courses should have become para-trained and used as supporting troops in air assaults into Zambia and Mozambique – not necessarily as assault troops, but in secondary roles like stop-groups. This would have taken a lot of exhaustion and pressure off the regular boys. Rumours did the rounds at one time that this was in the offing – and I think a grave mistake was made not carrying it through. Towards the end of the war, less and less men took on more and more tasks. It opened the floodgates of gooks into Rhodesia.

One evening I decided to go out and burn a few food storage bins – as well as bush lining the road to Jambezi from the north. I was irresponsible and foolish going in a single vehicle, but felt the risk was worth it because of the total lack of action in the area. In any case, I intended to stay relatively close to the keep.

We set off at dusk, with a view to travel to the main dirt road running west to east parallel with the Zambezi River gorge about 15 kays away. I left Roy Orchard in camp with a stick and put four or five guys on the back of my four-five.

Kenny was on the back – facing outwards with his MAG. Bomford, Duff and Corporal Kruger were just behind him – plus one or two other guys.

I don't know what made me do it, but I told the driver I wanted to drive – and he hopped onto the back of the truck. I settled into the driver's seat, stuck my rifle in its rack by the door and headed out into the darkening landscape.

The headlamps cast a yellowy-white glow into the bush as we proceeded. It had just finished raining an hour or two earlier and the sandy twin tracks of the dirt road had been swept clean of all tyre tracks and footprints. I felt confident that the road ahead was clear of all obstacles.

The keep soon disappeared behind us – and although it had been raining, the showers had been light and intermittent. I was confident that the tall grass lining the road would burn easily – as would the odd food storage bin I planned to set alight as provocation.

We entered a particularly heavily-wooded section of the road, with two distinct boulders either side of it. It was at this point that I noticed the spoor of a single barefoot adult in the soft, damp sand. I became engrossed by this lone pattern of footsteps and slowed the vehicle down to a crawl to see where they were going. The spoor was very fresh and had been laid after the rains – just a short while before. Someone was out and about after curfew. I planned to find the bastard and shoot him. I looked for signs of the road having been disturbed…

A great red flash with a sheet of sparks shot upwards to the left-front of where I was sitting. In that split-second, frozen in time, I saw the windscreen wobble and fold in on itself in slow motion. The headlights were snuffed out instantly. Everything was totally quiet. I couldn't see anything. I didn't know if I was alive or dead. A strong smell of vaporised rubber, oil and sand saturated my senses. I hadn't heard a thing, but I knew in a heartbeat I had either hit a mine or been rocketed by a RPG. I instinctively reached for my rifle, but it was gone. My seatbelt was still done up. Mild panic started to set in. I had seen documentaries of soldiers cooked to death in the cab of their vehicles.

I tugged wildly at the seatbelt until it suddenly came undone in my hands. Close-quarter firing broke out from behind me. Tracer zoomed off in all directions, but in a weird optical contradiction, I couldn't tell if the tracer was coming or going. Despite my initial panic, I felt totally calm; if this is what dying is all about, it's not so bad after all. I resigned myself to my fate.

Discovering I wasn't dead, I stood up on the passenger seat and pulled myself through the commander's cupola in the roof of the cab. Heavy firing was still pouring into the bush. I felt relieved it was my guys putting down suppressing fire into likely hiding places gooks may be lying in. I still hadn't a clue where my rifle had gone to.

"Cease fire!" I shouted at the guys – repeating the order before the last shot was fired. Total silence engulfed us. Smoke and cordite drifted slowly away – suspended in a red haze cast by the rear tail lights.

"Get off the back of the vehicle and stay in the tyre tracks. Walk back about 50 metres and get in all-round defence."

I felt totally naked without my rifle. It was a horrible feeling – and one of the reasons why I decided to carry a personal sidearm when I was called up in A Coy 2RR later that year; but that was a future nightmare waiting for me in Mozambique and Matibi 2 TTL, Crooks Corner and Mabalauta.

"For fuck's sake," I said to myself. "I don't even have a radio with me!"

"Fire some rounds into the air," I said to Duff and Bomford. They raised their rifles and fired. Red tracer streaked away like small laser beams – arcing slowly downwards before being snuffed out by the night. I hoped Roy had seen our call for help, but as it turned out, he felt rather than heard the landmine and was already on his way with two vehicles and a stick of men.

I felt ashamed and stupid. This was no way to act in an operational area – and my desire to draw gooks into some type of conflict had almost ended in disaster.

"Is everyone alright?" I said.

"Yes, sir. Sore eardrums, but we're all okay."

I shook my head in the darkness and cursed myself one more time. This would never, ever happen again.

We could see the headlights of the rescue trucks before we could hear them. A halo of light appeared to bob up and down in the distance – getting closer and closer. They arrived with Roy Orchard and a stick of men.

"You alright, sir?" Roy said.

"Yes. Thanks for coming to the rescue."

I felt mildly disorientated and confused. I guess you could call it shock. Landmines are quite often coupled with ambushes. We would have been sitting ducks, with no other men to back us up or assist us.

I decided it was bad news staying where we were. We should get back to camp as soon as possible. I very gratefully sat on the back of Roy's truck – ensuring all the other guys were okay and alert before we turned the vehicles around.

I have never been so relieved in my life – getting back to the keep. I was depressed by what I had done. I felt embarrassed and foolish.

"Ian," I said when I saw him coming out to ask what had happened, "can the guys have a beer each? I'll find a way of paying you back."

"Sure. What happened?"

"Know that thick bit of bush with two large rocks either side of the road – up towards the border road? Hit a biscuit tin there… Saw a lone pair of adult footprints just before it happened."

Ian looked at 'Nipple' and they nodded to each other – as if confirming something. I brushed past them and went into the small, shrapnel-scarred bathroom to do a piss and be by myself for a few minutes.

I caught a glimpse of my face in the mirror. It was completely blackened by oil – as if I'd put on camo cream for a night exercise. My eyes and teeth poked out from white sockets – rather like a white guy pretending to be black man in a musical (a black minstrel, so to speak). I shook my head and sighed.

❦

The next morning I'd recovered some of my composure and went out in the regulation 'two trucks' to look at the damaged vehicle. When we arrived, we approached it with caution – making sure the ground around the vehicle wasn't thick with anti-personnel mines (a favourite trick to injure and maim troops jumping off a truck after it had been blown up).

I circled it and had a look from the front. The left front wheel was gone, with stubby metal bits hanging over a huge hole in the sand. I figured the crater was nearly a metre deep and two metres wide. The chassis rested on white, powdery sand. Both headlights were blown out and the windscreen lay shattered inside the cab and below the front bumper. I hopped through the driver's door. My rifle was wedged firmly behind the double passenger seat. It must have been shot out of its holding bracket like a rocket, bounced off the cab roof and got stuck there. As I retrieved my rifle, I noticed the floor well in front of the passenger seat was peeled open like a sardine can. Bits of shrapnel had pierced the cab in the exact spot a passenger's head would normally rest. Thank God I had no-one sitting next to me. I would be on my way to his funeral now. In fact, if I hadn't insisted on driving, someone would be coming to my funeral because that's where I normally sat!

What the hell had I been thinking? Travelling at dusk on our own with no radio! What would have happened if we'd bumped into that 30-strong group of gooks? When would I ever learn? For the tenth time in 24 hours I felt foolish and immature. I circled around the rear of the vehicle. Bomford rested his forearms on his MAG – chatting to Duff 'Duffy'.

"Well done on returning fire last night. That was quick thinking. I thought your tracer was gook stuff coming at us, though. I nearly shat my pants."

"We did a bit of that too, sir," Duff said.

"Funny thing though, sir… My pack of smokes stayed on the seat just where I left them… Didn't budge an inch in the explosion," Bomford said. I smiled. The guys made me feel better – less of a prick.

"How about a photo, sir?" a voice said from behind me. I turned to look at Alan Currie with his ever-present camera.

"You'll go to prison one of these days, Corporal Currie."

"Nah, sir. This is history in the making."

"Come on you two," I said to Bomford and Duff. "Let's get your ugly mugs photographed."

We moved to the front of the truck and squatted near the left headlight socket – trying to look like heroes.

I walked down the road a short distance after that. To an observer, I was looking for spoor, but inwardly, I was thanking God that none of these fine young guys had died because of my stupidity. Indeed, I was glad I hadn't died.

Nothing happened after that. I made damn sure of it. I reduced our patrols and ambushes to easy tasks close to the keep.

The days passed into weeks, one day after another – repeating the same routine – patrol, ambush, patrol. Annoy the locals, burn things down.

The result? Absolutely nothing. I was relieved beyond measure when the day finally arrived to go back to Vic Falls for some local R&R – not a full 10 days off, but we would stay in camp for a few days to replenish our supplies and our souls and drain our loins, hopefully! I was so lucky I had Mally living in the village. What a great place to do my national service – in a holiday resort, where I had picked up a very pretty woman indeed. A woman I had fallen head over heels for.

I cherished those days when each camp would draw to a close – knowing full well I would be on my way back to welcoming arms, a home-cooked meal and a bit of normality; to sit on a loo again; to boil water in a kettle, in a nice kitchen; to watch TV and fall asleep on the couch; to drink a whisky while soothing music washed over you… Luxuries you only dream of. No camo cream; no straining your ears to listen for the footfalls of gooks – nothing like that at all – and to sleep in a soft bed with a warm woman next to you… Oh my word…

We reached camp late on a Friday afternoon. I chomped at the bit to be able to get out, but it was gone 1900 before I could shower and change into a clean uniform. I was pleased Von Stranz allowed all my guys out. Dino Quinn had taken over Pete Wells's platoon. They were out west by Chundu Island, but one of his sticks remained in camp for guard duty and as a reaction force.

I rushed out the back of the camp and headed for Mally's place. The days had become short and cool as we neared winter. I knew Mally started work at 8:00 p.m. – less than 20 minutes from now. I broke into a sprint – rushing into the dim glow of the suburbs. Music filtered out of the odd window as I ran – a silhouette of a family sitting in front of a TV flashing by.

I pelted around the last corner, along three houses and into Mally's driveway. My heart sank. The back door light was on, but there was no car to be seen.

"Shit!" I said to myself. I would have to walk to the casino.

I headed left out of the gate towards the shops and municipal campsite – cutting through the grounds. It was odd being in uniform without having to carry a rifle. I strolled past the post office, banks and tour offices. It didn't take a genius to figure out why adverts in the tour operators' windows, depicting flights over the Falls, were becoming faded and worn. Who wants to fly over one of the world's Seven Wonders and get shot at -something our little friends across the river were now engaging in on a random basis. Bastards. Why was there no outcry when we were shot at, injured and blown to bits?

I increased my pace when I came to the end of the shops – running over the main road into the Casino Hotel's car park. My eyes searched the cars. Her little black Morris wasn't there. I nearly panicked; thoughts of betrayal and desertion rushed around my head. Ignoring the receptionist, I streaked up the staircase into the machine room – bursting through the doors into the casino proper. Fred and two female croupiers looked up as I barged in.

"Slow down, boy. Looking for Mally?"

"Yes," I said, drawing in shallow breaths. "Where is she?"

"Bulawayo."

"Bulawayo? What the heck's she doing there?"

"Went to see a doc…"

"What's wrong with her?"

"You're not going to be a dad, if that's what you're worried about," Fred laughed. "She had a couple of nasty moles removed from her back, that's all."

I felt so relieved, then angry. Why didn't she tell me?

"Why didn't she tell me?"

"She has, so to speak," Fred said before plopping an envelope on the table in front of me. I picked it up – splitting the flap with my fingernail.

My dear sweet Tony,

If you're reading this card, you have returned to the village during my trip to see the doc in 'Bullies'. You know those two moles I've shown you on my back before? Well, they've got really sore and itchy in the last couple of weeks and I'm worried about them.

I hate not being there to welcome you back, but I haven't been able to contact you for weeks now. I know how angry and frustrated you must feel at the moment – and I too share those feelings.

I've missed you more than words can say. I'll be back on Tuesday, 14th April and I hope with all my heart that you'll be there when I return. I worry when you are away and miss you like crazy. You can phone me at my friend's house in Bulawayo on 19-81537 if you get a chance.
Fondest love,
Mally

I rested the card on my lap and looked at the floor. I felt relieved and crushed to the bone at the same time. I batted away tears that tried to escape down my cheeks.

"How long has she been gone?" I croaked.

"Since Monday morning. I drove her to the airport in her car. It's parked at my place at the moment."

"Damn!" I said quietly. "Shit luck."

"Will a drink perk you up?"

"Yes, Fred. Cheers, my friend. Is there any chance I can use a phone to call her?"

"No problem. Back through the doors; first office on the right."

"Thanks, Fred. Much appreciated."

I walked back the way I had come – through the swing doors and into a small, dusty office with lots of papers and files lying around. I sat in Fred's green leather chair and picked up the receiver. The phone rang the other end at my first attempt, but no-one answered. I dialled again to make sure I'd got it right and let it ring a long time before returning the handset. I stared at a piece of paper on the desk without really seeing it. Thoughts of betrayal and suspicion floated to the top of my consciousness again… What friend was she with? Who was she – or even worse, who was he? The thought of her making love to another man made me feel physically ill. I wanted to vomit – and all of a sudden, I felt hot and claustrophobic in the small office. I was just standing up when Fred came in with a whisky. He must have sensed my mood – or recognised the look on my face – because he was calm and reassuring for once.

"She'll never hurt you, Tony. You can trust me on that. Mally loves you to bits…"

My bottom lip quivered, and suddenly I was crying – flopping back into the chair like a lump of meat. Fred rested his hand on my shoulder. I was hurting like hell inside, but I was also letting go of stress I guess; the sight of Pete and the others being injured… Kazungula… the landmine… the dead civvy with chickens pecking at his brains… it was all too much for me. I felt guilt and shame for my irresponsible actions as an officer to date.

Great, heaving sobs wracked my chest and stomach… Shame, poor old Fred's desk got a real workout with piles of snot and slime landing on it, but I felt much better – and on occasions like this, I normally start laughing to hide my embarrassment. I wiped my face on the back of my hand – looking up at Fred and accepting the drink he held out to me as I chuckled away.

"That's my boy," Fred said, with his Mexican smile back.

"Thanks, Fred."

"You get through to Mally?"

"No," I said, shaking my head.

"You know what women are like. They're probably out having a meal or at a cinema. Who knows?"

"Who is this friend of hers?"

"Not sure. Someone she worked with long ago."

"Mmm…"

"I'll have to get back. Coming in for a chat?"

"I think I'll pop over to the Falls Hotel for a braai."

"Don't blame you," Fred said, looking quickly over his shoulder. "The food sucks here!"

I smiled, tilted my head back and swallowed the golden whisky all in one go. It warmed and soothed its way into my stomach, where it relit the fire I'd had earlier; the one of horny anticipation of meeting Mally again.

It's a short walk back to the Vic Falls Hotel – down a tree-lined road dappled with shadows from the street lights.

The hotel foyer looked bright and inviting, with the colourful doorman smiling a greeting at me. He was a renowned doorman – frequently photographed by tourists because of the hundreds of tiny metal flags he wore on his uniform donated by tourists from all over the world.

I walked along a softly-carpeted passageway until I reached the patio. A bar off to the right was crowded with suntanned people of varying ages.

The large hardwood trees overhanging the braai and dance area were brightly lit by green floodlights. Waiters dressed in white milled about the place and cooks with high, white chef hats tossed meat onto smouldering embers – creating delightful aromas that floated upon the cool air. The usual, very competent band was playing a good interpretation of an ABBA song, with corresponding well-dressed or scantily-dressed people moving to the beat. The bridge over into Zambia was brightly lit under orange floodlights. What an idyllic place this was…

I bought a huge piece of steak for a few dollars, handed it to the cook on a plate and made small talk with him and his assistants while it cooked. I like steak slightly under-done, so it wasn't long before it was handed back to me on a clean plate. I piled salad, bread and baked potatoes on top of the steak until it looked like a small mountain of food. It was such a rare treat to eat like this that I wanted to make the most of it. I ordered a beer and sat facing the dance area.

"Expecting a famine?" a voice said from the table next to me.

"Pardon?" I said, swivelling in my chair. A young woman with dark hair looked intently at me. She was American.

"Expecting a famine?" she repeated.

"No," I chuckled while chewing, "the army doesn't provide food like this."

"Do you mind if I join you?"

"Not at all." I stood – pulling a chair out for her.

"I see chivalry hasn't died in Africa."

I smiled and sat opposite her. I was fascinated by the American female. They are so forward and liberated. This would just not have happened with a local Rhodesian girl. Indeed, at this point in my life, I hadn't even dated one.

"I'm Tony," I said, before shovelling some food in my mouth.

"Yvonne. Yvonne Covino."

"New York?"

"Yes."

"Let me guess… the Bronx?"

"How'd ya figure that? Been there?"

"No, would love to. My ex-girlfriend was a Yank and tried to teach me the different accents there."

"Yank… You guys," she chuckled.

"My manners, sorry. Something to eat? Another drink?"

"I'm okay," she said raising her glass. "Eaten back at the camp."

"Camp?"

"Yeah. The campsite."

"Backpacking around Africa?"

"No," she said sipping her drink. "I'm in the Peace Corps."

"What?"

"The Peace Corps, hun…"

"What's that about, then?"

"We do voluntary work in underprivileged communities around the world. It's popular in the States."

"Rids you of your guilt, huh?"

Her cheeks and neck went dark red. Her smile faded slightly; her eyes locking on mine. I think I had hit a nerve there. I looked at her closely. Despite her hippie style of dress, there was breeding and intelligence behind those dark, unfathomable eyes. Her hair was jet-black; skin mildly olive; her 'eye' teeth slightly larger than the others.

"You're part Red Indian, aren't you?"

"For a guy who's never been to the USA, you sure know a lot. Yes, one-eighth Indian."

"I'm just curious, that's all."

"Does my race offend you?"

"No, on the contrary. I admire the Red Indian people and think they're lovely."

"What do you do?"

"Lieutenant in the infantry."

"Lootenent, hey? That's an officer?"

"Mmm," I agreed, sipping some beer. "What are you in Rhodesia for?"

"To see the Falls. We're based in Durban, South Africa."

I chuckled inwardly at the Americanism of stating the city as well as the country. You know – Paris, France or London, England. We would simply say Paris or London. In a way though, because of a heavy indoctrination of American television, we were probably closer to being American than British in our mannerisms and culture. We may have come from British stock, but we acted like Americans, really. Perhaps it was the wide open spaces we shared in common.

"What are you doing in Durban?"

"Supporting an agricultural extension programme," (pronounced 'program') "and assisting in a school there."

"Think you'll change Africa?"

"You go for the jugular, don't you?"

"Just trying to understand your mindset."

"Mindset?"

"Mmm… what makes you tick. Why do you care?"

"I do, that's all."

"You'll never change these guys. They'll always go backwards."

"So you think it's a waste of time trying to change them; uplift their way of life?"

"Maybe. Tell me how many times have they said 'thank you' to you?"

She took a large gulp of her drink and looked down at the table. She seemed to be fighting an inner battle of some sort.

"You Yanks are kind and generous people, but you'll get little thanks from our indigenous mates here… They despise generosity."

"So it's better to kill them?"

Now it was my turn to feel heckles rise. How could I explain our position to her?

"We're not fighting a racial war. Seventy percent of our regular troops are black volunteers. We're fighting an evil system. I don't care what colour they are. If our enemy was white, so be it."

"You're fighting to prevent majority rule. That's white supremacy, isn't it?"

"If we can get blacks that are like-minded to rule with us, we would welcome that. We know our enemy is Marxist and from a line of 'liberators' that has ruined the rest of Africa."

"Yeah sure, but…"

"We're doing no more than your own government did in Vietnam, Yvonne – trying to stop communism. If we can defeat that ideology, I have no doubt we can start power-sharing."

She went quiet then – looking into her glass. My steak had gone cold. I took a bit of time to study her. She was a lovely-looking girl actually – slim-waisted with roundish hips and medium-sized boobs. I decided to change the line of conversation.

"What's your impression of the Falls, then?"

"Just awesome." Her eyes lit up a bit. "I've been to Niagara Falls, but this place makes it look kinda stupid… Also, this hotel… it's just so old and romantic."

"It is beautiful, isn't it? I'd like to have a holiday here sometime."

"You should."

"A year to go until I'm a civilian again."

"You're still very young; lots of time. What's it like out there?"

"The bush? It's okay; not as frightening as you would imagine. Quite boring actually, with the odd bit of terror thrown in."

She smiled – the white of her teeth contrasting with her olive skin. I ate a few more mouthfuls of steak before putting the knife and fork to one side.

"Dance?" I said. She nodded and smiled. We wove our way through tables to the dance-floor. I was relieved it was a fast number; no body contact needed.

The music gave me a chance to clear my head, look at the surroundings; at the other couples dancing… people sitting at tables lit by shrouded candles. The high colonial façade of the building was lit up to the left. What an amazing place; what an amazing setting. It was probably one of the most romantic hotels in the world. My eyes drifted over to the bridge, and then back at Yvonne. She was staring intently at me. I swallowed involuntarily – breaking off eye contact. An electric thrill ran down my spine. I knew what was coming, but I was totally powerless to stop it. I shut my eyes – hating myself. The music changed gear – slowing down to '*Nights in White Satin*'.

I hated myself… wanted her… couldn't have her… Mally…?

"The army gets rooms for almost nothing here," I said, hoarsely. She squeezed my hand – pulling me from the dancefloor to our table where she retrieved her handbag. We walked in silence back to the reception area. Yvonne stood slightly to the side – looking at the floor as I paid for a room. The receptionist looked at her, then at me – a sarcastic twist on his face – before handing me the key.

I felt happy and guilty all at once as I strolled back to camp in the early hours of Saturday morning. It had been a wonderful night of intense passion, with deep kisses – hands exploring one another.

What on earth was I going to do on my own until Tuesday when Mally got back? Would I be able to face her – look her in the eyes?

I was in for a real shock when Von Stranz joined me for breakfast. His face looked ruddier than normal. For a split-second, I thought Rootman had died.

"Your platoon has been transferred to 1 Indep," he said, out of the blue. He looked at his food while he spoke.

"Sir?"

"Orders came through from brigade last night. 1 Indep is under-strength and we'll be getting guys from Intake 155 soon."

My heart went cold. That meant being based in Wankie – back in that hot hellhole of a town – away from Mally. I also knew that their operational area was Binga on the shores of Kariba Dam – operating inland in the Mavuradona Mountains and national park. There would be no civvies up there; no braais; no flitting liaisons with sexy American Peace Corps workers. I put my knife and fork down – dreading the answer to my next question.

"When do we go?"

"First thing Monday morning."

"You're joking, sir?"

"No joke," he said looking at me, while he stuffed bacon and egg into his mouth. I could've hit him. Why me? Why not Phil or Dino?

"Can we delay that by a day, sir? I want to meet Marilyn. She's been in Bulawayo having an operation."

Von Stranz looked at me as if some of his egg had landed on my nose before shaking his head.

"No way. There's a war on, you know?"

I sat back in my chair – pushing the plate of food away from me. I suddenly felt nauseous.

"I'm sorry Tony, but that's the way it is. Your guys can have the day off today, but you must spend tomorrow preparing to leave. Do a proper handover with the new guys that'll be arriving about lunchtime. Your counterpart is a lieut called Kingsley-Jones."

"Yes, sir," I said sullenly.

I walked outside and kicked a stone off the pathway as hard as I could – sending it spinning into the kitchen tent. Two wide-eyed cooks looked briefly at me before turning back to their duties. I was full of rage. I just didn't give a shit about anything anymore.

I tried doing the rounds of various hotels like I used to do with Mally, but the village felt odd and indifferent somehow. It was too cold to swim. Even being with the ever-upbeat Fred and the 'kuds' did nothing to liven up my spirits. In the end, I went to bed early with a couple of beers under my belt.

The next morning, I woke late to a camp full of troops. A platoon from Intake 155 had arrived to replace us at Victoria Falls. I looked at them in their fresh uniforms with mixed feelings. They would be here in the barracks we helped put together – sitting on our chairs on our patch of lawn that we grew. They would be going to the casino at night where Mally worked – looking and lusting at my girlfriend.

Guilt swept over me when I thought of Yvonne. I'd gone looking for her at the campsite the next morning, but she was either on a tour of the Falls or gone somewhere else. I never saw her again – although I did get a letter a few weeks later from her base in South Africa. It was a warm letter with an invitation to meet again one day in New York, but it never happened.

I strolled outside into the crisp winter day, had a shower and dressed into a fresh uniform. I felt mildly ill-at-ease thinking about transferring to a new company and being sent to one of the wildest and most remote parts of the country.

A young subaltern was enjoying a breakfast when I walked into the officers' dining room.

"Tony Ballinger," I said, extending my hand.

"Derek Kingsley-Jones."

He was only a kid. He was even wearing a Churchill High School tracksuit top.

"So… Looking forward to your stint up here? You couldn't wish for a better place."

"Good. Beats the south-east anyway."

"Churchill School, hey? I left there in '72."

"Your brother was a prefect, wasn't he? Brian?"

"Yes," I said.

"Where you from?"

"Out Centenary way… Tobacco farmers."

"You should've joined PATU instead of the army, then?"

"Nah, I'm in the army and that's fine by me… Better training."

"Who was your course instructor at Gwelo?"

"Theo Williams."

"You're joking? 'The Smiling Shit'?"

"The very same… You're the guys that donated an extra drum to take up that bloody hill?"

"'Felicity'? Yes, a companion for 'Felix', hey?"

"Thanks a stack! We carried the bloody thing up that hill a hundred times!"

"It's a pleasure," I mocked. I sat next to him and piled fried eggs and bacon onto toast. Who knew when I would eat like this again? A shadow darkened the doorway – causing me to look up. I instinctively stood up to face the sergeant major that stood at the door. It was Mally Foulkes from Llewellin. We always used to stand rigidly to attention whenever he came anywhere near us. Habits die hard, I guess.

Commissioned officers outrank sergeant majors, so I covered my embarrassment of standing to attention by shuffling over to the tea urn – saying a polite "Morning, s'aren't major."

"Morning, sirs," he said, saluting. "Can I have a chat when you've finished breakfast?"

"Ten minutes," Kingsley-Jones said.

"What the hell is he doing here?" I said when he was gone.

"He's our CSM."

"Good luck, Derek!"

"Tell me about it. Treats us like kids."

I didn't want to remind Derek that we *were* kids. I had barely turned 21 and Dave Matthews, one of my troopies, was the oldest at 25. His nickname was the 'old man'.

Anyway, poor young Derek would have to put up with a CSM (or Company Sergeant Major) in his midst. So far, we had been spared that dubious honour. Troopies and officers alike normally trembled when a CSM or RSM was about. After all, it was their job to instil discipline among all ranks.

The last image I have of Derek Kingsley-Jones was of him sitting on the chairs outside the officers' mess, chatting to Mally Foulkes. It was the last time I ever saw him. Barely a week later, that nice young man with good manners lay dying in the bush a few kays west of where he sat now. He was shot in the femoral artery in a contact and bled to death because Mally Foulkes would not allow a rescue ambulance down that same track I'd first deployed on months before for fear of hitting a landmine. That moment of poor judgement cost Derek his life – and our respect, if we ever had any, for CSM Foulkes. What a waste of a fine young man – a life full of hope and promise... snuffed out.

We left Vic Falls early on Monday morning. I had tried, unsuccessfully, to phone Mally the night before. The lack of contact with her was like a knife churning in my guts. My suspicions about her mounted. Alternatively, had someone seen me with Yvonne and told her about it?

After arriving at 4 Indep in Wankie, we handed in all our kit at the quartermaster's store before driving a few kays back the way we had come to 1 Indep. It was just about dark and I was exhausted from the travelling, admin and general supervision throughout the day. I no longer had a platoon sergeant due to Kevin Torode's desertion, so I had to do everything myself.

The admin staff had gone home by the time we drove through the gates of the run-down camp. It was a much older military base than the modern complex at 4 Indep and its red brick walls under corrugated iron reminded me of Llewellin. I felt thoroughly depressed.

I made sure the guys had a place to sleep and tracked the cook down to make them something to eat. The more he protested, the angrier I got – until he gave in. I eventually located the officers' mess and an empty room to bunk down in. By 2200 I was fast asleep – suitably warmed by a large steak the protesting cook had made for me.

The next morning, the admin staff arrived at a very leisurely 0800 – by which time we'd all eaten and were standing idly around in the weak morning sun. Clouds of vapour escaped our mouths when we spoke. I was surprised that Wankie got so cold in winter.

Later on, I was called into an office by a very attractive young lady with sergeant stripes on her freshly pressed, sand-coloured uniform.

"Lieutenant Ballinger?"

"Yes," I said, smiling at her.

"Morning, sir. I've got your movement orders here."

She handed me a clipboard with 'Memo' printed at the top. Neatly-typed instructions told me to take my platoon up to Binga, on the shores of Kariba Dam. I was to draw enough ammo to fill our magazines – plus one day's rations. Radios and batteries would be issued by the 1 Indep quartermaster. A map, radio frequencies and call-signs were issued. It was as simple as that.

We drove out the gates as soon as I was satisfied all was in order. I made sure the radios worked; that each stick leader knew his radio frequency and call-sign; that each truck had fuel and drinking water; what we would do in an ambush; and so on and so forth. I felt uncomfortable with my new rifle – it wasn't zeroed in yet. It's funny how familiar the feel of your rifle becomes. You could put 10 down in a pitch-black room and select your own with ease. It sort of becomes your lover.

We turned right out the main gate – heading south-east towards Bulawayo. Our three-vehicle convoy drew a few stares from the locals as we drove by, but apart from that, nothing stirred in that dusty hellhole. The green patch of grass with the big steam locomotive on display came and went. It was also the turn-off to where Pete Wells lay in hospital with his two men. I wondered how they were getting on.

The trucks curled around the high hill with the Baobab Hotel on it – a short while later, zooming past the front gates of 4 Indep. A few 'regulation' cat-calls and insults were exchanged with the guards on gate duty as we disappeared into the dusty wilderness ahead of us. What little grass there was, was now yellow like corn at harvest – the hills bare of leaves on many trees. The odd 'upside-down' tree passed by – the familiar baobab – and although the bush was dry and dusty and full of goats, it was beautiful... as all of Africa is.

The 200-something-kilometre journey to the base camp at Binga – on the shores of Lake Kariba – gave me ample time to think over things. The name 'Lake' was a misnomer. Kariba was a dam – its 5,000 square kilometres of water held back by 120 metres of reinforced concrete – built by the Italians in the late 1950s. Several Italians still lay entombed in the dam wall, having fallen in during concrete pours – a process that could not be paused once it commenced. The mighty Zambezi rebelled against being dammed – allowing monstrous floods to destroy temporary coffer dams during the wall's construction in the early '60s.

But now, the dam waters lay quiet in all their majesty – 5,000 square kilometres in extent, 40 kilometres wide in places and over 280 kilometres long. The water backing up behind the wall was so heavy that minor earthquakes occurred as the Earth's crust adjusted to the load.

The dam was a natural barrier between Zambia and Rhodesia, but the shores and 'lake' had to be patrolled and protected nonetheless. To this end, a small 'navy' had been formed by the Rhodesians and Zambians to patrol this small inland sea. A large converted ferry patrolled the deeper Rhodesian waters, while fast attack craft tethered to her would strike out at enemy boats her radar detected.

Binga – the military camp and village we were heading for – was a small outpost situated three-quarters south-west down the dam. It was built on a ridge above a bay that looked something like two index fingers not quite touching each other, while both thumbs made contact.

The gap between the two 'index fingers' allowed boats to come into a perfectly-protected bay, where fishing vessels were tied up. The 'naval' base was on the bend of the 'knuckle' of the right 'index finger' – facing open water to the north-east. The army base stood on a high ridge to the south-west of this.

We were passing the Lupane Catholic Mission now – about 20 kilometres south-east of Wankie. It was built above the dry Lupane riverbed – surrounded by thorn trees and scrub. The place reminded me of a cordon and search we'd done through its buildings earlier in the year. The Catholic Commission was well-known for its sympathies towards our enemies – and we had suspected for a long time that more than the gospel was being taught there.

And so, an hour before daylight, I had led a cordon and search of the mission station. A couple of platoons of troops were involved, as well as a Lynx – an armed 'push-pull' aircraft flying overhead, with the company commander directing operations. It was another 'lemon' and no gooks were found – although I kick myself to this day for not shooting a shadowy figure that tumbled out of a dimly-lit window above me… darting into the bush. I was slow to react for some reason – and I have no doubt the man was indeed a gook making a hasty retreat when he discovered troops were searching the mission.

A few kays further on, we passed a huge clear patch of dusty ground that looked like a parking lot off the highway. This was yet another reminder of operations in the area in February, when a large contingent of security forces attacked a ZIPRA base camp in the hills to our left. I still remember the long row of helicopters that deployed us as stop-groups shortly before a Lynx came in to drop a load of 'frantan' (or napalm) on the camp. Exit one gook; all that planning, expense and effort to kill a single poor sod that was roasted blacker than toast by the burning jelly that snuffed out his life. One memory of that day was a black and white safari coach full of tourists that stopped to take pictures of our helicopters deploying us into battle. The contradiction of tourism and war in the same landscape had struck my senses like a thunderbolt. I remain amazed no tourist coach went up in a landmine.

Memories of that heli-borne assault reminded me of a tour of duty on Fireforce at Wankie, where we lazed around helicopters playing with a resident monkey and a large horn-billed bird called Harvey that adopted us – or adopted our food, rather. The monkey was an irrepressible pest – stealing our food and running off with it to mock us from the heights of a wire cage surrounding the helicopters. We got our own back one day by building up a pile of freshly-cut grass for the monkey to jump into – neatly hiding bricks under it. A severe headache put paid to its antics for a week or so!

The nights in the air force pub were memorable too, with music of the day adding to the feel of the place… ABBA, Hues Corporation's 'Rock The Boat', Donna Summer's 'MacArthur Park'… America, The Doobie Brothers, Carlos Santana… Getting mildly pissed on our ration of beers and talking and laughing long into the night with sun-bronzed men of a kindred spirit. The large painting on the wall of a Fireforce action was one of the most vivid and evocative I have ever seen – in such detail that many men spent hours with their faces up-close to it. I was only deployed five times by helicopter – and all of them were 'lemons'… gooks, zero; Rhodesian dollar expenditure, many millions.

The driver slowed the vehicle to turn left towards Kamativi tin mine and on to Binga – rousing me from my reverie. I checked with everyone by radio that they were still awake, and it was time to 'switch on' again. This was new territory to me – not only as a soldier, but as a Rhodesian. I was heading for a part of the country I had never seen before.

The bush certainly got drier and sparser the further inland we headed, with steep hills all around us. You could literally hide a gook army in there and no-one would ever find them. I am sure that in days gone by, it was good elephant country – but now, it was over-grazed and overpoked… especially around Kamitivi, as we roared past the little mining village on our left.

A short distance down the road, we stopped for a piss and then we were off again. Although we couldn't see Kariba Dam at this point, you had the feeling that it was nearby – 'just over there', so to speak.

I remember looking at Dave Kruger on this trip. I'm not sure why he was in my platoon now. Perhaps it was because 4 Indep was basically breaking up at that point and some guys were shipping off to join other units. Dave, who I remembered clearly from Churchill High School days, was a loud, boisterous guy always ready for a laugh and a piss-up. He was a superb bagpipe player and had represented our school in many international events – even in Scotland, where our school won high praise for its professional band. As I looked at him though, it struck me that he was unusually quiet and pensive on that trip up to Binga. He was dead less than a month later – blown up by a landmine that killed two other fine men in my platoon; Corporal Roy Orchard and Signaller Tom Shipley. Some people say that you can sense your death coming – and in Dave's case, I have no doubt that this is true. He was deeply troubled all the time. What a bloody waste. The same mine also injured Albie Louw and 'Colm' Colman, who was paralysed. Colm died a broken man a few years later in an accident in his specially-adapted car for the disabled.

But that was in the future – and for now, our journey to Binga was drawing to a close. I wondered what our new company commander would be like and what lay ahead for us; an easy time, or days filled with gut-ripping fear? I missed Mally like hell and regretted my time with Yvonne, but that's a man for you. The 'little head' rules!

I met Major Don Price at breakfast the next morning. The officers' mess was an open-sided building with asbestos-cement roof sheets. The building's designer no doubt had summer in mind, but the first morning I was there was in the middle of winter – and a chill, moist air drifted over me while I buttered some toast.

Don Price turned out to be a good-looking man in his early-thirties with dark hair, green eyes and a moustache. His broad shoulders complimented his tall, lithe frame and suntanned skin.

"Tony, welcome," he said, reaching for a chair. I stood to attention, but he waved me down. "It's informal at the breakfast table."

"Yes, sir," I said, sitting. A couple of other officers joined us – one I assumed was his 2 i/c.

"Tell me about yourself," he said, leaning back in a canvas chair.

"Well, sir, I'm from Intake 152, as you know. I've been based up at the Falls since I arrived in August."

"I've read your file. What scenes have you been involved in?"

"Nothing much, really... A landmine, Kazungula... Jambezi..."

He raised an eyebrow and sipped his coffee before saying: "Contacts?"

"Not yet," I said, shaking my head.

"Think you'll cope?"

"No-one can answer that question, sir," I said after a pause.

"I've read Captain Williams's report about you."

"That's me sunk," I joked, but no-one smiled.

"He said you're soft on your guys."

"Maybe, but I reckon I've matured... It's a learning curve."

He nodded – leaning forward to load a fork with scrambled eggs. I felt ill-at-ease in the silence that followed, so I looked out at the camp. It had been almost dark when we arrived the day before, so I hadn't had time to study the place. My first impression was that it was a very temporary affair, with tented accommodation and simple A-frame shelters making up most of the camp. A run-down shed with a greasy mechanic sipping coffee in the sun nestled in the corner by some trees. Apart from my own troops, I had no idea who was in camp. Who were these guys scoffing their breakfast down in silence? I groaned inwardly. Months of this without Mally.

The view out the other side of the mess hall was nothing short of breathtaking, though. The vast blue waters of the dam disappeared over the horizon to the north-east – narrowing by Chete Island. I had heard that the island belonged to Zambia and that her troops were keen on firing at our civilian ferries that plied the very narrow gap between the island and mainland Rhodesia. The water to the north-west of the island was vast and open, but the early surveyors obviously made the Zambezi River the boundary between Northern and Southern Rhodesia, so the border now followed the tiny gap at Chete Gorge.

I ate some food and drank some coffee while I waited for Major Price to speak. He seemed in no hurry to do so.

"I'll give you a briefing after breakfast," he said at length. I merely nodded.

That was the beginning of my relationship with a rather controversial figure in the Rhodesian Army. He was accused, in months following, of spending more time hunting elephant with helicopters than he did chasing down gooks. This, of course, was denied – but he never explained away the truckloads of animal hide I saw heading for Wankie on occasion.

On the way to a sunny ops room, I called in to see my men to make sure they'd eaten and were okay. Dave Kruger was still very quiet and distant – although Roy Orchard and Tom Shipley appeared in good fettle.

"Take a seat," Major Price said in the ops room. A radio operator sat in the corner reading a *Scope* magazine. How us army boys loved that South African magazine, with scantily-clad women covering most pages. Good visual stimulation in an environment full of flies and 'munts' shuffling about.

"Chete Island… The brass want us to invade it," Don said suddenly. My heartbeat accelerated slightly; that would be a fantastic military operation.

"Because of the attacks on ferries?"

"Yup. It's still in the planning stages, though; probably use the RLI as the assault team."

"What will our role be?"

"No idea. Some type of support. The bugger is I can't deploy you guys elsewhere until we know for sure."

He went on to briefly explain the recent military activity in the area, where our boundaries were and what friendly forces operated around us. Two companies of 1 RAR patrolled the land to the east of Binga, from the Chete-Siabuwa Road as far as the Sengwe River on the western edge of the Matusadona National Park. Our area of responsibility spread from Chete Island, south-east along a dirt road to Siabuwa, east to Chizarira National Park, south through Kamativi to the main tar road running from Wankie to Bulawayo, north-west to the Deka drum turn-off, up that road and then west to the Matetsi River. Beyond the Matetsi River was Jambezi – the keep where we provoked 50 gooks to attack. Our northern boundary was the Zambezi River and Kariba Dam.

This was a vast, vast area to cover – and without any exaggeration, an entire corps of 30,000 men could be hidden in the Chizarira National Park without ever being seen – and we had about a hundred men to patrol this enormous expanse of savannah, gorges, rivers and swamp. The place was infested with lion and elephant and was probably one of the most remote areas in Southern Africa. I just didn't fancy the idea of operating here at all.

As soon as the briefing was over, Major Price suggested we go to the 'naval' jetty and have a look at the ferry that had been converted into our navy's flagship.

We hopped into a two-five and took off down the hill without an escort, but in this area it seemed okay. It was relatively civilised with little or no grass to hide gooks. Pity – I had nothing to flick matches into!

Our vehicle freewheeled down the steep, curving hill past the Binga Sports Club until we eventually came to the harbour. The large ferry we'd come to see was parked in pride of place, with its attendant strike craft tethered to her like calves sucking teats. A couple of police boats bobbed up and down in the water nearby.

The ferry had a couple of 7.62mm machine-guns up by the wheel house, with one each at the stem and stern. One of the complements was a 12.7mm anti-aircraft gun. A radar dish revolved slowly on top of the wheel house.

"Not exactly the Sixth Fleet," I said to Don. He smiled – revealing white, even teeth.

"No fear of a Pearl Harbour here."

We jumped down from the truck and sauntered around a bit. Don saw the boat's captain and went off for a chat. It was a wonderful opportunity to lean against the bobbing craft and soak in some of the sun and scenery. I've always liked boats and planes – and it was a pleasure to be in this type of environment. I was vaguely amused to see that some of the 'navy' boys were dressed in white, with their rank displayed in gold bands on their shoulders – unless they were customs and immigration officers, of course. I couldn't tell the difference. How embarrassing for them. Other men moved this way and that – filling up fuel tanks, cleaning weapons, loading provisions or sun-tanning in various attitudes of indifference.

When Don finished chatting, we drove back up the hill – stopping at the sports club to have a cool drink. The club had a quaint bar with a veranda overlooking the view – and like the world over, a couple of frilly-panted women hacked away at tennis balls; the kwa-thonk of their tennis racquets echoing around us. One of the ladies saw Don, paused in mid-serve and winked at him – smiling. I figured elephants weren't his only trophies.

It was close to lunch when we got back to camp. I called the corporals together and instructed them to tell the guys to clean their rifles and then organise two volleyball teams to occupy their time. Keeping men busy is essential – or else they bicker and argue, become lazy and slothful and discipline starts to slide. Sport is an excellent way to let off steam. I also got Major Price to agree to us zeroing in our rifles later in the day.

When a man gets a new rifle, it's essential that the sights are adjusted to the way his eye looks down the barrel. I once challenged a friend of mine who farmed in Wedza to a shooting competition. I knew he was a good shot and his beers would be a well-earned prize at the end of the day. However, we only had my rifle – and it had naturally been 'zeroed' to my eye – so try as he might, Rich just couldn't hit the target like I did. You have to drop the front sight a notch or two if the rounds fell short of their target. Similarly, the rear sight had to be moved to compensate for a horizontal error.

It was a great, noisy way to end the first day there. Apart from zeroing a rifle, it's essential a soldier fires it regularly, or else he becomes 'gun-shy', which results in him pulling the trigger too quickly in a situation where aiming is necessary. Your expectation of the weapon firing makes you jerk the trigger prematurely. Regular usage overcomes this.

We trundled back into camp towards sunset – thinking we were heroes for blasting a couple of thousand rounds into an unsuspecting mound of earth. Ants that occupied several towering nests on top of the butts had been blasted to hell. The massive ball of orange sun sinking to the west, magnified by winter's dust, was just too awesome to describe – and to our right, the blue waters of the lake turned black against the darkening mountains to the east. What beautiful, wild country – a land that man had barely tempered.

A few days of training followed while we waited for the green light to invade Chete Island. We practised anti-ambush drills, advance to contact in section and platoon strength, as well as withdrawals – although hopefully, we would never have to do the latter.

By the end of the third day, I was bored with the routine: up at 0600 to do a run and pokey drill, breakfast, weapon cleaning, various drills, volleyball or range work, or a drink at the club in the afternoon. I was getting irritated with Com-ops for keeping us in suspense – and then, all of a sudden, the op was off.

"The politicians are shit-scared," Don said at lunch on the fourth day, "worried it may escalate into something bigger."

"I'm sure we could handle anything those tossers can throw at us," I said. Don flicked an odd look at me. I was pissed off because I knew it meant deployment 'out there' into unknown territory.

"You'd best get your R&R out the way before you start for proper up here."

"Sir?"

"R&R. Your platoon is due R&R according to the files Sean Von Stranz sent me."

My heart leapt with joy. I could barely contain myself. A smile crept across Don's face.

"There's a PRAW plane leaving for Wankie in two hours. Best be on it."

"Shit, that's awesome, sir. Thanks. What about my guys?"

"They can go back on the resupply run tomorrow. Don't worry. I'll sort their passes out."

My emotions had swung from a low sense of foreboding to a 'high' in a few seconds. A great gob of adrenalin shot into my system at the thought of seeing Mally again. I packed my clothes in a daze – and after making sure my guys were informed and squared away, I was given a lift to the airstrip. I didn't know it then, but it was the last time ever that I saw Binga – and in just four weeks' time, three of my guys would be dead, with another three seriously injured.

The Police Reserve pilot shook my hand before throwing my bag onto the back seat of the small, single-engine Cessna aircraft. It was a bumpy and noisy flight back to Wankie, with massive quantities of heat boiling up from valleys and hills – tossing the plane around like a toy. If it wasn't for the calm deportment of the pilot, I would have puked all over the control panel.

I couldn't believe my luck when we landed. I was sitting around the Fireforce mess wondering how to get to Vic Falls, when I heard an Islander pilot mention he was heading for Vic Falls to do a casevac. I leapt at the chance – and after some persuasion, was allowed to accompany him and a medic on the flight up there. The Islander is a bigger, twin-engine aircraft with its wings situated above the fuselage, so it was a comparatively smooth flight, but too noisy to talk. Instead, I slumped in the back of the plane and contemplated meeting Mally. I felt excited and apprehensive all at the same time.

Although it was June, it was only a couple of months after the most spectacular period to witness the Falls in all its awesomeness. April is the time of the year when the river swells with billions of tons of rainwater – collected in Zambia, Angola and Botswana from November onwards – spilling itself into the gorge at a rate of 500 million litres per minute. We could see a column of spray towering up into the sky long before we could see the river or village itself – making a perfect beacon for errant pilots and pedestrians alike.

It was close to 1700 when we landed at Vic Falls airstrip – a modest tar runway with a few buildings at the end of it. I noticed artillery had moved into the area since the last time I was here. Perhaps half a dozen ancient British 25-pounders were staggered around a central fire-control vehicle at the far end of the runway. Red and white aiming poles had been pegged into the ground in an arc around them – and tents and vehicles sprawled beneath leafless trees.

Although the guns were old and had a modest range, they were still highly effective weapons in the right hands. Someone waved at me and I gave him a thumbs-up. We taxied back down the runway to where an ambulance waited for the plane to come to a halt. I climbed off quickly while medics helped two bandaged black soldiers on board. Their wounds didn't look life-threatening, but they grimaced in pain nonetheless. I wondered what that was all about.

The pilot gunned the engines – and in a short while, the plane was airborne once again – banking left in a big circle until it was heading south-east back to Wankie. I threw my bag over my shoulder and made for the gate – passing a hangar with a technician working on a red aircraft. A twin-engine tourist plane with RUAC markings pointed at what looked like an office or clubhouse of some kind.

When I got to the main road leading to the airport, I became indecisive about where to go. I no longer had a room at the army base – and there was no guarantee Mally would be home, but that's where I had to go; I had no choice. I turned right towards the Wankie Road – picking up my pace as I went. The air was cool and crisp; the sky to the east a dark purple bordering on black – a golden glow behind me silhouetting naked branches like petrified fingers. It was such a thrill to be back in town. The place was so familiar to me now.

I walked past Peters Motel on my right – trying to see if they'd repaired the boundary wall at the far end after Ncube's attack – but the view was blocked by cars and flowers. It dawned on me at that point that I was actually walking in a big circle, so I trotted down the hill towards the village – cutting across the grass at the back of the curio shops – turning left onto the circular drive that led to Mally's house. It was just about dark when I trotted through the gate of her property. I was gutted. The light at the back door was on, but her car wasn't there. I felt angry and confused. Hiding my bag under a small bush, I ran as fast as I could back to the casino – but there was no sign of her car there either. I looked at my watch. She would be starting work in just under an hour.

The casino looked more run-down and seedier than ever. I guess the reduced flow of tourists was beginning to have an effect on its cashflow. I ordered a whisky on the rocks and flopped down into a chair to wait for Mally. 'I Love To Love' by Tina Charles played over the hotel sound system – and the effect of the music and alcohol made me relax considerably. I didn't have long to wait. After less than 20 minutes, I could hear Mally and Fred walking up the staircase from the staff dining room. Of course, that's where she'd been! I saw Fred first – his smile widening instantly when we made eye-contact. He nudged Mally and pointed in my direction. I stood up – shaking like a leaf. Her face remained set as she climbed the steps – looking down from my gaze. My heart went cold. What had happened? Fred said something to me, but it didn't even enter my consciousness – and realising we needed time together, he carried on into his office, turning the light on. I looked at Mally, but she kept looking at the floor – and I could see her lip was trembling as she fought emotions within her.

"Mally…" I said simply, pulling her into my arms. Her back shuddered as great sobs left her. Tears dripped onto my collar. I just let her cry until it was all out of her. "What's up, babe?"

She shook her head and wiped her nose on the back of her hand. Her mascara had run – making her look like a panda bear.

"I've just missed you so much... You'd gone to Wankie by the time I got back from Bulawayo, and I couldn't contact you. I hadn't heard from you for ages... I thought it was all over with us, somehow."

"Never," I said, pulling back and looking into her eyes. She smiled and started crying some more. I just held her until the emotion was over. I felt so relieved there wasn't anything else between us – no mention of Yvonne. "Where's your car?"

"Outside..."

"I didn't see it. I was frantic trying to find you."

"I had a drink with Fred at the Falls Hotel, then a quick bite downstairs."

"I've missed you so much," I said, pulling her into my arms again. We stood like that for a long time until she left me to help Fred set up the tables for the night's gambling.

It was freezing cold at 2:00 a.m. when we finally got to bed. It was an incredible sensation climbing naked into bed with her – feeling her warmth and softness after the privations of the army; to see her trinkets and things on the dressing table and the familiar old air-conditioning unit – now silent – on the wall. Despite our urgency for each other, we chose to snuggle and draw in each other's warmth before falling fast asleep into a dark, formless void.

We woke at 10:00 a.m. the next morning to a crisp day with a pale-blue sky. I love the winters in Rhodesia. It rarely rained and the temperature mostly hovered in the low to middle seventies. It was just too cold to swim, but warm enough to sunbathe. We made love until it hurt – until our passions had drained away to a warm contentment.

Later, we made breakfast and mugs of coffee – deciding to eat in bed rather than the dining room. Experiencing freedom like this is something a lot of people the world over take for granted.

"I tried contacting you three times in Bulawayo, you know?" I said, licking marmalade off my fingers.

"I can't believe we kept missing each other. I tried twice too – hoping you'd be with Fred."

The roar of the jet engines shook us out of our reverie. I flicked myself off the bed and rushed to the window. I just managed to see two Hawker Hunter fighter-bombers banking sharply to the west – their throaty rumbles echoing down the valley long after they'd disappeared.

"That's unusual to see them so close to the border," I said, looking back at Mally. She propped herself up on the pillows – pulling a sheet up under her chin.

"It's getting creepy living here."

"It's not that bad."

"Says you… You weren't here when Ncube attacked Peters the first time – nor the mortar attack while you were at Jambezi."

"I had my own fun to contend with."

"It's not fun. Never has been, never will be."

"You know what I mean… Do you think we should build a bunker in the garden? Everyone else is doing it."

"Haven't thought about it, really."

"I think we should. It'll give me something to do while I'm on R&R."

"Okay… but what do you know about building?"

"Not a helluva lot. It'll be fun though, don't you think?"

Building that bunker was a noble idea, but an onerous one. My hands were the only ones to put it together. We lay in bed late the first morning until the air was warm, and then I set about digging a hole two-and-a-half metres long by two metres wide, by the same depth. I had stone, sand and cement delivered by a local builder – using it to mix a 60 millimetre-thick floor slab the second day. It was hard, sweaty work – but I thoroughly enjoyed it. I would break to have lunch with Mally, and then we would drive around in her little black Morris to beg materials from wherever we could find them. I got timbers from the local African compound – as well as good, homemade bricks formed from baked ant clay. The goods were delivered in old rickety vehicles that had seen the better part of 30 years' service. I admired the entrepreneurial spirit of the local black population and their determination to succeed and feed their families whatever the cost.

Sean Von Stranz was more than obliging – giving me sandbags to pile on top of the timbers, but generally found the whole thing amusing and took the piss out of me when we came to collect the bags in Mally's car. The base camp looked good and our patch of grass was still green and neatly-cropped.

By the afternoon of my eighth day on R&R, the bunker was complete. It was a rickety affair, with its timbers resting on four wobbly brick columns. The earth walls still had to be bricked-up.

"A toast to our home in the event of a mortar attack," Mally said, passing me a beer. We gingerly climbed on top of the sandbags and chinked our bottles together – the last rays of sunlight glinting off the bottles.

"Think it'll survive a hit?" I smiled at her.

"Who knows? Surely the iron roof on the house is just as good?"

"Might stop a mortar shell penetrating, but if it went off, the shrapnel would tear you to bits down below…. This is definitely a better bet."

We swigged our drinks down – and for the next two evenings, we ate our meals on top of the sandbags – toasting each other with wine.

I only had four days of leave left – and the thought left me mildly depressed. I'd spent more time than I wanted to on the bunker, but it had been fun, really – and after all, it was interspersed with the odd booze cruise and trip up to Elephant Hills to pull slot machines. They were great days, I suppose; I never really appreciated them until too late.

I don't know what made me decide to do it, but I stayed home on the second to last night of my R&R while Mally went to work. I hadn't had any time to myself for literally a year and I wanted to just chill out and read, listen to some music and maybe watch a bit of TV on Mally's fifth-hand set.

"Be good," Mally said, as she bent down to kiss me. She smelled so good and was all soft under her black evening gown.

"Sorry I'm not coming with you. I just need a break from sitting around at the casino."

"It's okay. Business is quiet… I'll see if Fred can let me off early."

"That'll be nice."

I almost regretted staying at home when she closed the front door behind her. I sat motionless until the sound of her car died away – wondering whether I should go to the casino after all. In the end, I decided to have a bath and went to bed to listen to radio 702 from South Africa.

Radio 702 was an icon for most Rhodesians of my age. I would often get home from school and lie in the sun listening to 'Spin Out' on LM Radio with Gerry Wilmot – a man reputed to be the fastest talker on earth. I would listen to the hits of the day – tapping my feet on the grass as I sunbathed, dripping in sweat. Mungo Jerry's *In the Summertime*; *Love Train* by The O'Jays; *Fantasy* by Earth, Wind and Fire; *Boogie Nights* by Heatwave and so on.

When the Portuguese were overthrown in Mozambique in the middle of the 1970s, Gerry Wilmott and crew moved to South Africa and continued broadcasting from Radio 702. I now lay in bed with the lights off – waiting for 'Spin Out' to start at 10:00 p.m. It was June 1977.

I was halfway between sleep and consciousness when I heard a faint kwa-kwa-kwa coming from the direction of Elephant Hills. I sat up in bed, resting on my elbows – not quite sure if I had heard it. A bright flash lit the room – followed shortly by a massive, echoing explosion that rolled down the valley – and then, a sound like someone slowly tearing paper filled the room. My heart accelerated its beat – pumping massive quantities if adrenalin into my bloodstream. I raced to look out the window just as another flash and thud rolled down the valley once more. There was no way I could see Elephant Hills from my room, but the odd green tracer sped upwards like miniature rockets at a fair.

I ran into the passage and turned on the light. It gave off enough illumination for me to find my rifle and webbing. I ran out the back of the door in a T-shirt and shorts. Frikkie Blauw was already standing next door – drawing deeply on a cigarette.

"This is bad for business, my friend. Very bad."

"Elephant Hills, Frikkie?"

"Ja…I suppose I better get to the cop station to see what I can do."

"Give me five minutes and I'll come with you," I said.

I rushed back indoors – and after scrabbling around for a while I found my boots, denims and combat jacket. Frikkie was waiting in his car for me – sitting in one of those little Renaults with the gearstick in the dashboard. They always reminded me of a pop-up toaster.

We zoomed off in the direction of the police station. Frikkie was a field reservist – and if trouble started anywhere in the village, he'd been commanded to report to the police station (as indeed the 30 or so other eligible males in the village had also been instructed accordingly).

Flashes – and a distant report of dozens of weapons – could be heard above the high revs of the car's small engine.

We sped off left and then sharp-right at the municipal campsite – accelerating past the shops on my right. The street was devoid of humanity. A car sped uphill in front of us at the next T-junction. Someone else was also heading for the police station. When we arrived, at least 12 other men were there waiting for the chief superintendent to arrive, which he did shortly after us.

It was a motley collection of men that gathered around the police chief as we listened to him telling the men what to do. Some had grey hair, others had long hair, some fat and some thin – hardly poster material for the Rhodesian security forces – but one thing they did have in common was their ability to shoot. Most police anti-terrorist men were farmers or hunters in this area of the country. They had been weaned on rifle grease and could hit a coin at 70 metres.

"Phil," the chief said to a section officer next to me, "take the boat and the Browning and patrol upriver. Anyone here know how to use the Browning?"

I looked around, but no-one put up their hand, so I decided to have a crack at it. After all, how difficult could it be to load and fire a machine-gun?

"Try and intercept any gooks rowing back to Zambia."

"Yes, sir."

Four of us went outside, round the back to the armoury and picked up the Browning .303 machine-gun and three metal boxes of ammo. It was one of those guns with holes down the outer casing of the barrel. Looking at in the bright glare of the armoury lamp made me wonder whether I could indeed fire it. Cracks and thuds were still going off in the middle-distance to the west – each thud preceded by a burst of light that looked like a large camera flash at a wedding.

My body had now accepted the rush of adrenalin, and I felt calm and able to reason. We ran to the front of the building, where I half-expected to get into at least a Land Rover or a two-five, but instead we headed for Frikkie's pop-up toaster.

"We're driving into a war zone in that?" I said, coming to a halt. The three of them turned and looked sheepishly at me. Phil shrugged his shoulders.

"It's the only transport we have."

"You do realise that the turn-off to the police jetty is beyond the hotel, which is still being revved by gooks? We could drive straight into an ambush."

"It's a risk," Phil said, and climbed in the car – as did the other three. I wondered what the hell I was doing. After all, I was on leave!

"Shit!" I spat as I slammed the door shut.

There we were – four lunatics driving down the road in an unarmoured vehicle with rifle barrels hanging out the window to prevent digging holes in the upholstery. Talk about the charge of the pop-up toaster. I just couldn't believe it!

I really shat myself that night – roaring down the road to the police boat jetty, where two very fast 'push-pull' boats were moored. The bush was cold, dark and ominous; the poor headlights of the 'toaster' casting a weak halo of light ahead of us. I was expecting an avalanche of tracer to tear us to shreds at any second. I pointed my rifle out the side window as best as I could – cocking it.

The towering Elephant Hills Hotel soon appeared on our left – and I was immediately relieved to see armoured cars and troop carriers climbing the hill up to its summit. Thank God for the army's reaction. At least this section of the road was clear. The attack had obviously stopped now because there was no return fire from the army – nor the sounds of explosions; just a deathly hush.

We turned right at a disused caravan park – and in a few seconds, we were at the jetty. We unloaded the car as quickly as possible. Phil and Frikkie positioned the Browning on a pole fixed to the port side of the boat – slipping a box of ammo into a tray before feeding it into the machine-gun.

"Just pull the trigger," Phil said to me, moving forward to start the engine. Why on earth didn't any of the other 12 men back at the police station volunteer to just 'pull the trigger' themselves? I shook my head and sat on the engine cowling – handing my rifle to a police reservist who had come along with a handgun only. What he proposed to do with a handgun in a possible contact was anybody's guess. I felt really angry with myself for volunteering for this crappy mission. I could be in bed tuning back into Radio 702 while I waited for Mally. She was probably going to freak out coming back to an empty house. I hadn't thought of her feelings at all.

Our boat's engine sounded powerful when it started with a throaty roar. The current looked very strong – being only two months after its highest level; dark and brooding. Trees on the island opposite us were faintly silhouetted against a starry backdrop.

Phil threw off the mooring and gently eased the throttle forward – pushing it most of the way home as soon as we were free of the jetty. The bow rose up – and in a few seconds, we were racing upstream. The tourist jetty where the booze cruise launched from came and went – and so did the A'Zambezi Hotel; its bright lights undimmed after the nearby attack. Rumours did the rounds that the A'Zambezi never got burned down during various attacks on the village because it was staffed by terrorist sympathisers and eyed by senior members of ZAPU to take over after the war. Just a rumour... well, maybe.

The island on our right came and went – and soon we were in open waters at a very wide section of the river.

"Go down the Zambian side of the island," I yelled at Phil. He nodded – banking the boat right. We sped downstream at an amazing speed – the dark bushes of the island flicking by. Stars reflected off the calm water ahead of the bow wave – just like they did when we attacked the Zambian Army officers' mess at Kazungula with that nutcase, Steve.

"Slow down, Phil. We'll never see anything like this."

He cut back on the throttle – but even so, the current and combined forward motion of the boat meant we kept up a rapid pace. This was pointless, in my opinion. In any case, the machine-gun I manned could only face one way – and that wasn't toward the island!

At the southern end of the island, the river opened up again and the Elephant Hills Hotel was clear for all to see through the palm-fringed bank – lit up like a spaceship. What a beautiful target the gooks had chosen. I learned some weeks later that there was virtually no damage to the building, but one of the cooks had hidden in a walk-in deepfreeze and was almost frozen solid when they found him.

We'd drifted about 400 metres east of the island when Phil decided we'd better turn around and try searching around Kandahar Island. Spray from the Falls was clearly visible about two kilometres away – the dark waters moving past us at a breakneck pace as it became channelled towards Devil's Cataract.

Phil punched the accelerator handle forward – the engine revs rose to a scream, but we went nowhere.

"Oh shit, shit, shit!" Phil said in a panicky voice. "Weed in the jet... Row like hell for that island, or else we're going over the Falls!"

The cop with my rifle grabbed hold of a paddle and started digging madly into the water, while Frikkie did the same on his side.

"No, no, no... Both of you row on the same side, man, or you're just making us go faster... Here, on Frikkie's side! Tony, use your rifle butt like a rudder at the back and head for that clompie of trees."

I scrabbled forward to get my rifle – making sure it was on safe – and did as Phil said. Phil ripped off the fibreglass cowling that covered the engine – pulling a knife from nowhere to start hacking at the weed inside the jet nozzle. It was coiled thick and tight in a rope the size of my forearm.

I leaned over the stern of the boat, and using the back of it as a fulcrum point, pulled the rifle barrel forwards – the butt going backwards on the side opposite Frikkie. It had an immediate effect, and the bow of the boat started to swing towards the small island diagonally ahead on our left. We were moving at an incredible speed – and I knew that in less than 10 minutes, we would be plummeting to our deaths. I was scared shitless.

"Tony, row on your side!" Phil said, looking up at me. His voice was edged with panic.

I went a few paces forward and dug as deep as I could – pulling back hard. A rifle butt makes a very awkward paddle – and a rather ineffective one, at that.

"Frikkie... Tom.... Row like mad, now!"

There was a noticeable movement to the left – a bit like a crab walking diagonally forward to its hole in the sand.

"Harder guys, harder!" Phil shouted. We rowed like lunatics. It didn't take a genius to realise that if we missed this little island, we would either grind to a halt on the lip of the Falls, or be swept sideways into the cataract. I was absolutely terrified.

The bushes we were aiming for were suddenly upon us – fringed by tall reeds. Phil cut the engine. We reached out at the reeds – shrieking in pain as they cut into the palms of our hands – letting go to grab another one until we began to lose way and slow down. Tom grabbed onto a low, overhanging branch and tied the bow rope onto it. The stern spun around sideways – almost capsizing us. We came to a halt with a sudden jolt as the slack on the rope was taken up. I collected up a large armful of reed and tied the stern mooring rope around it – pulling the knot tight.

"Shit, that was scary!" Frikkie said, the white of his teeth showing in the grey light. "I'll need a dop or two when I get home."

"If we get home," Phil said.

Phil continued to hack away at the coil of weed in the jet's nozzle for over half an hour before he could find no more.

"There's bound to be some in the last section. I'll have to get into the river to do that."

"You're nuts," I said, but Phil ignored me and stripped down to his underpants. He did one of the bravest things I have ever seen in my life that night – climbing into those dark, swirling waters to hack away at weed just at the bottom of the boat.

"Can you guys move to the front so that the back lifts up slightly?"

We crawled forward – Frikkie going over the windscreen to sit on the bow. Tom and I rested against the dashboard. The only thing I could see of Phil was the top of his blonde head bobbing up and down every now and again. He pulled himself aboard about 15 minutes later.

"That's the best I can do, guys. There's just one problem now."

"What?" said Frikkie, standing next to me.

"I can't risk starting the jet in these weeds. We'll have to drift out into the river to do that."

"And if it doesn't work?"

"We're dead meat… It's up to you, guys. I think we can pull it off, though."

We paused for a while – lost in our own thoughts. If the engine couldn't push the water out the back of the nozzle, we would most certainly die. I don't know how many other people had faced the prospect of flying over a gigantic waterfall in a boat, but we would possibly be the first.

"Let's do it," Frikkie said for all of us – although for a different reason. "There's no beer here, man."

We chuckled and nodded our heads.

"Okay, it's agreed. Sit near the middle of the boat, you guys."

We took up our positions. Tom and I had to cut the ropes off the reeds and overhanging branch because the knots had been pulled too tight. We surged forward like a human bomb at a circus. As we left the small islet, it became horrifyingly clear that we would get sucked into the Devil's Cataract – less than a kilometre away – if the engine failed us.

Phil sat hurriedly on his seat – turning the ignition switch at the same time. The powerful motor kicked into life; so far so good. He gave us a quick look over his shoulder and pushed the accelerator lever all the way forward. The engine screamed as the revs increased, but we barely moved at all. Phil spun the wheel so that we were facing upstream – keeping the revs high all the time. We were just making headway, but at this rate we would either burn out the engine, run out of fuel or blow something up.

"Come on baby, come on!" I said under my breath. Phil angled the boat towards the western edge of the small islet we had just left so that if the worst came to the worst, we could become marooned there and wait for rescue the next day.

We were just about level with the western edge of the little clompie of trees we had anchored ourselves to when something must have cleared in the nozzle. The revs dropped slightly, but the stern bit deep into the water – the bow rising sharply. Frikkie, Tom and I landed in a laughing pile of humanity on top of the engine cowling.

"Yes, yes…yesss!" Phil shouted triumphantly – raising his right arm. We soared up the river like a scalded cat – leaving a high column of water in our wake. I patted Tom and Frikkie on their backs – as they did mine – before we leaned forward to pat Phil. He felt cold and wet, so I looked for his shirt and helped him put it on.

"Well done, Phil. Well done, man. That was brilliant!" I shouted above the rush of wind. We could relax now.

Phil waited until we had passed the A'Zambezi before throttling back so that he could dress again. The rush of adrenalin was exciting and addictive; at that point, you could take on the world.

"Keep going upstream, almost as far as Kandahar Island," I said.

Tying the last knot in his shoelaces, Phil sat up straight and floored the engine one more time. What a beautiful, fast boat. The wind flicked through my hair – and although it was cold, it was invigorating. I didn't know until much later that as we sped upstream, we were almost taken out by armoured cars ambushing the river. This was typical of the poor liaison between the army and the police. They thought we were Zambian Army personnel. What an irony that would have been: getting shot up by my own guys while on R&R.

The river widened – and then narrowed somewhat. It was hard to calculate our speed because we had little reference of nearby, static objects. Whatever speed we were doing, it was damn fast. I was fascinated by the mirrored stars ahead of the boat and sort of became mesmerised by them. Something touched the shiny surface about 20 metres in front of us. At first I thought it was a fish snatching an insect, but there was another splash – and then another and another. I snapped out of my daydream in the same split-second that Phil shouted back at me.

"We're being shot at!"

I sort of crouched down – as did the others – peering over the side of the boat towards the Rhodesian shoreline. There was no indication of barrel flashes coming from there. I adjusted my body and looked at the Zambian bank about 300 metres away. It was alive with little lights winking on and off – and now the all-familiar speeding green lights flicked past us at a dizzy rate.

"Zambia! It's the Zambian side!" I screamed into the wind. We were advancing rapidly into what looked like a solid wall of tracer. Tom and Frikkie were both below the water line. I couldn't bring the Browning to bear because it faced the Rhodesian bank. It could only ever face to the left (or port) of the vessel. Whoever designed the mounting needed to be shot. The wall of tracer advanced – then passed over us in a bent, optical illusion – and was suddenly behind us.

"Bank right, Phil. I want to have a go at them!"

"You're nuts!" he shrieked at me, but turned back anyway. The boat turned right in a slow arc – the left-hand side where I stood banking upwards – making the Browning totally useless. I had to wait until the 180° turn was complete before the boat levelled out again. Once more, we were heading for lots of tracer. I sited as best as I could down the Browning's barrel – pushing an odd little button rather than a trigger, as such. The weapon coughed and roared into life. Red tracer sped away – hitting the water about 200 metres away. I adjusted the angle of the barrel and fired a long, long burst towards the Zambian bank. At that point, although I was terrified, the work I had in hand took the fear away; I was concentrating too hard. I paused for a while to make sure I was firing in the right direction, but to be honest, I'd been made night-blind by the muzzle flash of the machine-gun, so I depressed the button and emptied the entire metal container into the dark smudge at the water's edge. It didn't seem to slow the line of green tracer down very much – and I was now fearful we would be caught in it. One of us could die.

"Go upstream again!" I yelled at Phil. He didn't need any prompting and swung hard-left – completing the U-turn in a few seconds – flooring the boat to maximum speed. The odd tracer attempted to follow us, but their line of flight soon fell far behind us. Phil throttled back – looking at me with wide eyes. Tom and Frikkie made their first appearance.

"Shit, man. I need a dop," Frikkie said, trying to light a fag.

"For fuck's sake, put that out," Phil shouted at him. "What now, Tony?"

"Let's anchor on that island there and make a plan."

The boat angled right – and then left – until we were keeping a neutral position in the speeding river. Phil inched the wheel over until Tom jumped up and tied the remainder of the front mooring rope to a thick overhead branch. The deep rumble of the engine was replaced by the sighing and gurgle of the water as soon as Phil cut the engine.

"Shit, that was mean," Phil said.

"Bad, very bad," Frikkie concurred – using possibly the only two adjectives he knew.

"Shh… Listen," I said, raising my index finger to my mouth.

There was the unmistakable sound of trucks moving on the Zambian shore – lots of them. Faint voices carried over the cool night air. I wasn't sure if this was Kandahar Island, but quickly rejected the idea because there appeared to be no civilian jetty here – indeed, no sign of it being used as a tourist destination in years gone by. The island was thickly-wooded with tall hardwood trees.

"Let's go have a look," I said to Phil. "You guys stay here and keep your eyes peeled."

I took my rifle back from Tom and climbed into the thick branch anchoring our boat. Phil followed as I walked precariously up to the main trunk, and then down to the ground. The place was heavily-wooded, but fortunately the grass was short.

"Follow me," I whispered to Phil. We walked slowly forward – rifles at the ready – until we reached the northern bank of the island about 50 metres away. Heavy trees with low boughs – similar to the one we'd anchored to – lined the bank of the island. It made it almost impossible to see anything in Zambia – now less than a hundred metres away. We stood silently listening to the voices and revving engines. A red tail light from a truck briefly appeared before being snuffed out.

"Loads of Zambian Army guys," I said to Phil. He nodded his agreement. "No point in hanging around here."

We retraced our steps – whistling as we approached the boat. I was quite sure Frikkie would shoot us simply because he could act thick, so I made darn sure he'd heard us before we crossed back to the boat.

"What now?" Phil asked when we were back on the boat.

"Maybe we can cross to our shore and get picked up by a truck?"

"Good idea," Frikkie piped in. "This is a bad idea, staying out here all night."

I grimaced, and so did Phil – his white teeth appearing briefly in the gloom. He started the engine and accelerated only fast enough for us to angle sideways to the Rhodesian shoreline.

As we approached home territory, I suddenly became aware of where we were. We were at the mouth of Hippo Creek – probably the largest tributary running into the Zambezi in this area. The entrance to the tributary was a darker smudge against the backdrop until the water heading inland appeared like a silver spear disappearing into grey and formless trees. We tied up left of a large bush that looked as if it was floating on the water.

"Phil, call your base and ask them to get hold of the army for uplift."

He nodded and called several times before he got hold of the police signaller less than 10 kays away in the village. The message was repeated and confirmed – and that was that. I added one more thing: that we would be on the same frequency on the radio as we moved inland, and that the army should tune into our frequency rather than us try and figure out theirs. It was only after we disconnected the boat's radio that we came to the painful realisation that we had no co-ax aerial for it. We might be able to transmit for half a kay if we were lucky, but that was all. It meant walking towards friendly forces in an area possibly swarming with gooks, with no radio to warn them of our approach.

Phil took out the rotor arm from the boat's engine before pulling the Browning off its mounting. He clipped two belts into it and handed it to me on the shore. Tom had my rifle once again. He hadn't spoken a word the entire time since we left the police station earlier in the night.

"Know how to use it?" I nodded towards the rifle.

"Sure."

"Okay, listen in. I'll lead the way. Phil, you back me up; then Frikkie; then Tom, okay?"

They nodded agreement and picked up their weapons. I pointed the Browning ahead of me and started walking slowly into the gloom. Every tree looked like a gook poised to strike – the complete absence of definition compounding the feeling. My heartbeat accelerated slightly as we moved inland to the main dirt road that serviced the national park, less than a kilometre away.

We'd gone barely a hundred metres when a massive red-yellow flash went off to our left. A split-second later, a rolling shockwave hit us – continuing down the valley like thunder after a lightning strike. Phil, Tom and Frikkie had thrown themselves flat, but for some reason, I just stood there. I am not particularly quick to react to anything. This was borne out later in the war in Mozambique when 2nd Battalion was operating along the banks of the Limpopo River, near the power lines from Cabora Basa. There, I had simply watched a Lynx aircraft getting stonked by a 12.7 and RPGs without warning the pilot on my radio. It was only through the quick thinking of Sergeant Cloete that the pilot escaped unharmed.

"Someone's hit a mine," I said. "Keep your wits about you."

The words had barely left my mouth when a dozen or so weapons opened up from behind us. I was more fascinated by the way the tracer arced than any fear entering my senses. I don't know why, but I am simply built that way. The other three guys were still lying in the prone position – preparing to fire their weapons. I levelled the Browning at the flashes and pushed the firing button. Nothing happened. Now I was really scared – and I rapidly knelt down.

"Stoppage!" I hissed at Phil. "How do you overcome that?!"

"Beats me," he said.

I chucked the weapon down and grabbed my rifle back from Tom. He tried to resist, but I yanked it away from him. As I stood up to fire, I realised the gooks were about 50 metres away and were firing in our general direction – not quite knowing where we were. Fortunately, most of the tracer was high and wide. I followed the angle of the tracer back down to the base of a large clump of tall trees on the other side of Hippo Creek. I made sure the safety catch was off and aimed 'open-sited' down the barrel before emptying the entire magazine into the general area in closely-spaced single shots.

When the last doppie flung itself out onto the dusty soil, I could distinctly hear the gooks shouting back at me and running into the gloom. I will never forget the sound of their feet rustling in the grass as long as I live.

"Give me another magazine, Tom!" I hissed at him. He looked wide-eyed up at me.

"I left them in the boat..."

"For fuck's sake!" I spat.

We started walking towards the main dirt road again. I felt calm and exhilarated for some reason, but feared that we had a machine-gun that didn't work and three rifles with hardly any ammo. We were virtually defenceless. At least Tom had taken the handgun out of its holster – holding it by his side.

I started walking again until we reached the main road less than five minutes later. Phil passed me the radio and I set about trying to make contact with the army column coming to rescue us. I was amazed our aerial-less radio made contact first go – although somewhat faintly. We were instructed to walk east along the road until we reached the rescue vehicles.

"Make sure your guys are all, I say again, all informed we are coming down the road." I said.

"Copied. Come along now, we're waiting for you."

"Copied... out."

I handed the radio handset back to Phil and started a slow walk down the wide, dusty track. The sand looked white in the faint starlight – and we had no trouble making our way along the road at all. We were in an extremely vulnerable position, and any ambush waiting for us in the darkened shrubs either side of us would cut us to bits. Strangely, this was when I felt the most scared – not while the contact was going on. Our soft footfalls were the only sound we could hear apart from our laboured breathing – laboured from adrenalin more than effort.

About six minutes later, I saw the first vehicle around the bend in the road. It was in complete darkness, but there was no mistaking its profile. The weak signal on our radio had given me the impression the rescue column was a lot further away, but in fact it had been less than 300 metres away. I stopped and called the column commander before we continued our progress.

"Hurry up, will you? We have a badly-injured man."

"Copied that. I have you visual and am approaching from the west on the road now."

"Got you visual," the column commander said. A dark figure detached itself from the vehicle and came towards me.

"What happened?" I asked rhetorically, looking at a Ferret Scout car that had been blown up by a mine.

"Boosted mine I reckon... Let's go. The Ferret commander is all smashed up."

"No seatbelt?"

"I reckon... Anyway, you guys go back in the two-five that's got him aboard."

"Thanks for coming to get us, man. It's been a bit hairy out there tonight. I owe you."

"It's okay. Let's go."

"I know you, don't I?" I said, staring at his face in the gloom. "What's your name?"

"Watermeyer."

"Laurie?"

"Yes," he said, coming closer to my face. "Tony Ballinger?"

"The very one."

"Good to see you, Tony. We'll chat later. Let's get that guy back to base."

"Sure..." turning to the police guys, I said: "Get on that truck, there."

We helped the injured man, whose head had been wrapped in white bandages, onto the passenger (or right-front) seat of the Unimog 2.5. We strapped him in as best we could. I climbed in behind him – propping him up with my hand – after quickly tugging my seatbelt tight. It was damn cold, so I pulled a balaclava out of my combat jacket and pulled it over my head. As the powerful diesel engine kicked into life, so the driver commenced a 'three-point turn' to go back the way he had come. Laurie was in another vehicle behind me with a stick of infantry in it. I was glad to be going back to the village. Enough of this heroic bullshit; I was supposed to be on R&R. In less than half an hour, I would be tucked up in bed again – the terror of the night being eased by a whisky and Mally. I was mildly surprised seeing Laurie again. The last time I'd seen him, he'd been shot through the buttocks by a gook that was lying on the other side of a tree trunk that he stepped over. The gook got a 'third eye', but also a pile of shit from Laurie's intestines when his bowels emptied from the shock of being shot at from so close. The PRAW pilot that casevaced him landed on the main Vic Falls to Wankie Road – against orders – and I admire the man for that.

I looked to my left as the vehicle was about to pull away – turning briefly to say something to Phil sitting next to me. I never started the sentence. A massive shockwave – like an open-handed smack from a very strong man – smashed into the left side of my skull. In the same frozen second in time, a white light – followed by red and orange sparks – shot upwards and outwards in slow motion. The bandaged form next to me lifted off his seat like a human cannonball in a circus and sailed away into the rapidly-enveloping dust cloud. I had just hit my second landmine.

A fine mist rained down on me – probably the water from the tyres, which is put in them to absorb shockwaves in an explosion. It smelled of oil. For a few brief seconds, I felt disorientated, but recovered rapidly. No-one had opened fire to clear potential ambushers from the shrubbery around us.

"Open fire!" I shouted. A MAG coughed into life from the back of the truck – the only weapon to start firing. Red tracer sped off like angry hornets into the black night. Laurie's stick opened up in support of us, but almost as quickly as it started, it finished. Once again, I had no idea where my rifle was. I had rested it on the side of the truck when I put on my balaclava.

"Off, off, off…. Get into the tyre tracks behind us!" I yelled. We scrambled and tripped over each other to jump off the tailgate – taking cover immediately. I felt lopsided on the left side of my head; my balance was buggered.

"Everyone okay?"

The odd head nodded in affirmation. There was a strong smell of spent explosives, oil and vaporised rubber hanging in the air.

"Where's the injured guy?" a voice said from far away. A sound like a plane taking off coursed through my head.

"Dunno," I said – standing uneasily to my feet. Laurie brushed past me and went to help the armoured car guy – as did two other men. He was in a bad way – moaning and groaning on the dusty soil. Laurie suddenly stood up from a crouching position and looked towards Zambia.

"Mortars!" he shouted.

We dived to the ground – waiting tensely for the shells to land. You cannot imagine the horrible feeling that creeps up your spine when you are waiting for a mortar round to land. About 20 seconds later, a bright-yellow flash went off down the dirt track where the damaged Ferret lay at a lopsided angle in the ditch.

We stood to a man and started running wildly into the bush – two guys dragging the wounded man behind them. I caught a brief glimpse of my rifle lying a few feet from the truck – snatching it on the run. It had no ammo in it, so it was totally useless anyway.

The bush looked like an alien landscape – intimidating and frightening. We had no idea if we were running towards more gooks retreating from Elephant Hills or what; we were a disorganised rabble. Thorns tugged at my face and clothes as we ran. In a short space of time, we'd left the injured man and his two assistants way behind us.

Every few seconds after that, Laurie shouted at us to take cover. I couldn't hear the primary charge 'popping' as the mortar shell left its tube in Zambia, but Laurie could. He was my 'ears' now. I realised then that I had lost my hearing in my left ear – and some of my balance with it. I staggered along behind Laurie like a drunkard.

One shell after another landed. The bush lit up with bright flashes – some far away and some close by – but thank God no-one was injured. It looked like an act on a stage where a giant kept using a flashgun on his tiny victims. Each spur of light momentarily lit up the land-scape – enabling us to run for a few seconds before we crashed to cover again. Despite the cold,

I was sweating profusely. Smoke and the smell of spent explosives drifted on the light breeze – causing successive flashes to look like they were coming through a haze of frosted glass.

I didn't count the bombs that fell that night, but I figure perhaps 20 did – maybe more. By the time it was over, I was fatigued, sweaty and swaying on my feet. My immediate concern was the injured man and any other potential casualties. Laurie did a quick head-count with his men – as I did with Frikkie, Phil and Tom.

"Let's back-track and look for him," Laurie said. I nodded – tasting blood in the back of my throat for the first time.

"Can you spare me some ammo, Laurie?"

He flicked a full magazine at me from his webbing. I took the empty one off my rifle and put it inside my combat jacket – slipping the full one into position, cocking it. I was relieved to have some form of defence again.

We back-tracked a surprisingly long way until we found the injured man and his assistants. Despite the assault on him, he was lucid – and even smiling thinly. Seeing the two sitting there made me wonder why we had bothered running at all. I mean, who was guaranteeing we were running from the shells rather than into them?

With Laurie in the lead, we gingerly made our way back to where our two-five had been blown up. The three abandoned vehicles looked like a scene from the lunar landings – cast in the silver-grey of night.

"Get the guys in all-round defence," Laurie said to his sergeant. "I'm off to A'Zambezi to phone for help."

"Don't you have a radio?"

"I do, but it's not working. Maybe the shockwave from the first landmine…"

"What about driving back in your two-five?"

"Too risky… We've already hit a mine two other vehicles missed."

"Okay, I'll come with you," I said. He looked me and nodded.

"Let's go."

Laurie is a big man with wide shoulders. He started off at a stiff pace – heading for the A'Zambezi Hotel about six kays east to use their phone, calling for yet more backup. It was an eerie feeling walking down that dirt road with darkened bushes all around us. Everything was totally silent apart from our footfalls. I walked about 10 paces behind Laurie – battling like crazy to stay upright. Blood thickened and congealed in the back of my throat. I felt mildly afraid because I didn't know what the injury meant to me.

We followed the twisting and turning dirt road for what seemed ages until at last we came to the turn-off to the warden's house. I caught up with Laurie and tapped him on the shoulder.

"Warden's house," I said, pointing to my left. "There's a phone there."

"Okay. Let's give it a go."

We turned left down a track that had been churned to white powder by heavy trucks. After a couple of hundred metres, we came to the security fence surrounding the homestead. The gate was securely padlocked. Laurie rattled it and called out several times, but it remained in darkness.

"Probably thinks we're gooks," I said. Laurie nodded agreement.

"Let's carry on."

I felt slightly firmer on my feet now as we pressed eastwards at a fast pace. The next lot of buildings we came to were the tourist chalets – one of which I'd mistaken for the warden's house that time we invaded Chundu Island. A kay or so further, we reached tar – and then the thatched offices that spanned the road at the entrance to the national park. Not far to the A'Zambezi now. I felt a bit more relaxed being this close to civilisation again.

I couldn't believe my eyes when we walked into the A'Zambezi Hotel. All the lights were on and people milled about outside a bar as if nothing had happened just down the road from them. A smartly-dressed male receptionist was on duty under the open-sided thatched reception area – even though it was now 1:00 a.m. in the morning. His eyes widened in fright as our camouflaged forms materialised out of the inky blackness in front of him.

"I need a phone and the police station's phone number," Laurie said without introductions.

The receptionist pushed a phone forward – pointing to the number on a nearby clipboard.

The phone rang for a long time before it was answered – soliciting a 'fucking useless cops' comment from Laurie. He spoke at length and then put the phone down. I had difficulty following what he was saying; I had that buzzing noise come back into my left ear again.

We waited an hour or so, but eventually the second rescue column arrived to collect us – this time with a police 'Pookie' leading the way. The Pookie was designed to detect landmines electronically – sensing their metal canisters as one would detect a coin on a beach with those handheld metal detectors.

"I'll wait here, Laurie. I think I've lost my eardrum," I said.

"Okay. We'll pick you up on the way back."

He hopped onto a four-five with three men on it and another Ferret as escort behind the Pookie. The red tail lights soon disappeared into the black night. It was nearly an hour before they returned – and the loud rumbling explosion of another mine I'd been expecting never came. While I'd been waiting, I returned to the receptionist to try and get through to Mally at the Casino Hotel, but the casino's receptionist told me they had closed shortly after the mortar attack. I was still trying to get through to Fred when Laurie returned with the guys we'd left behind. I hung up and ran to join him.

We drove in silence to the army base – passing the brightly-lit Elephant Hills Hotel on our right. An ambulance was waiting when we arrived – and an Islander aircraft was at the landing strip ready to take the injured Ferret commander back to Wankie. If things hadn't been so organised, I would have had time to run to Mally's house and tell her I needed to see a doctor. I scribbled a note and asked Laurie to give it to Fred as soon as possible. Everyone knew Fred, so that was the easiest route.

I was surprised I had to convince the medic in the ambulance that I was injured, but after a short discussion, he agreed to let me fly to Wankie also. We took off at 0345 and I soon fell asleep at the back of the plane in a warm cocoon devoid of sounds entering my left ear.

The diagnosis, as I expected, was a shredded left eardrum. I spent two days in hospital sleeping the stress off – mildly amused that I was in a ward two down from Rootman and next door to Pete Wells. I had a very pleasant visit from a servicemen's support lady, who gave me a toothbrush, toothpaste and some magazines to read. I really admired those women for the way they supported men in the operational areas. They ran canteens where you could always stop for a hamburger and coke and a chat with either a nice-looking girl, or a pleasant motherly woman who reminded you of your mom and happier times of sitting in a kitchen while she baked cakes.

I spent the third night at 1 Indep officers' quarters – and by lunchtime the next day, I was on a train for Bulawayo (and ultimately, Salisbury). I was still in my hastily-arranged uniform, but fortunately it had been washed at the hospital and felt fresh and clean. I'd made contact with Fred at last, and he promised to tell Mally where I was and what had happened.

"It scared the crap out of her coming home to an empty house," he said over the phone.

"I'm sure. Tell her I love her and I'll call her from Salisbury. Tell her I'm sorry too."

"She's got a big heart. You just get better 'Bomber Ballinger'."

I smiled at my nickname and put the phone down. Mal and I just couldn't get our act together. We were always getting separated by fate... Even my leave had ended with a bang!

It was great seeing my folks again – and sleeping in my childhood bedroom, with model aeroplanes and ships stuck on the pelmets, was like going backwards in a time-warp. It's almost as if they had not wanted the feeling of their kid to leave the room. My mom related how she had almost fainted when a chaplain had visited her to tell them about my injury – fearing I'd been killed.

As familiar as Salisbury was, the normality of life there felt alien somehow. It made me realise how small Vic Falls was; how isolated we were – and indeed, that the ever-present threat of an attack had become a way of life now… forming an oppression at the back of our minds.

I had an appointment set with an ear specialist by the name of Dr Fine for the third day after my arrival – and in the meantime, I sunbathed the time away in the warm wintry sun, listening to Radio 702. It was like being a kid again – and my mom's baking and abundant food made it that bit harder for the top button on some old shorts to get done up, but it was great being there and I thoroughly enjoyed lying on the sofa watching TV at night. It was a time when each news broadcast would bring reports on the war – and as the years passed, the frequency of announcements beginning with: 'Combined Operations regrets to announce the death in action of….' increased rapidly.

The visit with Dr Fine came and went. It was his diagnosis that the tiny shred of eardrum left would encourage the rest to grow back on its own – and that I would have to come back in three months for a check-up. I was told not to swim in that period and I had to tilt my head to one side when showering or washing my hair.

"If it doesn't grow back, I'll remove some lining from a vein and put in an eardrum for you," the Doc said, concluding our appointment.

A few days later, I was watching TV at about 7:00 p.m. when my mom called me to the phone.

"Someone called Pearce, Tony," she said, holding the receiver.

"Major Pearce?"

"I think so," she said, handing me the phone. My heartbeat quickened under a spurt of adrenalin.

"Major Pearce?" I enquired.

"Yes, Tony. How are you?"

"Getting better thanks sir, but my left eardrum's gone."

"I believe so." There was a short pause before he continued. "Look, I'm sorry to trouble you while you're on sick leave, but I thought you would want to know…"

"Know what, sir?"

"Tony, I'm sorry to be the bearer of bad news, but three of your guys died in a landmine explosion two days ago."

My skin went cold – a shudder running through me. I sat down by the phone – expecting the worst.

"Who?"

"Roy Orchard, Tom Shipley and Dave Kruger..." he said, after a heavy pause.

"Oh no!" I gasped, leaning my forehead on my palm. "How... Where?"

"I can only say in an operational area. Phones have ears... but you know where they were based."

"Yes, I know... Shit.... Three of them!"

"I'm sorry, Tony. Really."

"How?"

"Well, no harm in telling you that, I suppose. They got on a police Land Rover to get back to base after a long patrol, and it wasn't mine-proofed."

"Anyone injured?" I said, horrified by visions of carnage.

"All of them, one way or another... Colman, Albie Louw, Nick Wilson... Rob Maggs..."

"Where are they now?"

"Wankie, but they'll probably be transferred to Andrew Flemming in Salisbury, soon."

A long, heavy silence followed – broken only by the odd bit of static on the phone. I could hear my mom and dad laughing at a comedy on the TV next door.

"I'm terribly sorry, Tony."

"Thanks for phoning, sir. What about me though? What do I do?"

"I'm sure Don Price will get hold of you shortly and tell you what's up... Well, I'd better go now."

"Thanks again, sir," I said and hung up. I sat staring at the phone for a long time after that. I was utterly crushed. Those poor, young men – just at the start of their lives... dead. I just couldn't believe it. I felt responsible and angry with myself that I hadn't been there for them. Why on earth had they got on an unprotected Land Rover? It was the biggest 'no' in the military.

I stood up and walked slowly down the passage towards my bedroom – feeling a large lump forming in my throat and tears welling up in my eyes. I flopped onto my bed and let out great heaving sobs of grief and anger – the sound of it deadened because my good ear was on the pillow.

And so began 30 years of anger towards Don Price because someone told me – incorrectly at the time – that he had ordered them to get on that Land Rover to react to a store robbery and that they had died because of his arrogance and stupidity. I am glad to say, for Don's sake, that I have learned the truth – and only the youth of those three men is to blame; youthfulness that also made me do stupid things – the consequences of which were far less than the penalty those lovely young men received.

Chapter Nine

I was temporarily medically downgraded during the last three months of my national service and was assigned as an admin officer at 1 Indep in Wankie. I have no idea what happened to my platoon – although I learned later that many of them were reassigned to other units, like Hugh Bomford going to mortars and so on. I think my faithful and trusty driver, Bert Furmston, stayed with 1 Indep. Max and Kenny and Duff and the others… I am ashamed to say I simply lost track of them stuck in that hot hellhole of Wankie.

I spent the daylight hours doing reports, being paymaster, ordering supplies and chatting to the very pleasant-looking sergeant who always dressed so neatly in her sand uniform. The chemistry was there – and I knew that if she hadn't been married and I didn't have Mally, we would have become lovers. The flirting made the days easier to bear, anyway.

At night, I would be duty officer at the JOC office or go to a movie in the village or visit the power station's clubhouse. On other occasions, I went to the officers' mess at 4 Indep to listen to the old, resident major relate hunting stories from the '20s and '30s – he was *that* old. In fact, he helped shoot out most of the game in Mashonaland to get rid of tsetse flies so that commercial farms could be opened up. So much for stealing land from black people; they didn't live there in the first place because 'sleeping sickness' carried by the fly kept them at bay.

I missed Mally like crazy, so it came as a wonderful surprise one day when she drove through the front gate in her little black Morris.

"You drove all the way here in that thing?" I said in horror and disbelief.

"Relax. We came in a small convoy. Karen Blauw kept me company."

It was pleasantly embarrassing to kiss her in front of 'my' sergeant girl. Needless to say, she looked daggers at Mally.

I led her to the officers' mess, where we had a late lunch of roast beef, potatoes and vegetables followed by Dairy Maid ice-cream.

"I can see why you're popping out your uniform," she giggled. I gave her a discreet 'middle finger', which she swiped away before holding my hand. "I've missed you so much. You like scaring me to death with all your antics, don't you?"

"At your service," I said, pulling her down the corridor to my room. The place smelled of fly spray and beeswax – the 'regulation smell' of all government buildings, it seemed.

My room was clean and adequate; the décor a bit dated, but it was private and I could do my own thing after hours. I often felt sorry for my guys who had to bunk down in barracks, but I guess youth and dormitories make for good fun.

We spent the entire weekend in bed – only leaving the room to eat and drink. It was a time in my life I will never forget – of youth, virility and powerful sexual desires. We made love to the music of the day – particularly Donna Summer, who we both loved... her haunting, romantic voice helping us get totally lost inside each other. I felt drunk with contentment when I had to report for duty on Monday morning, and it was agony watching Mally drive away again – leaving me with a lump in my throat as her little black car disappeared among the thorn trees.

Towards October 1977 my national service came to an end in a drunken orgy at 1 Indep Barracks – as well as the Baobab Hotel on top of the hill. It was a night of mixed emotions, with feelings of sadness and joy competing with each other. It was great to see my guys again – as well as the other two platoons – and I laughed and joked with them until the early hours of the morning. It's hard to describe how close you get to men in war; they literally become like brothers. There was a lot of back-slapping and hugs and alcohol. I think it was Max Cochrane who suggested we try and drink the 'top shelf down' of spirits in the hotel bar. There were whiskies, liqueurs, brandies and so on. It was reported that no man had gone beyond the middle of the second shelf before collapsing in a drunken heap on the floor. I barely managed the top shelf before losing part-consciousness. Rumour had it I went and pissed all over the African beer hall behind the hotel in retaliation for the many nights we lay in ambush around the building earlier in the year.

I remember one of those ambushes at the beer hall, when we lay in silence in the shrubs opposite – trying to see if any gooks were having a night off. Several of our guys could speak either Shona or Ndebele and we were hoping that copious quantities of beer would loosen tongues enough to give themselves away.

We were about two hours into the ambush when two very large African women came waddling towards us – laughing and slapping each other on the back. At first I thought they were heading for a nearby path to go home, but at the last second, they walked into the bush where I was, spun around, hoisted up their dresses and dropped their knickers. There I was – blackened up in camo cream – less than two feet from the biggest, blackest arses I've ever seen... and to top it off, buckets of hot piss shot out of them like a waterfall – splashing and bubbling all over the flash-hider on my rifle. The stench of fermented urine was overpowering! I looked sideways at Max as this was happening. His face was contorted with suppressed laughter – tears running down his face. So I can say in all honesty, that was the quickest ambush I ever conducted!

The next morning we stood in a line with thumping heads – taunted by nausea – while the Q.S. slowly and deliberately took back every single item of military equipment (bar our uniforms) that we'd ever possessed. It would have made a fine cycle of events if Pete Wells had stood there in the queue with me as we had done at Llewellin so long before, but he, Rootman and Brown were now back in Salisbury – no doubt somewhere near the men injured in the landmine.

As soon as that long-winded exercise was over, we signed copious forms, received our final pay, train tickets and were officially civilians once again. My guys took their last shot at being able to take the piss out of me – no doubt organised by Max. They came to me one after the other to shake my hand – deliberately calling me by my Christian name to annoy me. For 18 months it had been 'sir' this and 'sir' that – and now they filed past me saying: "thanks, Tony" or "where are you going now, Tony?" I think Abbott was the most successful in annoying me because he used my name about 12 times in one sentence, but it was all good fun – and in less than an hour, we parted ways… never to serve together again. I felt sad and heavy-hearted as I watched them clamber on a four-five to take them to the station.

❧—❧

I arrived in Vic Falls the next day by train. Mally was waiting at the station and we decided to go to the Casino Hotel for a drink by the pool before going home.

"I have a surprise for you," she said, as I eased into a deckchair. It was a hot day; the pool crowded with tourists and their kids. Mally opened a plastic carrier bag and pulled out some clothes. "For you, my love!"

"Mally, they're lovely!" I said, holding up several new shirts and shorts. "Just what the doctor ordered."

"And some slops and rafters for your feet…"

"That's so sweet, love…" I bent forward and kissed her. "I was wondering what I would wear."

It was really weird being a civilian again – and already, the first nagging thoughts of how I would support myself had set in. The army had been like a strict mother to me – providing everything I needed – and now I was supposed to support myself and think and plan finances. I wasn't very good at that. Mally had a mischievous smile on her face.

"What's up, babe?" I smiled at her. She looked behind me and smiled widely before focusing on me again.

"You'll see..."

"A man of leisure," the familiar voice of Fred said from behind me.

"Fred, good to see you." I stood, shaking his hand. He flicked his wrist at a waiter and ordered drinks all-round.

"Time to celebrate the good news!"

"Good news? You mean being a civvy again?"

"Yes, that as well," Fred smiled at Mally before continuing, "plus the job I'm offering you."

"Job?" I flicked my eyes from Mally's smiling face back to Fred's. He looked like a cat in a cream factory.

"In the casino. I want you to work in the casino with us... as a croupier."

"You're joking, of course? Me? A croupier? I know nothing about it."

"Naturally, but I'm sure Mally's taught you a thing or two already, hey?"

He laughed his Mexican laugh while Mally smacked him on his knee. I couldn't believe this was happening. It was a very generous offer and was the ideal solution for staying at the Falls and being with Mally.

"I don't know what to say Fred..."

"Just say 'yes'," the two of them said together. I thought about it for a while and then nodded.

"Okay. Thanks very much, Fred."

"Don't thank me, thank Mally. It was her idea; never entered my head!"

"Thanks Mal," I said, leaning forward to kiss her. She looked flushed with excitement.

"You can start Monday night. Your pay will be 300 plus tips – and one free meal before work."

"That's very generous, Fred. Thanks so much."

"It's okay. Nice to have you aboard... Anyway, I'll leave you two lovebirds."

The drinks arrived just as Fred left us. We sat in the sun sipping the golden liquid – revelling in our newfound freedom and the perfect solution to all my cares. I felt liberated and happy for the first time in many, many months. I could genuinely relax now.

"There's something else," Mally said, as she picked up another packet – pulling out a black evening suit – "your uniform."

I took it from her and held it up to look at. It was beautiful.

"How did you know what size I am?"

"Your clothes at home. I remember which ones looked comfortable on you and sent the measurements to an Indian tailor in Wankie – one of my errands that time I came down to see you."

"You're amazing," I said, before kissing her on the lips. "Thank you..."

The seasons had done their full cycle – and it was now incredibly hot in October. Clouds threatened rain every day, but nothing materialised. Sensing the pending onslaught of rain, flowers and trees burst into a profusion of colour – a little like May in the northern hemisphere. After all, this was our spring.

Bougainvilleas – ranging in colour from pink, to purple, to red, to peach – simply exploded all over the place. Cannas reached up high – buds popping. The odd msasa tree turned red before going green. Jacarandas dripped mauve flowers – competing with flamboyants to carpet roads in an orgy of colours – and in some of the more colonial residences and hotels, roses bloomed by the hundred. The air was liquid and sweet with smells of every description. Frangipani and lavender perfume drifted over the whole village.

In other cases, some indigenous trees smelled of rotten meat – using flies to carry their pollen from flower to flower. Not pleasant on the nostrils, but equally beautiful and special in its own unique way; God's splendour in all its glory.

It was on one of these aroma-rich, warm evenings when Mally and I strolled to work for my first appointment as a croupier. The sky was an orange smudge behind us and dimly lit by a silvery moon to the east. What a perfect setting for a romantic walk, at our leisure, to work.

We took a shortcut through the municipal campsite, with brick chalets dotted between the odd caravan and tent. I wondered who the people were in those tents, or sitting by a fire having a braai – the divine scent of cooking meat filling the air. Who were these brave people driving up to our little outpost in the middle of nowhere to have a holiday and see one of the world's greatest natural wonders? Who were they to be ignorant of Albert Ncube, who still stalked the bush out there? Where was that bastard?

I was intensely embarrassed to walk into the casino after our staff meal and felt totally ill-at-ease, uncomfortable and stupid. As soon as the doors closed behind me, I turned and walked out again – with Mally in hot pursuit.

"I can't do this, Mal. It's not me…"

"Of course you can. You look so sexy in that suit… Come on, we all felt like this the first night."

"I don't know, honestly. I'd rather be in a contact."

"You won't be dealing to customers for a long time, babe. Please come in." She tugged ineffectually at my hand.

"I need to think about this a bit."

"Think about what?" Mal's voice indicated her own nervousness – perhaps a fear that I wouldn't go through with it; that it would jeopardise our relationship.

"Come on, please… for me."

I pursed my lips before smiling at her. The fact that I didn't have to be a dealer for a while took the edge off. I nodded once before walking hand-in-hand with her through the doors like a lamb to the slaughter.

"Got cold feet?" Fred laughed. Ivor Ring, the assistant casino manager, stood next to him – smiling. Ivor wore glasses that reflected the overhead lights like 'The Smiling Shit's'.

"Welcome, Tony," he said, extending his hand. I shook it firmly before he introduced me to the other croupiers. Liz was a 30-ish Scottish girl, blonde and busty; Lesley, slightly round-shouldered, was also blonde with shoulder-length hair. Linda came next. I had instant chemistry with her. She was short, with brown hair down to the bottom of her shoulder blades. Her lips were full and sensual – her eyes large and inviting. Danny looked like a school kid and Gavin was about 30 with a permanent sheen of sweat on his top lip. His handshake was limp and clammy. Needless to say, I took an instant dislike to him.

"So, what now?" I said to Fred.

"Go over to that spare roulette table with Mally and she'll start teaching you how to deal."

I adjusted my bow-tie with my forefinger – unused to the restricted feeling around my neck. All my army shirts had been open and comfortable; now I felt like a penguin all trussed up.

"See, it's not that bad," Mally said, leading me by the elbow to a table on the far side of the pit. Music filtered through the air. People laughed and joked at the corner bar. A few punters sat down to be dealt by Lesley. Linda smiled at me when our eyes met.

"She's trouble," Mally said. "Keep your distance from her."

"Is that you or the green monster talking?"

Mally smiled and slapped me hard on the bum.

"I can see I'm gonna have to screw you to death to keep your eyes off the other girls."

"Looks like a lot of lusting coming up, then."

"Bastard!' She pecked me on the cheek. "Remember, I have eyes in the back of my head…"

"Mmm. All the better to see me with."

"Want a drink?"

"You mean a beer?"

"No… coke, orange juice… a softie."

"Fanta please."

Mally ordered us a drink each and waited for it to arrive before she settled down to show me how to deal on the roulette table. She was a good tutor and I learned quickly. She showed me how to spin the ball, rotating the wheel in the opposite direction; how to place called bets like 'orphans' or 'splits' or 'straight-ups'; how to quickly calculate pay-outs in my head and so on and so forth. After a couple of hours, I was getting the hang of it.

"See? It's not so bad, is it?" Mally said, squeezing my bum – then whispering in my ear: "I feel so horny looking at you in that suit; wish I could do you on the table."

"It's a date," I said, looking nervously back at Fred – who thankfully wasn't aware that I existed.

It was 3:00 a.m. when we finally staggered through our front door. The house was cool because we had left the air-conditioner on in our absence. It was so lovely to hear the familiar old rattle and buzz of that faithful old machine. How it worked with half the front face missing – as well as most of its knobs and buttons – I'll never know, but the sound of it made me feel at home, like coming back to old slippers.

I eased down on the couch. My feet were hurting like hell and every muscle in the small of my back and legs screamed at me.

"Shit, Mal. This is worse than pokey drill. How the hell do you do it night after night?"

She didn't say anything, but came quickly towards me – that familiar glazed look in her eyes.

"You look so sexy in that suit," she breathed into my mouth before pulling back. "I saw the way you and Linda looked at each other. You won't ever cheat on me, will you?"

My heart skipped a bit – thinking of Yvonne.

"No... never," I lied.

"I know I'm older than you. Linda is your age... young... sexy..."

"Shhh, I love you and I'll never hurt you. I promise."

"That's all I wanted to hear," she said, resting her head on my shoulder. "I would die without you."

"Look forward to a long life, then," I said, stroking her hair.

The next two months at Vic Falls were the best I experienced there. The weather was hot. Lazy days were spent by the pool of various hotels, playing tennis or having a braai at home – sitting on top of the bunker at sunset, licking the taste of chicken off our fingers. We also went on the odd booze cruise, where the liberal dispensation of alcohol would ensure us racing home to make love on the first surface available after the front door slammed shut – our sweaty bodies sliding over each other.

On other days, we would drive out to the croc farm and watch crocs being fed; or pull a few one-armed bandits at Elephant Hills; or drive past the baobab tree and sit in silent wonder – watching millions of litres of water pouring into the Devil's Cataract.

The build-up of heat brought threatening black rainclouds and a sense of electricity and expectation into the air. We would lie on the bed under the cooling effect of the air-conditioner – satisfied and sleepy – waiting for the rains to come. Thunder rolled and echoed down the valley most afternoons.

The feeling of anticipation was mirrored and highlighted by the Rhodesian Corps of Engineers moving into the village to start the onerous task of building twin, four metre-high security fences around the entire village. Situated six kays from the town centre, it was designed to put the suburbs out of range of gook 82mm mortars, which had a maximum five-and-a-half kay range. The 80-metre gap between the two fences was liberally sprinkled with anti-personnel mines and 'ploughshares' that would blow anyone to bits if triggered. As the name suggests, the device was made from shaped explosives that looked like a ploughshare. A wire would be stretched – spring-loaded – to a nearby tree about 10 metres away. If a human or animal bumped into this wire, it fired a detonator which set off the charge – directing steel ball-bearings into a deadly cone that would literally cut a human in half.

Only three breaches existed in the minefield: one on the road to Wankie, one on the road to Kazungula and the last one on the dirt track running parallel with the Zambezi River into the national park. Each of these breaches was manned by PATU men – and part of their job was to search each and every vehicle that came into the village. Daily patrols by foot or vehicle ran along the inner or outer edge of the fences – looking for holes or footprints.

The village was now an island in a sea of hostile bush in the middle of nowhere – and the realisation of this was tangible. Many of the local population started to 'look over their shoulders' all the time. Levels of stress increased. We basically felt like prisoners in a very big cage.

The minefield was a superb move to curtail incursions into the village, which would almost certainly have increased with the arrival of the rains. There were at least 150 gooks operating between Jambezi and Vic Falls – a large enough number to cause chaos and panic if they wanted to.

The barrier also released surplus troops to patrol the hinterland – troops that would normally just sit in camp waiting to react to an attack. Some of these men were posted to the airport, as rumours swirled around the village that Albert and his gang of merry thugs were going to shoot down a civilian airliner – or sneak in at night to blow parked aircraft and other infrastructure sky-high. Troops and Ferret armoured cars would race alongside a plane about to take off or land to deter gooks lying in the surrounding bush from opening fire. The war was definitely taking on a more 'classical' phase, where terrorists operating in small numbers were joining forces for possible large-scale attacks against the village.

Although the local population felt hemmed-in or in prison, they also felt much more secure with the fence in position – and constant armoured car and vehicle-mounted patrols created a profile of intense army protection. You couldn't really go anywhere without seeing army personnel doing something.

Frustrated by their inability to attack the village from inland, the gooks' Zambian backers decided to start a war of nerves with us from across the river in Zambia. Barely a day passed without one of the tourist aircraft being shot at, or the odd mortar bomb being tossed into the village on a Saturday night when the Zambian Army was a bit pissed-up. Nothing big or serious ever happened – just enough to frustrate, scare and irritate us.

The minefield was also a severe test of our nerves. It was an alien object to the local animals – and the ploughshares exacted a very heavy toll on birds and monkeys, in particular. Larger animals soon realised that the fence meant death and stayed away, but the good old 'bobbo' (as we called the baboons) came over in ever-increasing numbers to get blasted to bits; and vultures would circle and land – setting themselves down on the wire that fired the mines – only to get blown to smithereens also. The stench of death and the buzzing of flies lay heavy in the hot afternoon air.

"Shit, there goes another one!" Fred said, as we sipped sundowners at his house one evening.

A thud and echo rolled down the valley – barely fading before another went off.

"'Bobbos' having a tea party," quipped 'the wife'. We all laughed.

"It's driving the 'kuds' nuts," Fred said. "They won't come outside anymore."

A small column of dust could be seen to the west of us where the mines had gone off.

"You hear about the elephant that stood on a mine down the road?" Mally asked.

"Mmm…" we all nodded. News travelled fast in a small town.

"Terrible," 'the wife' said – her buck-teeth looking more pronounced than ever. "Poor animals; these buggers have no shame, man!"

We all nodded in agreement before sipping our drinks. The feeling of being in an open jail was overpowering – sitting prominently in the back of our minds. More civilians than ever walked around with handguns now – either in a bag in the case of ladies, or holstered by men.

The laying of a landmine so close to the village indicated not only a change of tactics, but clearly demonstrated that the gooks had been stymied and were frustrated. The village jewel that lay bare before them had been snatched away. I wondered what they would do in response – and I guess that question hung over everyone's lives. A strong rumour persisted that Joshua Nkomo wanted Vic Falls, Wankie and Bulawayo at all costs to prove himself a worthy opponent to Mugabe and to re-establish Ndebele supremacy in Matabeleland – something that had been interrupted by the arrival of the white man.

I personally enjoyed that 'closed-in' feeling. I'd always loved military stories as a child – particularly stories that depicted small bands of men fending off thousands of attacking warriors. I really envied the bravery exacted from those defenders and the heroic deeds they carried out to save their friends and companions. I think the movie '*Zulu*' inspired me so much that I longed for the day when I too would be surrounded on all sides by the enemy. Well, that day had arrived in full force. We were on an 'island' 400 kilometres from the nearest major city – and if the Zambians or gooks chose to attack us in strength, we would be a relatively easy target.

"The minefield still has one weakness, Fred," I commented at length.

"What's that, then?"

"If the gooks want to get into the village, they can still cross anywhere along six kays of waterfront. It's wide open."

"Now you tell me," 'the wife' said, looking unnerved. "I was just beginning to feel a bit safer until you said that!"

Fred pursed his lips when our eyes met, slowly shaking his head, so I mouthed a 'sorry' to him.

"But, it also means less river to patrol," Mally butted in quickly. "More chance to catch the buggers…"

"That's right," Fred and I said together, trying to cheer 'the wife' up, but she didn't look too convinced. The sound of the kids laughing in the lounge broke the tension.

"It's Friday night. The cameraman's pissed again on Zambian TV," Fred chuckled. "At least that remains a constant in our lives… if nothing else!"

I had long overcome the initial embarrassment of being a croupier. The first night I served the public was embarrassing and cumbersome, but I soon got into the rhythm of things – and in a short while, it started to get boring in its repetitiveness.

Working in a structured environment is not for me, really – and wearing anything around my neck, like a bow-tie, is sheer hell. Having someone as my boss – even as congenial as Fred – was restrictive too. I feel that most bosses are idiots who give stupid instructions – and I, therefore, champ at the bit as an employee. I want to take control – and if I can't do so, I sort of give up.

It was with this type of mentality that I slipped into my role as a croupier – demonstrating keenness and ability even when I was intensely bored inside. The confines of a hot casino and the lack of freedom and excitement I had in the army sort of draped itself over me like a heavy coat. I wanted to kick it off and be free.

I knew in my heart of hearts that being a croupier wouldn't last long, but for Mally's sake, I was prepared to go along for the ride… for now. A day would come when I would throw off that coat of boredom and go charging out the building, but it had its compensations. The lifestyle was idyllic. We rarely worked beyond 1:00 a.m. because of the downturn in tourism, and we would race home in 'our' little black car to make love or go to one of the endless croupier parties that one casino or the other organised. Fred and Ivor invited us to join their tennis circle and we lazed away many days at the casino swimming pool before strolling over to the tennis courts to compete with each other. They were really good days with no pressure; no money either, but that didn't seem to matter. I was young, in love and had my own place with the woman I loved. I really had it all – something many couples search for all their lives.

Each party blended into the other until the faces became a blur; the thumping head in the morning commonplace; the longing looks from Linda when Mally and I danced together. We would then stroll home – hand-in-hand – under a full, silvery moon… scents and perfumes hanging in the liquid, hot air; lightning flickering in distant clouds.

The old, familiar air-conditioner would be battling and rattling away to lower the temperature in our bedroom. We would lie naked on top of the bed looking out the window in silence – moon-dappled shadows covering us. We would caress each other and gets lost in our own heaven for a few hours… Idyllic days.

In late October, the rains came – and not the grey drizzle that you get in Europe. I am talking rain that is so heavy, you cannot see your hand in front of your face; rain that turns your driveway into a muddy river in three seconds flat; rain that tops the back door and floods into your lounge; rain that strips trees of its leaves.

Many times we would be caught in it and would run screeching with delight into a hotel foyer, or run like mad for our back door – a pointless exercise because we were already sopping-wet – or we would just stand in it and get drenched… holding hands and kissing; Mally holding her shoes in one hand.

The lightning and the explosions in the minefield created a tension in the village that was palpable. We often went to bed – and would just be falling asleep – when a loud bang would go off. It took a long time and a discerning ear to tell the difference between lightning and an explosion – especially one that was in the middle-distance – but after a while, I could tell the crack of thunder versus the thud of an explosion. It wasn't so easy for Mally though…

"What's that? Thunder or a mine?" she would ask, her hand tightening into a fist on my chest.

"Thunder my love. Take it easy, okay? Even if it's a mine, it would mean some gook bastard's just met his maker."

Mally giggled and snuggled closer into the crook of my arm. Rain started to patter on the metal roof – and in the space of a few seconds, it sounded like a million toy soldiers running from one side of the roof to the other. The sweet perfume that the rain carried washed over us. I looked at my bedside table to make sure my handgun was there.

"Do you like pets?" Mally said suddenly.

"Yes, especially dogs."

"Cats?"

"Can't say they're my favourite, but I'd put up with one."

"Good, 'cos Ivor's got a kitten for us."

"I've a feeling I've been left out of this plan?"

Mally giggled again, nuzzling into my neck. "We pick up Tookie at 10 tomorrow."

"Tookie?"

"Mmm… I've given the cat your nickname."

"Tookie, hey? Well that's okay, I guess. Anyone or anything with my nickname can't be that bad, hey?"

Mally rolled over to face me – pulling my face down in a cupped hand to kiss me. I responded willingly – kissing her slowly and tenderly – and all the while, the rain thrashed on the roof and the air-conditioner battled away in our private little cocoon of love. As long as we were together, all would be okay. The dark bush out there and all its fears could wait for a while.

We woke naturally – without alarm clocks or kids ordering us into consciousness. The rain from the night before had left a cool temperature in its wake. Bees were buzzing under a blue sky; the rich smell of flowers wafted into our room. We stretched leisurely – finally deciding who would get up and make the coffee by flipping a coin. I won – slapping Mally's naked bum as she reluctantly left the warm sanctuary of our bed to go and make it. I snuggled under the sheets – delaying the day as much as possible. I still couldn't get over the sheer joy of being in a bed; being free – just doing what I wanted to do. The smell of coffee and toast preceded Mally's return by a minute or so. We ate and drank in silence – watching steam from the mugs curl lazily into the air – licking fingers free of the last few crumbs.

"We better get dressed," Mally said, looking at her watch. "It's 20 to…"

We showered quickly together – and after slipping on shorts, T-shirts and flops, we drove out the gate to Ivor's house. He lived with his wife in a crescent-shaped road – one down from us – quite a long way down in the direction of Elephant Hills Hotel. We hadn't seen his place before and looked forward to seeing something new.

I cherished the short drive and enjoyed the profusion of flowers, butterflies and colour that abounded. We turned right, then left again – banking left along the arm of the crescent. We parked under a shady tree in his driveway and walked together hand-in-hand towards the front door. Ivor and his wife responded together after a brief knock on the door.

"Hey!" Ivor said, smiling. "Come in, come in. This is Judy… Judy, Marilyn and Tony."

"Pleased to meet you," we said, shaking her hand.

I loved that about our little country. We were old-fashioned and innocently backwards in our customs – still formal.

It was a lovely, relatively modern house with high pine-panelled ceilings, lots of plants, paintings and large windows which gave an airy, clean feel to the place. That familiar smell of beeswax polish filled the air. We followed Ivor and Judy out into the garden, which although not big, was immaculately-kept – and the view of Elephant Hills and Zambia was stunning, being as elevated as we were.

"Tea? Coffee?" Judy enquired.

"Coffee please," we replied together. Judy smiled and headed for the kitchen.

"I know what you want to see," Ivor said to Mally. "Back in a second."

We looked at each other and smiled before sitting on comfortable, well-padded patio chairs under an umbrella.

"Lovely place," I commented.

"For a prick," Mally said, from behind her hand. We chuckled at the private joke. Ivor was a real womaniser – and even bedded a rather loose female behind the bar area at the back of the casino near the slot machines. I felt sorry for Judy. She was really attractive – innocent-looking. Nice. I think Ivor fancied himself as God's gift to women – with his designer glasses and suave, prematurely-grey hairstyle – but he was still a prick; someone who loved himself.

"Here comes loverboy," I said quietly. He was carrying a box, with a distinct mewing sound coming out of it. Mally stood up to meet him as he approached – opening the lid, smiling.

"Tookie!" she said, holding the black and white kitten up at arm's length. "Isn't he beautiful?!"

"Yes, he is," I said, standing up to scratch him behind the ear. The kitten meowed some more – its back legs trying to get to grips with Mally's forearm. The three of us stood there smiling at the petrified animal. Tookie must have thought baring our teeth was a prelude to eating him, because he twisted suddenly before being dropped unceremoniously back into the box.

"Tough cookie, hey?" Mally said.

"Scratch the birds around our place."

"You can say that again if he's anything like his dad," Ivor agreed.

I looked up at Ivor and smiled. Judy came walking out the kitchen with coffees and tall, frosted orange drinks. We sat while she did the rounds with sugar and biscuits.

I was just stirring my cup when a large whooshing noise came from my right. I didn't pay any attention to it because I knew steam engines often let off surplus steam when they climbed into Rhodesia after crossing the bridge from Zambia.

A massive kwa-thoom shattered the silence a few seconds later to my immediate left – in the direction of Elephant Hills Hotel.

"What the hell was that?" Ivor said, as we all stood to our feet. We pushed our chairs back and walked quickly to the end of the manicured lawn. A small spiral of smoke curled up from the base of the huge thatched roof of the hotel.

"What the hell was that?" Ivor repeated, shielding his eyes against the glare.

"Sounded like a rocket," I said. My heart beat a bit faster. I couldn't believe what was unfolding in front of us.

Slowly but surely, the plume of smoke grew thicker and darker – taking on a type of dance as the wind caught it in a vortex. An orange glow in its depths got brighter and brighter until a ball of flame shot several metres into the air.

"Oh my Lord!" Judy said, putting a hand on her forehead.

We stared mesmerised by the spectacle. Flames were leaping over each other to gain height. Sparks curled back and formed more fires on the roof. Someone ran out of the hotel – driving a white car away just as the thatched reception area collapsed. More and more people ran into the open – waving their arms and shouting at each other.

Despite the distance, the crackle and snap of the inferno reached us high up at our view-point. The four of us were totally speechless and horrified. A multi-million-dollar hotel with exquisite furnishings, restaurants, gambling halls, slot machines, convention centres and dozens of bedrooms was dissolving into ash right in front of our eyes. The ugly, wild flames roared perhaps a hundred feet in the air.

"Do you think someone's phoned the fire brigade?" I said at length. Ivor looked at me quickly before running towards the house.

"Good thinking!" he shouted as he sped away.

Mally came close to me and nestled into my shoulder – her left hand held up to her mouth. Judy was shaking like a leaf. None of us said anything. We felt totally useless and helpless.

In less than 15 minutes, it was almost over. That massive hotel that looked like a beacon from the dark waters of the Zambezi at night, or like a lighthouse to the men in the bush just west of here, was going... burnt to a frazzle – rafters blackened and caving in; smoke and flames pouring out of blackened windows.

"I hope no-one's been hurt," Mally said.

"Mmm," I agreed. Ivor came back to join us.

"Got through to the cops... eventually. They already knew about it."

"And the fire engine?"

"On its way from the airport."

"Airport?! That'll take half an hour."

Ivor merely shrugged – turning his focus back to the ruins below him.

"One good thing about this..." Ivor said, without looking at us. "We've got the monopoly on gambling in the village, now."

Mally and I looked at each other – pursing our lips – shaking our heads quickly in disbelief.

"Wanker," Mally breathed into my ear.

"Maybe, but he's right, you know."

The kitten, cool drinks and coffee had been totally forgotten. We continued standing there in silence for perhaps another 40 minutes – watching the comings and goings below us. The fire engine made a very belated appearance to dampen down hotspots. Even if it had been right there, it would have made no difference to the outcome; you simply cannot put an inferno out with one or two hosepipes.

Guests milled this way and that – their cries of anger and grief clear for all to hear. The police and a stick of army guys did a slow sweep through the immediate surrounds of the building – and as time wore on and the heat died down, they ventured further and further into the ruins... no doubt looking for bodies.

"Should we go down to have a closer look?" Mally said, looking up at me.

"Better not, honey... They've got enough to deal with right now."

I looked at my watch. It was only 1:30 p.m. In less time than it takes to eat a good meal, a large hotel had disappeared off the face of the Earth. The sky was still as blue as ever; the bees still buzzed and small spirals of smoke from cooking fires lazed up into the air over in Zambia. The river looked serene and inviting. It was like nothing had happened.

Judy's domestic worker came out and told her lunch was ready. We sat at the table when he returned with piles of chicken and mayo sandwiches and fresh ice for the now-warm orange juice.

I felt sorry for people who had just had their holiday trashed; for employees that may become unemployed; for the owners of the resort; and indeed, for our little village that depended so heavily on tourism. The whole country was getting chewed at bit by bit. Everything that was nice and normal and moral and upright was being snatched away in front of our eyes. The idyllic days we had grown up with were becoming jaded – and no doubt would fade to a mere memory one day.

"This is bad news," Ivor said after a long silence. The excitement of coming to get our new pet had vanished – to be replaced by a sombre, inward-looking silence.

"Looks like this is the gooks' answer to the minefield," I said. Ivor nodded in agreement.

"Yup. They'll just plaster us from Zambia. No need to sneak into the village anymore."

"What caused that explosion?" Judy said.

"Dunno. Something bigger than an RPG, that's for sure. I reckon the hotel's too far from Zambia for that," I replied.

"Surface to air missile?"

"Not sure if the Zambians have any… Probably an anti-tank weapon… a B-10… something like that."

"Which means they can hit every building in the village?" Mally said.

"Correct," I nodded.

"What'll the army do?"

"Probably send in the SAS to monitor the situation; maybe hit back with Arty or attack a few of their gun positions from the air, that type of thing."

"So the war's escalating?" Mally said, wide-eyed.

I hadn't noticed it before, but she looked strained somehow – a little thinner in the face… more gaunt… smudges under the eyes.

"I'm afraid so, Mal, but it'll remain low-key, I think. Zambia can't afford an all-out war with us. They know they'll lose."

We sipped our drinks in silence. Mally got lost in the kitten a short while later – probably more as a defensive reaction than adoration of the black and white fur-ball.

The doors to the casino swung open before closing automatically behind two punters that strolled up to the roulette table I was dealing on. They ordered drinks before sitting down to watch.

As usual, few people came gambling anymore – even though Christmas was only seven weeks away. Less and less foreign tourists arrived, but they were fortunately replaced by a regular flow of locals intent on putting life's financial worries behind them – but in most cases, they left broke and depressed or pissed (or all three). How many of those idiots who followed me into the gents' toilet to bribe me to help them win, I'll never know. I tried vainly to explain that the tables were not rigged, but a cloud of suspicion still hung over us. The punters wanted to know how the house won most of the time. How could that be if it was just luck for both punter and dealer? No! The casino had to be fiddling somewhere. The temptation to become corrupt was therefore very intense – especially when we earned low salaries and handled large sums of money.

Fred tapped me on the shoulder as soon as the two punters started placing bets. He replaced me with Mally – bringing scorn and ridicule down on his shoulders, which he absorbed with charm and alacrity. The punters knew they had a hard battle ahead to win any money off her.

"C'mon, Fred. Put the 'Turk' back on," one said with a wide sweep of his arm. I hated the nickname 'Turk' that prick had given me. He thought that just because he owned Peters Motel and lost a lot of money in our casino almost every night, that he had some type of privilege to verbally abuse our staff. I glared at him before moving to stand just behind Fred. Linda smiled at me as she moved in to chip-up for Mally.

"I'll beat the crap out of him one day," I whispered into Fred's ear. He half-turned – shielding his mouth with his hand.

"Not if I get in first!"

We both chuckled and it made me feel a bit easier. I sipped on my orange and water while I watched people moving around the place. Lesley was dealing to about six people – one of whom owned the croc farm. Ivor was dealing blackjack to a similar number of people. Danny helped Lesley chip-up and Warren was on a break.

"Still no sign of us getting busier since Elephant Hills burned down," I said.

"It'll come. The village drained of just about everyone when that happened. We'll be busy in a week or two, so enjoy it while it lasts."

I relaxed against a table – enjoying the music, sights and sounds around me. 'Nights in White Satin' was playing again; I wished someone would buy a new tape. We only ever seemed to listen to George McRae and Donna Summer. Like everything else in sanctions-hit Rhodesia, things were hard and expensive to come by.

The doors opened and perhaps a dozen off-duty soldiers strolled in. Their stable belts revealed which regiments they belonged to: Grey's Scouts, Armoured Cars and Artillery – one officer, three sergeants and the rest corporals.

"I just love this war," Fred said, smiling back at me.

"Should we open another table?"

"Nah. Two tables can handle this merry lot. Ten bucks they drink and don't gamble."

Linda turned to smile at me – followed by a quick glare from Mally.

"She's got the hots for you, that Linda has," Fred said, turning to face me. He had a naughty glint in his very dark eyes – a smile under his trimmed moustache.

"I'd be skinned alive. Mally's like a friggin' tiger underneath… but I wouldn't mind under different circumstances, I can tell you."

Fred turned to face Linda again. We both studied her very sexy body from behind. To me, a woman's backside is the most exquisite part of her body – and the evening dress she wore hugged the pert and well-formed buttocks like a second skin. The dress had no back and lay suspended just at the top of her backside. Her brown shoulders supported two narrow strips of cloth tied at the nape of her neck – just covering her ample breasts. She was one really good-looking woman. Her hair had been coiled up in a loose ball at the back of her head, with one of those large wooden clips women stick a pin though. Little shards of loose hair dangled down towards her shoulders. Her lips were full and inviting. The army guys had a very hard time trying to look at her without gawping – and that gorgeous girl kept giving me the come-on… Dear oh dear, the trials of life…

It was around 9:00 p.m. when I first sensed it. Not a bang or a rumble, but rather a vibration coming through the floor of the casino.

"Fred," I said, pulling him gently to one side. "Do you feel that?"

"What… What are you talking about?"

"Can you feel a faint sort of vibration?"

He cocked his head to one side as if to hear – looking down at the floor at the same time. I noticed, out of the corner of my eye, that one or two soldiers were doing the same thing.

"That's just vibration from the Falls, Tony."

"It's too late in the year for that, Fred. The river's low."

"Beats me," he said, straightening up – and then: "Oh crap," when he saw the soldiers filing out the casino doors.

"Someone's getting mortared upstream, Fred."

He cocked his head again – trying hard to listen – but the sound system and laughing punters drowned everything out.

"Let's go on the roof," I said. Fred thought for a second before shaking his head.

"I'm needed here. You go along and let me know what's happening."

I headed for the gap in the tables, which led to the casino door. Mally frowned at me – mouthing 'where you going?' I pointed upstairs. Warren had possibly sensed what was going on because he looked very tense – his top lip sweating profusely. I learned later that as a territorial soldier, he had been involved in many contacts – and was highly-strung as a result.

The swing doors flapped shut behind me as I left the casino at a trot – turning right into the staff exit before running downstairs, along a long corridor to a set of lifts that took me to the Summit Bar. The doors hissed shut – the lift taking me silently and swiftly to the fourth floor, where the Summit Bar was.

A cool breeze washed over me when I left the stifling lift. It was a gorgeous view from up there. Lights twinkled over in Zambia – and the large pool to the right was lit up with various-coloured party lights. The Falls Bridge, just visible through the trees, was illuminated in a halo of orange searchlights.

I turned left – walking perhaps 10 paces to a railing that faced west. In very recent times, the Elephant Hills Hotel would be just visible in the distance through the trees, but the area where it stood was now a blackened void.

I cupped my eyes to block out the glare of lights from the car park below – staring into the inky darkness to the west. I stood like that for about 20 seconds before I saw a very faint flicker of light, followed a good deal later by a mild vibration. I knew from the weeks and weeks of mines going off around the village and the crack and rumble of thunder that what I was listening to was no storm. Storms move and don't repeat their lightning strikes in a regular, spaced interval. Only Man makes noise like that. It was too far to be the minefield around the village, so what on earth could it be? One of the hunting concessions to the west getting hammered? Or one of the army call-signs who still patrolled the bush out there? Surely not, though. That was really big stuff firing. It went on and on and on until even the few people at the Summit Bar came over to look west, also.

"Someone's getting hammered," a powerful-looking man with an Afrikaans accent said, standing next to me.

"Yes. It's big stuff too, by the sounds of it."

"What's the target?"

"Good question… Nothing but bush out there. I'm sure it's not Kazungula; it's too far."

"Sound carries at night."

"Mmm…"

We remained there in silence for a long time, but there was no cessation to the faint rumbles. What on earth was it? I felt a bit uneasy when I took the lift downstairs again. This was just another piece of a jigsaw puzzle called 'fear' slotting into place. Was it the combined ZIPRA and Zambian Army invading? Why did those soldiers leave the casino so quickly?

It looked like nothing had changed when I walked back into the casino pit; perhaps fewer people were gambling. Mally and Fred strolled over to me.

"What's going on?" Mal said.

"Someone's taking a real hammering out west… Big stuff, possibly artillery."

"Artillery?!" Fred said with his usual over-exaggerated facial expressions. "What type of artillery?"

"No idea. I can only imagine it's Kazungula, but that's 60 or 70 kays away. It just doesn't make sense."

"So what's happening, then? An invasion?"

"Can't see it, Fred. The Zambians don't have the logistics for that."

"What about Russians or East Germans, then?"

I flicked my eyes at Mally. She'd gone slightly pale.

"Nah. The South Africans wouldn't accept Rhodesia becoming a Soviet base camp. We'll just have to wait and see."

"This place is beginning to give me the shits," Mal said.

"Mmm. I know how you feel. It's pushing up the pressure on us, hey?"

I gave Mally a kiss on the cheek before walking over to relieve Danny from chipping up next to Linda. Mally positioned herself so she could keep an eye on us – a thin smile of triumph on her face. I mouthed 'I love you' to reassure her, but inwardly I could feel an amazing electric current run through me standing so close to Linda. Whenever she brushed against me, a tingle ran down my spine. I wanted her so bad – even though I was satisfied in every way with Mally – but that's the universal male, isn't it? We're designed to spread seed, aren't we? I was young and wanted to do some more spreading! The first glimmer of dissatisfaction of being tied down was creeping into me… just me. I think Mally would say 'yes' if I popped the question.

"You've got the hots for Linda," Mally said suddenly as we drove home at two in the morning.

"What's brought this on, then?"

"As if you don't know, you bugger. You'd shag her on the roulette table if you had the chance."

"Come on, Mal. Don't start. It's late and my back hurts."

I was beginning to think the landmines I hit may have done damage to the discs in my spine. My back hurt more than usual and got tired quickly. My ear was buzzing – no doubt a frayed nerve doing its thing. I would be going back to Dr Fine in a few weeks' time – as well as an army doc to see if I would be upgraded to 'A' category once again. If the answer was 'yes', I would soon be called up. The thought made me irritable.

"I'm sorry," Mally said a short while later when we slid into the cool, crisp sheets on our bed.

"I'm sorry too, Mal. I know I flirt, but I don't mean to hurt you. I guess the psychological tension's making us all a bit crazy."

A mine thumped off to the east – and then another to the distant south. It felt a bit like aliens trying to invade the safety of a spaceship – the exploding mines representing another attack on the ship's hull. Mally snuggled into my arms and we lay there silently – listening to the thump and thud of mines, clearly audible above the rattling and creaking air-con. All that was missing was a violent thunderstorm to top it off – and we both felt we were going a little crazy.

❦—❦

Two days later, we were cooling off after a steamy tennis game when Fred walked down the path to join four of us at our table by the pool. He leaned forward – talking in low undertones.

"Those explosions the other night were Kazungula." He looked sideways before continuing – enjoying the role of drama queen. "Went on for 33 hours, with big stuff firing from Zambia. The police camp there took a serious beating. Our artillery had to respond, and get this: the SAS had to go over to calm things down."

"Where the hell do you get all this info, Fred?" I said incredulously.

He tapped the side of his nose and said: "My pal in CIO…"

"You're full of shit, Fred," Ivor butted in.

"When have I ever lied?"

"Well, maybe…"

"I'm telling you guys, it was really serious. I reckon it was payback for what you did there," Fred said, looking at me. Everyone's gaze turned in my direction.

"I'm sure the Zambians still came off second-best. Don Price is up here. He'd sort them out."

"It feels like a noose is closing around our necks these days," Mally said, as she sipped her ginger square.

"We've got nothing to worry about. Our army is more than capable of dealing with any threats from Zambia."

"Arty used their 105mm Howitzers," Fred said flatly. "That must've been the big thuds we felt, and get this: my pal reckons the Zambians used Green Archer."

"Green what?"

"Green Archer, Mal. It's a mobile radar system that can detect where enemy fire's coming from. It allows you to strike back very accurately."

"Probably explains why the return fire at the police camp was so deadly."

"Who fired at Zambia from the police camp?"

"Armoured cars, possibly mortars…"

"What a stupid thing to do," I said. "Talk about inviting trouble!"

"They had to, Tony. They reckon armoured cars just like ours were firing at the police camp from Zambia."

"If that's the case, they might have been South African Elands captured in Angola."

"Never heard that happening," Danny cut in.

"Does that mean the Angolans are coming this way as well?" Mally asked.

"Nah. Jonas Savimbi and the South Africans are in the way."

"Typical bloody Brits. Green Archer could only have come from them, the bastards."

"They're not all against us. There's plenty of support for our cause over there."

"We need that Labour left-wing prick… What's his name… Wilson? We need to get rid of that bastard and get Maggie Thatcher in."

"I'm telling you, that Wilson's a commie. Wouldn't surprise me if he's in Mugabe's pay-book."

"My wife's putting me under pressure to leave," Ivor said.

"That's 'cos she's sick and tired of you shagging everything in a skirt," Fred said, and then: "Sorry, Mally. No offence."

"None taken, Fred."

"Piss off, Fred… Nah, she wants out. Not just from the Falls, but from Rhodesia."

"Joining the chicken run?"

"Maybe the owl run. They're wiser!"

'Piss off, Ivor!" we said in unison.

But maybe Ivor was right. Rumours had it that over 2,000 whites a year were emigrating. With our population down to about 220,000 from an all-time high of 275,000 we were running out of 'reflective' skin.

"Just listen to what we talk about these days," Mally said at length. "War, emigration, call-ups, danger, insecurity, a lack of future… Do you think people in London or New York worry about things like that? We're living a twisted life here."

"We're at war, Mal. What must we do? Roll over and give up?"

"No honey, but can't we talk about anything else? You know, has anybody heard a new LP lately that they like?"

"Don't like the modern stuff," Ivor said.

"That's 'cos you're a bloody fossil," Fred retorted.

I realised the alcohol we had been steadily consuming for the last hour was beginning to kick into gear – so when the going gets tough, you talk about sex.

"Shagged anyone lately, Ivor?" Danny said suddenly.

"You know, one of these days I'll smack you, Danny!" Ivor's face flushed red.

Danny was a provocative and annoying 19-year-old brat with a permanent smile at the corner of his mouth – you know, the type that stays there even when he's being threatened, which makes you even angrier – and as it turned out in the not-too-distant future, it was me who flattened him in the casino – sending him and a tray of betting chips flying across the floor. He had called me 'Turk' just one too many times. It would be an occasion when everyone else had little smiles at the corners of their mouths…

A long, long time later, I came to know that when the SAS went over into Zambia to 'calm things down' at Kazungula, they did so on 5 November 1977 in an operation called 'Partisan'. Among other things, they seeded the area near the conflict with landmines. The first casualties were a Zambian Army officer and a non-commissioned officer killed, with five others wounded… Take that, you bastards. Now you and yours know how we felt when Roy Orchard and the others got blown up near Binga. Shit happens – and what goes around comes around!

The weeks rolled by. The rains settled in and storms arrived in mid-afternoon like clock-work – repeating the show most afternoons. It was hot and humid, but life just burst forth everywhere. Flowers bloomed in abundance; trees became weighed down under countless tons of leaves; grass grew; animals got fat and lazy and plentiful. It was a time of new growth – of life and renewal. Why then did those bloody bastards across the river have to keep buggering things up?

Their favourite trick was to lob the odd mortar round towards the golf course or fire occasionally at an RUAC tourist plane showing visitors what the Falls looked like from the air. It wasn't uncommon to hear the sudden burrrrpp of a 12.7mm anti-aircraft weapon fire off a few pot-shots at the circling plane. What the hell gave those boogs the right to do that? Those people were innocent tourists!

Naturally, when this type of thing happened, everything else stopped and it would be the talk of the town for a few days – and the odd ambush on the road to Wankie (courtesy of Albert Ncube, no doubt) once and forever made us feel cut off, isolated and forgotten. Perhaps other border towns like Umtali and Kariba felt the same way we did? Yes, no doubt they did, but somehow, perhaps because of the minefield that corseted us into place, we felt the most vulnerable. It was like the population of the village was sitting there every day just waiting for a breach or a landing along the waterfront and another atrocity to barrel at them out of the night.

Paranoia set in – and quite honestly, I wasn't prone to the effects. I would often sit up at the Summit Bar when off duty at night and stare at the town of Livingstone over there in Zambia – all lit up like jewels on a neck. I would sit there with binoculars and study vehicle movements down to the bridge. I reasoned with myself that if a long row of headlights aimed for the bridge, it was military and should be reported. By strange coincidence, the C.O. of artillery eventually cottoned onto the idea of using the hotel as an observation post – and by the middle of December 1977 it was manned by uniformed personnel at night and then by men dressed as civilians by day. A regular record of vehicle movements was monitored night and day from then onwards. It was comforting to see forward fire-control observers with radios and plotting boards sitting up there at night. I often had long chats with them. Zambia's immediate environs were marked and targeted – and would be blown to smithereens if they continued to push their luck.

"Mmm, this is delicious, babe," Mally said, licking her fingers. We were sitting on top of our bunker towards sunset one day – eating braaied meat, salads and drinking wine. I loved the effects of wine; it made me randy. I was sort of numb from three-quarters-of-a-bottle of Green Valley when a twin-engine Cessna belonging to RUAC zoomed over at low-level – giving us both a huge fright.

The plane had barely exited our vision when two very fast streaks of white light that looked like a laser beam flashed past – followed instantly by a loud cracking noise.

"Did you see that, Mally?" I said, still looking up at the sky. "Mally...?"

I looked down at her, but she was gone. Only her feet were visible – angled upwards from the bottom of the bunker. For a split-second, I thought she'd been shot. Wine sploshed over my shirt as I bounded after her.

"Mally! Are you okay?!"

She didn't answer, but I could see from the quivering of her body that she was crying silently – her head buried in her forearms. Her shins were bleeding from her fall down the steps into the bunker.

"Mally, babe… What happened?" No answer – just muffled sobs and sniffs.

"What happened, honey?" I sat next to her. She rolled over and put her head on my lap.

"I just freaked a bit. The tension… the wine… I guess I'm just wired-up!"

I let her cry while I held her – stroking her temple – letting the sobs slowly fade away until she was almost silent. I felt totally sober now.

"I love you honey…"

"I know, Tony, but Ivor's got me thinking: maybe it's time to leave here."

My gut went cold. I couldn't think of anything worse. That would mean starting over – looking for a new job; a new house – and what if this was just a wartime romance? I had read many accounts of men in other wars who had fallen in love with a woman in days of heady excitement, only to find that the burdens of peace were too much – their marriages ending in divorce. In a funny way, the war and the village were synonymous with my relationship with Mally. They were inextricably linked. I knew in my heart of hearts that when we left the village, our time together would be over.

"It's not that bad, Mal," I said, trying to encourage both of us. "We still have good life here, don't we? No-one's actually been killed since the minefield was built… We're pretty safe, you know. Even the odd mortar bomb and go at the tourist planes have had no effect whatsoever."

"I know. It's just the waiting; the unknown." and then: "Ow, shit. I've really scraped my knees."

"Come on. Let's wash you off," I said, pulling her up. I supported her as we climbed the steps up to grass-level – escorting her towards the bathroom. The sky was still blue and Tookie was chasing a butterfly. The normality around us softened Mally a bit. We walked arm-in-arm to the bathroom.

"Ouch, that stings!" Mal said as I gently cleaned the bleeding flesh with antiseptic. "Damn!"

"Your own personal war injury… You'll get a Purple Heart and pension!"

"Taking the piss, hey?"

I cleaned her shins until the bleeding stopped – and then we held each other for a long time.

※—※

Fred's prophecy that the casino would fill up came true. The recent horrors of Elephant Hills burning down and the odd mortar attack on the village had recessed into the short-memory span of the type of fickle human that liked gambling.

While workmen slaved away to convert a conference hall at Vic Falls Hotel next door into a temporary casino, people piled into our run-down place by the score. By 9:00 p.m. each night, our few, understaffed tables were heaving with people of all description. Foreign tourists made a brief comeback – particularly South Africans. It was nice to see foreigners. They looked different; were well-dressed – chic and affluent. They played with hard currency that our country so desperately needed instead of the 'dead' Mickey Mouse Rhodesian dollar that local villagers used.

Since roulette was my forte, which I actually became quite good at, I was more or less glued to a table for hours on end without a break. It was sheer agony on my feet, back and shoulders – as well as my brain. There's a lot of mental arithmetic going on in a croupier's head. My ear buzzed a lot – and on one humorous occasion, I turned right in ever-decreasing circles without any control over my body whatsoever – sprawling a tray of betting chips all over the casino floor. You see, your inner eardrum controls your balance – and my eardrums were shot. My balance was shot, so I often staggered around – falling over – without any ability to help myself.

It became the norm to go home to bed at daybreak. We would drive home like tortured zombies, feed Tookie, switch on the air-conditioner and die for the whole day. I despise that feeling of waking in the afternoon, when the day has mysteriously disappeared and the sun is diving towards the western horizon.

The rains were heavy and persistent that season – and on more than one occasion, we were woken by thunder crashing and booming around us. Being in that semi-awake state made it difficult to determine if the bang was a mine or thunder, so our sleep was often cut short. Tempers became frayed and we got on each other's nerves. It was about this time that I smacked Danny to the floor after the casino had closed – much to the amusement of Fred, who feigned horror by my actions.

The few remaining weeks leading up to Christmas 1977 passed in a type of blur. The casino was making good money for a change and we looked forward to the possibility of a generous Christmas bonus. Maybe we could go on a holiday, buy clothes or something for the house like a new TV or stereo.

Christmas is also a time of frivolity and joy – a time to forget; a time to celebrate with friends and relatives; a time to have fun; to have a braai and chat to friends over a beer or glass of wine – and stuck here, in our little 'spaceship' 400 kilometres away from civilisation, we had to make our social life work.

We became very close friends with several people – and their lives became entwined with ours. They were simple days of simple pleasures: swimming together, partying together, sitting on the ruins of Elephant Hills to watch spectacular sunsets, going for walks, playing golf and getting tipsy on the booze cruise... Wonderful days of youthful vigour and energy – and no responsibilities – but at the back of our minds we knew we were at war; that there were gooks 'out the wire'; that you could get shot to bits driving your car; or killed in your bed by a stray mortar bomb. It added that element of friction and tension to a unique situation in a unique country. I knew how the Israelis must feel, with the whole world out to get you.

"It's really heaving tonight," I said to Fred.

"Mmm..." was all he could manage. He was so busy chipping up for me – as well as doing the rounds as manager, cashier and all-round charmer.

It was Christmas Eve and I'd managed to secretly buy a new handbag, perfume and make-up for Mally. We planned to open our presents when the casino closed – even if that was 8:00 the next morning.

I had a charming group of Italian, French and Germans at my table. They were exceptionally generous with tips, which was great for the staff as it made up most of our wages – and behind them, people stood three-deep waiting for a chance to bet. All of them were 'tanked up' and in a party mood. The music was drowned out by many loud voices; by laughter and general merrymaking. Our few waiters were rushed off their feet.

"Think Don will give us a bonus for all this hard work?" I said to Fred as I helped chip-up after sweeping the table clear of betting chips – referring to Don Goldin, the casino owner.

"He bloody better, or else I'm gone."

"Serious?"

"Nah," he said, smiling the Mexican way. "I honestly don't think he has the bucks to pay us."

"Come on, Fred. Look at this lot. We're making a fortune."

"Maybe, but the hotel's almost gone bankrupt twice this year."

"I didn't know that..."

I turned back to face the punters, who were piling chips all over the table, but few had covered 35 black – an unpopular number. I rolled the ball slowly from opposite the number on the roulette wheel. The ball spun around the rim for a few circuits before I called 'no more bets'. It bounced twice – landing squarely on the number. I raked dozens of chips away and paid out only a few splits.

"Well done," Fred said under his breath before looking up to disarm the punters with his smiley face.

"I bloody better get a bonus, or else I'll be the one pushing off," I whispered into Fred's ear. My back hurt like hell and my shoulders felt like barbs of hot steel had been shoved into them.

The first explosion was far enough away to be mistaken for someone slamming a door in the next room – or something like a deepfreeze lid falling closed – a thud; a vibration; an echo.

Very few people noticed it, but I did – and so did Warren. We stared open-mouthed at each other – both of us nodding our awareness of the cause. Warren started to take his apron off.

"Fred, the village is getting mortared."

"Bullshit, man. Just concentrate on..."

The second bang was close and really loud – cutting off the end of his sentence. I stood frozen at the table. I couldn't believe that the punters weren't alarmed. Well, who could blame them? No bombs had fallen in Europe for 32 years.

"Shit!" Fred said – and after a brief pause, reached for the top drawer in the pit boss's table – pulling out a huge handgun and quickly shoving it into his belt.

"Attention! Attention!" Fred shouted at the top of his lungs. The place quietened down a bit, but not enough – so he had to bellow it again.

"Attention! Please! We are under attack. Will everyone move towards the doors in an orderly manner?"

Looks of dumb disbelief crossed most punters' faces. Some laughed... Maybe it was a party prank? A very loud explosion that shook the building changed their minds. At least two dozen people flinched instinctively – ducking down. Chips clattered to the floor. A woman or two screamed – and then, there was absolute pandemonium. People stood up en masse and charged for the door – pushing and shoving each other to get away first.

"Don't panic!" Fred screamed – barging into the middle of them.

"Follow me to the basement... PLEASE! Don't panic... Follow me!"

I stood mesmerised watching this happen – as if in slow motion. Then, my brain triggered a response. I looked sideways for Mally and the other croupiers. At first I couldn't see them, but they were all under a table. I dived down and belly-crawled over to them just as another massive explosion shook the building. Mally and Lesley were wide-eyed and close to panic.

"Stay here! Nobody move until the explosions become more distant!"

"We'll be killed!" Danny said next to me. I hadn't even seen him.

"No we won't. The roof will detonate any mortar rounds. I'm sure the wood on the table will protect us!"

"Sure? It's just wood, man!"

"Yes, two inches of solid mahogany. Now just stay still!"

The pandemonium of loud voices and chairs being turned over had receded – the doors flapping back and forwards as the last person exited the room. We lay there in breathless anticipation. My back crawled with nerves – waiting for something to rip me apart. Donna Summer sang 'MacArthur Park' over the sound system.

Mortar shells fell with relative frequency after that. Each thud and vibration made the four of us shiver and duck involuntarily, but they were definitely moving away – further south towards the post office.

"Time to go," I said, half-dragging Mally behind me. The others followed.

We followed the exact course I'd taken previously, when I went up to the Summit Bar to listen to Kazungula getting bombarded.

"Where the hell are we going?" Danny yelled as we hurtled along a back corridor.

"Basement!"

The girls' shoes thwack-thwacked rapidly on the concrete floor – mirrored by the softer footfalls made by Danny and I. A very bright flash went off to our left, over by the tourist offices and banks – making us crouch low as we ran… As if that would help! Shrapnel kills you standing up or crouched; makes no difference, but it's an instinctive reaction to get down.

We turned sharp-right at the end of the corridor, down a small ramp and then left into the foyer leading to the annex. The staircase to the basement was on our immediate left. The four of us barged down the stairs – turning back on ourselves on the next flight before bursting into a room packed with people. They stared wide-eyed at us – probably thinking we were gooks. We joined the other croupiers and Fred. A loud buzz of conversation died every time the upper windows lit up with a flash – followed by a loud bang or rumble depending on the distance from us. More people packed themselves into the hot and humid basement. Some sat on beer crates and others lay on old, disused carpets. I had visions of gooks coming down those stairs and killing all of us, like they did to those people in the Congo back in the '60s. I vowed I would never come down here again unless I was armed.

"I've got to get back for 'the wife' and the kids!" Fred said wide-eyed – making a move to go. I restrained him forcefully.

"No point, Fred. This isn't a gook attack. This…" a loud bang cut off my words. "This is coming from Zambia. They'll be in the bunker, not so?" He stared blankly at me. "Not so, Fred?! You've told them to go in there, hey?"

"Yes…"

"Well that's okay, then. There're no gooks in this one. It's a plain mortar attack, that's all… She'll be safe!"

I held onto him until he started to calm down. He was sweating profusely and had suddenly gone pale. I looked at Mally then. She was staring at something far away – mouth slightly open – breathing rapid, but shallow; classic signs of shock.

"You okay, babe?" No answer. I shook her gently – pulling her into my arms.

"You okay, babe?"

"Yes, yes, I'm good," she said softly. Her body shook – well for that matter, so did mine.

"Danny, Lesley, you guys okay?" They nodded and smiled nervously. "We're safe down here, so everyone just relax."

"We'll have to put a pub down here for next time," Fred said suddenly. We smiled at the thought of it.

"Where's Warren, Ivor and Linda?"

"Ivor's probably shagging Linda," Danny cut in. Under different circumstances I would've punched him again, but down here, any form of humour was welcome. We smiled and nodded at him.

"Good one, Danny."

The thuds and rumbles went on for maybe another 10 minutes – and then stopped as suddenly as they'd started. Everyone stared at the ceilings in silence – another human oddity, like submariners looking up at the hull during a depth-charge attack. You will never see what kills you, so what's the point?

"Fred, I think it's okay to go upstairs now. You should tell the folks," I said. He came down to earth then, breathed in deeply and spoke in a loud, authoritative voice.

"Attention, please!" Everyone became silent and looked at him. "I think it's okay to go upstairs now. You can either go back to your rooms, or join us in the casino for one free drink each!"

A loud cheer went up, followed by relieved smiles, back-slapping here and there and a rapid increase in noise as all started to talk at once. We made slowly for the doors, like cinema-goers leaving after a movie. Some movie!

"You okay, hon?" I said to Mally, taking her hand. It was cool and clammy.

"Fine."

"You don't sound very convincing."

"I said I'm fine, so let's leave it, okay?"

"Okay…" I let go of her hand and put my arm around her waist – gently leading her towards the exit. The air was sweet with the perfume of flowers – cool and crisp – but a distinct smell of expended explosives caught me in the back of my throat.

"Tony," Fred said next to me, "Find Ivor. Tell him to take over for me. I'm going back to the house. Tell Ivor to tell the barman to give each person one drink each – preferably a beer. Spirits are too darn expensive…"

"Okay, Fred. I've got the drift. I'll sort it out for you. Coming back?"

"Later, once I've settled 'the wife' and kids down."

"Okay, you go on. I'll sort the rest out."

He pulled ahead from us – and in a few seconds, his big frame had disappeared out the nearest exit. Poor bugger. I reckon it would be the end of him soon. He was already under a lot of pressure to leave the village.

By the time we got back to the casino, I was amazed to see that Ivor, Warren and Linda were already starting to deal to the punters again. The chairs had been up-righted and spilled betting chips squared away – no doubt some into the odd pocket or two. I told Ivor what Fred said and he nodded before going over to the barman in the corner. The latter was already hard-pressed to serve drinks people demanded from him. In the end, Ivor went behind the bar counter to help serve.

The human race is amazingly resilient. Here we all were – a few minutes after a major mortar attack on a tourist village – and yet everyone was laughing, drinking and gambling in high, festive spirits. It was like nothing at all had happened. The news of the free drink had swollen the ranks of punters from before the attack, and now the place was heaving. Maybe the mortar attack was a good marketing strategy thought up by Fred!

"Where did you get to?" I said, standing close to Linda as I helped chip-up for her.

"I went into the office with Warren and Ivor," she said, casting me a quick smile.

"Wise move. Went into the big safe?"

"Mmm…"

"Good move. Got a roof of reinforced concrete over it. I'll have to remember that next time."

"Look forward to that," she said, with a smile in her eyes. I glanced at Mally, but she was hunched over the blackjack table dealing to a full house. Lesley and Danny dealt at the second roulette table – and a short while later, Ivor came back to open a second blackjack table. By the time Fred got back, it was 2:30 in the morning, but the place was still heaving.

"We need more attacks," I joked. I was pleased to see that he smiled his big Mexican smile, which meant everything was okay in Fred's world.

"Wife and kids okay?"

"Yes, thank God. She did just as I told her: ran into the bunker, shut the door and turned on loud music. The kids were still half-asleep, so they just carried on as if nothing had happened."

"You got beds in there now?"

"Sleeping bags, pillows, food and water… torch, candles… They're always in there."

"Why the hell didn't we hit back, Fred?"

"Maybe we did. We wouldn't have been able to hear anything in the basement anyway, but I'll find out from my mate. I promise you, if we don't hit back next time, I'm packing my bags and I'll make it plain to the cops here that they'll have no civilians left one day."

After that, none of us spoke – or even moved from the place we stood at. Fred opened a third roulette table all on his own, but was more than able to do so with his knowledge, speed and dexterity. He even had time to chat and banter with the punters. I loved that man. He would eventually leave the village – like we all did – and became the bar manager for the half-dozen or so bars at the Royal Hotel in Durban, where I saw him several years later – still smiling and still in love with 'the wife' and 'kuds'…

We drove home in silence through eerily quiet streets at 8:00 in the morning. Normally, tourists would be ambling around – perhaps going for an early breakfast at the Wimpy bar or looking at curios or standing in a line waiting for the post office to open – but there was no-one to be seen.

As we slowed to turn right at the Wimpy bar, a car full of people – bags packed on top of the roof rack – bounced out of the municipal campsite in front of us. Our income and wealth was leaving the village with them. I could just hear Frikkie saying: "This is bad, man. Very bad."

My eyes shifted from the accelerating car to the plate-glass windows of the Wimpy bar. They were all shattered and lay in gleaming shards all over the place. Even a couple of windows in the flats above the restaurant were shattered.

"Must have been a direct hit," I said, but Mally merely stared ahead.

"You okay, babe?" I said, my stomach knotting a bit.

"I'll be okay. I'm just tired."

We continued along the road – lost in our own thoughts. I was worried and concerned for Mally. Some people can take this type of thing in their stride. To be honest, I found it incredibly exciting and didn't want it to end. I had arrived at 'Rorke's Drift' in my mind; I was living my own version of 'Zulu', where the few battled the thousands – and then there are others, perhaps like Mally, who fold and fade very quickly. I knew that her folding and fading would be the end of us living here – and in turn, that would spell the doom of our relationship.

When we got home, I retrieved the Christmas presents from the boot of the car – where I'd secreted them – and made some coffee and toast, while Mally showered. She came out looking all pink and fresh – her hair caught up in a towel, turban-style; her body wrapped in a white dressing gown. She sat on the couch and looked out the window. Tookie meowed once before jumping up on her lap. She stroked the ball of fur silently – not looking at me once. I was beginning to panic inside. I didn't want this to happen. I ran to the kitchen, pulled a tray off the cupboard and arranged her coffee and toast alongside her present. I tugged open the back door and yanked a rose off one of Frikkie's prolific rose bushes hanging over our fence. I didn't get the reaction I wanted.

"That's nice," she said, looking at the tray as I put it on a table in front of her. I tried to sound upbeat and happy, but I was screaming inside.

"Happy Christmas, Mal." I bent to kiss her, but was offered her cheek. I felt tears well up in my eyes. My voice croaked a bit when I said: "I love you babe."

"I love you too…" she smiled thinly as the wrapping paper came off – saying a simple 'thank you' before going over to the sideboard to get a small, brightly-coloured package for me.

"Happy Christmas, Tony."

Tony, huh? She normally only used my Christian name when she was angry. I took the gift with a heavy heart.

"It's lovely, Mal. Just what I needed," I said, looking down at a shiny new watch.

She looked indifferently through her presents without a comment and then stood up.

"I'm exhausted. I'm off to bed."

"I'll come just now, okay?"

"Mmm."

"Love you," I said to her back, but there was no answer. I sat there totally stunned, with Tookie rubbing his body against my leg. Suddenly, everything was falling to bits.

❦—❦

Later in the day, Mal had picked up a bit, but was still noticeably quieter than normal. The odd thump of a mine going off had become a routine reminder that we were surrounded by our enemy. It was playing on everyone's nerves.

We met Fred later and bought ice-creams from the small kiosk behind the one and only supermarket. The place was reasonably crowded and the glass from the Wimpy restaurant had been swept up. I think the patrons welcomed sitting at tables in a building with no windows – letting in fresh air for a change. Almost as an act of solidarity, locals and tourists alike had come out of curiosity to see the damage all over the village – and by default, actually increased business for the local traders.

"Not one plane of incoming tourists has cancelled," Fred said, before licking his ice-cream.

"Masochists?"

"Perhaps," he chuckled.

We walked past a small hole in the pavement where the mortar bomb that demolished the windows had exploded. Police and forensic teams had come and gone – tell-tale chalk-marks were scribbled on the pavement where a piece of shrapnel had been found. No doubt they had photographed the incident, as well.

The post office had also been hit – a direct one, at that – but the damage to the roof structure had been minimal, and only a few broken tiles and shredded gutter bore evidence of the impact. A privately-owned house next to the national parks office had shrapnel-marks and windows missing too. It was weird going on this tourist excursion looking at war damage.

Further down the road next to the bank and Hertz car hire, another set of windows was missing, with more shrapnel-marks radiating upwards.

"That's only four impact craters, Fred. Where's the rest?"

"All over, I guess… People's gardens, fields, all over… Who knows?"

"They must have fired 50 shells or more."

"Mmm, the bastards… and get this: we didn't retaliate. Arty was told not to escalate the attack."

"Escalate, my ass. What about defending us?"

"As I said, I told my mate to get onto his superiors. There's going to be hell to pay if our security forces don't respond next time."

"Next time?" Mal said.

"Sorry to alarm you Mal, but yes, they'll try it again. Remember we said they can't get at us directly, so they'll find another way?"

"Great way to spend Christmas!"

I pretended to want to see something with Fred and said we'd meet Mally down at the casino pool in a short while.

"Fred," I said out of earshot as Mal walked away. "We need a holiday from this place. Can we get some leave early in the New Year?"

"Sure, as soon as business gets slow."

"Good, because Mal's about to crack up."

"'The wife''s not far behind. She handled last night well, but it scared the crap out of her."

"She putting pressure on you to go?"

"Yes."

"And?"

"I love it here, and love my job too. It'll take a lot more than this to make me go... A massacre in the village, maybe."

"Let's hope that never happens."

We strolled down to the casino. Mally wasn't that far ahead really, and I could see she had changed somehow – even from this distance. There was no spring in her step for a young woman. What on earth was going through her mind? I wish she would open up to me – scream, shout, protest or anything... anything but silence.

When we got to the pool, we saw Ivor and Linda over by the tennis court, so we decided to join them. I wondered if Danny's cryptic comment about Ivor having an affair with her was true? But I somehow doubted it. Why would she go for an older man like him? She could have anyone in the village. I was amazed she was still unattached. She smiled up at me when we approached the table.

"What'll you have?" Fred said to Mally and I, then Linda and Ivor. We ordered drinks from a hovering waiter and sat back to enjoy the warmth of the sinking sun. Pink bougainvilleas had covered one end of the tennis court wire – and high above, seed pods cracked and splattered – sending their seeds flying in all directions. I'd been hit in the head more than once by them. The msasa tree pod is unique in that it twists as it matures until the tension is so great, that it literally explodes – sending seeds off like small missiles all over the place. What a wonderful way to 'spread your seed'. Us humans have to wine and dine before doing that!

Linda looked directly at my eyes for longer than necessary before looking away again. For once, it went unnoticed by Mally, who sat staring at her fingernails.

"Fred," Ivor said.

"Mmm?"

"We need to make a plan if an attack happens like that again."

"Like what?"

"Have a notice put up, you know; move to the basement in the event of a mortar attack."

Fred found that quite funny and threw his head back in laughter – his heavy jowls and bouncing belly joining in.

"I can just see the reaction a Frenchman would have to that! 'Oui, madame, misseur. Pleez proceed to the bomb shelter. Wine and caviar will be served shortly... Misseur, what is a mortar? Is it some type of cement? C'est le vie, non, non – it is a type of bread!'"

"They'll be dead by then!" Linda laughed. Even Mally looked up and smiled.

"Okay, big joke," Ivor cut in, "but I'm serious. We need to know what to do."

"You're right," Fred said, leaning forward – the broad smile on his face slowly fading as he became serious.

"I know one thing for sure. I'll not go down that bloody basement again without a weapon," I said. "I felt like a rat in a cage." Ivor and Fred nodded.

"The safe is full of Don Goldin's hunting rifles. I think we should dish them out to anyone with military or hunting experience."

"Good idea... and form an armed group to protect the basement."

"Yes, agreed then. Ivor, you have an Uzi, don't you?"

"That and a 9mm handgun."

"Can you make sure both weapons are here all the time?"

"I'll commute with them. I need them at home too."

"It gave me the shits being herded into that place," I said again. "That's how all those people died in the Congo. Can you imagine the mess if gooks got amongst us last night?"

I felt stupid as soon as I said it – and looked at Mally for her reaction, but she was staring at the bush on the far side of the tennis court. She was building a wall around herself. Probably just as well.

"Okay. Ivor, it's a good idea, actually. I'll get instructions printed out and put up in every room in the hotel – including the casino. It'll tell people where to go and what to do," Fred said.

"It was pretty dark and miserable down there," Mally chipped in.

"Mmm... Okay, I'll organise more lighting."

"And sandbags around the ground-level windows. We don't want shrapnel or bullets coming in there."

"What about refreshments – a bar or something?" We all laughed at that. "We'll have to give the place a name, like 'The Bunker' or something like that."

"Okay, a bar also. There's a fridge down there, anyway."

"Sorted then, Fred?"

"Yes, no problem."

"What about the army, Fred?" Linda asked. "Why don't they send men to guard places when that happens?"

"Too thin on the ground," I replied for Fred. "Anyway, they're mostly interested in intercepting them down by the river or outside the wire."

"Just a guard or two?"

"Times a dozen public places, that's a whole platoon of infantry all fragmented; no radios and lots of transport needed. No, it's better they do their job, or at least stay in a bunch to react to something."

We sat in silence for a while and watched a couple of tourists hack away at a tennis ball.

"We're living in a false paradise," Mally said at length. I looked at her – pursing my lips. I knew she was right, but didn't want to deal with it. I was quite happy to carry on with the things the way they were. I for one would not leave the village that easily.

"Time to go home to get ready," Fred said, downing his orange and soda. "Would you and Mal like to come back for a bite? It's going to be a long night."

I looked enquiringly at Mal – and was surprised she nodded her head. We finished our drinks and stood up to follow Fred. Linda smiled at me – and this time, jealousy flooded Mal's eyes. Good! She was back again! Not some zombie from 'The Twilight Zone' anymore! Maybe things were going to be alright, after all?

❧—❦

The nights between Christmas and New Year's Eve were packed with tourists. I found my dinner suit and bow-tie hot and restrictive – and the press of rude, loud people infuriating. I generally don't like people that much – and crowds of sweating, half-pissed humanity drove me to the edge… And we never closed before daybreak. The small staffing levels that we'd been reduced to in lean times meant we rarely got a break before 4:00 a.m. – and by then, my back would be a screaming mass of muscles and my ear would buzz and disorientate me. If work was like this all the time, I'd have to give it up; it was just too demanding – but I knew at the back of my mind that as soon as the temporary casino at Vic Falls Hotel was completed, we would become a quiet, boring place for locals again. What would be worse: boredom or madness like this? Well, at least in this press of humanity, there were some beautiful foreign women here. Olive-skinned Italians and blonde Germans; foreign, exciting – but why was I thinking of other women like this? I had a lovely girlfriend that adored me and would do anything for me. Maybe it was the fact that another relationship would mean freedom from this one – one that was becoming smothered by an abnormal reality. I had to get things squared away in my mind, or else I knew things were doomed between Mal and I. It was time to reinvent the wheel with her; to take her mind off the current situation and to make her feel as normal as possible – so I set about doing just that. I would not let boredom creep in – nor inactivity to allow depressing thoughts to take hold – so I got us to do the garden together; to turn it from a weed-encroached wasteland into something pretty and homely. To begin with, we both found it hard-going and didn't know what to plant where, but as time passed, our efforts bore fruit. The effort forced us to go places to look for plants and rocks, which in itself channelled us into new ventures – taking time out to look at curios, carvings and other things we may need in our venture… and walks – lots of walks to find driftwood and ferns and odd-shaped bits of wood.

We would take a picnic basket and sit on the banks of the river – sipping wine and munching cheese and bread – or go up to the ruins of the 'Hills Hotel' and have a swim and lunch. We expanded our sport to golf, but after a few rounds, decided that was best left for the professionals – but at least we had made the attempt and felt good about that. I saw and enjoyed a new glow in her eyes.

"This is fantastic, Tony," Mally smiled at me as we chugged up the river on an evening booze cruise one day. It was my favourite time of the day: orange and gold colours everywhere; the feel of evaporating heat on our brown skin; the company of foreigners talking in strange languages; wearing clothes we had never seen before – nor dreamed of ever wearing; the smell of exotic perfumes on the women and large cameras around the necks of men – cameras our war-torn and sanction-hit country had not seen for nearly a decade now – but it was just sitting quietly in a chair on the upper deck of the launch, watching the Africa I loved so much drifting by; feeling Mally slump back against me – moulding perfectly in the crook of my arm; watching elephant and buffalo and hundreds of buck come down to the water to slake their thirst. I just loved this land more than words can describe.

"Is that the minefield?" Mally said, pointing at two high fences separated by a span of ploughshare-infested ground.

"Yup. That's what keeps us awake so often."

"Seems harmless from here."

"Try walking in there."

"What's that red sign on the fence?"

"International minefield markers; skull and crossbones."

I felt a bit of a shiver go through me looking at the minefield – and I sensed a vague change in Mal's mood as she studied the ground dividing the two wires. I decided to distract her.

"Why don't we go to the croc farm tomorrow? I hear a tea garden's opened there?"

"Okay, that sounds good," she said, cuddling her head under my chin. We sat in silence for the remaining 40 minutes of the cruise – lost in our thoughts and enjoying the amazing beauty of Africa. How much Man had set his face for war in this amazing 'Dark Continent', where less than 100 years ago, the indigenous population had seen a rifle fired for the first time – and in that period, here in Rhodesia at least, we had paved thousands of kilometres of road; built dams and cities; tamed wild bush to create some of the best farms in the world; and built railways and bridges – a modern world in a crazy continent. Could it last?

When we got to the car, Mally turned towards me and kissed me for a long time.

"I love you babe," she said when we parted. I held her tight against me and said nothing, but she knew my embrace was an affirmation of my love for her.

When we got home, we switched the TV on. We still had some time before work and sat and watched a bit of 'Peyton Place', with Tookie purring between us – a mug of coffee caressed by chilled hands.

"It's going to rain," I said.

"What's new?" Mally said, sipping her coffee. I looked out the doorway at our garden and was proud of the way it looked. The rains and fertiliser and heat had made everything we planted explode into colour. I had a real sense of belonging sitting there – and I know Mally did too. We felt like a normal couple for once – and I hoped any military action against the village would stay at bay long enough for this new normality to become ingrained; to stabilise both of us.

We woke at three the next afternoon – mainly because Tookie was making a racket wondering where his food was. I've never liked sleeping during the day – and found night-shift I did years later a horrible time for me. I hated that feeling of disorientation and emptiness I experienced for the first five minutes after waking. It was like I'd woken from a coma and the world had passed me by.

"We still going to the croc farm?" I said, rolling my tongue around a stale mouth.

"Uh-uh," Mal said. "Let's just stay at home and read a book."

"I think we should, you know. Hanging around here gets boring."

The sun was hot and the air clear after the storm the night before. For some reason, the exploding mines bothered us less and less. Maybe we were getting used to them, or maybe there were less of them as animals became wary of the minefield. Either way, we slept really well these days. I figured good sleep also helped us a lot; it's so important to mental health.

The pool at the Elephant Hills ruin looked unusually busy as we drove past in our little Morris on the way to the croc farm – and the A'Zambezi Hotel was packed with cars and zebra-painted tour buses.

"Things are picking up, hey?" I commented.

"More sore feet tonight."

"Mmm."

"I was thinking…"

"What?"

"We need to name the car; give it a nickname."

"How the female mind works… From talking about more tourists to naming a car!"

"Piss off," she said, slapping me. "C'mon, what's it to be?"

I thought for a while – my mind turning back to Charlie Pope's 'Pickles'. It seemed an important thing indeed to name one's car. After all, a whole movie had just come out about a VW called 'Herbie'!

"What about 'nigger'?"

"Piss off, Tony…"

"It's black, isn't it?"

"Racist…"

"And you're not?"

"No."

"Bullshit. Would you sleep with a black man?"

"Change the subject. We're supposed to be thinking of the car's name."

"You see, Miss White African, we're all the same."

"It's not their skin colour; it's class distinction. Our British heritage has rammed that into us."

"We agree on something, then."

The hot bush sailed by as we drove along the bouncy tar road to the croc farm. I had a handgun between my legs just in case the next thing that jumped out the bush wasn't an animal. What a way to live! Tourists thought us locals were either gun-crazy or a bunch of looneys. How nice to be ignorant – to fly home to London or Geneva to security and comfort.

"'Bush Pig,'" Mally said suddenly.

"Where?" I said, looking out the window.

"No, silly; the car's name."

"'Bush Pig'? That's two words. Doesn't roll off the tongue easily."

"'Pig', then. It's a squashed-up little car, anyway; looks piggy from the front."

"Okay," I said, beaming her a smile. "'Piggy' it is then."

I held her hand and gave it a quick squeeze – smiling into each other's face.

"'Miss Piggy' would be better."

"Like '*The Muppets*'?"

"Yes!" she said, clapping her hands.

"Okay, you daft woman. 'Miss Piggy' it is!"

The entrance to the croc farm was cool and welcoming under large indigenous trees. Green grass carpeted itself either side of the walkways; a curio shop full of tourists nestled under a shady tree.

We walked hand-in-hand into the farm and were pleasantly surprised to find we'd arrived at feeding time. We watched in awe as crocs, large and small, had chunks of meat thrown at them. The result was chaos and pandemonium as snapping jaws grabbed at this and that. In one case, we saw a croc with the top half of its jaw gone – no doubt bitten off by a bigger croc that mistook the jaw for meat.

"Just like school boarders at mealtime," I quipped.

"Poor buggers," Mally said, without looking at me.

"Who? The crocs or the boarders?"

"Both."

We followed the tour guide to the breeding pens, incubators, 'juniors' tank, the teenage tanks and then the odd mature croc. It wasn't the farm's plan to let the crocs mature – that cost too much in meat – although a croc could live many weeks off a good meal. The aim was to 'farm' them to a point where they would be killed for their skins – taken mainly from the soft underbelly. The skin was then tanned and shipped off to countries all over the world – no doubt labelled 'a product of South Africa' to avoid sanctions imposed upon our tiny little country. How many Italians wore croc leather belts and shoes that originated from here – and that hard currency would buy bombs and bullets and fuel to keep our war effort going.

"I'm looking at 10 litres of diesel there," I said to Mal, explaining my train of thought.

"Funny bugger. Croc-skin selling to buy diesel."

"And bullets."

"And bombs."

"And birth control pills…"

"Let's hope they don't forget those!"

"You've never given kids a thought, then?' Mally said, leaning on a wooden fence – looking back at me. Her eyes were dark-green and serious.

"I'm still a kid myself. Can't see me breeding until I'm at least 27."

"Another five years… I'll be an old woman by then."

"What's this all about, then?" I said, as we sat at a table in the picturesque tea garden. A waiter dressed in white with a red fez on his head moved towards us. We ordered tea and scones with fresh cream and strawberry jam. How colonial.

"Penny for your thoughts, Mal…"

"I dunno. My internal clock's ticking, that's all."

"I had no idea you thought that way about us?"

"Marriage? Kids? Yes, I have. It's natural for a woman to think of these things… and time's running out for me."

"Okay. I'll wait until you're 30… another three years."

"Stop taking the piss."

"I'm dead serious," I said, leaning forward to take her hands in mine.

"If we're still together when you're 30, we'll have kids. I rather fancy the idea of firing live rounds into you!"

"You bastard," she said, smiling. She looked like Tookie finding a pot of cream.

In my mind though, I thought of me being a dad. I wasn't sure if I was ready for them – even at the tender age of 25. I had a lot of desire to move and travel again, like I did with Jess. I fell deep into thought about Jess and wondered where she was these days.

"A penny for your thoughts," Mal said, buttering a scone.

"Just trying to get my head around nappies and school runs," I lied. She smiled at me and licked some cream off her finger.

❧—❦

"I'm jealous of Mal being allowed to start later than us," I said to Fred. He'd decided to let some of the staff start later in the evening – when it got really busy – so that it would be less of an endurance mission to go through the whole night. In addition to that, we had 'borrowed' three croupiers from our 'sister' casino up at the Montclair in Inyanga – situated in the eastern part of the country; a place of hills and rivers filled with trout – the 'little Switzerland' of Rhodesia; a place I had many fond memories of.

"Gives us a chance to get to know each other a little better," Linda butted in. I smiled at her – swallowing involuntarily. I knew she would be bad news for me if I did something stupid.

The place was filling up. It was New Year's Eve, 1977 going into 1978 – and in less than three hours, it would be packed with partygoers and diners cramming into the casino to sing the traditional songs, linked arm-in-arm at midnight. A bit of cash had been splurged on the place – and some new curtains, paint and a false ceiling over the bar area made it look more upmarket than usual. Party hats were in free supply and a few ragged decorations had been pinned to the walls. The owner, Don Goldin, must have been feeling a little generous these days – perhaps a bit less threatened by bankruptcy than before. It boded well for a good year-end bonus, as well. I could just smell the sea at Durban, where we would spend our bonus money on holiday. All in all, there was a great festive mood in the air – and I felt good and light-hearted.

"Hope the gooks or Zambians don't stuff it up," Fred said.

"Just thinking the same thing… Is the safe ready to be opened if we get attacked?"

"Yes… and the basement's packed with chilled beers."

"The guests seem to be ignoring your notice about what to do if we get attacked."

"They'll have to learn the hard way, then."

I discarded the thought of an attack. Christmas Eve was just a go at us on a public holiday – a way of saying: "we are still out there" or "we don't care much for your white God"… Who knows? I doubted an attack tonight; gooks and Zambian Army personnel would want to be somewhere celebrating something – maybe a year closer to the end of the Chimurenga war; a year closer to Zimbabwe rising out of the ruins of Rhodesia? A place where the majority ruled and all people would have big houses and farms and a good job, with bellies swollen by food and drink. This is what they had been promised by Mugabe, not so? Gullible bastards.

The first thud sent a tremble through the building, but not loud enough to frighten anyone – but my skin went cold and I felt the blood drain from my face. Fred and Danny stared wide-eyed at me. I nodded.

"Yes," I said to Fred. "It's happening again!"

My toes seemed to curl up in my shoes; my back tingled while I waited for the second explosion – and when it came, it was very, very loud and frightening. Laughter and gaiety died instantly – to be replaced by a look of confusion on the tourists' faces and shock and horror on the locals' faces.

"Please stay calm!" Fred bellowed. "I want you to follow this man here to the basement." Fred pointed at Ivor, who in turn, pulled on a handgun from the cashiers' desk and headed for the door.

You cannot stop panic and chaos in a situation like this. I'd experienced it in Australia two years before when the front wheel of the plane I was travelling in collapsed as we were being wheeled backwards onto the taxiing ramp. The panic had been total, with people clawing and climbing over each other to get out the plane. Tonight was no different. It started with a woman screaming directly after another near-miss – and then that was it. People simply lost their dignity and pushed and shoved like animals to get out of the casino. Ivor got swamped in a mass off heaving humanity – and soon disappeared from sight. Adrenalin had kicked in and I stood rigid – my body shaking and quivering uncontrollably. I decided to wait until everyone had left the place. What was the point being blown to bits in a congested pile of humanity? Only Fred and I stood upright. The three temp croupiers – plus Lesley, Warren and Danny – were under the table; Linda was at my feet. Thumps, vibrations, loud bangs and flashes of light were going off all around the building. This was much more serious than last week's attack.

"Let's go!" I shouted at Fred and the others – pulling Linda up by the crook of her arm. We ran as one out the doors – over spilled betting chips, discarded jackets and party hats.

"Danny, take the others down to the basement!"

"But…"

"Just do it!" I yelled at him, pushing Linda forward. Her eyes were wide with panic – and they remained fixed on me as Danny pulled her away. Fred and I rushed to open the large walk-in safe to collect weapons as agreed.

"Where's Warren?" I shouted. Fred shrugged. I went back towards the casino to look for him. He was part of our three-man group that would be armed in case gooks came into the hotel. No Congo slaughter for us.

"Warren!" I shouted into the now-darkened casino area. Silence greeted me. I was just about to turn away when I noticed a ghostly figure drift towards me from out of the gloom – gun in hand, pointing straight at my chest. Warren had flipped. I felt shit-scared. I knew this guy had been on the edge for a long time. He was always nervous and sweating heavily whenever I saw him.

"Warren! It's me! Tony! Put that bloody thing down, man!" There was little recognition in his eyes. If there was ever a case of post-traumatic stress syndrome in a former Rhodesian soldier, this was him – pointing a 9mm Browning at me.

"For shit's sake, Warren! You're scaring the crap out of me! Who's this talking to you, man? Where are you in your head?!"

There was a mild form of recognition then – and his eyes started to focus. He looked drugged, bleary-eyed and was sweating profusely. I'd nearly got shot by an idiot fellow employee. I waited a second or two, with bombs crashing around the village, while this clot calmed down enough not to murder me.

"What's going on?" Fred said from behind us – a load of rifles in his arms.

"Nothing. All's okay... It is, isn't it?" I said, facing Warren again. He nodded – shaking like a leaf. I walked back into the bright lights of the one-armed bandit room and took a rifle and bandolier of ammo from Fred – putting the belt diagonally across my chest over my left shoulder. Fred offered a rifle to Warren, who took it nervously from him. We ran down the staff staircase towards the basement. In all the panic and haste, I'd completely forgotten about Mally. No doubt Fred was worried sick thinking of his wife and kids too.

The sight that greeted me in the basement was unforgettable. There was no quiet, desultory air of resignation like last week; this time around, everyone was in a party mood. The older folk were singing 'Roll Out The Barrel' or 'It's A Long Way To Tipperary' and Ivor and the barmen from upstairs were selling alcoholic drinks like water. It was certainly the right way to squash fears of what was happening 'out there'.

A lot of folk seemed to be cheered by the sight of three men armed to the teeth – even though we were still in our evening suits and bow-ties. We probably looked like cloned versions of James Bond. I went and sat with Linda for a few minutes.

"Where's Mally?" she asked.

"With a friend at the Falls Hotel... I'm worried about her."

"You should go get her. She may not be safe out there."

"I dunno. It seems pretty serious, this attack."

"Go get her, Tony."

I pursed my lips and shook my head slightly. It wouldn't be a joke running around out there. A slow – but steady – rain of bombs was falling around the village.

"What the hell is our artillery doing?" Fred said. "We should be plastering those bastards by now!"

"Who knows? Look, Fred… I need to go find Mally. She's at the Falls Hotel next door."

"You're nuts."

"I've got to. I'll see you back here, just now."

I got up and rushed towards the small flight of stairs, with Linda and Fred saying: "be careful" from behind me. I was mildly amused to see a lone soldier with an Uzi on guard at the top of the staircase – accompanied by a civilian with a massive rotary anti-riot shotgun cradled on his lap.

"My night off," the soldier said sarcastically, as I looked at him.

"No such thing," I replied and ran off down the open-sided hallway, up the ramp, left along another corridor and into the hotel proper – arriving in the reception area. Another soldier and Robin Ellis, the hotel manager, stood next to a huge plate-glass window looking at the flashes outside. It reminded me of curious onlookers gazing at an approaching electrical storm – except in this case, the flashes were being generated by high explosives. Each arc of light momentarily lit up the trees and car park like a large flashgun had just gone off. It was surreal and eerie. Also, any one of those bushes could be hiding a gook – waiting for the order to attack and kill civilians.

"You guys are nuts standing next to that window! Any idea what that glass will do to you if a mortar shell lands outside?!" I shouted at them. They both saw the sense of my comment and moved rapidly into the interior of the building.

"Robin, I need the keys to your Land Rover. Mal's over at the other hotel."

"Look who's nuts now! You want to go out in that?" Robin said, pointing.

"I have to. Can you help me?"

"C'mon," he said, gesturing me to follow him. It was such a weird feeling watching the lights flicker on in his office, with the normality of a desk and files and a swivel-chair in the glaring light, when it was madness and war out there.

"Here," he said, tossing a bunch of keys at me. "Reverse is a bit dodgy."

"Thanks, man. I owe you!"

I ran out his office, turned sharp-right, down a hallway that led to the kitchen and out the back door. A bright flash and kwa-thoom went off ahead of me through the trees some distance ahead – and in the same direction of the hotel I was heading for. I flung open the door of Robin's rickety Land Rover, threw the rifle on the spare seat and jumped in behind the steering wheel. I was shaking so much I fumbled around for ages to get the correct key into the ignition switch. I had this overpowering fear of someone walking up to me and shooting me in the head.

Eventually, the engine kicked into life – but as Robin forewarned, I battled to find reverse. It would've been quicker to run over to the hotel, but more risky, perhaps. Who knows? An army detachment lurking in the shadows may have shot me.

I shoved the gear lever into first, gunned the engine and wheelied out the side gate of the hotel – turning sharp-left onto the tar road that led past the station to Vic Falls Hotel. By the time I'd covered the 400 metres, I was doing close to 50 and almost took out a car parked near the front gate. Another crump and thud went off on the other side of the hotel as I screeched to a halt in front of the reception area.

I ran into the large foyer where several receptionists normally stood, but now the place was deserted and silent – but not the hallway off to my right; the hallway that led to the East Wing bedrooms. It was in partial darkness and heaving with humanity. Young kids were crying, and most people sat holding their loved ones for comfort. There was no sign of soldiers or armed civilians here – and if gooks appeared with automatic weapons now, there would be masses of dead. I often wondered why they never tried something like that; the gutless bastards. I looked down at my rifle – and although it gave some of the onlookers cheer, I realised I hadn't a bloody clue how to load or fire it. In fact, it was unloaded!

"Mally!" I bellowed at the top of my lungs. The noise died down partially, and then started up again before I shouted her name one more time.

"Here, Tony! I'm here!" Mally's voice called back. I waded through legs and arms down the claustrophobic passage until at last, I met up with her. She stood up and fell into my arms – shaking like a leaf. I squeezed her tight.

"C'mon. Let's get the heck outta here."

"Out there? Isn't it safer to stay here?"

"No," I said without explanation, tugging her after me. We half-tripped, half-slipped over feet and legs on the way back to the vehicle.

"I don't want to go out there," Mally said, resisting me.

"Look at me, Mal," I said, looking straight into her eyes. "Do you trust me?"

"You know I do…"

"Well, now's the time to put it to the test." A flicker and rumble of light to our left made us flinch slightly. The horizon near the airstrip lit up – silhouetting the tree line. "That's our artillery opening up, babe. We'll be okay now."

We could both hear the whistle of shells sailing off into the night to our right, followed by louder, deeper bangs than we'd heard all evening. I opened the passenger door, shoved Mally forcefully inside and handed her my rifle, which she held like a snake in front of her.

"It's not loaded," I said, slamming the door. She looked at me as if I was nuts – opening her mouth once to say something, and then closing it again.

I accelerated as hard as I could – and in less than a minute, we screeched to a halt outside the back of the casino kitchen.

"C'mon," I said, pulling Mally out the passenger door. Only the odd mortar bomb was falling now, but not knowing where it would land was simply terrifying. Mally felt like a bar of lead as I tugged her behind me. I retraced my steps back to the basement with what appeared a reluctant and resentful person behind me, but her mood lightened immediately when she saw the basement and high spirit of the people in there.

"This is better," she said.

"Go to Fred and the others and I'll get you a drink."

I elbowed my way to Ivor and got her a brandy and coke. She knocked back half of it before coming up for air.

"You okay, now?"

"Yes, thank you. Thanks for coming to get me."

"I had to. I was worried sick. How's things here, Fred?"

"Good, but I need to get back home. As soon as the last bomb's dropped, I'm going."

"I dunno, Fred. What if there's an attack by gooks?"

"All the more reason. I'd rather die with my family than down here."

To the outsider, this situation may seem surreal – but at the time of the attack, we were all genuinely worried about enemy forces rushing in and murdering all of us. It would have been an amazing coup for the forces of evil – and it was something we all took very seriously.

"Mal, I'm no good down here with this thing," I said, tapping the hunting rifle. "I'm going up to the foyer to make sure no gook gets near this place."

She merely nodded and took another large swig of her drink. I eased my way through a hot press of people reeking of booze and climbed to the top of the steps. The soldier and civvy were still on duty.

"You're lovely targets with this light on," I said, flipping a switch. The foyer fell into darkness, with the only illumination coming from the swimming pool lights about 30 metres away.

"Which unit you from?" I said to the soldier. I should have known by his stable belt, really.

"Armoured cars."

"Off duty, huh?"

"Mmm. What a way to go."

"Just as well. The folk down there are shit-scared. You're performing your best duty ever." He smiled in the gloom.

"And you?" I said to the heavily-armed civilian.

"From Jo'burg," he said with a thick South African accent.

"That's one helluva weapon you got there."

"American anti-riot shotgun."

I'd never seen anything like it. The barrel was short, with some type of rotating drum underneath it. It looked like an oversized Russian RPD machine-gun, but with a short barrel.

"Well, I'm glad you're here too. Sorry these bloody gooks are ruining your holiday."

"It's the best holiday I've ever had," he said, tapping the weapon. Well, okay. I was talking to some fruitcake in the same mould as Warren.

"I'm just popping upstairs to the Summit Bar," I said.

"You're mad. It's not over yet. There's no protection up there."

"I plan to live a long time," I said, heading for the lift. The doors closed behind me and I glided upwards in a silent cocoon. I hoped I didn't get trapped in here, though. I was borderline-claustrophobic.

The doors swished open – and I was immediately confronted by an armed trooper. He gave me the scare of my life.

"Sorry, army personnel only," he said forcefully.

"I'm Lieut Ballinger."

"Who?"

"Lieut Ballinger. Did my national service up here. I know this area backwards. Perhaps I can be of some help?"

He looked uncertain and turned to consult with an officer I hadn't noticed in the gloom. I also hadn't noticed the tables, radios and radio operators sitting next to him.

"It's okay," the officer said. "Let him in."

The guard stood to one side – allowing me to stand next to the artillery officer without hindrance. He took a quick look up at me and smiled – no doubt because of the way I was dressed.

"Don't tell me your name's Bond? It'll be too much…"

"No, Tony Ballinger. I was a lieut up here during my NS."

"Okay," he said disinterestedly.

"You gonna hit back at those shits?"

"We already have. One more salvo to go… and it'll be tickets for them."

He'd barely finished speaking when the horizon to the south-west flickered a few times. Moments later, shrieking whistles flew overhead from our left to right. Bright red flashes went off in Zambia – followed a short while later by rewarding thuds and explosions. I wondered how they knew what to fire at. Perhaps the SAS were over there feeding back info? Who knows? War's a mysterious art – and half the time, you don't have a bloody clue what's going on.

My body trembled with excitement watching all this. I wished I had come up here earlier. It was like some type of game – being detached and aloof to the actual killing going on out there. This was my scene – and formed the seeds for requesting a transfer to a support company during my next call-up.

"How come we didn't retaliate last week?"

"Weren't allowed to, but the brass have given us carte blanche from now on."

I stood transfixed for about 10 minutes – watching and learning how the forward fire-control officers worked, with their plotting boards and charge/range sheets laid out in front of them. I was hooked, I liked this very much indeed. I was determined never to set foot back in the bush ever again as an infantryman.

The bombs landing in the village had stopped altogether now – and apart from the static on the military radios, there was an absolute, ghostly silence. Less than five minutes later, Fred's car zoomed away from the hotel at an amazing speed for such an old vehicle. Poor bugger; he must be worried sick. I decided to go downstairs again. The two sentries were still there – and had been joined by one or two curious onlookers. I stared out into the gloomy bush on the other side of the tennis court and wondered what we could do if a determined gook attack was put in against us. If they could raise 50 men to attack Jambezi, they could certainly do the same – or more – here. Also, rumours had abounded for months that they planned to come across the bridge en masse and slaughter every white in town. Perhaps just idle fears, but something our unusual lifestyle fed on. Rumours often become fact in one's mind under stressful conditions.

I looked down at my rifle and belatedly decided I had better know how to use it. I slid back the bolt action and fed five rounds into the internal magazine – a bit like an SKS, but with a bolt action instead of a cocking handle. I guessed it was a .3006 calibre, with a rounded soft-point head. I slid the bolt forward and pushed a button onto safe – all the while facing it out into the bush. I figured all I had to do was take it off safe, aim and pull the trigger. A couple who came up from the basement watched me with growing unease as they realised their storm-trooper guard had only just loaded his weapon. I felt like a complete dork – and faced the bush out of embarrassment. Some James Bond!

I waited until my cheeks had stopped glowing red before I went downstairs again. It was as hot as hell in there, and people lay all over the place – some looking bored and others drunk out of their skulls. I waded through them over to Ivor.

"What's going on, Ivor? Fred's pushed off. Is he coming back?"

"No idea."

"Are we opening the casino again?"

"Not 'til Fred gets back. He's got the keys to the safe." I sensed the others standing next to me, and turned to face a small group of croupiers behind Mally.

"What's up?" she said, her cheeks flushed. She was pissed.

"Who knows? But it's as hot as hell down here."

Turning back to Ivor, I said: "I think shut this place down and let's go back upstairs?" He nodded 'okay' – making his glasses reflect light like 'The Smiling Shit's'. I took Mally by the hand and led her back to the cocktail bar outside the machine room, where we all proceeded to down half the bar's stock. I was startled to see it was only 11:00 p.m. Fear and the inrush of adrenalin distorts time – and what seems like hours when something horrible is happening, turns out to be a few minutes in the end. I was simply staggered that only an hour and 50 minutes had passed. I was almost past caring when Fred staggered up the staircase at 20 minutes to midnight.

"Let's get the show on the road," he said in a bored voice.

"You can't be serious," Ivor responded. "We're all pissed... and knackered."

"Skip it, come on. We've got a living to make."

We rose like drugged zombies and staggered through the throng of people towards the casino door, which was being guarded by a waiter with a black fez on his head.

"Thanks, Philemon," Fred said. I looked at the old waiter and smiled. He was one of the old-school – courteous and loyal. A sort of cheer went up when people saw us entering the gambling hall.

"This is bullshit," Danny muttered.

People, in varying degrees of sobriety, followed us inside – some heading for the bar and others straight to the tables. We had to work quickly to scoop up dropped chips and issue new ones for cash. A few tourists griped that their betting chips had been moved, stolen or lost, but what could we do? Fred issued 20 dollars of chips to each complainant, and that was that.

We'd just started to get into the swing of things when someone started the countdown to midnight. Party hats came on and people started to pull back to form an interlocked, gyrating circle. I walked up behind Mally and put my arms around her as the countdown went from 10 down to one. I wasn't in the mood for this – and nor was Mal. We just stood there silently – looking at this crazy mass of humanity doing their best to forget what had just happened. To them, it was just an exciting life experience; to us, it was another nail in our coffin. I stood there – totally indifferent to the madness in front of me.

"Five..."

"Four..."

"Three!"

"Two!"

"One!"

"Happy New Year!" the crowd chorused. People moved to and fro to kiss each other before forming a twisting and turning, arm-locked circle to sing *'Auld Lang Syne'*. I turned Mally to face me and looked deep into her glazed eyes.

"I love you," I said. "Happy New Year, love."

"Love you too babe, love you too…" We squeezed each other until a tap on our shoulders separated us. It was Fred – beaming a slightly less enthusiastic smile than normal. He knew how we felt; we were more like combat veterans after a battle than civilians at a party.

"Love you both," he said, giving us a bear hug. I hugged him back and Mally kissed him fondly on the lips.

"You can bugger off now," he said playfully to me – giving Mal a big, singular hug.

I shook Ivor's hand. "Happy New Year, Ivor."

"Same to you. Thanks for making us feel secure earlier."

"What a joke. The rifle wasn't loaded." He laughed and slapped me on my shoulder.

"Well, it was good for us psychologically, Tony. I probably would've shot myself in the foot if anything had happened." I smiled and patted him back.

The room was still going crazy, with heaving humanity all over the place. I really didn't want any of this.

"Fred," I said, pulling him away from Lesley. "Mal and I need some time off. She's had it – and so have I, for that matter."

"I know," he nodded. "I can see it in her eyes. You can take 10 working days from the fifth of January."

"Thanks," I said, patting his shoulder. I went over to Mal and told her the good news. "We'll go to Durban… get some sea air and prawns into us."

"Thank God! That sounds lovely! I feel like a compressed spring."

I pulled her into my arms and gave her a long squeeze – and an even longer kiss.

"I was worried sick about you tonight," I said, looking into her eyes.

"Me too. For you and me."

"Sounded like some of the bombs landed pretty close to the Falls Hotel."

"I think a couple hit it. We'll go look tomorrow?"

"Mmm."

"It was the flashes that scared me the most, like big cameras going off. They seemed to illuminate everything in a weird light."

"I know what you mean. I was terrified driving over to you."

We remained hugging each other for a long while – lost in our own cocoon – wondering what the immediate future held for us. What would 1978 bring us as a couple – and the country in general? Would the war intensify to the point where it became a classical war, with planes and tanks attacking us, or would it forever be a low-intensity civil war like it was now?

Fred tapped us on the shoulders – jerking his head sideways once. It was time for us to go back to work. I didn't want to serve these crass people – with my nerves frayed – and I resented having to show any type of manners or hospitality to them. I knew that I was fed up with the job – mainly because I was exhausted, but also because I knew it would go nowhere… and it all worried me a little.

We eventually got to bed at 8:00 a.m. – and I was more tired than from any army operation I'd ever been in. My feet were lumps of bruised meat; my back muscles knotted; my fingernails black from handling dirty currency. When we woke at 4:30 p.m. I staggered through to the bathroom and soaked for nearly 40 minutes, with Mal joining me for the last 15.

"Oh, that's lovely," she said, lowering herself into the steaming water. "I feel 80!"

It was just gone 6:30 p.m. when we arrived in 'Miss Piggy' at the Falls Hotel. We, like many other locals, did a tour of the town to see damage after a mortar attack.

"There were two massive bangs down by the pool," Mal said, as we walked through the reception area – past two thickly-carpeted lounges to the outer patio. I simply loved this hotel – and it was a long time since I'd seen the place. Soft and subtle green lights shone up into the leafy trees – and already, as if nothing had happened the night before, people were queuing up to eat braaied meat and salads at their tables under the stars. The majestic Falls Bridge – framed by a wall of trees either side – was illuminated by orange security lights in the middle-distance.

Then we saw the damage. The cocktail bar's window on our right was gone; a small impact crater could be seen on the patio floor, with shrapnel-marks radiating outwards.

"A woman lost her elbow last night," a voice said from behind us. I turned to see Phil, the blonde-headed cop from long ago – the one that had dived overboard to clear our boat engine of weed.

"Phil," I said, shaking his hand warmly. "Great to see you again, my friend. You remember Mal, don't you?" Phil nodded his head. "This is the fella I told you about who jumped into the river that night to free our boat's engine of weed."

"Impressive," Mally said, pursing her lips.

"A woman lost her elbow, you say?"

"Mmm. She was sitting just inside the window, there."

"Ouch. That must've been bloody painful."

"I vaguely remember seeing her; an elderly woman in a floral dress," Mal said.

"Bastards," I said.

"They also hit the laundry; almost killed one of the staff."

"What other damage in the village?"

"Nothing."

"You're kidding?!" Mal and I said in unison. "There must have been 40 or 50 shells dropped on us," I said.

"I know it's hard to believe," Phil shrugged, "but that's the truth of it."

"Unreal," I said, looking at Mal. "How's your wife taking it, Phil?"

"Wife?" he smiled, "I'm still looking." He cast a quick glance at Mal.

"Thought you were married, for some reason. Think tourists will leave now?"

"Not yet. Just look at them all. I think they'll go when the holiday season's over... maybe a day or two, now."

"Any locals leaving?" Mal asked.

"Not that I know of. Most are drunks anyway... probably don't even know we've been mortared."

We smiled at him. He was right, of course. A lot of people hit the bottle pretty hard around here – an easy way to forget being locked up in a jail the size of a small city.

"I went up to the Summit Bar during the attack... well, near the end. Artillery was just firing its last salvo."

"I know, and I can promise you, those buggers over the river won't do it again too soon."

"Who was it then? Gooks? Zambian Army?"

"I dunno, Tony, but I doubt gooks have heavy weapons lying around this close to the border... more than likely a Zambian effort."

"We should bloody well invade them," Mal said.

"It may come to that. Anyway, I better go. Got reports to hand in before I knock off at 10."

"Well, nice meeting you again, Phil,"

"You too." We shook hands and Mal and I walked over to have a light meal near the dancefloor. We chose our meat and sat down to wait for it to be cooked and delivered to us.

"I just can't believe there's so little damage in the village. It's almost a non-event, like we had a bad electrical storm or something," Mal said.

"Tell that to the woman with the elbow missing."

"I know, but crumbs... one injury and no deaths."

"Wonder what they did with her, the old lady? There's no hospital around here."

"Probably flew her straight to Bulawayo."

"So where do you think this is going, Tony?"

"Not sure, Mal," I said after some thought. "Where should we go on our holiday?"

"I thought we'd agreed Durban?"

"Okay, sounds good… Any ideas?"

"I've heard the Blue Waters Hotel is okay… Probably in our price range."

"Okay, we'll book it tomorrow. I can't wait to get into the sea."

"And some decent shops!"

"Knew you'd say that. We'll have hardly any foreign currency left."

The drinks and food arrived together. We ate the delicious steak with relish. I have yet to eat nicer steak than that reared on the grassy veld in Africa; not that water-induced pulp you get in Europe – stuff that boils away in front of your eyes when you try to fry it; and that delicious bit of fat along the edge that has been nicely browned over the coals.

The band started playing quietly in the background – and for all intents and purposes, life was normal and good – although at any second, a bomb could shatter our enjoyment. It would take just one serious incident in a hotel here, or the death of a few civilians some-where in the village, and that would be the end of our tourists; our lifeblood. It didn't take a rocket scientist to realise the gooks were out to destroy our economy as much as our army. In fact, economic collapse would probably cripple us quicker than a military defeat. By lobbing a few bombs at Kariba, Umtali, Inyanga and Vic Falls, they could virtually wipe out our tourist industry – an industry vital to our survival.

I was quite surprised by Mal's response to the attack. I honestly thought she would flip and head for greener pastures, but something had matured in her – or hardened her resolve. Maybe she too realised that the village is our relationship. Leave here and who knows what would happen?

The promise of a holiday in a country where there was no war – or the threat of a gook killing us – had livened her up no end. We could drive a hired car without having to worry about a shortage of fuel, and could walk into a shop to buy chocolates and perfumes and clothes – the likes of which we hadn't seen for a long time now. I planned to eat two whole bars of nut chocolate before anything else.

By the third of the month, the tourists dried up like a tap had been turned off. We had loads of people in on 2 January – suffering another night of tortured feet – but on the third, they were gone. Back to Salisbury; back to America, Italy, France or South Africa. The whole village just drained itself of foreigners. We packed our bags on the fourth – and by the afternoon of the sixth, we were in the Blue Waters Hotel in Durban... the north-ernmost hotel in the long strip of hotels on the Durban beachfront.

I cannot describe that feeling of having a press taken off our shoulders. It was like the wind-up handle on a toy soldier being let go at last. All we did for the first three days was eat, sleep and make love – but definitely more sleep than the other two. It was lovely to wake at our leisure, stretch lazily and go down for a late breakfast; to stroll over the causeway to the beach and sleep there all day under an umbrella; to go back to a cool room and make love in the afternoon. By early evening, we would be bathed and refreshed – and would go for a stroll to another hotel to eat or have a drink on the veranda overlooking the sea. Life seemed so normal and relaxed here – even though deep down, South Africa was simmering towards her own eventual Uhuru... but not freedom for all. The povo – the poor – would always be badly-off in Africa.

For now, we luxuriated in a white-run paradise in Africa and enjoyed the fine cuisine the country had to offer. Good wines, good seafood and lots of good sex. It was a holiday I shall never forget. I loved the bar under the side of the swimming pool, with windows allowing you to look up and into it while you sat in the comfort of soft chairs – sipping something new and tasty.

We returned 10 days later – refreshed, invigorated and, in a strange way, glad to be back. It was lovely to see Tookie and our garden again – and to be able to kick back and sit on top of the bunker while having a chat. The absence of pressure on us was profound, but we could detect that same 'wired-up' feeling we'd left behind in others. There was a brown envelope pushed under the door on our return. The sight of it sent shivers up my spine. I was to report to a military doctor in Salisbury within 10 days. The date stamp gave me four days to respond to the order. I had to leave for Salisbury soon.

"What's that all about?" Mal asked.

"They need to know whether my ear's healed. It'll determine my posting."

"Posting?"

"I'll be due for call-up again soon."

"Shit! When's this going to end?"

Two days later, I was sitting in front of a doctor in KGV1 Barracks in Salisbury. My dad waited outside while the doc examined me. An assistant did a sound sensitivity test before he slid one of those things with a light on it into my ear. He poked around for a few seconds before straightening up.

"Your eardrum has a scar on it, but basically, it's healed. I'm upgrading you to 'A' category."

"Great," I replied sarcastically.

Less than two weeks later, another brown envelope arrived under the door. I looked at it for a long time before slitting it open. I was filled with dread. I was told in simple, unemotional language to report to 'A' Company 2nd Battalion, Rhodesia Regiment in one week's time. A return train ticket was enclosed.

The two weeks since my trip to Salisbury had allowed me to be lulled into a false sense of reality. I'd got back into the routine of closing at midnight – or two in the morning at the latest – to wake to a leisurely breakfast, a read of the newspaper and a day doing what I wanted to do. Actually, the life of a croupier was brilliant. It was easy and laid-back – unless you had to work until daylight; then, it was a nightmare.

Our gook mates and the Zambian Army had been good boys; they only dropped one or two mortar rounds while we were in South Africa, which we didn't witness, and nothing since. That was a whole month of no tension. Even the thuds in the minefield had quietened down – and the other casino had opened to replace the one lost when Elephant Hills burned down. Life was a dream, until that bloody envelope arrived. I felt sick and nauseous with fear. I was going back to the army.

It wasn't only me that had taken the call-up news badly. Mally had just about gone to pieces and slumped into a depression virtually overnight. I knew this would happen, so I kept the call-up notice private until the last moment. How many other couples all over the country were going through the agony of opening call-up letters? How many businesses would fail because the only guy that knew how to run it was being shoved off to the army for six weeks? How many marriages broke down because of adulterous affairs during this forced separation? And how many men kissed their wives and kids goodbye to never see them again? Our parting was full of tears and feelings of emptiness.

My uniform was decidedly tighter than four-and-a-half months earlier – and I felt slightly stupid waddling around in it. I had lots of time on the train journey down to Bulawayo to ponder my new posting. What would my OC be like? Would he be supportive and helpful, or a plain bastard? It was usually one or the other, like a lottery draw.

Sitting on a train – rolling through the flat Matabeleland bush – brought back so many memories from two years earlier, when I first reported for duty. It was happening all over again now – except this time, I was trained and already an officer – but I was rusty and very much a civilian again. I knew that a period of retraining was ahead of me.

On arrival at the red-bricked Brady Barracks, I was shocked – and mildly confused – by the news that my company had already departed for our operational area. I looked at my call-up papers, but couldn't find fault with the arrival date printed on it. I showed a clerk, who went away to the adjutant – coming back about 15 minutes later.

"Admin error," he said. "We'll fly you down to Buffalo Range. You can link up with Colonel French there and he'll get you to your company, somehow."

"Exactly where is that? My operational area?"

"Mozambique."

"Excuse me?" I said – my pulse racing. The clerk appeared to enjoy my discomfort.

"Your company operates from the Rhodesian border to the power lines coming from Cabora Bassa."

Cabora Bassa – a big hydroelectric dam hundreds of miles north-north east of our patrol area. I vaguely knew that the power lines ran parallel with the Rhodesian border, along the Gonarezhou National Park border towards South Africa, which the dam supplied power to. That was an operational area of perhaps 30 kilometres deep by about 100 kilometres wide – a huge area for 130 men to operate in.

"You've got to sign for these," the clerk said, bringing me back from my daydreams. He handed me a new set of epaulettes. They had two pips on them. I was now a First Lieutenant. Big deal.

I didn't enjoy the next six weeks at all. I found our Company Commander (or OC) overbearing and patronising. His name was John Bissett – and his company had been given the nickname 'Bissett's Bastards'. He was a good soldier; I just didn't like him. I hated the bush we operated in; I hated the flies and smell of death whenever we passed through the minefield into Mozambique; I hated it when Rob Hickey – one of our sergeants – was crushed to death by an elephant in bush so thick, you couldn't see a man five metres in front of you. The barren wasteland of deserted Portuguese farms depressed me. Is this what farms in Rhodesia were heading for? It was six weeks of tension, contacts and the sights and sounds of death; of exploded heads and maggots eating into dead flesh; of bluebottle flies buzzing out of the mouths of rigid, rotting corpses – or us having to massacre herds of cattle to deny gooks the opportunity of feeding off them.

I hated the heat, the ticks, the food and the loneliness of that vast tract of flat land. Death stalked everywhere – and I realised often that I'd had it cushy up at Vic Falls during my national service. This was where the *real* war was – and when I came away from that call-up, I wasn't at all convinced we were winning it either. There were sections of Matibi 2 Tribal Trust Land that, in my opinion, were 'liberated' by the gooks. It was Zimbabwe already down there – a place of death and decay. Was this an omen for the future of our land?

It got to the point where we had to operate in platoon-strength. The gook spoor we followed often numbered 30-plus. Every day, I could hear a contact in the distance or be instructed to rush to the assistance of friendly forces to act as stop-groups or whatever. I must have seen two or three para-deployments in that short period – and then, the inevitable horror happened to me during a contact... of sorts. I don't remember seeing gooks or anything like that – just lots of firing, chaos and an injured woman lying in front of me... a woman whose head I blew off her shoulders with a single shot to her forehead. I remember standing there, feeling mildly amused by the way the back of her head got sucked off her face – leaving a death mask with no eyes staring back at me... you know, like a mask you would wear at a Mardi Gras festival.

I always thought those Vietnam movies – where cruelty and horror abounded – were beyond the pale, but here I experienced it for myself. I will never forget the sight of my platoon – wearing a mixture of 'cunt caps' and camouflaged headbands – burning down every hut we encountered in that wasteland... right as far back as Matibi 2 and beyond... And we had some excellent men – men that stuck to tracks until they made contact with gooks. One sergeant followed spoor for two days until he saw a gook guard dozing under a bush. He despatched him with a bayonet in case the main body of gooks was nearby. He was certainly the only territorial soldier we knew that killed a gook with a bayonet – and was naturally labelled with various nicknames that suited the occasion... something to do with killing 'Piggy' from *Lord of the Flies* if I remember right.

By the time I'd finished that call-up, I was a changed man – changed in the sense that my mind had been warped; not changed by anything spectacular I'd done, because I hadn't done anything spectacular at all. Killing a half-dead woman wasn't spectacular.

I met Mally at the Holiday Inn in Bulawayo six weeks and three days later. I was thin and my legs were a mass of bites and festering sores. I stank and felt like a stranger to her and civilisation. I think she was shocked by my appearance – the way my eyes had sunk into their sockets from a dose of heat-fatigue.

Climbing into bed that first night at the hotel – feeling the exquisite pleasure of the soft, clean sheets and the warmth and tenderness of her lying next to me – is a memory I will never forget. I barely spoke – and nor did she – but the level of communication between us was incredibly intense and special. It was one of the most tender nights of lovemaking I have known; of deep passionate kissing – just knowing we were okay and back together again.

We flew back to Vic Falls – and I was beside myself with joy seeing Tookie and our house again. I loved the sunsets, when dappled rays of warm sunshine would filter through the lace curtains on the lounge windows – casting shadows on the wall behind me... A time to read a book and sip whisky or sit on a loo again! What heaven! I know that many, many men who returned from military service must have felt the same way I did when they got home. No ticks or death here; nothing waiting to kill you. I came home with a deep respect for regular soldiers who faced death and injury all year round. I could understand now why some snapped and went nuts, or why so many drank or took drugs to kill the nerves – the pain and the memories of what they experienced.

Chapter Ten

In those days, pressure on manpower was intense. We had such a small population to draw soldiers from, that our call-ups came down to six weeks in and six weeks out. Other armies called up men for a year – and then their tour of duty was over for a long time… maybe even for good – but in Rhodesia, in the heady days of 1978, we were scraping the bottom of the manpower barrel. The disruption to peoples' lives was gruelling. You can imagine trying to run a business, support a wife and kids – and then go away to fight again every six weeks! A lot of marriages broke down. A lot of people emigrated. The 'chicken run' had begun – a name we gave to emigrants; people who left us behind to carry the can.

Nationally, the country was undergoing major changes both politically and militarily. On the political front, we had just gone through a referendum asking whites if we should allow a black government to take over – or at least, share power with us. The vote was overwhelmingly 'yes'. People were tired of war. Ian Smith had long been grooming Bishop Abel Muzorewa – a Methodist clergyman – to take over the reins, at least symbolically. There was a view among white people that Muzorewa was a 'soft touch' and we whites would be able to pull his strings – rather like a puppet. Naturally, the real gook leaders like Mugabe and Nkomo despised him as a traitor and 'sell-out'. Even though we were tired of war, the prospect of Rhodesia becoming a black-led country horrified most of us – and we all knew the precious name of our country would change, which it did in 1979 – becoming a horrible hybrid called 'Zimbabwe-Rhodesia'.

On the military front, gook incursions were not only increasing – with larger and larger formations of the enemy moving over our vast, sparsely-protected borders – but running parallel with this, larger and larger conventional formations were being formed by the enemy in preparation for the 'final push', which they now sensed like hounds chasing a terrified fox.

There were rumours of large military formations moving towards the north-eastern border, in the Op Hurricane area – formations that had to be attacked by the air force. My mate from Churchill High School, Kevin Pienke, got killed early the following year when he went to bomb one of those huge FRELIMO/ZANLA convoys. His Canberra bomber took hits – and being the fighter that he was, he tried to nurse his plane back to Rhodesia and died in the attempt. In the days of sanctions, applied against Rhodesia by former

Allies, a military aircraft was a very precious weapons platform indeed – and my mate died trying to coax it back to be used again on another raid. On another occasion, I spoke to a woman who offered her help in a forces canteen – and her and her colleagues had been called out at short notice to feed upwards of 3,000 of our men enlisted to face a potential invasion from Mozambique, down along the Mtoko Road to Salisbury.

All over our borders, massive raids were taking place into the heart of ZANLA in the south-east of the country, where I had been – raids deep into Mozambique around Mapai and Barragem (some columns going almost as far as Maputo!). Naturally, the world condemned us. We were failures at scoring points in the press – and the enemy took full advantage of it – just like the Israelis in their conflict with a few nomadic Arabs that conveniently gave themselves a title one day: calling themselves 'Palestinians'.

In Zambia, large bridge demolition operations were being undertaken, with big camps being attacked on a regular basis. Our enemies were entering the final phase of their war against us. They were forming into conventional armies and preparing to invade our homeland.

Here, in our village – in an operational area called 'Tangent' – we faced aggressive insurgents and heard more and more rumours of a potential invasion to be carried out over the bridge at Vic Falls. Rumours – whether true or false – swirled around the village that Cubans or East Germans were going to attack us; that tanks were coming from Angola to help Nkomo; that he had 20,000 troops ready to march at a moment's notice. As I said: some rumour, some fact – but it had the intended result of winding us all up once again. Things were getting serious – and a bit frightening. Rhodesia could handle one front at a time, but if the enemy attacked on four fronts, we would really struggle to contain them. Official statistics at the time listed our national troop strength at 69,000 men – of whom only 5,000 were regulars – and perhaps another 10 battalions of territorials were actually young enough to fight effectively. That's 15,000 men supplied with dated weapons and ageing support aircraft to fight off whatever Africa and the commie world could sling against us.

It was against this backdrop that another brown envelope arrived in our post-box five weeks later. Mally handed it to me – her face strained. I stared at it like it was a cobra about to bite me. I slid my fingernail under the flap and pulled out the contents. I had been transferred to Support Company 2RR – under command of one Captain Roy Pritchard. My eyes scrolled down the page.

"Shit," I said. "I don't believe it."

"What, babe?"

"I've been transferred to a mortar platoon."

"And that's good news?" Mal said, looking at the smile on my face.

"You bet! No more foot-slogging for me… and it gets even better…"

"Go on, then!"

"I'm to report for duty here at Vic Falls!"

"Oh honey, that's fantastic!" Mally said, hugging me. "You're not joking, I hope?"

"No! Look here…" I handed her the paper.

"I can't believe it! This is amazing!"

"Me neither! What are the chances of me being posted to where I live?"

"You can come home just about every night!"

"Let's hope so…"

"What do you mean, hope so?"

"Vic Falls may just be the admin base. Who knows?"

"Bull, Tony. You know as well as I do there's no other place to defend than right here."

"Mmm…"

I took Mally in my arms and squeezed her ecstatically – feeling a rush of relief and joy sweep over me. We did a little pirouette on the lawn.

"This calls for a celebration," she said, grabbing me by the hand – pulling me into the house. We made wild, almost angry, love – as if to celebrate and reassure each other at the same time.

Later, as the breeze cooled the sweat off our bodies, she rolled over and picked up the call-up notice one more time.

"You have to report Monday next week at 4 Indep base camp."

"Fantastic! My old turf…" I said, stretching luxuriously. Tookie jumped up on the bed – purring and sniffing here and there.

"We have three days off before you go back. What should we do?"

"I dunno," I said, putting my hands behind my head.

"I wouldn't mind a trip to Bulawayo."

"Good 'ol Bullies… Ja, why not?"

We worked two more easy shifts, lazed around pools and played tennis until Fred drove us out to the airport on the third day. I felt free from the threat of going back to an area of death and destruction; of maggots in wounds; of a death mask staring at me in frozen horror.

We booked into Grey's Inn – and after unpacking, we walked down the wide, wide streets of Bulawayo. I have always liked the city and had many fond memories of going there to visit my uncle and aunt from my mom's side of the family. I had several cousins in the town and we often went fishing in dams in and around the Matopos National Park.

They had been good, sunny days of innocence; days when my brother and I would strip down to underpants and swim out into the middle of the dam – trailing a fishing line each to drop bait in the deepest part. We caught monster fish by doing this – and had many pleasant meals eating the slightly-muddy-tasting flesh. I only came to realise many years later that our cousins' snigger as we entered the water each time was because they knew there were crocs in there – and we didn't. Days of stupidity and fun and beers under the African sun – to be there forever? For the next generation?

Mal and I did some shopping; went to a cinema to watch a movie – a rare event for us; went to the Sun Hotel for a drink; Holiday Inn for a meal; and to the Zambezi Bar to get slightly pissed – kissing and laughing on our way back to our hotel… Memorable days – making good memories.

❧—❦

I reported for duty on the date indicated on the call-up papers. My OC, Captain Pritchard, would arrive the next day – and I was instructed to meet my platoon on the day of my call-up and organise temporary billets for them. I knocked on the door of the OC of 4 Indep's office.

"Morning, sir," I saluted. "I'm here to meet a platoon from Support Company 2RR."

"Are you?" he said, wrinkling his forehead. "That's news to me. Typical bloody army." He stood up and shook my hand.

"Where's Captain Von Stranz, sir?"

"Major Von Stranz… back in Wankie. I'm his 2 i/c."

He didn't give his name – and for that reason, it never stuck. He sounded Australian.

"2RR Support Company, hey? How long have you been in mortars?"

"About three hours," I said stupidly, and when he frowned, I explained why: I had just received my transfer.

"I'll have to learn in the field, I guess."

"Mmm," was his answer.

"I was based here for a year during my NS."

"Oh?"

"We turned this place from an overgrown jungle into what it is today. My guys planted the grass out there," I said, flicking my wrist in the direction of the door.

"Local knowledge, then?"

"Very much so."

"Could come in handy, that."

"What's the latest around here?"

I knew he couldn't tell me much because I had been here during every major event that had taken place. It was like hearing a history teacher tell me my own life story. After a while, he figured I knew more about the history of the place than he did – and we entered a period of stilted silence.

"I think I'll get some coffee if that's okay, sir?"

"Sure. Tell the cook to send me some, also."

"Yes, sir."

I walked outside into a cool breeze, ordered the coffee and retreated to the white metal chairs on the grass. It was surreal being here again – in a uniform decidedly tighter this time. I would have to exercise and get the fat off. I looked up into the leafy green tree above me and let my mind roll back over the period I'd spent here.

I remembered the day I had first arrived at the Falls – so full of pride and youthful innocence; proud to be an officer in an army fighting for a country I loved like a lover – or maybe even more so. The days at Jambezi; of landmines; mortar attacks… Kazungula… memories… memories of Dave Kruger, Tom Shipley, Roy Orchard and Derek Kingsley-Jones… the wounded too. It all came flooding back – down the halls of my mind. It made me feel disjointed and out of place – still being here when none of them were. Where was Max, Kenny, Abbott, Bomford, Fisher, Bert Furmston, Phil Laing, Dino, Pete Wells, Gomo, Dave Matthews, 'Duffy', 'Mabrook'… Where were all my mates and buddies?

I was far away in deep thought and distant memories when at about lunchtime, a small convoy of five vehicles pulled into the camp. I stared at them as if from far away – looking at and admiring the tough-looking unit that had just arrived. A lead Unimog vehicle – a two-five – pulled up in front of me. Its cab-less windscreen was up – and two weather-beaten guys with goggles stared down at me. They looked like something from 'desert rat' movies I'd seen. I dropped my eyes to the emblem on the door below the driver, and saw a mortar bomb with two wings on the tailfin, with '2RR Support Coy' stamped underneath it. They were my platoon!

I shot self-consciously to my feet before strolling as casually as possible over to them.

"Lieut Ballinger?" a dark-haired, powerful-looking man said to me.

"Yes. I figure you're the guys I've been waiting for?"

"Yes, sir. I'm Sergeant Van Der Merwe, and this is Sergeant Accorsi," he said, flicking his wrist at the passenger beside him. Perhaps it was Accorsi's glasses reflecting light like 'The Smiling Shit's', but I took an instant dislike to him. I didn't know whether they would salute – and I stood there stupidly waiting for it. When it didn't come – and their faces had turned to puzzled expectation – I told them to park to the right of the cookhouse and set themselves up for the night.

When Sergeant Van der Merwe had instructed his men what to do, he strolled over to me to have a chat.

"Have the guys eaten, sarge?"

"Yes, sir. We got some burgers at the caff in town."

I smiled inwardly. I loved the way Afrikaner people called a 'café' a 'caff'.

"Good. Perhaps you can give me a 'rundown' on how many guys we have and what their ranks and responsibilities are."

We walked over to the chairs on the grass – a clipboard in the sergeant's hand. "What's your first name?"

"Johan."

"My mom came from an Afrikaner family," I said.

"Oh," was his reply. The lack of further enquiry embarrassed me. I was trying too hard.

We spent 40 minutes or so going through the men's names, ranks and responsibilities. There were roughly 36 all-told, with a contingent of about 12 black support troops included. The platoon had two 106mm recoilless anti-tank rifles, which the Israelis used to great effect in their 1973 war against her Arab enemies. We also had three 81mm and two 60mm mortars – plus supporting machine-guns.

"What do you know about mortars?" Johan asked.

"Only what you're going to teach me. I was with 'A' Company last call-up; did my NS up here with 4 Indep. And you?"

"Been around them a few years."

It was a profound understatement, I learned later. There were few people in the Rhodesian Army that knew more about mortars than him.

"I'd like to meet the guys," I said. He nodded and shouted to Accorsi to form them up. They came to attention in two ranks of 18 men as I strolled over to them. I caught the OC of 4 Indep looking at me from his office door. I felt it unusual that he wasn't a part of what we were doing. However, the arrival of my OC the next day revealed that we were in fact an independent formation – and would only meet with the Australian captain during our weekly Joint Operations Command (or JOC) meeting.

I walked down the rank of men as they stood facing me, while Johan read out their name and rank. A black corporal in charge of the support troops came to attention in a spectacular display of boot-stamping and rapid arm-movements. I smiled inwardly before asking his name, where he was from and how his family was doing – a sort of traditional greeting with the indigenous. Well, at least it felt the right thing to do.

I focused on the faces of all the troops – trying to remember their names against faces – but I knew it would take some time to get to know them. In the end, I gave them a little talk – telling them who I was and that I was their new platoon commander and that our duty would be to protect the village – at least, I assumed that was our role. I gave them a brief rundown on the history of the area – and promised them they would definitely see a bit of action up here. I told them that the casinos were out of bounds to men below the rank of corporal, which sent sighs of distaste into the hot afternoon air. What a way to start my command – reviled by my troops!

"You can take a break today and go to the Casino Hotel for a swim." This brought a couple of smiles to suntanned faces.

"Dismissed." They made a half-hearted attempt to break ranks correctly before sauntering back to the shelters they were rapidly erecting. It was threatening rain again – well, what was new up here?

"Sort yourself out, sarge. I'll be back later."

Johan raised his eyebrows, but I ignored him and walked out the back of the camp to Mally's place. She was reading a book, with Tookie curled up on the couch next to her.

"My warrior returns," she said, looking up – then: "What's the matter?"

"I feel a real prick when I'm talking to my guys. I have no self-confidence. It drives me nuts. I know I'm not a coward – I've proved that to myself."

"You treat everyone like a friend. Just be their boss and leave it at that. Who gives a shit what they think?" I smiled then – and felt relieved by her advice. I guess I'd just got all wound-up waiting for my call-up to start and what it would hold for me.

"You back for long?"

"Long enough to eat something… I'm starved. They got some wanker in charge of 4 Indep – and he obviously doesn't want us eating his rations."

"Tut-tut," Mal said, heading for the kitchen. She came back a while later with an ice-cold coke and a platter of ham and tomato sandwiches. I looked up at her, looked at my surroundings and quietly thanked God that I was here during my call-up. It was unbelievable, really. I still hadn't got over the reality of it all. We chatted and relaxed until about four in the afternoon, when I strolled back to camp. Johan was fast asleep under his bivvy – a small piece of nylon sheeting soldiers were issued with to keep the rain off when in camp. They formed a sort of tent with no sides. He must have suspected my presence – opening his eyes to look up at me.

"Sorry, sir. We left Bulawayo really early this morning."

"Not a problem at all. What plans for food tonight?"

"The guys that went swimming will look after themselves; the others have been given rat-packs for the cook to rustle up some grub."

"How will you recall the guys if something happens?"

"They're all at one hotel. Accorsi has a radio."

"Good. Listen, there's not much I can do here until the boss arrives tomorrow. I live with my girlfriend in town. Go out the back exit, over the intersection, turn right at the T-junction and it's the third house on the right – the one with the nice garden."

He repeated the instructions – and I said: "Good. See you tomorrow morning. Make sure the guys are back by 2200." The last thing I saw of Johan was him rolling onto his side on his stretcher – nestled among several other sleeping, reading or dozing comrades.

⁕—⁕

Captain Roy Pritchard arrived the following day at about lunchtime. He was a rounded man with thinning dark hair and glasses – in his mid-thirties, I guessed. I immediately liked him, which was great. I just couldn't stand the macho competition you get with some guys in the army. He put me at ease straight away. I knew I could work more efficiently if I felt I didn't have someone breathing over my back all the time. I filled him in about my background and what I'd done. To be honest, I was surprised that Major Bissett had agreed to transfer me to a mortar platoon, but I was forever grateful that he had.

"I've cleared it with 1 Brigade that we can base up behind the Elephant Hills ruins," Roy said.

"Superb views, sir. It'll make a great base – and the showers still work at the golf club."

"So do the squash courts," he smiled.

I was glad I had an accountant playing captain as my OC. I had long come to realise that I was a civilian playing soldier too.

We spent the next three days establishing a camp about 100 metres behind the Elephant Hills ruins. Mortar pits were dug, a fire command bunker built and ammunition lowered into two widely-separated trenches about 15 metres behind the mortar pits. I let Johan do his thing in this regard, and spent my time organising the infantry side of things – siting machine-gun nests around the perimeter of the camp and allocating places for the men to sleep, ensuring each had a shell-scrape nearby. We also set up our canteen and a mess hall for the senior NCOs and myself. A big deepfreeze had arrived, with pre-packed fresh food – and it wasn't long before the cook was churning out excellent meals. One beer per man per night went down very well too.

That was a period in my military career I enjoyed the most. Support weapons were 'right up my alley' – and I thoroughly enjoyed learning how to use a plotting board and issue instructions to mortar teams (as well as learn the intricacies of loading, aiming and firing the 106mm anti-tank gun). This was my scene; this was professional – and for the first time since I'd put a uniform on a couple of years before, I felt proud, confident and in charge. I blossomed under Roy's guidance and encouragement; the relaxed atmosphere he generated helped too – not that he wouldn't come down on us like a ton of crap if we stepped out of line… and so a great team was formed.

But, in all good organisations, there's always a fly in the ointment. In this case, it was Sergeant Accorsi. I found him sullen and subversive; well, it wasn't hard to see why. I'd taken the position he was hoping to get promoted to. He was jealous – plain and simple. It didn't take long for things to come to a head – and a good dressing-down put him in his place. I reminded him that the promotion he craved had to be endorsed by me – and that soon shut him up.

I spent a long time becoming proficient in my new role, and would end the day – beer in hand – sitting on top of the hotel's ruins with either Johan and Roy as company, or later, the pleasure of my schoolmate, Barry Munroe, who was artillery's forward fire-control officer. The old 25-pounders he spotted for were based up at the airstrip a kilometre or two behind us on the escarpment rim.

It appeared that our army was gearing up for all-out war with our enemy – judging by the various units that now inhabited the village. We had an extra company of infantry, artillery, two squadrons of armoured cars, 'Black Boots', PATU and a couple of troops of Grey's Scouts billeted in and around the small village. We were literally an island in a sea of hostile territory – and the reality of this added a magical atmosphere to the town and its inhabitants. We were, in essence, like the American troops that beat off Germans in Bastogne during the Battle of the Bulge in December 1944. Surrounded; cut off, so to speak. It was a great thrill.

I loved the sight of the two squadrons of armoured cars – in their billets at the municipal campsite – at night. Tourists no longer weighed down the beds in the cramped cottages. The new occupants were smart young men in black tank suits with the head of an eland deer as unit insignia on their shoulders. Gas lamps lit up young, eager faces under large trees that sheltered their heavy steel vehicles – the long barrels pointing accusingly into the dark night. Faces that reflected the yellow glow of fires; laughing and joking; having the single regulation beer at sunset; a military encampment in waiting…

Sitting there, high above the valley, drinking my beer – and watching the massive pink-orange sun sink slowly towards the western horizon – was absolutely magical. I drew great cheer from sitting with comrades in arms – chatting, laughing and telling jokes, or just being quiet; to absorb the haunting magic of Africa laid before us; a massive smudge of black bush out there, with the silver spine of the river in the middle-distance and the orange lights of Livingstone twinkling beyond that – a beautiful, peaceful sight that belied the dangers that lay on the other side. That darkness sheltered an enemy determined to crush us into submission; an enemy that grew stronger by the day, while we, in all reality, grew weaker.

Our mortar platoon also used the casino's Summit Bar as a forward fire-control centre – alongside artillery – as the height of the hotel offered panoramic views of where our enemy sat across the river from us. The irony of being based on top of the Summit Bar didn't go unnoticed by me. After all, this was the very rooftop I went up to on Christmas Eve to watch the artillery exchange with Zambia. I was now on the inside of this exciting set-up – and it thrilled me to bits.

This idyllic posting allowed me to swim at the casino during my time off. Roy was very pleasantly surprised to meet Mally. He fitted easily into my circle of friends – and I couldn't be more happy and grateful for being here; it was a dream come true – but even better news was to follow… It soon transpired that Roy had only come up to the village to make sure I settled in okay – and once he was satisfied that everything was in order, he got on a plane and flew back to Bulawayo. I was on my own – running my own independent command! This was totally unreal – fantastic! I just couldn't believe it – and my girlfriend lived and worked here too. What more could a man ask for?

It was a thrill to walk into the casino that first night in my freshly-pressed uniform; to chat to Fred and Mally while they worked – and to revel in the 'glad-eye' I got from Linda. It was weird beyond description to be sitting as a guest in my own place of work – and thankful I didn't have to put up with the drunken abuse croupiers so often had to contend with.

"The town's filling up with troops," Fred said, leaning on a small bureau between two roulette tables.

"And emptying of tourists," I replied.

"Who's here these days, army-wise?"

"Geesh, Fred. I really can't tell you. It's confidential, you know."

"Balls. I'm a police reservist. I'll find out from my mate, anyway. Thought you could save me the time."

"You a spy or something, Fred?"

"What a joke! Poorest bloody spy in the world, then!"

I waited most nights to escort Mally home, and stayed with her more often than not – always making sure I had a radio turned on next to our bed in case of an emergency, or phoning my whereabouts to the duty controller on the Summit Bar. On a few occasions when I was duty officer, I slept on the Summit Bar roof – neatly tucked up in a sleeping bag on a stretcher – gazing up at the star-drenched heavens above… twinkling in their infinite mass. The spray from the Falls would often spiral upwards above my head – reaching hundreds and hundreds of feet into the sky… forming a type of ladder up to the sparkling stars above. They were nights of great tranquillity and reflection for me – a time to think about my life, my destiny, the future of my country and my relationship with Mally. They were the best days of my life, without doubt.

A few days later, I was summoned to an urgent JOC meeting at the 'Round Bar' in the now closed-down and shuttered A'Zambezi Hotel. The hotel had been taken over by the army and used as a communications base and meeting place for the various military and police detachments in the area.

It was a bright, sunny day when Johan and I arrived at the conically-shaped building with its high, sloping thatched roof – fans spinning lazily to stir liquid air. An armed guard saluted us as we entered the double doors. The room was taken up by a very large, rectangular-shaped table with perhaps a dozen or so officers sitting around it. I took a seat with my back to the door – a neat card with my name typed on it placed in front of me. Pencils and notepads had been supplied to all of us – and a jug of cold orange juice did the rounds. Unfortunately, Johan had to sit against the wall behind me because in essence, I was the platoon commander – but he was still needed to answer technical questions if they came up. I was introduced to the police, CIO, army and air force reps before the meeting got under way.

A brigadier stood up to address us – and since we came under 1 Brigade's operational area, I assumed he was our overall commanding officer who had come up from Bulawayo for the meeting. He cleared his throat and said something like this…

"We've received reliable information that ZIPRA plans to shunt about 1,200 gooks across the bridge, in a train, to take out the village in the dead of night." He paused to look at our faces. You could have heard a pin drop. "Their initial target is to secure the bridge to let a large armoured column enter shortly afterwards."

I looked at the other men sitting around the table – noticing a common trend in their facial expressions. All of their lower jaws were slightly limp; perhaps 'hanging down' would be a better description! We were all shocked to the core by the news. Everything we feared and suspected had suddenly been thrust upon us – and by one of our senior commanders at that. I felt a cold hand of dread take hold of my spine… Mally, the women and kids in the village… they would all be raped.

"Once across, they'll join up with other forces that'll head south to Wankie and Dete, then east through Mashonaland to capture Salisbury; another group heading straight for Bulawayo."

"What numbers are we talking about?" a captain not known to me asked at length.

"Twenty-thousand-plus. Nkomo intends to become the first black President of Zimbabwe... by force if necessary." The brigadier pronounced 'Zimbabwe' with contempt.

"Shit," someone said. A loud buzz of conversation started up before someone else said: "Twenty-thousand... How the heck does he propose to defeat the Rhodesians and Mugabe's ZANLA with so few men?"

"By surprise. Nkomo knows he'll have perhaps 36 hours to succeed or fail. I guess air force bases will be top targets."

"What about direct Russian, Cuban or East German involvement?"

"There's nothing confirmed, but I'm pretty sure our South African friends won't allow that."

"So how are we going to be reinforced?" the Australian captain asked. The brigadier picked up a notepad and adjusted his reading glasses before replying:

"We'll be sending another company of infantry from 9th Battalion, plus enough explosives with engineers to blow the bridge to hell if they try to cross. We have a plan to turn the railway line at the bridge into a killing field. The RSM from Llewellin Barracks has a lot of experience positioning troops in this type of scenario."

"What other forces will cross, and where?" I asked.

"We suspect some of the force will cross upstream near Kazungula, possibly using a pontoon bridge supplied by the Russians. Other crossing points will be the dam wall at Kariba."

"Will the Zambian Air Force get involved?"

"Yes, no doubt, but we have a little surprise waiting for them," the brigadier smiled. He seemed totally relaxed about the whole thing – and it led me to believe he knew a lot more than we did. After all, how could only one company of reinforcements have any effect at all?

"What about troops in Wankie?" a major from Grey's Scouts asked.

"There'll be at least two companies there, with a battalion on standby in Bulawayo."

Small forces, I thought. A company here, a company there, one battalion on standby... against 20,000 conventionally-trained troops with air and armour support. In a twinkling of blind panic, I felt like running out the door to warn Mally and Fred – and all the others – to get the hell out of town, but all I did was sit there trying to look macho. I swivelled in my chair and was encouraged by a lazy smile that crossed Johan's face.

I figured if the bridge was blown, then Vic Falls would become redundant to Nkomo's aims – and perhaps that's why the brigadier had resolved to put only one more company of infantry into the tiny area the security fence encompassed. Heavier forces would be needed inland to combat an enemy that would swarm beyond our village.

At the end of the brigadier's briefing, a refined regimental sergeant-major about 60 years old stood up to address us. I recognised him as the RSM from Llewellin – and he spent the next hour briefing us where our security forces would be positioned in the days ahead.

From the air, the railway line leading up to the bridge to Zambia looked like a 'lizard's head' – with a long neck behind it – facing north-east. The 'nose' of the 'lizard's head' was the point at which the steel railway tracks actually met the bridge. A set of remote-controlled cameras would be set up there to watch the bridge night and day – and enough explosives would be laid at this point to physically dislodge the bridge from its Rhodesian foundations under the 'nose'.

Halfway down the 'lizard's head' – on the right (or eastern) side – two large and heavily-fortified bunkers were built to face inwards (or to the west). They were filled to bursting with machine-guns and infantry. The railway track ran down the 'spine' of the 'lizard's head' – and a tall, existing fence separated the bunkers from the railway tracks.

On the left (or western) side of the 'lizard's head', a new, coiled barbed wire fence was erected and liberally sprinkled with claymores and other nasty surprises – and at the end furthest from the 'nose' (by the 'neck') was another set of bunkers and a control room where the remote-control TVs operated from.

Just short of the control room, a series of 44-gallon drums full of sand had been erected in a herringbone fashion for more infantry and machine-guns. Two of these positions had been reserved for our two anti-tank guns, with a clean line of fire down both the railway tracks and the tar road on the left-hand side of the 'lizard's head' that snaked towards the bridge.

To put it simply, if any train tried to cross over – packed with enemy like a Trojan horse – it would be easily halted and its occupants cut to shreds by dozens and dozens of automatic weapons and anti-personnel mines. Our mortars and artillery were co-ordinated to hit the far end of the bridge as hard as possible to deter any reinforcements trying to join in the 'fun' – and no doubt the air force would smash any armoured column heading our way. It was a daunting task for the enemy to undertake – and even if any of them escaped the immense firepower we were building up, they would have nowhere to run. After all, the left and right side of the 'lizard's head' was a sheer drop to the riverbed hundreds of feet below.

We spent many days setting the whole thing up – and practised racing our 106's into position in the dead of night and doing dummy mortar runs in pitch-blackness. I managed to iron out a lot of potential mishaps this way, but I was really worried by the lack of proper night sights for the 106's – and put pressure on Roy Pritchard to get it sorted out – but in the end, our ever-pressed and broke army came up with nothing and I had to contend with aiming through ordinary sights at night. I stocked up on flares to illuminate any enemy column that may break through. That would be better than nothing.

Not knowing how to actually fire the 106, I asked for (and got permission) to fire two of the very precious rounds out in the middle of nowhere – taking pains to 'zero' the weapons at the same time. It was a proud day for me when I drove out in the lead vehicle with the 106's covered by tarpaulins – our faces tanned – goggles over our eyes to keep the sting of bugs at bay. The police reservists guarding the breach in the minefield looked at us in awe as we arrogantly drove through their position to go and test-fire the weapons. Kids with toys...

It was an exciting experience I will never forget, firing the 106. We set up empty drums about 1,000 metres away – and I fired the second of the two rounds. You sit at right-angles to the weapon, looking into the sight – getting the range as best you can. You then pull a lever towards you, which fires 12.7mm anti-aircraft rounds as a method of zeroing in on the target. Once they strike the target, you push the same lever – and the massive missile fires. A large orange flame appears on the periphery of both eyes... a thump in the kidneys from expanding gasses... and whoomph! The target is smashed to bits far away. We drove down and had a look. We'd both missed the drums, but the angle of error was so small that if it had been a tank, it would have been a direct hit. We decided not to alter the sights. Firing that awesome weapon reminded me of stories about Arab tank crews abandoning their vehicles the moment the 12.7mm 'sighting' rounds hit their tank – fired, of course, by very aggressive Israeli soldiers!

However, I remained very ill-at-ease about our proficiency in the use of those weapons – and I hoped we never had to fire them.

The village soon became one large military encampment. It came with great cheer and humour when I caught sight of Max, my old MAG gunner, among the 9th Battalion troopies – and we had a long chat about this and that. He was a real piss-cat, that guy, and looked hungover whenever I saw him – but I sort of felt all my old comrades hadn't vanished into thin air after seeing him!

The village was laid out something like this now: one entire company occupied the bunkers and trenches in the rainforest, while another continued to do normal patrols inside and outside the security fence – rather like I did when I first arrived. The plan was to recall them at a moment's notice if there was any indication of a build-up on the other side of the river. No doubt the SAS – or possibly the Selous Scouts – were already over in Zambia watching the road leading into Livingstone from as far away as Lusaka – or even Angola.

A 26-man troop of Grey's Scouts, the equivalent of cavalry, also patrolled the bush in and around the village – as did a company of Police Support Unit (nicknamed 'Black Boots'). Two or three Police Anti-Terrorist Unit (or PATU) sticks were based at the police station.

Then there was my mortar platoon up on the hill – and behind us, a battery of ageing British 25-pounders that made up our artillery support. Our main punch, of course, were the two squadrons of Eland 90mm armoured cars based at the municipal campsite.

The stage was set – and the clock was ticking. Political and military pressures made it pretty certain that something was going to happen in the near future – and we, the residents of the village, became rather like a group of parents waiting for our kids to commence play on-stage... wondering when the curtain would go up – except, in this case, it wasn't a pleasant feeling of anticipation, but rather, one of dread; a dread many drowned in parties, sex and alcohol (particularly witnessed at croupier parties when the casinos closed for the night).

⚜—⚜

"What's up, Mal?" I asked as we sat on top of the bunker, sipping wine one evening. She took a long time to answer.

"I think I've known you long enough to know when you're hiding something from me."

"Hiding something? From you? What do you mean?"

"You never talk about what you're doing up here. When you did your national service, you always told me what happened... you know, Jambezi, Kazungula... but nothing here."

"It's hard to talk about nothing, because that's precisely what's happening... nothing."

"I'm not stupid, Tony. There are hundreds of troops in the village; tourists aren't allowed into parts of the rainforest anymore... Why? Everyone's asking: 'Why'?"

I shrugged my shoulders and stared into the pale-green depths of my glass of wine. What was I supposed to say to her? That 20,000 terrorists were poised a few kilometres away – ready to invade, rape and pillage. I knew she would be on the first plane out. We had also been sworn to secrecy by the brigadier at the end of our briefing.

"Mal, all low-key terror wars eventually get to a point when large bodies of men come together to fight conventional battles. We're just getting prepared, that's all."

"Bullshit, Tony. You know as well as I do that our economy's too small to have hundreds of troops loitering around unless something's brewing. Please tell me. You know I'm not the type to shout my mouth off. You owe me that much."

"You'd probably wet your pants if I told you."

"Well, you've blown it now. How the heck do you expect me to shut up after a comment like that?"

"Okay… Listen. I think it may be wise for you to know… We can plan accordingly."

"Well?" she said, leaning forward – looking me in the eye.

"We're expecting an invasion," I said simply. Mally recoiled as if a cobra was about to strike.

"An invasion? What do you mean?"

"The whole of Nkomo's Army is poised to invade. He knows Mugabe will be the first black President if he doesn't get his act together."

"How many men does he have?"

"Upwards of 20,000."

"What?!"

"Mmm, 20,000."

"You're joking? It's not funny."

"It's no joke. You asked me to level with you."

"*Twenty-thousand*," she said, with emphasis, "and we have a few hundred protecting us?"

"If that," I nodded.

"Hell, Tony…"

"We'll blow the bridge if they try to cross."

"Big deal. They'll get over somehow."

"They won't waste time and manpower trying to sort us out. Salisbury's their target."

"Your folks and brother are there."

"And yours in Que Que. They'll have to pass through there at some stage."

"Wow, I had no idea. No wonder you didn't want to tell me. What should we do?"

"Well, there's nothing I can do. I'm here 'for the duration' as the Yanks say, but you must have a bag packed at all times, with your passport and other documents ready to go."

"I won't go without you."

"You must. I couldn't do my job knowing you were here. If there's any early warning of an invasion, you go – and that's all there is to it."

Mally looked down at her hands – and her bottom lip started to tremble slightly. I worked my way over to her until we sat with our legs crossed – facing each other – my arms around her shoulders.

"It'll be okay, Mal. The air force will destroy any major column – and I suspect Mirages from South Africa will come to the rescue as well."

"I dunno," she said simply as a single tear splashed onto my kneecap. "I'm finding the whole thing a bit stressful."

"I know," I said, tilting her face up with a finger under her chin. She had such lovely eyes – and the golden sunlight sparkled off the tears in them. "I'll never let anything happen to you or us, okay?"

She nodded – and we kissed tenderly until the passion rose in us – and we went inside to make love. Our lovemaking in those last days became deep and forceful, as many lovers must have experienced in wars through the eons. We didn't know the future, and we couldn't plan normal things like pensions and holidays and retirement… Life had sort of come down to one day at a time; we never knew what tomorrow would bring.

It was impossible to keep news like this secret – and before long, there were subtle signs of change in the village. Fred organised bags full of clothes and food for 'the wife' and 'kuds'; Ivor's wife left the village altogether; and Warren resigned from the casino. Smaller businesses 'on the brink' suddenly closed overnight. Our one and only chemist indicated he may be leaving as well. The small school emptied of kids in a few weeks. Tourists dried up. We had become a military base – and nothing else.

It's difficult to try and maintain a normal life under circumstances like this, but we did our best. Three of the six hotels in the village were either shut or burned down. Fewer and fewer tourist planes flew overhead. The Falls were off-limits beyond the 'rainforest' – and generally, things started to grind to a halt.

We spent the hot and humid days when I was off duty by the pool of the Casino Hotel or the Vic Falls Hotel – both now virtually empty – or I would dress in civilian clothes and go on the booze cruise as the duty forward fire-control officer, with a military radio in a camera bag slung over my shoulder so as not to alarm the few tourists that remained. My job would be to bring down mortar fire on any terrorists that fancied ambushing the booze cruise.

They were great and exciting days, in my opinion. The large claps of thunder, heavy rain and exploding mines in the cordoned-off bush added just a little more flavour to the tense situation we were in, but it was telling – and our sleep patterns became altered… often leaving us quirky and irritable with each other. I found our garden a great source of peace and contentment, and would often scratch around in it or stand with a hosepipe watering the flowers. It was very therapeutic.

"We haven't had an attack within 100 kays of the village for weeks," Mal said one evening as we sat down to supper.

"I know. Our JOC meetings are non-events."

"What can you read into that, then?"

"Who knows?" I said, sweeping Tookie off the table. "Maybe they're regrouping, or shagging themselves stupid before the bell rings."

"No feedback on any build-up?"

"You'll be the first to know, I promise... Can't we change the subject?"

"Yes, sorry. You know..."

"I know honey, but there's squat we can do. I hear Ivor's resigned as well, now?"

"Mmm, though in his case, I think he wants to patch it up with Judy."

"Stupid bugger. What he did to her was off-sides."

"What's it with men and their dicks?"

"Your bodies! You drive us insane, you women. We just have to conquer you. It's what defines us as men. We get a tremendous sense of power when a woman submits."

"Like spearing us with a weapon? Some type of carnal thing from hunter-gathering days?"

"Perhaps," I said, feeding Tookie a piece of steak. "It's a hard drive to suppress. Some of us make it, and others don't."

I was just about to scrape some more peas and mash onto my plate when the long, tearing sound of a machine-gun went off in the middle-distance to the north-west of us... Beyond Elephant Hills – and even the A'Zambezi Hotel. At first, I thought it could be an accidental discharge by someone from my camp because the direction the sound came from was correct, but it happened again – and this time, more weapons joined in. I went cold on the inside and Mally's eyes went wide – her mouth half-open with food in it. Her face became ashen instantly.

"What the hell?" she said, swallowing her food. "Is this it? Is this the invasion?" She stood up rapidly – pushing her chair backwards.

"Relax Mal," I said, heart thumping massively in my chest. "It's the wrong direction for a start. They couldn't get close to the bridge without the SAS spotting them. Must be a contact..."

"Where are you going?"

"Back to camp. You'll be okay."

"You're leaving me here on my own?"

"You know I have to," I said, reaching for my rifle. I was always in uniform, so there was no need to change or anything like that.

"Fred will probably go straight home when he hears this. Take your emergency bag and go to his house."

Mally froze momentarily before spinning on her feet and rushing towards the bedroom. I was just getting into my two-five when she came running out the door – bag and car keys in hand. Her eyes were wide with fear. She raised herself up on her toes and kissed me quickly through the open window. More and more weapons were ripping into the night now – and both of us shook like leaves.

"You'll be okay, Mal. Just do whatever Fred says, okay? You okay?"

"Yes, yes," she nodded vigorously, "I'll be okay. Please be careful. Please!"

"I plan to grow old and grey!" I pushed the start button on the dashboard – and the throaty diesel engine burst into life. The radio I always carried crackled into life as various military call-signs started to make contact. Someone's voice was high with adrenalin and sounding a bit panicky.

"Dozens of them on the river…"

I gave Mal one last fleeting kiss and engaged reverse gear – churning up the stone-chip driveway as I raced backwards out the gate. The last image I had of her was her struggling to get the car door open – and then, she was lost from view. I was as nervous as hell and shook like a leaf as adrenalin flooded into my system, but I was also relieved and excited. The long, long wait was over.

I turned left one house after Frikkie's – accelerating over the intersection along 70 metres or so of housing – and into the back gate of 4 Indep's camp. A startled guard waved me hurriedly inside, and in a few brief moments I was out the other side – turning sharp-left on the tar road towards Elephant Hills. There had been a lot of activity in the army camp I'd just driven through, with men running here and there – no doubt readying themselves to respond to whatever was happening.

It was a warm starlit night with few clouds around – and under different circumstances, it would have been one of those nights you would take your lover for a stroll, but instead, I drove into inky blackness – focusing on the pool of light the headlamps cast. I was looking for any signs of the enemy – or more likely, a bloody great elephant standing in the road. I had nearly rammed into them more than once; you just cannot see an elephant at night.

I turned left up the road that led to the ghostlike ruins of the 'Hills Hotel' – knowing that artillery's forward fire-control personnel would be watching me drive up the hill. It had been agreed that we would drive past the ruins at night with headlights off to prevent the enemy in Zambia becoming aware of vehicles travelling up here. I stopped briefly, switched the headlights off and waited a few seconds for my night vision to adjust before carrying on up the hill – the tall walls of the hotel passed by on my left, like the sails of a ghost-ship, as I drove higher and higher.

A guard in battle dress waved me into camp. I parked next to the canteen and set about finding Johan, who was on duty that night. I found him in the command bunker listening to one of two radios we had. One radio was for our own net, and the other was linked into JOC Headquarters down below at the A'Zambezi Hotel. They, in turn, would be in overall command of all the forces in the village.

"What's happened, Johan?" I said, sitting next to him.

"Large crossing by the minefield."

"Shit. Who intercepted them?"

"Not sure…"

At that moment, a long, ripping noise of a machine-gun echoed up to us from the west. Johan picked up the radios and we ran over to one of the machine-gun nests that had a commanding view of the valley below. It was an awesome sight that unfolded before us from the elevated position we were in – a vast sea of grey-black darkness extended to the west as far as we could see… blending with an undetermined horizon. The luminescent river came out of this blackness – wide and silver under millions of stars… silhouetting tall trees along its bank. The only sign of humanity was a couple of lights at the Grey's Scouts camp – as well as one or two from JOC Headquarters at A'Zambezi.

"What's our condition, Johan? How many guys are in camp and are they all stood to?"

"Everyone's here except a stick of guys on liberty run. Sergeant Accorsi's gone to get them."

"Good comms with the Summit Bar?"

"Affirmative," he nodded in the gloom.

Another rip of automatic fire rolled up the valley towards us. This time, it was joined by the distinct hollow clatter of communist weapons. We could just see tracer zipping back and forth in both directions, like angry fireflies having a go at each other… Then something much, much heavier opened up from the Zambian side – sending long streams of white needles racing for the Rhodesian side.

"Some type of support weapon," I said. "12.7 by the sound of it."

There was a lot of yelling and shouting on the radio net – and after a few minutes, I determined it was an armoured car call-sign that was doing all the shooting. The voices of the young operatives were high on adrenalin.

"Do we have the range to offer support, Johan?"

"Yes… Just. I figure the punch-up's by the minefield."

"I agree."

Then came a call for artillery support. That 12.7 was obviously causing alarm and despondency – and it was time to sort it out. I sat there in absolute fascination – watching all this unfold in front of me. It was like watching a pair of gladiators fighting in an arena – and I had the best seats in the house.

The horizon flickered behind me – and a few seconds later, the sound of artillery shells whistling overhead could be clearly heard above the rattle of machine-guns. It was an awesome thing to hear – straight out the movies. The carump of the primary charge; the moving whistle… a flash… a huge bang rolling up the valley… and then more flickers; more whistling and more bangs… tracer going this way and that. I was shaking like a leaf watching all this. It was exciting and horrible all at the same time.

"Shit, this is unreal," Johan said. I nodded in agreement. I looked sideways and saw at least 10 of my men lining the lip of the hill we were on – standing there in mute fascination as the whistles, bangs and flashes of light lit up the valley below us. It was a surreal sight. Each flash momentarily illuminated the vast expanse of bush to our left – freezing images of grey-green trees in my eyeballs. It was like watching a vast, advancing electric storm – except this storm was raining death and shrapnel down on some poor unfortunate sods. The white, darting lights of the 12.7 rose to a crescendo. Explosions overlapped each other. It sounded like the valley floor was coming apart. My guys whooped and cat-called into the night – and then, it stopped abruptly… as quickly as it began. It was over; it was just one of those oddities of war. Smoke rolled down the valley into the inky blackness to the west – and the odd shot rang out – but apart from that, there was total silence.

"Okay, the show's over," I said to the guys loitering around. "Back to your posts."

The armoured car call-sign started to give their report over the radio, which was fascinating. It appeared that dozens of gooks had tried to row across the river – roughly where the minefield ended in the river. They'd scarcely believed their eyes – looking at a river full of dinghies. What a horrible sight it must have been – out there; alone; isolated; in the dark, where every bush looks like a gook; where the weakness of human night vision makes every person look like two. It must have been horrific.

"We're being called," Johan said, picking up the radio handset. "Go ahead."

"I want two of your tubes mobile at first light. Take them to JOC Headquarters, where I'll brief you," an Australian voice said.

"Copied. Anything else?"

"Negative," came the reply.

"That's the Aussie captain from 4 Indep," I said.

"Mmm."

I did the rounds of the camp then – making sure everyone was at their post and that they were okay. Several mortar men sat nonchalantly around their tubes, smoking. I guess this was old hat for these guys. They had seen plenty of action at Villa Salazar on the 'Russian Front' in the south-east of the country, where I'd done that bloody awful call-up.

Why we Rhodesians nicknamed it the 'Russian Front' I'll never know. After all, it was Chinese-backed ZANLA gooks belonging to Mugabe that infiltrated the area. Maybe it's because Russia was to the east of Germany in that long-forgotten war – just as our 'Russian Front' was to the east of Rhodesia.

The adrenalin pumped into my body – and kept me awake until 0200. None of us knew if the fight was over; whether the action we'd just witnessed was round one or the end of it. We were all keyed up. I stood the guys down at 0200.

I got to bed in the camp at 0300 – tossing and turning on my camp cot – wondering how Mally was and what was going through her head right now. I was sorely tempted to go check on her, but that wouldn't be a very good example for the guys. Everyone was back in camp – and the sound of men snoring mingled with the whine of mosquitoes and the soft footfalls of the guard doing his rounds. I eventually slid down a long, black tunnel into a deep sleep.

⁂

Cloud threatened rain when we met the Aussie captain at first light the next morning. Johan remained in camp to keep a smooth handle on things there, while Accorsi and I took two mortar tubes and 10 men down to JOC Headquarters. The Aussie quickly briefed me, while I stood by the vehicle I'd arrived in.

"Upwards of 60 gooks tried to cross last night. An armoured car call-sign engaged them here," he poked his nicotine-stained finger at a point on the map near the minefield.

"Were they trying to cross into the village or what?" I asked.

"More than likely. I don't see the point of crossing so close to the village unless that was their target."

"What do you want us to do, sir?"

"Well, no doubt you heard that 12.7 firing last night?"

"Yes, sir."

"They fired from here, this spit of land." He indicated a long finger of land next to an estuary on the Zambian side.

"Our guys are doing a follow-up in and around the contact area, and your job is to suppress any fire from Zambia or anywhere else. Understood?"

"Sir."

I made a few notes about friendly forces in the area – and their radio channels – before moving off. I think Accorsi was glad to have me along because I had local knowledge of the area – and his map-reading was up to shit according to Johan. I reasoned that we would need visual contact with the Zambian target as we had no forward observers in the area – and I figured the best way to get that was to drive through the gap in the minefield and then turn left up the service road towards a small hillock a quarter of the way up the escarpment face. I just hoped and prayed that no landmines had been laid by any gook survivors from the night before.

It was a weird sensation entering the gap in the minefield. The road was channelled through the cordon by two high fences – creating a sort of alley that we drove through. It was the first time I'd seen the minefield up close – and it didn't take the eye of an eagle to see all the tripwires and claymores inside it. I stopped the two vehicles at the exit and told the guys to buckle up and switch on. My vehicle took the lead – and I immediately became conscious of my toes clamping involuntarily in my boots. It was the first time since my last brush with a landmine – on this very road – and I sat in a contorted heap waiting for one to go off. I was drenched in sweat by the time we reached the top of the small hill. I hopped down from the cab, and Accorsi stood next to me. I had to defer to his experience with mortars – and we looked down the valley together.

"Right spot?" I enquired.

"Couldn't be better, sir."

"Good. Set the guys up here, then."

He barked a few orders – and before I could say 'bullshit', the tubes were erected and ammo crates broken open. I watched the guys in mute fascination; they were very efficient indeed.

Picking up a set of binoculars that belonged to Accorsi, I strolled over to the road we'd just driven up and focused the glasses on the river some two kilometres below us. The spit of land in Zambia – heavily treed in the distorted image – was clearly visible, but I couldn't see anything like weapons or men. The bright-blue waters of the river – speckled with white rapids – filled the middle of the image. Bare tree-trunks stood out in sharp contrast to green foliage everywhere else. I decided that if any firing came from the spit, I would plaster it with a lot of ammo. Accorsi cleared his throat and handed me a map that he'd clipped on a board.

"Confirm this is where we are," he said, pointing at a grid reference that would put us about a kilometre further away from where we actually were.

"No. This is where we are."

"Are you sure, sir?"

"Positive."

There was no detail about the minefield on the map – and Accorsi's mistake was easy to make. Only my local knowledge made me feel confident I'd indicated our correct grid reference.

Having established where we were, it was easy to set up the plotting board, read off co-ordinates and prime charges on the mortar shells that corresponded to the distance from the target. However, as we had direct visual contact with the area we were to bomb, we could virtually fire without using an aiming pole – and in the end, we discarded the plotting board – sitting down to wait and see what would happen. I found a nice comfy rock and rested against it – radio next to me – elbows resting on raised knees as I studied the Zambian bank very carefully through binoculars. There was no sign of movement, but I could clearly see our guys moving around the relatively treeless shoreline on the Rhodesian side. It came as a mild surprise that the area I was looking at was just upstream from where I'd been shot at on the river several months earlier. I made radio contact with the troops below me – telling them we were there for support – and then shut my gritty eyes to give them a rest.

I'd almost fallen asleep when a loud rustling sound came out of the grass to my left. I sat up with a start when 10 horse-mounted Grey's Scouts came out of the bush – line abreast. It was perhaps the most awesome sight I'd ever seen. There is something magical about cavalry, in my opinion – and the sight of those tough-looking men covered in weapons and ammo, blackened up with camo cream, horses snorting, looked really terrifying. They looked down at us and smiled – their white teeth contrasting sharply with the black cream on their faces. I could imagine the terror in the eyes of Matabele warriors a century before when horse-mounted infantry hunted them down in the Matabele uprisings – a truly awesome sight.[1]

We sat there most of the day – and eventually, we got the all-clear to go back to camp at about 1500. I looked at my watch when I got back to camp and debated what I should do: go see Mal, or hang around until something else happened? My indecision was brought into sharp focus at about 1600 when we got a message from our forward fire-controller on the booze cruise that gooks could be seen on an island roughly where we got weed caught in our patrol boat's engine that night, long ago. Johan stood the mortar crews to – and quickly worked out aiming co-ordinates and the range to the island. We heard that a platoon of troops was speeding down to the jetty to get on board a standby booze cruise, while the one full of tourists was steaming as fast as possible back to the safety of

---

1   I did not realise until years later that the troop commander of the Grey's Scouts in this encounter was none other than 'The Smiling Shit' himself – and it was he that brought down fire on the enemy crossing the river. Why he never called upon our mortars to help suppress the crossing remains a mystery to this day. The only conclusion that I have come to is that there was a mortar team attached to the Grey's Scouts, and it was their weapons he called upon for support – forgetting about our 81's in the heat of battle.

its departure point. I decided to leave Johan there and raced down to meet my forward fire-controller to get a first-hand account from him.

"What news?" I asked of him as a group of terrified tourists made their exit from the tour boat.

"Definitely gooks. About 10 or 12. They were waving at us to attract our attention."

"You're joking?"

"No joke, sir. They look like shit… Shivering, bleeding and half-dead."

"Survivors from last night?"

"No doubt, sir."

"Okay, thanks. We'll hang around and watch them come in."

About an hour later, a boat literally heaving with troops pulled into view. The top deck had machine-guns pointing outwards – and a dozen or more rifle barrels tilted upwards on either side of the lower deck. The water sighed against the hull of the boat – and a gentle breeze rustled the palm leaves above me; a delightful tourist spot bedevilled by war.

Then, they came off… the gooks, that is – about 10 of them. It was the first time I'd seen living examples close-up before. They looked like pathetic, scared heaps of humanity – their eyes wide with terror. Some hobbled, helped by comrades; others skipped along on one foot, with crusted blood on swollen feet. I felt more pity than hate for them – and wondered why I'd feared this pathetic lot in the first place. Well, I guess it was the fear of the unknown. They were escorted away by the platoon to an uncertain fate. Some would be made an 'offer they couldn't refuse' and would join the Selous Scouts to fight for Rhodesia, and others – convicted of any crimes they may have committed – would swing from the gallows.

There was one thing that struck me about them, though… They were all dressed in a plain, brownish-khaki uniform with black boots. This was most unusual for gooks, who depended upon blending in with civilians by looking just like them. Why were they in uniform?

It was gone 9:00 p.m. that night by the time I'd showered and changed – heading down to the casino to meet Mal. She shrieked with delight when I walked through the doors – enveloping me in a big bear hug.

"Thank God you're okay, Tony."

"You too," I said, kissing her. "I missed you so much." She smelled all womanly and fresh. I just love that in a woman.

"Fred," I said, shaking his hand. "Thanks for looking after Mal. How did 'the wife' cope?"

"Fine," he beamed his Mexican smile. "We got a bit pissed in the bunker."

"We did, at that," Mal nodded. "It was fun actually, apart from the drive up there. I nearly wet my pants driving around in the dark like that. You really live in a scary part of town, Fred."

"That I know. Bloody dark, it is; puts the shits up all of us. Come, sit. Let's have a drink."

We walked over to some easy chairs near the bar and sat, while Fred ordered drinks. The place was totally empty except for two people at Danny's table, so Mal joined us. Linda winked at me when our eyes made contact.

"Listen to this," Fred said, as he sat down – leaning in close to us: "The crossing last night was supposed to open the front door for the invasion."

"What are you talking about?"

"The gooks from the crossing; they were going to attack our guys at the bridge. As soon as they'd captured it, the train was going to cross."

"Bullshit, Fred. Where do you get this? Oh, don't tell me... your mate in CIO?"

"Mmm," he nodded. "I'm telling you. They were going to land, and then walk along the riverfront all the way to the bridge – cutting through the fence by Livingstone's statue – and attacking our guys from the rear, so to speak."

"They would've got wiped out. There's a whole company of troops there."

"Their objective was to destroy the control room for the explosives on the bridge, that's all."

"Shit. That explains it..." I said.

"What?"

"Why they were wearing uniforms instead of civilian clothes. They were a regular formation."

"You see!" Fred said triumphantly.

"Why the hell weren't we put on alert? Surely the SAS or Scouts are watching the other side?"

"Who knows?" Fred shrugged.

"You okay, Mal? You seem a bit quiet."

"Just thinking, really. It's a bit of a scare, the whole thing – plus I'm a bit knackered from the stress coming off."

Fred agreed Mal could go home with me – and towards midnight, we crawled into bed. The air-conditioner buzzed away, while a torrential rainstorm with lots of thunder and lightning rolled over the village. One loud bang of thunder brought Tookie sailing onto the bed with us – and before long, he was curled up – purring away and kneading my arm with his paws. I felt secure and at peace lying there in Mal's arms, with the blue-white lightning bolts lighting up the room every now and again, while millions of tiny drops hammered the wrought-iron roof above us.

The next day was very bright, with an eye-scrunching blue sky and fluffy white clouds floating lazily by. The garden looked glorious, and bees and butterflies buzzed around – doing their bit for nature. I arrived back at camp at 1000 after a leisurely breakfast with Mal.

"Have you heard the news?" Johan said when I strolled into the mess for coffee.

"No?"

"About 15 gook bodies have been recovered so far. They're down at the cop shop."

"Killed on the river?"

'Yes, fished out like trout; some half-eaten by crocs; two dead in the minefield; and another three killed by Grey's Scouts."

"Shit. Should we go have a look?"

"Why not? There's stuff-all going on here."

We hopped into my two-five and drove back into town. The place looked deserted – and only a handful of tourists ambled around empty curio shops.

"The place is dying," I said, but Johan didn't hear – probably didn't care anyway. It wasn't his home.

We turned right at the Wimpy bar – accelerating briefly uphill before turning left into the police camp. Entering the place brought back memories of arriving here nearly two years earlier, when Intake 146 was camped under the trees at the back of the buildings that made up the complex.

We hopped down from the truck and strolled around the main building to the left, and through a large security gate that enclosed an electrical substation and car park. A few police and military vehicles were parked in the shade of high trees. Quite a mob had collected to look down at two neat rows of bloodied bodies lying on the hot tarmac. The corpses I looked at were all very young. In some cases, it was obvious why they had died. Brains hung out crushed skulls, with flies licking at blackened blood; others had heads missing altogether – while on some, you could see no wound at all. Perhaps the latter had drowned? Most though, seemed covered in tiny holes; small entry holes and big exit wounds.

I was just about to turn away when one particularly tall corpse attracted my attention. My heartbeat accelerated as recognition dawned on me. There were the big feet, the wild woolly hair, the matted beard and one yellow eye staring accusingly up at me. The other eye – and most of the head with it – had been blown away. Was I staring at the corpse of Albert Ncube[2] – my foe of long ago? Could it be him? It looked just like him – although a

---

2 For many years, I remained convinced that I'd seen the corpse of Albert Ncube at the police station that day. However, a nurse I knew at Morris Depot once told me that he died from

death mask often makes recognition impossible. I bent over and stared at the corpse for a long time – remembering what that man meant to me as an individual and to the village in general. Farmers murdered; hotels attacked… Comrades of mine shot up. I felt no hate for the man. He had died for what he believed in – just like friends of mine had died for what they believed in – but still, he was a gook to me and an evil bastard. I stood up – feeling a bit shaky.

"That's Albert Ncube," I said to Johan.

"Who?"

I looked at Johan and shrugged inwardly. How could I expect him to know my nemesis and the history of the area like I did?

"Just some gook we chased for a year…"

"Oh," was all he said before we walked back to the truck.

I remained lost in thought most of the day – and when my duty officer time was up later that evening, I went to see Mal and Fred at the casino.

"I think I saw Albert Ncube's body today," I said simply.

"What?" they said in unison. I nodded – sipping my whisky.

"Sure it was him; down at the cop shop… one of the gooks killed in the crossing the other day."

"How can you be sure?"

"I was one of very few people that actually laid eyes on him when he was alive. The corpse had the same physique as Ncube; the same hair, beard… and that yellow eye."

"Eye?"

"The other's croc food."

"Yugh," Mal said, puckering her lips.

"Albert bloody Ncube," Fred said. "This calls for a celebration." He ordered drinks for all of us – and we sat around talking about the previous year and what had happened. We all sensed a chapter had closed in our lives. Albert was dead and an invasion of the village had been foiled.[3]

---

insanity in a Bulawayo mental hospital – and then, to top it all off, when Gloria Olds was killed in March 2001 the assailant was named as Albert Ncube, aged 47. The name and age certainly pointed to the man I knew. Also, his method of 'overkill' was used on Gloria – not only killing her, but all her dogs too. Maybe the bastard is still alive?

3   I caught up with Theo Williams many years later – and he told me that the boats that crossed the river that night were just the first wave of hundreds of terrorists waiting to be ferried across the river. In his own words, he said it was a 'brigade-sized attack'. The old 25-pounders that brought death and destruction down on the terrorists waiting to embark resulted in many scores being killed, with artillery rounds landing in a rolling pattern that followed them into the bush as they made a hasty retreat. Theo commented that they were burying bodies in Livingstone

In the end, we left the village – not because of the threat of an invasion which never came, but for purely economic reasons. We got lousy pay over the Christmas prior to my first call-up on the 'Russian Front' – and big bonuses we expected from the Bulawayo Trade Fair never materialised. We resigned in protest – as did most of the casino. Fred left a short while later – and in the New Year, Don Goldin (the owner of the Casino Hotel) lay dead in the Umniati Viscount aircraft – shot down on 12 February 1979.

One day we were enjoying our garden, and the next day we were packing up to leave for good. My heart felt heavy – and Mally often burst into floods of tears. When the last load of furniture was taken by the removal people, we got into 'Miss Piggy' and did one last tour of the village. We drove slowly down to the Falls – walking hand-in-hand beneath the canopy of trees – then to the Falls Hotel, and finally, the ruins of the Elephant Hills Casino. We sat quietly for a long time – looking at the beautiful view below us – lost in our own thoughts… sad and empty.

We both knew the end of the village as part of our lives would affect our relationship – and we knew that what we felt was mirrored by the entire nation of Rhodesia. Something had died – and it would never be recaptured ever again. Our way of life, farms of lush green tobacco and swaying corn would be gone for good. Our innocence was trashed – and an entire nation would be forced into exile abroad or fealty at home.

Images of dead friends like Dave Kruger, Roy Orchard and Tom Shipley waved before my mind – and I knew it was time to leave the land I loved so dearly.

It's all ghosts and memories now.

The End

---

for many days afterwards. The artillery barrage was truly spectacular – and is something I will never forget.

Epilogue

A couple of people who read the manuscript before I got it published said I should add a footnote about what happened after I left Vic Falls.

Mally and I moved to Que Que – where her parents lived – and I got a job as a shift operator at Sable Chemicals. I hated the job – particularly the shift work – and it brought a lot of pressure down on our relationship. We finally broke up in mid-1979. I was gutted for a long, long time after that – and in a funny way, I am still in love with her.

I did one last call-up at Vic Falls in 1979, where I met my first wife – Diane Faulkener – at a party some army guys held at A'Zambezi Hotel. It was strange being back at the Falls – and I occasionally drove back to 'our' house to look at the garden, which was now all weeds. I swore I could see Tookie chasing butterflies there!

At the end of 1979, I joined the police as a regular and was posted to Morris Depot to instruct PATU trainees in the art of war. It was while I was attached to them that I was selected to be Indira Ghandi's bodyguard during her visit to Zimbabwe's electoral birth. I stood just to the left of Prince Charles the night the Union Jack (not the Rhodesian flag) was lowered on 18 April 1980.

The 'chicken run' had now been renamed the 'owl run' because only the wise left the country – and so at the end of 1980, I emigrated to South Africa. Five years later, I divorced Diane and returned to Zimbabwe with my second (and current) wife – Coral – in 1986. I started a construction company with my brother that same year, and eventually left Zimbabwe in 2002 when my business failed due to Bob's thuggery on the farms.

I now live in Salisbury on 'Mud Island' (the UK). How's that for irony? Living in a city with the same name I was born in! But it's not the same – and never will be.

CPSIA information can be obtained at www.ICGtesting.com
Printed in the USA
BVOW11s0900221115

427864BV00002B/2/P